PRAISE FOR
INTERNATIONAL FREIGHT TRANSPORT

'A great book which not only covers issues in international freight transport but also gives detailed insight into key corridors and markets which would be essential for people working in this sphere.'
Michael Nielsen, Transportation Manager, India-ASEAN, Caterpillar Inc

'The perfect companion not only for someone who wants to deeply understand how international freight transport operates but also for someone who wants to update his or her knowledge. The book provides an excellent synthesis of current and future issues affecting international freight transport based on cases with a truly global footprint.'
Dr Stavros Karamperidis, Assistant Professor of Shipping and International Logistics, Heriot-Watt University, UK

'This book is a vital contribution to the ongoing debate about the importance of international freight transport in the context of the ever-growing influence of globalization and will become a significant text for academics, researchers and practitioners in the coming years. Containing contributions from across the globe, the case studies presented place the dynamic international freight market in its varied context reflecting the wide range of commodities and transport media that are involved. With a strong theoretical as well as practical basis, and supported by a substantial and wide ranging literature, a clear understanding of the economic, social and political contexts, and a thoroughly researched case study base, it will be welcomed as both a topical and practical guide to the sector.'
Professor Michael Roe, Chair of Maritime Governance, Plymouth University, UK

'*International Freight Transport* is a comprehensive compendium of practical research in this fast-evolving area. As an academic and practitioner with over 40 years of worldwide experience in the industry, I found the assembly of papers in this book to provide a broad and, most importantly, up-to-date background on the industry's main segments along with several case studies from around the world. The review and assessment of future trends, included in the last chapter,

is of special interest, shedding light on critical issues facing the industry, such as the subsiding of freight volumes, change in direction due to re-relocation of production and consumption, and the respective difficulties in providing reliable forecasts. Altogether, I highly recommend this book as essential reading to practitioners as well as researchers in port authorities, port operators, shipping lines, logistic providers, government agencies involved in transport and logistics, and academic institutes – and anyone interested in our dynamic industry.'
Dr Asaf Ashar, Research Professor (emeritus) and Independent Consultant, National Ports and Waterways Initiative (NPWI), USA

'This book provides comprehensive coverage of the most important contemporary ideas and issues in international freight transport and logistics. These are conveyed through an eclectic mix of applied contexts that add significant interest and relevance to the underlying concepts. The geographical scope of the content spans the globe and the list of contributors is impressive. Expertly edited, this book is a thoroughly absorbing read that comes highly recommended for both students and practitioners.'
Professor Kevin Cullinane, Professor of International Logistics and Transport Economics, University of Gothenburg, Sweden

International Freight Transport

Cases, structures and prospects

Edited by Anthony Beresford
and Stephen Pettit

KoganPage

Publisher's note

Every possible effort has been made to ensure that the information contained in this book is accurate at the time of going to press, and the publishers and authors cannot accept responsibility for any errors or omissions, however caused. No responsibility for loss or damage occasioned to any person acting, or refraining from action, as a result of the material in this publication can be accepted by the editor, the publisher or the author.

First published in Great Britain and the United States in 2017 by Kogan Page Limited

Apart from any fair dealing for the purposes of research or private study, or criticism or review, as permitted under the Copyright, Designs and Patents Act 1988, this publication may only be reproduced, stored or transmitted, in any form or by any means, with the prior permission in writing of the publishers, or in the case of reprographic reproduction in accordance with the terms and licences issued by the CLA. Enquiries concerning reproduction outside these terms should be sent to the publishers at the undermentioned addresses:

2nd Floor, 45 Gee Street	c/o Martin P Hill Consulting	4737/23 Ansari Road
London	122 W 27th St, 10th Floor	Daryaganj
EC1V 3RS	New York, NY 10001	New Delhi 110002
United Kingdom	USA	India

www.koganpage.com

© Anthony Beresford and Stephen Pettit, 2017

The right of Anthony Beresford and Stephen Pettit to be identified as the authors of this work has been asserted by them in accordance with the Copyright, Designs and Patents Act 1988.

ISBN   978 0 7494 7434 8
E-ISBN   978 0 7494 7435 5

British Library Cataloguing-in-Publication Data

A CIP record for this book is available from the British Library.

Library of Congress Cataloging-in-Publication Control Number

2016056964

Typeset by Integra Software Services, Pondicherry
Print production managed by Jellyfish
Printed and bound by CPI Group (UK) Ltd, Croydon CR0 4YY

Dedicated to Maritime Studies and International Transport 1974–2000

CONTENTS

About the editors xiii
List of contributors xv
List of abbreviations xxv

Introduction: cases, structures and prospects 1
Anthony Beresford, Cardiff Business School, UK
Stephen Pettit, Cardiff Business School, UK

PART ONE Trade and the transport environment 11

01 **Demand, supply and freight rates: the shipping of global trade** 13
Hassiba Benamara, UNCTAD, Switzerland
Jan Hoffmann, UNCTAD, Switzerland
Frida Youssef, UNCTAD, Switzerland

Introduction 13
Demand: drivers and trends 14
Supply: the key players in international shipping 27
Freight rates 36
Outlook 53
References 54

02 **Trade and customs procedures in international freight transport: requirements, issues and trends** 57
Andrew Grainger, Nottingham University Business School, UK

Introduction 57
Trade and customs procedures 58
Customs management practices 63
The case for trade facilitation 66
What does compliance cost? 67
Fixes and reform 68

Conclusion 71
References 72

PART TWO International freight transport in practice 77

03 Multimodal transport solutions for grain exports from Kazakhstan 79
Timur Bimaganbetov, Ministry of Healthcare and Social Development, Republic of Kazakhstan
Anthony Beresford, Cardiff Business School, UK
Stephen Pettit, Cardiff Business School, UK

Introduction 79
Grain exports from Kazakhstan 81
Principal grain routes 83
Discussion and conclusion 94
References 97

04 The transport of oil and gas 100
Hance D Smith, Cardiff University (emeritus), UK
Azmath Jaleel, Cardiff University, UK

Introduction 100
Development 100
Technology 105
Environment 112
Political economy 114
Governance and management 118
Conclusion 120
References and resources 121

05 Global container transport 123
Rolf Neise, International School of Management, Germany

Introduction 123
History of containerization 124
Global container trade 126

Maritime Container Transportation Chain (MCTC) 131
Information and communication technology (ICT) 148
Conclusion 152
References 153

06   Car shipping 158
Paul Nieuwenhuis, Cardiff Business School, UK

Introduction: the car shipment market 158
Moves to more localized and regional flows 161
Industry developments 164
Environmental impacts 167
The future car carrier 170
Conclusions 171
References 172

PART THREE Trading regions 175

07   International freight logistics in South East Asia: The Indonesia–Malaysia–Thailand Growth Triangle (IMT-GT) 177
Ruth Banomyong, Thammasat University, Thailand

Introduction 177
IMT-GT trade flows 180
Analytical framework 182
An analysis of freight logistics in IMT-GT's corridors 184
Conclusion 199
References 202

08   North America's evolving international freight transport: challenges and responses 204
Michael Ircha, University of New Brunswick, Canada

Introduction 204
Integrated global transportation 206
Continental international transportation 208
Canada's gateways and trade corridors 211
Canada Transportation Act review 222

Conclusion 226
References 227

09 International freight transport in South America: the case of Colombia 231

David B Grant, Hull University Business School, UK
Rodrigo Britto, Universidad de los Andes School of Management (UASM), Colombia
Juan Pablo Soto, Universidad de los Andes School of Management (UASM), Colombia
Marcus Thiell, Universidad de los Andes School of Management (UASM), Colombia

Introduction 231
The nature of international freight transport 232
The international freight transport market in Latin America 237
Colombia: background, facts and figures 239
International transport of Colombian cut flowers 244
Transportation of oil in Colombia 248
Conclusion 253
References 253

10 International freight transport in Southern Africa 256

Christopher Savage, University of Huddersfield, UK

Introduction 256
Trade, logistics, transport and corridors 257
Demand and supply: trading volumes 263
Trade agreements 266
Infrastructure 268
Ancillary factors 272
Conclusion 273
References 274

11 Freight transport in Korea and Taiwan 277

Su-Han Woo, Chung-Ang University, South Korea
Po-Lin Lai, Chung-Ang University, South Korea
Doori Kim, Chung-Ang University, South Korea
Jungeun Kim, Chung-Ang University, South Korea

Introduction 277
Freight transport in South Korea 278
Challenges and responses in the transport sectors
 of Taiwan and Korea 289
Discussion and conclusion 294
References 295

PART FOUR Challenging environments and transport futures 297

12 Overcoming international freight transport challenges in a disaster response context 299
Peter Tatham, Griffith Business School, Gold Coast, Australia
Gyöngyi Kovács, Hanken School of Economics, Helsinki, Finland

Introduction 299
The humanitarian context 300
Access to the disaster area 303
A complex system of humanitarian transport services 305
New technology in humanitarian transport 307
Grand challenges 310
References 312

13 Transport futures: reconciling the on-demand economy with global production chains 315
Peter Wells, Cardiff Business School, UK

Introduction 315
Technologies, transitions, varieties and elites: a theoretical
 framework for transport futures 317
Freight transport: bridging the spatial separation of production
 and consumption 320
Forecasting in a chaotic and diverse world 325
Conclusions 327
References 328

Index 333

ABOUT THE EDITORS

Anthony Beresford

Anthony is a Professor of Logistics and Transport in the Cardiff Business School, Cardiff University, UK. He graduated with a BA in Geography from Manchester University and was subsequently awarded his PhD in Environmental Sciences at the University of East Anglia in 1982; his research was focused on climate change in East Africa. He has subsequently travelled widely in an advisory capacity within the ports, transport and humanitarian fields in Europe, Africa, Australasia and North America. He has been involved in a broad range of transport-related research and consultancy projects including: transport rehabilitation, aid distribution and trade facilitation for UNCTAD and, for example, the Rwandan Government. His cost model for Multimodal Transport has been widely used by UNESCAP Corridors in South East Asia, Africa and elsewhere. He has also advised both the United Kingdom and Welsh Governments on road transport and port policy options.

Stephen Pettit

Stephen is a Reader in Logistics and Operations Management at Cardiff Business School. In 1993 he was awarded a PhD from the University of Wales and he has worked at Cardiff Business School since 2000. He has been involved in a range of transport-related research projects, notably a groundbreaking project for the Department for Transport, analysing the UK economy's requirements for people with seafaring experience. This work highlighted important issues relating to the decline in the number of UK seafaring officers. Subsequently, he has been involved in a range of transport-related research projects for EU DGTREN, including the 'Economic Value of Shipping to the UK Economy', an 'Analysis of the Cost Structure of the main TEN Ports' and 'Work Organisation in Ports'. His most recent research work has considered aspects of humanitarian aid supply chain management. Stephen's teaching-related activity has been focused in two main areas: port management and the application of information and communication technology in the fields of transport, logistics and supply chain management. Stephen has written a large number of journal papers and conference papers, and has contributed to a wide range of reports, many of which relate to port development, port operations and port policy. Stephen is co-editor of *E-Logistics: Managing your digital supply chains for competitive advantage*, published by Kogan Page.

LIST OF CONTRIBUTORS

Ruth Banomyong
Ruth is currently an Associate Professor at the Department of International Business, Logistics and Transport Management at the Faculty of Commerce and Accountancy, Thammasat University in Thailand. He received his PhD from Cardiff University in 2001, in the field of International Logistics. He won the James Cooper Cup in 2001 for the best PhD dissertation in logistics from the Chartered Institute of Logistics and Transport (CILT) in the United Kingdom. Ruth's main research interests are in the field of multimodal transport, international logistics, logistics development policy and supply chain performance measurements. He has published widely in journals such as the *International Journal of Physical Distribution and Logistics Management*, *International Journal of Logistics Research and Applications*, *Asia Pacific Journal of Marketing and Logistics*, *Journal of Applied Sciences*, and *Maritime Policy and Management*, and he has co-authored 10 books. Since 1995, Ruth has been a consultant for a number of international organizations such as the United Nations Conference on Trade and Development (UNCTAD), the United Nations Economic and Social Commission for Asia and the Pacific (UNESCAP), the World Bank, the Asian Development Bank (ADB), and the Association of Southeast Asian Nations (ASEAN). His particular area of expertise is currently the strategic and operational aspects of transport corridor development in the Asian Pacific region.

Hassiba Benamara
Hassiba is a shipping and trade specialist with extensive professional experience in the field of transport and trade logistics. She joined UNCTAD's Division on Technology and Logistics over 10 years ago and has been working on various issues including maritime transport and trade. She is a co-author of the UNCTAD annual *Review of Maritime Transport*, focusing in particular on international seaborne trade issues. Other relevant areas of work include climate change (mitigation, impacts and adaptation in transport/seaports), energy market developments, shipping costs, transport, supply chain security and sustainable freight transport.

Before joining UNCTAD, Hassiba worked for the Canadian Ministry of Transportation in both the international shipping and trade divisions. Areas of work included marine insurance and liability, arrest of ships, maritime liens and mortgages, maritime security, antitrust immunity and liner conferences, cabotage as well as transport and logistic services trade liberalization. She represented the Ministry at various International Maritime Organization (IMO) Legal Committee meetings, as well as at the World Trade Organization (WTO) and relevant bilateral and regional trade negotiations.

Timur Bimaganbetov

Timur is currently a Senior Specialist at the JSC Workforce Development Centre of the Ministry of Healthcare and Social Development in the Republic of Kazakhstan. He was formerly a Director of the Department of Partnership Development and Public Relations at the JSC Republican Scientific and Methodological Centre for VET Development, and was a Senior Manager at JSC Kasipkor in the Ministry of Education and Science, Republic of Kazakhstan. Currently his main areas of work are to develop an effective national qualification system, and to develop and implement state incentives in the field of employment and social assistance. He was awarded his BSc in Customs Affairs from the Eurasian National University in 1999, and his MSc in international transport from Cardiff University in 2012.

Rodrigo Britto

Rodrigo is an Assistant Professor in the Department of Strategy at Universidad de los Andes School of Management (UASM), Colombia. He obtained his PhD in supply chain management from the University of Maryland, College Park, MD. His research interests have focused on operations management in emerging markets, transportation management, and efficiency and productivity analysis. Rodrigo has published in the *Transportation Journal, Transportation Research Part E: Logistics and Transportation Review, International Journal of Physical Distribution and Logistics, Journal of Operations Management,* two Chilean academic journals and several Colombian academic journals. He has also co-authored two books in Spanish: *Introducción a la Programación Lineal con Aplicaciones en Administración de Operaciones* and *Análisis envolvente de datos: Herramienta de optimización para la medición de la eficiencia y la productividad.*

Andrew Grainger

Andrew is a Lecturer in Logistics and Supply Chain Management at Nottingham University Business School. Prior to this, Andrew worked as Deputy Director at SITPRO, the former UK trade facilitation agency. He also served as the Secretary for EUROPRO, the umbrella body of European trade facilitation bodies, and was also a member of the European Commission's DG TAXUD Trade Contact Group. Andrew has worked as a consultant with the World Bank Group, and has also provided consulting services to the European Commission, the European Parliament, the UK's businesslink.gov.uk programme, and the governments of Bangladesh, Lao PDR and Ethiopia. He has also advised a large number of private sector companies and research organizations. Andrew's current research interests include trade logistics and trade facilitation; trade and customs procedures, administration, law and regulations; port and border management; trade documents and standards; electronic trade and customs systems; and supply chain risk, security and resilience.

David B Grant

David is Professor of Logistics at Hull University Business School and Distinguished Senior Fellow at Hanken School of Economics, Helsinki. He has recently held visiting appointments at École Supérieure du Commerce Extérieur, Paris and Universidad de los Andes, Bogotá as the Silla Corona Distinguished Visiting Professor. David obtained his PhD from Edinburgh University and his thesis, which investigated customer service, satisfaction and service quality in UK food processing logistics, received the James Cooper Memorial Cup PhD Award from the Chartered Institute of Logistics and Transport (UK). His research interests include logistics customer service, satisfaction and service quality; retail logistics; and reverse, closed-loop and sustainable logistics. David's business experience includes retail, corporate banking, technical design and consulting, and recent applied research has investigated on-shelf availability and out-of-stocks, total loss and waste in food retailing, forecasting and obsolete inventory, service quality and fulfilment in internet retailing, and consumer logistics. David has over 185 publications in various refereed journals, books and conference proceedings and is on the editorial board of a number of international journals.

Jan Hoffmann

Jan Hoffmann joined UNCTAD in 2003. As Chief of the Trade Facilitation Section he is currently in charge of various trade facilitation programmes in Africa, Asia and Latin America. He created and co-edits the quarterly *Transport and Trade Facilitation Newsletter*, is co-author and coordinator of the *Review of Maritime Transport*, initiated the *Maritime Country Profiles*, and created and produces the annual *Liner Shipping Connectivity Index*. Previously, Jan spent six years with the United Nations Economic Commission for Latin America and the Caribbean (ECLAC) in Santiago de Chile, and two years with the International Maritime Organization (IMO) in London and Santiago. Prior to this, he held part-time positions as assistant professor, import-export agent, seafarer, translator and consultant. For eight years, he worked part-time for a family tramp shipping business, registered in Antigua and Barbuda. Jan has studied in Germany, the United Kingdom and Spain, and holds a doctorate degree in economics from the University of Hamburg. His work has resulted in numerous UN and peer-reviewed publications. Jan is a member of the advisory and editorial boards of AJSL, IJSTL, INCU, JST, MEL and MPM, and the Committee of the Propeller Club of Geneva. In 2014, Jan was elected president of the International Association of Maritime Economists (IAME).

Michael Ircha

Michael is a Professor Emeritus in Civil Engineering and Associate Vice-President Dean Emeritus at the University of New Brunswick (UNB), Canada. He was an integral part of UNB's Transportation Group and earned an international reputation in the area of ports and shipping. His work as a civil engineer and his service to the profession earned him Fellowships in the Canadian Society for Civil Engineering and in the Engineering Institute of Canada. Michael has also received numerous awards, including a New Brunswick Merit Award for Community Leadership and a Lieutenant Governor's Award for Excellence in Public Administration.

Azmath Jaleel

Azmath is a researcher at Cardiff University and a consultant to Seafarers' Rights International, London. His research interests include maritime and marine management with a focus on the welfare and human rights of seafarers. He has a PhD in transport policy from Cardiff University, an MSc in shipping management from the World Maritime University, a technical diploma in marine engineering from Singapore Polytechnic, and is a Class 1 Marine Engineer and Chartered Marine Technologist. He has seagoing experience and has also worked in maritime administration, where he was responsible for seafarers' education, training and licensing, as well as carrying out statutory surveys of ships including PSC inspections. Dr Jaleel has provided consultancy services to a number of organizations, including the

Asian Development Bank and the European Commission, on various maritime and marine environment-related projects, and has published academic papers and contributions to books.

Doori Kim

Doori is a PhD researcher in the Department of Trade and Logistics and also works at the International Logistics Experts Network Center at Chung-Ang University. She received a bachelor's degree in business administration in 2012, and a master's degree in international trade from Chung-Ang University in 2014.

Jungeun Kim

Jungeun is an MSc researcher in the Department of Trade and Logistics and also works at the International Logistics Experts Network Center at Chung-Ang University. She graduated from Chung-Ang University with a BA in international logistics in 2015.

Gyöngyi Kovács

Gyöngyi is the Erkko Professor in Humanitarian Logistics at the Hanken School of Economics in Helsinki, Finland, and the subject head of Supply Chain Management and Social Responsibility. She is a founding editor of the *Journal of Humanitarian Logistics and Supply Chain Management*, and has served as the Director of the HUMLOG Institute since its foundation until 2014. She has published widely in the field of humanitarian logistics and sustainable supply chain management.

Po-Lin Lai

Po-Lin is an Associate Professor at the Department of International Logistics, Chung-Ang University. He has also been a visiting professor for several universities. Po-Lin's research and teaching centres on the themes of transportation policy (focusing on aviation and shipping), logistics and supply chain management. Currently, he has extended his research interest into logistics relating to agricultural and aquatic products, and the so-called blue economy among Asian countries.

Rolf Neise

Rolf has a degree in Economic Engineering from the Technical University of Berlin, and a PhD from the University of Stuttgart. Rolf is a Visiting Professor at the International School of Management and a freelance consultant supporting multinational companies in optimizing their supply chain management and logistics structures. He was the Global Head of Logistics Operations at BAT (British American Tobacco plc), in charge of defining logistics excellence in the end-to-end supply chain. At BAT, Rolf held a number of operational and strategic roles across the group in Germany and the UK. Prior to BAT, Rolf worked in several consultancies where he gained in-depth experience in reorganization and optimization projects across the automotive, telecommunication and chemical industries.

Paul Nieuwenhuis

Paul is a Senior Lecturer in Logistics and Operations Management at Cardiff Business School, Cardiff University. He joined the Centre for Automotive Industry Research (CAIR) at Cardiff University in 1991 and became one of its two directors in 2006. He was a founder member of the ESRC Centre for Business Relationships, Accountability, Sustainability and Society (BRASS) and is an associate of the Sustainable Places Research Institute. A client study in 1999 led him to investigate the car shipping industry, an interest he has kept up since and which has led to a number of conference papers and publications on this topic. In all, Paul has produced around 300 publications, ranging from books and academic papers to articles in practitioner journals, official reports for governments and international bodies as well as conference papers for both academic and business audiences, and even some journalistic pieces. Paul is a member of the Guild of Motoring Writers and the Society of Automotive Historians.

Christopher Savage

Christopher is a Senior Lecturer at the University of Huddersfield Department of Logistics, Operations, Hospitality and Marketing. He worked for 15 years in process industries such as pharmaceuticals, film and animal feed manufacturing as well as brewing, during which time he moved into logistics. This was followed by a further 15 years of logistics consulting working in the UK, Hong Kong, Europe and Australia before joining academia at Huddersfield in 2002. In 2011 he moved to Southern Africa to take up an appointment as Associate Professor and Academic Director of the Namibian German Centre for Logistics, which is now part of the Namibian University of Science and Technology, where he helped establish a logistics master's programme. While in Namibia, the emphasis of his research changed to focus on the state of logistics in Namibia, southern

African skills gaps, logistics hubs and clusters. He returned to Huddersfield in 2014, where he continues to teach and research, and completed his PhD in 2016. Chris is a Fellow of both the Chartered Institute of Logistics and the Higher Education Academy. His published research covers pharmaceutical supply chains, vehicle routing and scheduling, third-party logistics, transport geography, global logistics, supply chain relationships and high-capacity vehicle impact.

Hance D Smith

Hance was a Reader at Cardiff University until 2011, and is currently editor-in-chief of *Marine Policy*. His research interests include marine policy, the development of the world ocean, and marine geography. Within these broad fields, he has conducted research projects relating to shipping and ports, fisheries, coastal and sea use management, and marine spatial planning. From 1986 until 2000 he was successively Secretary and Chair of the International Geographical Union Commission on Marine Geography. He has published numerous academic papers, book chapters, and several books, as well as acting as editor for many journal special issues and several books.

Juan Pablo Soto

Juan Pablo is an Associate Professor at the Department of Strategy of Universidad de los Andes School of Management (UASM), Colombia. He obtained his PhD from Pompeu Fabra University (Spain). His research interests focus on closed-loop supply chains, reverse logistics and retail logistics. Juan Pablo has published in *Omega* and other academic and professional journals. He was the co-founder of the master's in International Retail at ESCI-UPF, academic director of Centro Español de Logística, and is currently the director of specializations at UASM. He has been the director of several consulting projects in both the public and private sectors as part of the UASM Strategy and Competitiveness Center.

Peter Tatham

Peter is Professor of Humanitarian Logistics at Griffith Business School in Gold Coast, Queensland. A former (UK) Royal Navy logistician, he served in a variety of logistics appointments during his career of some 35 years, in which he rose to the rank of Commodore (1*). Following his retirement from the Royal Navy, he joined the staff of Cranfield University, UK, was awarded his PhD in 2009 and subsequently received the 2010 Emerald/

EFMD Outstanding Doctoral Research Award. In the same year, Peter joined the faculty of Griffith University, where he teaches and researches supply chain management, specializing in humanitarian logistics. Peter is the Asia and Australia editor of the *Journal of Humanitarian Logistics and Supply Chain Management*, and is a member of the editorial board of the *International Journal of Physical Logistics and Supply Chain Management*.

Marcus Thiell

Marcus is an Associate Professor at the Department of Strategy of Universidad de los Andes School of Management (UASM), Colombia. He obtained his PhD from Friedrich-Alexander University Erlangen-Nürnberg. His research interests focus on supply chain management in emerging markets. Marcus has published in *Omega* and the *Journal of Cleaner Production*, and co-authored several cases about supply chain management practices and challenges in Colombia. As a consultant at the UASM Strategy and Competitiveness Center, he worked on projects related to supply chain management, for example in the oil industry, retail, and the public sector.

Peter Wells

Peter is a Professor of Business and Sustainability and Director of the Centre for Automotive Industry Research at Cardiff Business School, where his work has ranged across spatial industrial development, environmental economics, organizational theory, industrial ecology, technological change, and sustainability. Examples of Peter's specialist areas are the global automotive industry, transitions theory and the development of alternative business models. He teaches transport, mobility and business sustainability on the MBA and MSc programmes in the Cardiff Business School, as well as to a wide range of companies and organizations. Peter has produced a substantial number of publications targeting academia, industry, policymakers and stakeholders; his methods of dissemination include academic journal papers and books, internet publications and, more recently, webinars.

Su-Han Woo

Su-Han is a Professor in the Department of International Logistics at Chung-Ang University in South Korea. Prior to his current position, he worked for more than 10 years at the Korean Ministries dealing with transport and logistics policies. He received his PhD from Cardiff University in 2010. His research interests focus on effective management of international logistics and transportation, focusing on integration of transport and logistics into supply chain networks. He has published articles in leading academic journals such as *Supply Chain Management: An International Journal*, *Transportation Research Part A*, *Transport Reviews*, *Maritime Economics and Logistics* and *Maritime Policy and Management*.

Frida Youssef

Frida is Chief of the Transport Section in the Trade Logistics Branch of UNCTAD. She holds an MBA from Boston University, and an MA in International Affairs from the Haute Etude international, Paris. She has more than 20 years of professional experience in trade, finance and sustainable development, including 18 years in UNCTAD, which gave her the opportunity to build, lead and motivate research and technical assistance programmes covering a broad range of issues, including sustainable freight transport, transport corridors, commodity value chains, energy, finance, environment and climate change. She is also a co-author of the UNCTAD annual *Review of Maritime Transport*, focusing in particular on maritime freight rates issues.

LIST OF ABBREVIATIONS

ACI	Airport Council International
ACO	Air Cargo Operator
ACPA	Association of Canadian Port Authorities
ADB	Asian Development Bank
AEC	ASEAN Economic Community
AEO	Authorised Economic Operator
ANC	African National Congress
AOS	Accredited Operator Scheme
APGCI	Asia-Pacific Gateway and Corridor Initiative
APROC	Asia-Pacific Regional Operational Centre
ASEAN	Association of Southeast Asian Nations
BDI	Baltic Dry Index
BOPD	Barrels of Oil Per Day
BRIC	Brazil, Russia, India and China
BRICS	Brazil, Russia, India, China and South Africa
BYB	Beyond the Border
CAA	Canadian Airport Authorities
CETA	Comprehensive Economic and Trade Agreement
CEU	Car-Equivalent Unit
CFS	Container Freight Station
CIF	Cost Insurance and Freight
CILT	Chartered Institute of Logistics and Transport
CIMT	Centre for IMT-GT Sub-Regional Cooperation
CIS	Commonwealth of Independent States
CO_2	Carbon Dioxide
COMECON	Council for Mutual Economic Assistance countries
COMESA	Common Market for Eastern and Southern Africa
CPA	Canadian Port Authorities
CPR	Centre for Retail Research
CRED	Centre for the Research on the Epidemiology of Disasters
C-TPAT	Customs and Trade Partnership Against Terrorism
CTARC	Canada Transportation Act Review Committee
DDP	Delivery Duty Paid
DRC	Democratic Republic of Congo
EAP	East Asia and Pacific

ECOWAS	Economic Community of West African States
EPA	Economic Partnership Agreement
ERP	Enterprise Resource Planning
ETC	Electronic Toll Collection
EU	European Union
EXW	Ex-Works
FCC	(1) Food Contract Corporation
	(2) Fully Cellular Containerships
FDI	Foreign Direct Investment
FEU	Forty-foot Equivalent Unit (Container)
FOB	Free-on-Board
FTA	(1) Free Trade Agreement
	(2) Freight Transport Association
GATT	General Agreement on Tariffs and Trade
GDP	Gross Domestic Product
GHG	Greenhouse Gas
GTO	Global Terminal Operator
HCA	Hybrid Cargo Airship
HERO	High Efficiency Ro-Ro
HMT	Harbour Maintenance Tax
IADB	Inter-American Development Bank
IASC	Inter-Agency Standing Committee
IATA	International Air Transport Association
ICT	Information and Communications Technology
IFRC	International Federation of Red Cross and Red Crescent Societies
ILO	International Labour Organization
IMB	International Maritime Bureau
IMF	International Monetary Fund
IMO	International Maritime Organization
IMT-GT	Indonesia–Malaysia–Thailand Growth Triangle
INTERTANKO	International Association of Independent Tanker Owners
IOPC	International Oil Pollution Compensation
IP	Implementing Partner
IPO	Initial Public Offerings
IPSAS	International Public Sector Accounting Standards
ISO	International Organization for Standardization
ISTEA	Intermodal Surface Transportation Efficiency Act
ITOPF	International Tanker Owners Pollution Federation

JSC FCC	JSC 'Food Contract Corporation'
LAA	Local Airport Authority
LAC	Latin America and the Caribbean
LCL	Less-than-Container Loads
LCO	Land Cargo Operator
LDC	Least Developed Country
LE-RPAS	Long Endurance Remotely Piloted Aircraft Systems
LNG	Liquefied Natural Gas
Lo-Lo	Lift on, Lift Off
LPI	Logistics Performance Index
LSCI	Liner Shipping Connectivity Index
LSP	Logistics Service Provider
M&A	Mergers and Acquisitions
MCTC	Maritime Container Transportation Chain
MDC	Maputo (Development) Corridor
MOTC	Ministry of Transport and Communication (Taiwan)
MOU	Memorandum of Understanding
MPB	Maritime Port Bureau (Taiwan)
MTNet	Maritime Transport Network Portal (Taiwan)
MUNIN	Maritime Unmanned Navigation through Intelligence in Networks
NAFTA	North American Free Trade Agreement
NAS	National Airports System
NCER	Northern Corridor Economic Region
NDMO	National Disaster Management Organization
NEPAD	New Partnership for Africa's Development
NGL	Natural Gas Liquids
NGO	Non-Governmental Organization
NORAD	North American Aerospace Defense Command
NOx	Nitrogen Oxides
NPX	Neo-Panamax
NSR	Northern Sea Route
OBO	Oil–Bulk–Ore
OBOR	One Belt, One Road
OECD	Organisation for Economic Co-operation and Development
OPA90	Oil Pollution Act 1990
P&I	Protection and Indemnity

PCC	Pure Car Carrier
PCS	Port Community System
PCTC	Pure Car and Truck Carrier
POD	Points of Distribution
PSA	Port of Singapore Authority
PSC	Port State Control
PTA	Preferential Trade Area
RAC	Railway Association of Canada
RCEP	Regional Comprehensive Economic Partnership
RCH	Railway Clearing House
RENAMO	Resistência Nacional Moçambicana
RISDP	Regional Indicative Strategic Development Plan
Ro-Ro	Roll-on, Roll-off
RPAS	Remotely Piloted Aircraft System
RSA	Republic of South Africa
RZD	Russian Railways
SACU	Southern African Customs Union
SADC	Southern African Development Community
SCM	Supply Chain Management
SCRM	Supply Chain Risk Management
SDG	Sustainable Development Goal
SIDS	Small Island Developing State
SKUs	Stock Keeping Units
SME	Small and Medium Enterprises
SOx	Sulphur Oxide
SWAPO	South West Africa People's Organization
TEU	Twenty-Foot Equivalent Unit (Container)
TIR	Transports Internationaux Routiers
TKC	Trans Kalahari Corridor Secretariat
TOD	Transit Oriented Development
TOS	Terminal Operating Systems
TPP	Trans-Pacific Partnership
TTIP	Transatlantic Trade and Investment Partnership
UAV/S	Unmanned Aerial Vehicle/System
ULCC	Ultra Large Crude Carrier/Ultra Large Container Carrier
ULCV	Ultra-Large Container Vessel
UN	United Nations
UN/CEFACT	United Nations Centre for Trade Facilitation and Electronic Business

UNCTAD	United Nations Conference on Trade and Development
UNESCAP	United Nations Economic and Social Commission for Asia and the Pacific
UNHRD	United Nations Humanitarian Response Depot
VLCC	Very Large Crude Carrier/Very Large Container Carrier
VTS	Vessel Traffic Service
W&D	Warehousing and Distribution
WBCG	Walvis Bay Corridor Group
WCO	World Customs Organization
WEF	World Economic Forum
WFP	World Food Programme
WTO	World Trade Organization

Introduction: cases, structures and prospects

ANTHONY BERESFORD, Cardiff Business School, UK
STEPHEN PETTIT, Cardiff Business School, UK

The increasing emphasis on globalization in the context of production, least-cost sourcing, corporate structures and finance has stimulated a substantial increase in both information transfer and the physical movement of goods. Demand for products has also been steadily growing, with patterns of demand becoming ever more complex. The movements of raw materials, for example, which feed into manufacturing processes, and the markets for finished or semi-finished consumer goods are dynamic, with final assembly and other activities often moving downstream to locations closer to the customer, following the principle of 'postponement'. In the case of perishable products, long-distance transport is often designed to overcome seasonal availability constraints, to bridge the gap between the supply of, and demand for, exotic products, or simply to provide increased choice.

The quest for reduced costs, increased capacity or improved service is most visible on international routes and over the longest distances where scale economies are most important. This has driven up vehicle and vessel size in most sectors and has precipitated extremely ambitious infrastructural improvements, for example the Panama Canal widening, the St Gothard base tunnel in Switzerland (the world's longest and deepest transport tunnel with a route length of 57 km), super-high road bridges and rail routes in China and a variety of other capacity expansion projects elsewhere.

Regarding the transport vehicles, the biggest liquid bulk vessels – Ultra Large Crude Carriers (ULCCs) – ply the longest sea routes, the world's longest and heaviest trucks in the form of 100 m-long multi-trailer road trains move iron ore from Australian mines to the railheads, the longest container trains, up to 2 km in length, comprising as many as 160 double-stack wagons, operate on certain landbridge routes in North America and the world's heaviest trains (gross weight up to almost 100,000 tonnes) transport bulk iron ore to the export ports of Australia. The biggest container ships, currently 18,000+ TEUs, serve the Far East–Europe trade lanes, where the extremely large volumes of containerized freight justify the deployment of the biggest ships. Other routes, for example Trans-Pacific and Trans-Atlantic, are also served by extremely large ships. One of the biggest ships currently operating, the *Berge Stahl*, carries over 300,000 tonnes of iron ore in one shipment from Brazil to Rotterdam, squeezing into the only two ports in the world that can accommodate its 24 m draught. Even in the cruise ship sector, vessels are now bigger than ever before: the *Harmony of the Seas*, at 227,000 GRT, is the biggest passenger ship ever. The push for economies of scale is equally visible on the long-haul air routes with Boeing 747 freighters weighing up to 442,000 kg serving, for example the Europe–Far East trades. The Airbus A380 (maximum take-off weight of 573 tonnes) likewise serves a range of long-haul routes with freight piggybacking on its core passenger transport function. The heaviest freighter of all, the Antonov 225 (maximum take-off weight of 640 tonnes with up to 245 tonnes of freight), offers hire-and-reward services for one-off project cargo transport, which is beyond the capability of any other aircraft currently available, although experimental airships such as the Aeroscraft ML866 (potential payload of 60 tonnes, range of some 6,000 km) and the larger ML868 (potential payload 220 tonnes, range 9,500 km), may enter service for specialist purposes in the coming decades.

International freight transport is by no means dependent on the inexorable advance of globalization; very few trades are in practice truly global, but international freight transport operations are fundamentally about converging time and space across boundaries and borders, pressing down unit costs along the way. The methods and means of transport, and the infrastructure supporting transport operations, have become increasingly sophisticated and diverse.

Broadly, the longer the distance over which freight is transported, the more imaginative the solutions, and the more finely tuned information and documentation systems which bind the elements together become. Thus trading protocols involving partners, facilitators and suppliers, as well as the cargo owners, have been the subject of continuous review in order to keep up with both technological developments and the dynamics of the global marketplace.

International freight transport takes place on a range of scales: cross-border trade in some cases may be over only a few kilometres and transport methods may be extremely simple, eg by means of small truck, barge or sailing craft making use of the available basic infrastructure and prevalent physical conditions. The need in these cases is simply to bridge a small gap between the supplier and a customer. At a regional level, trading is over longer distances, transport solutions are more varied, procedures are more formal, and control protocols more rigid. The world's major trading blocs, such as the North American Free Trade Agreement (NAFTA), European Union (EU)/Schengen, Economic Community of West African States (ECOWAS), Association of Southeast Asian Nations (ASEAN), and the Southern African Development Community (SADC) have international transport at their heart and, although they vary in their structures, control mechanisms and context, they are all designed to facilitate or promote intra-regional movement of freight or people, or usually both. Within these blocs, and between the blocs and non-affiliate neighbouring states, much progress has been made in the areas of trade facilitation and transport efficiency, but tensions remain and progress is still required in pursuit of the free movement of goods without compromising security and control.

The great distances involved in some international transport operations invariably entail increased risk and uncertainty derived from time in transit, amount of intermodal handling, the number of operators or agents involved, and variation in operating conditions. But long distance transport also offers financial reward, especially for innovative solutions, by exploiting economies of scale and scope, and by offering value-addition activities.

International Freight Transport: Cases, structures and prospects brings together a number of self-contained studies which are themed around either a specific trade or a major trading region, compiled by experts in their respective fields. The intention is to illustrate and examine the richness and diversity of freight transport operations evident in different parts of the world, reflecting the variety of operating conditions, cargo characteristics, trading cultures and customer requirements which prevail.

Part One: Trade and the transport environment

Part One of the book establishes the principles for international freight transport. This introduction provides a platform for the global and regional cases which are subsequently presented. In Chapter 1, Hassiba Benamara, Jan Hoffman and Frida Youssef contextualize international transport with an emphasis on trade which acts as a key driver of freight movement. The authors show that trade has been steadily growing, and at the same time, patterns of movement have become more complex. They take a demand and supply perspective, showing that the further the supply region is from the market, the greater the demand for transport. Transport solutions then resolve into a selection of modal combinations and methods, with shipping dominating for the longer routes and for the trades which require the highest capacity provision. The chapter also considers trends in trade, and the commercial dimension, including profitability and the performance of freight markets. Longer-term patterns of movement, including the delicate balance between freight volumes transported and capacity provision, are highlighted in order to gain an insight into the link between maritime transport and the trade landscape. The prospects for maritime transport are assessed against continuing uncertainty in the world economy.

Chapter 2, by Andrew Grainger, highlights the importance of trade and transport protocols in the provision of efficient and sustainable transport operations. The author first presents an overview of trade and customs procedures and of the regulatory framework for international trade and transport, then considers the extent to which procedures impact upon cost, and suggests ways in which the trade and customs environment can be improved. This is particularly important in light of the reconfiguring of trade blocs and ongoing global trade reform; such issues are at the heart of trade policy and are regularly faced by international logistics and transport operators. The chapter includes guidance through the procedures involved in reliable fast-track port and border clearance, taking account of the varied nature of traded cargoes. Liabilities, cargo handling responsibilities and the ways in which risk is accommodated are also discussed.

Part Two: International freight transport in practice

Part Two presents a series of cases which focus on particular trades in order to highlight the diversity and richness of the international freight transport environment. The four chapters are focused on global trades involving continuous flows of raw materials or finished/high-value goods respectively.

Chapter 3, by Timur Bimaganbetov, Anthony Beresford and Stephen Pettit presents an evaluation of grain transport in Kazakhstan where operating conditions are complicated by historic connections to the former Soviet Union and by the fact that the country is severely landlocked. Kazakhstan and several of its neighbouring countries require access through adjacent maritime states in order to tap into global markets. The chapter examines the transport of grain exports, highlighting the unusual nature of the routes and the carrying methods. Kazakhstan is among the top six grain exporting countries in the world, and is comfortably world number one in terms of export tonnes per head of population. In particular, the chapter explores the interplay between distance, time, cost and mode alternatives using an analysis of existing and alternative routes available to Kazakh grain exporters. Both soft (intangible) and hard (tangible) dimensions are highlighted. A multimodal transport time-cost model is used as a framework to evaluate the effectiveness of both existing and potential routes.

The transport of hydrocarbons is central to the global economy due to the primary role oil and natural gas play in the world energy budget, the importance of hydrocarbon products in the supply of fuels for transport and power generation, and the contribution of oil and gas to the chemical industry. Chapter 4, by Hance Smith and Azmath Jaleel, recounts the temporal patterns of transport of oil, gas and products, and the basic elements and factors underlying these patterns. The chapter also presents an evaluation of the physical aspects of liquid bulk transport, including the use of tankers and pipelines. The environmental dimension, including geographical patterns of transport, routine operations and the random shocks deriving especially from accidents, shipwrecks and war, are also discussed. The political economy, geopolitical influences on the transport system, governance and management, and likely future trends in hydrocarbon transport are also discussed.

Containerization has been one of the greatest facilitators of change in the world economy over the last five decades. Today, consumers are connected with the lowest-cost production locations. Global outsourcing is based on containerization as well as on multi-location processing. Containerization enabled the standardization of port handling equipment, in turn increasing the speed of cargo handling and leading to the establishment of global liner networks and intermodal transport. Such developments changed the way that both manufactured and primary goods are shipped around the world. In Chapter 5, Rolf Neise examines the development of container shipping, outlining both current and future global trade perspectives looking ahead to 2030. Shipping networks, key origins and destinations, main routes and service types, as well as the main actors and their interactions with each other in the Maritime Container Transportation Chain, are described. The latest technological developments in terms of vessels, handling equipment and ICT support, complete what is a comprehensive overview of global container transport.

The final chapter in Part Two, by Paul Nieuwenhuis, provides an analysis of the international transport of cars. Chapter 6 considers in particular how the shipment of cars has changed in response to adjustments in both vehicle manufacturing methods and the markets. While cars have always been a globally traded product, for many years the flows involved very small numbers of complete units. Many companies transported components for local assembly at branch plants, but in due course the situation changed as larger flows of fully built, mass-produced cars and other vehicles began to emerge. Similarly, when markets for Japanese cars opened up in developed countries such as the United States, the larger European countries and Australia, higher-volume shipments of cars became necessary, leading to the use of dedicated ships and a reorganization of the logistics networks for the mass movement of cars. An interesting aspect of the expanding market for vehicle transport has been the emergence of mixed-method shipping embracing Roll-on, Roll-off (Ro-Ro) and Lift-on, Lift-off (Lo-Lo) via the deployment of combination vessels on certain routes, or by using containerization to 'anonymize' vehicles in transit, especially to protect classic or high-end marques.

Part Three: Trading regions

Part Three considers international freight transport from the perspective of trading regions. The five chapters in Part Three cover respectively South East Asia, North America with the spotlight on Canada, South America with particular focus on Colombia, Southern Africa, and Korea/Taiwan.

In Chapter 7, Ruth Banomyong provides an assessment of international transport in the ASEAN region with particular emphasis on the Indonesia–Malaysia–Thailand Growth Triangle (IMT-GT). The IMT-GT is a sub-regional cooperation initiative between the governments of Indonesia, Malaysia and Thailand developed to accelerate economic transformation in the region. Since its formation, the IMT-GT has grown in geographic scope and activities to encompass more than 70 million people. The IMT-GT provides a sub-regional framework for accelerating economic cooperation and integration of the member states and provinces in the three countries and promotes private sector-led economic growth in order to facilitate the development of the sub-region as a whole by exploiting the underlying complementarities and comparative advantages of the member countries. An economic corridor approach has been identified as a core strategy for accelerated development of the IMT-GT, and the development of these economic corridors is a Flagship Project of the IMT-GT. It is shown that for the economic corridor to be successful as a driver of development, freight logistics capability within these corridors will need to be enhanced, as in the case of the North–South Economic Corridor in the Greater Mekong Sub-region. The main purpose of the chapter is to provide a freight logistics analysis of key corridors in the IMT-GT using empirical data and then to propose policy recommendations to increase freight transport efficiency.

In Chapter 8, Michael Ircha reviews freight transport in North America with an emphasis on Canada. International freight moves continentally among the three NAFTA countries primarily by land – road, rail and pipeline. Global transportation and trade trends are examined along with how they affect commodity movements both within NAFTA and internationally. The chapter considers gateways and trade corridors, regulatory challenges and system liberalization in order to address transport friction generated by technical non-tariff barriers. The chapter also considers the 2016 Canada Transportation Act Review's recommendations to improve Canadian and North American international freight transport.

In the last few decades much attention has been focused on global trade and transport between developed western nations and Asia. But despite trade volumes being highly significant between these regions, trade with and across other continents such as South America, one of the economically fastest-growing regions in the world, has largely been ignored as to its potential, nuances and issues. In Chapter 9, David Grant, Rodrigo Britto, Juan Pablo Soto and Marcus Thiell discuss international freight transport operations in South America with particular reference to Colombia. Colombia's US $48.5 billion of exports include coffee, fresh flowers, natural resources and apparel with over a quarter of its products destined for the United States. The chapter provides an overview of Colombia's transport statistics in the context of its Latin American and Caribbean neighbours and the United States, and observations are made regarding the trade trajectory of Colombia in its South American context, with vignettes presented to elaborate on particular cases.

In Chapter 10, Christopher Savage considers freight transport across Southern Africa. The diversity of modern Southern African countries is first outlined, including the dynamics of the Southern African borders, groupings and alliances. Of note in the region is the prominence of commercial/customs unions which tend to encourage trade in particular directions. The UN and the Southern African Customs Union (SACU) define Southern Africa as the five countries of Botswana, Lesotho, Namibia, Republic of South Africa (RSA) and Swaziland, whereas the Southern African Development

Community (SADC) recognizes a larger group which comprises the five SACU countries plus Angola, Democratic Republic of Congo, Madagascar, Malawi, Mauritius, Mozambique, Seychelles, Tanzania, Zambia and Zimbabwe. The unusual physical and economic characteristics of the region offer both opportunities and challenges to the transport operators, especially those offering international services. The transport network binding Southern African countries together is examined and bottlenecks and inefficiencies are highlighted. While the chapter focuses on the SACU countries it also acknowledges that significant cross-border interaction with neighbouring countries such as Angola, Mozambique, Zambia and Zimbabwe occurs.

In Chapter 11, Su-Han Woo, Po-Lin Lai, Doori Kim and Jungeun Kim discuss the role of Korea and Taiwan in their regional and global transport context. While firms in this region have competence as producers of final products, they are particularly prominent in terms of their participation in global value chains. Freight transport systems in the two countries are summarized, with particular emphasis on modal split, capacity provision and development and the underpinning geopolitics influencing their trajectory. Both international and domestic transport are considered, and recent influences such as online purchasing and environmental considerations are highlighted, especially regarding their influence on the restructuring of distribution networks. The chapter thus reviews current transport developments in Korea and Taiwan and discusses how transport sectors respond to internal influences and external challenges.

Part Four: Challenging environments and transport futures

Part Four concludes the book by considering transport in challenging environments and transport futures. In Chapter 12, Peter Tatham and Gyöngyi Kovács look at uncertainty from the perspective of operating transport services in fragile or crisis conditions where there is the need to deliver freight, either as development cargo or emergency aid, to remote or unstable areas. The particular emphasis of the text is on highlighting strategies in the humanitarian context which are inherently challenging from a transport perspective. Whether as a result of natural disasters or wars, circumstances which individually or collectively impact on access corridors and command structures, capacity provision and routing options are examined. The chapter focuses on specific challenges that arise for transport operations in crisis conditions, together with emerging opportunities that have the potential to improve the efficiency and/or effectiveness of the logistic response process. A number of specific issues in humanitarian transport, namely achieving access to disaster areas and beneficiaries, the very complex nature of transportation services in this area, and the rise of new technologies are considered.

To conclude the book, in Chapter 13 Peter Wells assesses the future prospects for transport, and he speculates regarding the range of possible transport futures. He suggests that, looking back, both freight and passenger transport have enjoyed reasonable stability and continuity over the last 70 years, notwithstanding several generations of incremental, or step-wise technological improvements. The overwhelming narrative he describes is one of evolutionary growth, occasionally accelerated by a particular need or a particular innovation.

The chapter makes the case that, over the next few decades, transport will be radically different except for one key aspect: the majority of transport will remain a derived demand. Transport is used in order to achieve other things; freight, for example, feeds into manufacturing processes if it is in crude form, or into retail if it is finished product. Transport is shown to be at its most effective when unused space or waste mileage is minimized. This points towards a future for transport which will almost certainly be driven by waste minimizing or efficiency maximizing, with technological or operational innovation guiding businesses towards those objectives. In turn, this unites the thinking behind the achievement of efficient and low-cost production via exploitation of economies of scale, and the operation of global production chains. He highlights the fundamental tension between localized on-demand economies and global production chains that are linked by mainly low-geared maritime transport, and also in part by high-geared airfreight services with other modes performing link functions, collection and delivery. This chapter does not seek to answer the question, 'what is the future for transport?', rather it presents a stance whereby there is likely to be a multiple set of co-existing, complementary and contradictory futures in which the activity of transport is contested and politicized as never before. Transport emerges from these futures as a residual service function requiring considerable flexibility in order to respond to changes in the demand for transport provision, changes in technology, and developments in the governance and business models which underpin that provision.

PART ONE
Trade and the transport environment

Demand, supply and freight rates: the shipping of global trade

01

HASSIBA BENAMARA, UNCTAD, Switzerland
JAN HOFFMANN, UNCTAD, Switzerland
FRIDA YOUSSEF, UNCTAD, Switzerland

Introduction

With over 80 per cent of global trade by volume and 55 per cent to 71 per cent by value – depending on the data source and methodology – being carried by sea, maritime transport remains the backbone of globalization and at the heart of cross-border transport networks that support supply chains and enable international trade.

Maritime transport is the backbone of globalization and at the heart of cross-border transport networks that support supply chains and enable international trade. An economic sector in its own right that generates employment, income and revenue, transport, including maritime transport, is cross-cutting and permeates other sectors and activities.

Maritime transport enables industrial development by supporting manufacturing growth, bringing together consumers, intermediate and capital goods industries, and promoting regional economic and trade integration. The importance of transport has been further recognized by newly adopted Sustainable Development Goals (SDGs) which integrate infrastructure and transport as an important consideration.

Against this background, this chapter considers relevant developments affecting demand and supply of maritime transport infrastructure and services as well as related trends determining profitability and the performance of freight markets. While the chapter emphasizes recent trends unfolding in 2015, some longer-term patterns are also highlighted to gain greater insights into the overall maritime transport and trade landscape. An outlook for maritime transport is set out against the backdrop of continued global uncertainty and downside risks which have, since the 2008 financial crisis and the 2009 Great Recession, been weighing down on the world economy, trade and maritime transport.

Among other factors, slower global economic and trade growth, energy and oil price developments, advances in technology and digitization, the rise of e-commerce, chronic mismatch in ship supply capacity and demand, as well as growing environmental and sustainability imperatives are identified as key factors currently redefining the maritime transport sector and shaping its ability to effectively meet the growing demands of the 21st century, while at the same time maintaining profitability and competitiveness.

Demand: drivers and trends

Although a number of factors are increasingly redefining seaborne trade patterns, maritime trade flows continue to be largely determined by developments in the macroeconomic landscape. Over the past four decades, seaborne trade volumes have generally moved in tandem with economic growth, industrial activity and merchandise trade, albeit at varied speeds. Historically, world merchandise trade volumes have grown about twice as fast as world gross domestic product (GDP), but the trade-to-GDP growth ratio continues to decline, and in recent years, world merchandise trade has been expanding at a relatively slower rate either matching or below world GDP growth levels. In 2015, the trade-to-GDP growth ratio was estimated at 0.62, down from 0.94 in 2014 and 1.4 in 2013.

While international trade is still influenced by the remnants of the 2009 downturn, the question that arises is whether the continued slowdown in merchandise trade is resulting mainly from cyclical factors (weaker GDP growth and macroeconomic cycles) or a break in the long-term relationship between trade and GDP, indicating that structural factors such as slower growth in value chain may also be at play.

World seaborne trade: general trends

In 2015 and for the first time on UNCTAD's record, world seaborne trade volumes exceeded 10 billion tonnes (Table 1.1).

Demand, Supply and Freight Rates

Table 1.1 Development in international seaborne trade, selected years (millions of tonnes loaded)

Year	Oil and gas	Main bulks[a]	Dry cargo other than main bulks	Total (all cargoes)
1970	1,440	448	717	2,605
1980	1,871	608	1,225	3,704
1990	1,755	988	1,265	4,008
2000	2,163	1,295	2,526	5,984
2005	2,422	1,709	2,978	7,109
2006	2,698	1,814	3,188	7,700
2007	2,747	1,953	3,334	8,034
2008	2,742	2,065	3,422	8,229
2009	2,642	2,085	3,131	7,858
2010	2,772	2,335	3,302	8,409
2011	2,794	2,486	3,505	8,785
2012	2,841	2,742	3,614	9,197
2013	2,829	2,923	3,762	9,514
2014	2,825	2,985	4,033	9,843
2015	2,947	2,951	4,150	10,047

SOURCES Compiled by the UNCTAD secretariat on the basis of data supplied by reporting countries and as published on the relevant government and port industry website, and by specialist sources. The data for 2006 onwards have been revised and updated to reflect improved reporting, including more recent figures and better information regarding the breakdown by cargo type. Figures for 2015 are estimated based on preliminary data or on the last year for which data were available
[a] Iron ore, grain, coal, bauxite/alumina and phosphate. The data for 2006 onwards are based on various issues of the *Dry Bulk Trade Outlook*, produced by Clarksons Research

During the year, dry cargo shipments accounted for over two-thirds of total seaborne trade volumes while the remaining share was made up of tanker trade, including crude oil, petroleum products and gas (Table 1.1 and Figure 1.1). Growth in world seaborne trade by tonne-miles, which provides a more accurate measure of demand for ship carrying capacity as it takes into account distances travelled, also decelerated in 2015. Volumes increased at the modest rate of 1.6 per cent, down from 4.1 per cent recorded in 2014. World seaborne trade totalled 53.6 estimated billion tonne-miles, up from 52.7 estimated billion tonne-miles in 2014 (Figure 1.2).

Developing countries continued to contribute larger shares to the total volumes of international seaborne trade. In terms of global goods loaded, developing countries accounted for an estimated 60 per cent, while their

Figure 1.1 International seaborne trade, selected years (millions of tonnes loaded)

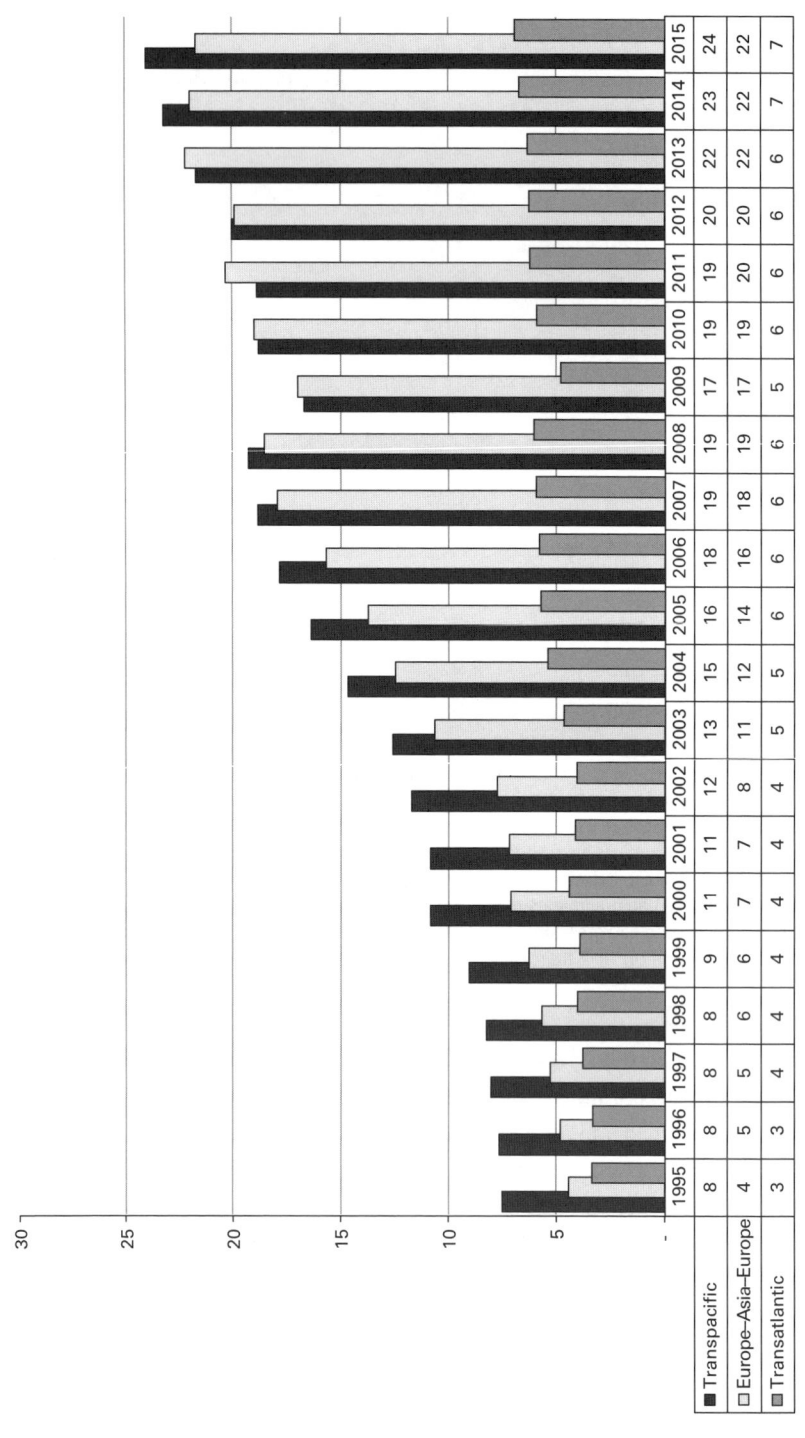

	1995	1996	1997	1998	1999	2000	2001	2002	2003	2004	2005	2006	2007	2008	2009	2010	2011	2012	2013	2014	2015
■ Transpacific	8	8	8	8	9	11	11	12	13	15	16	18	19	19	17	19	19	20	22	23	24
☐ Europe–Asia–Europe	4	5	5	6	6	7	7	8	11	12	14	16	18	19	17	19	20	20	22	22	22
▨ Transatlantic	3	3	4	4	4	4	4	4	5	5	6	6	6	6	5	6	6	6	6	7	7

SOURCE *UNCTAD Review of Maritime Transport*, various issues. For 2006–2015, the breakdown by type of cargo is based on Clarksons Research (2016b) and *Seaborne Trade Monitor* (2016)

Figure 1.2 World seaborne trade in cargo tonne-miles by cargo type, 2000–2016 (billions of tonne-miles)

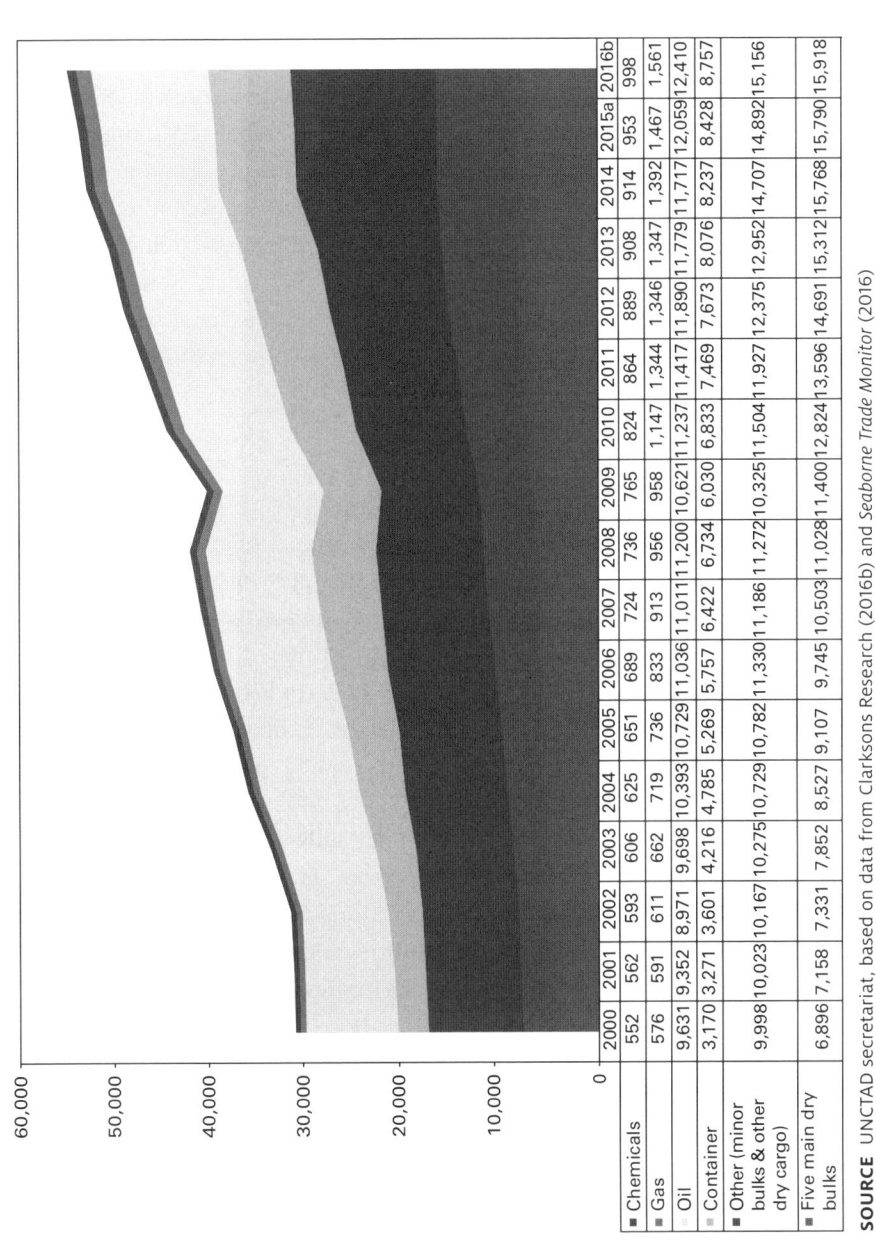

	2000	2001	2002	2003	2004	2005	2006	2007	2008	2009	2010	2011	2012	2013	2014	2015a	2016b
Chemicals	552	562	593	606	625	651	689	724	736	765	824	864	889	908	914	953	998
Gas	576	591	611	662	719	736	833	913	956	958	1,147	1,344	1,346	1,347	1,392	1,467	1,561
Oil	9,631	9,352	8,971	9,698	10,393	10,729	11,036	11,011	11,200	10,621	11,237	11,417	11,890	11,779	11,717	12,059	12,410
Container	3,170	3,271	3,601	4,216	4,785	5,269	5,757	6,422	6,734	6,030	6,833	7,469	7,673	8,076	8,237	8,428	8,757
Other (minor bulks & other dry cargo)	9,998	10,023	10,167	10,275	10,729	10,782	11,330	11,186	11,272	10,325	11,504	11,927	12,375	12,952	14,707	14,892	15,156
Five main dry bulks	6,896	7,158	7,331	7,852	8,527	9,107	9,745	10,503	11,028	11,400	12,824	13,596	14,691	15,312	15,768	15,790	15,918

SOURCE UNCTAD secretariat, based on data from Clarksons Research (2016b) and *Seaborne Trade Monitor* (2016)

a = Estimate / b = Forecast

import demand as measured by the volume of goods unloaded increased and reached 62 per cent (Figure 1.3). They remained key world importers and exporters in 2015 and have consolidated their position as suppliers of raw materials while also strengthening their position as a large source of consumer demand and major players in globalized manufacturing processes.

Over the past four decades, a compositional shift has occurred in seaborne trade, reflecting among others things the effects of globalized manufacturing processes, longer supply chains, developing countries' expanding energy and industrial commodity needs as well as their growing requirements for consumer goods and processed products. In terms of regional influence, Asia continued to dominate as the main loading and unloading area in 2015. For loadings, the Americas surpassed Europe, Oceania and Africa, while, as regards goods unloaded, Europe received larger volumes followed by the Americas, Africa and Oceania (Figure 1.4).

Seaborne trade by cargo type

Supported in particular by ample supply of oil cargo and lower oil prices, in 2015 the tanker sector experienced one of its best performances since 2008. Global crude oil trade reversed the 2014 trend and expanded at the rapid rate of 3.8 per cent, taking total volumes to an estimated 1.77 billion tonnes in 2015. Meanwhile, petroleum products and gas trade totalled 1.17 billion tonnes, an increase of 5.1 per cent over 2014. Global natural gas trade carried by sea in the liquefied form (LNG) accounted for nearly one-third of the world natural gas trade in 2015.

Estimated at 4.8 billion tonnes, global dry bulk shipments fell marginally (–0.2 per cent) in 2015. In sharp contrast to the average annual growth of recent years (7 per cent), dry bulk trade contracted due to a 1.3 per cent decline in the five major dry bulk commodities trades (iron ore, coal, grain, bauxite and alumina, and phosphate/rock). Shipments of the five major bulks totalled 2.95 billion tonnes in 2015. In less than 15 years, China's import volumes increased nearly seven-fold from 319 million tonnes in 2000 to 2.1 billion tonnes. The concentrated growth both in China and in two key commodities, namely iron ore and coal, heightened the vulnerability of shipping and seaborne trade to fluctuations affecting demand and to developments in China's economy. Iron ore seaborne shipments totalled 1.36 billion tonnes with import volumes into China, which accounted for over two-thirds of world iron ore imports, increasing by 2.8 per cent, a much slower rate than the 15 per cent expansion recorded in 2014. As for

Figure 1.3 Participation of developing countries in world seaborne trade, selected years (percentage share in world tonnage)

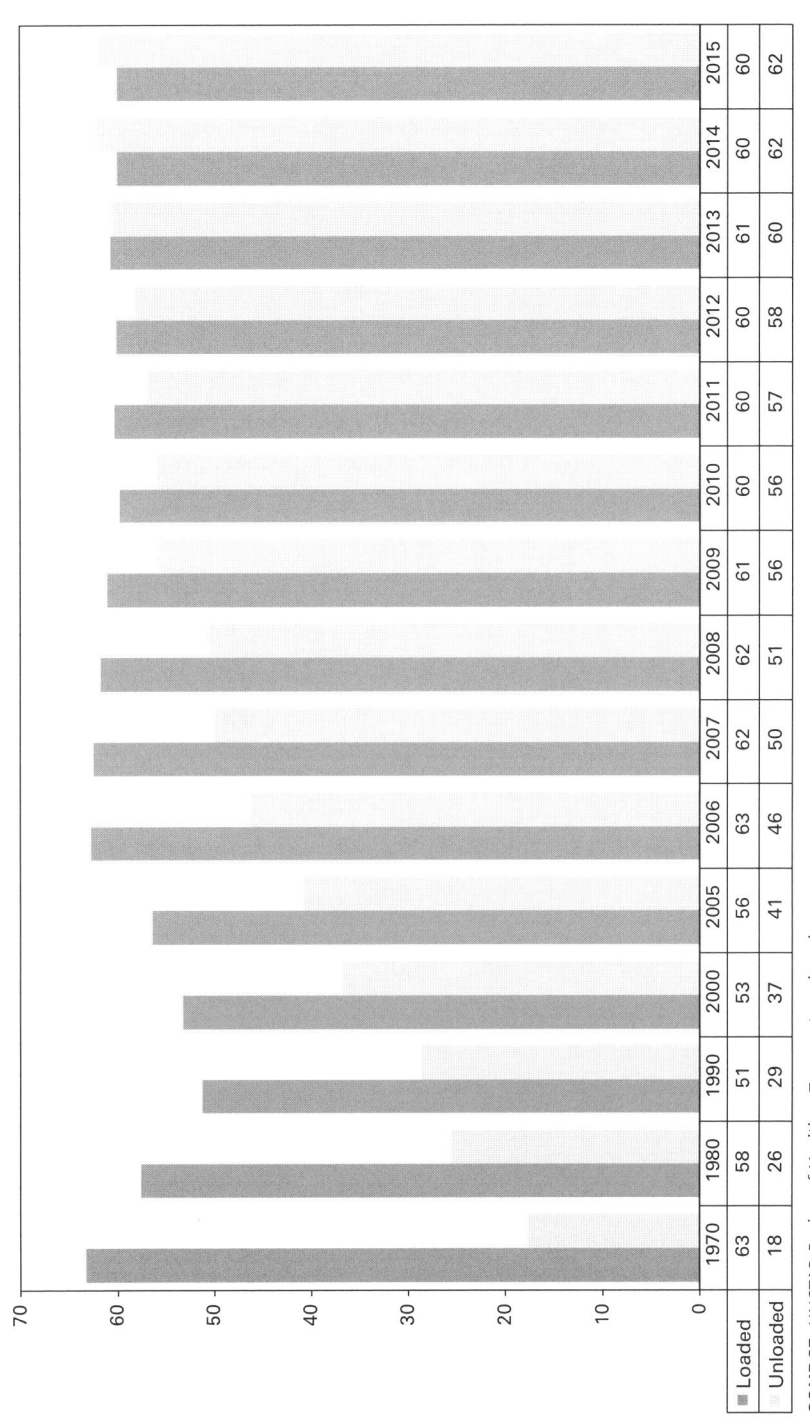

	1970	1980	1990	2000	2005	2006	2007	2008	2009	2010	2011	2012	2013	2014	2015
Loaded	63	58	51	53	56	63	62	62	61	60	60	60	61	60	60
Unloaded	18	26	29	37	41	46	50	51	56	56	57	58	60	62	62

SOURCE UNCTAD Review of Maritime Transport, various issues

Figure 1.4 World seaborne trade, by region, 2015 (percentage share in world tonnage)

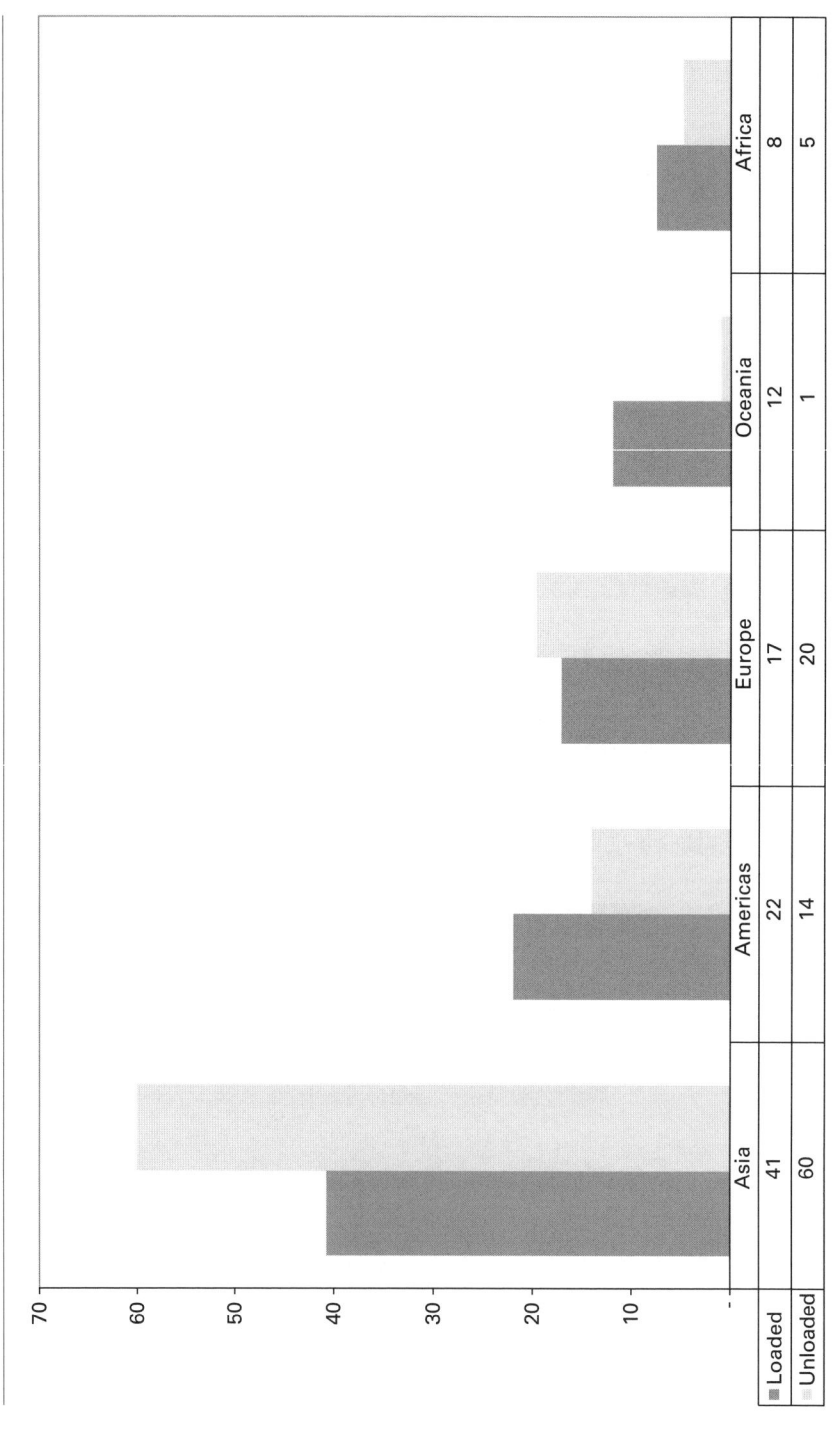

	Asia	Americas	Europe	Oceania	Africa
Loaded	41	22	17	12	8
Unloaded	60	14	20	1	5

SOURCE UNCTAD Review of Maritime Transport 2016, on the basis of data supplied by reporting countries and as published on the relevant government and port industry websites, and by specialist sources. Estimated figures are based on preliminary data or on the last year for which data were available

the coal trade, for the first time in about three decades, world shipments (thermal and coking) fell by 6.9 per cent in 2015 with total volumes falling to 1.13 billion tonnes.

The global grains trade (wheat, coarse grain and soybean) increased by an estimated 4.9 per cent, taking the total to 453 million tonnes in 2015. This performance reflects the high grain stockpiles as well as a weaker import demand in some of the largest grain importing countries, especially from Western Asia and North Africa. Meanwhile, bauxite and alumina trade volumes expanded at a rapid rate of 18.1 per cent in 2015, a stark contrast to the 2014 negative performance (−24.5 per cent). China's ability to secure sources of bauxite other than from Indonesia and its growing alumina production capacity have both contributed to the growth.

Minor bulk commodities trade increased at an estimated 0.4 per cent in 2015, with total volumes reaching 1.74 billion tonnes. Manufactures (steel products and forest products) accounted for 43.0 per cent of the total, followed by metals and minerals (37.1 per cent) and agribulks (19.9 per cent). While manufactures and agribulks increased by 1.9 per cent and 2.9 per cent respectively, shipments of metals and minerals declined by 2.4 per cent.

Containerized trade

In 2015, total containerized trade volumes recorded a dramatic slowdown, with volumes increasing at the modest rate of 2.4 per cent and reaching 175 million twenty-foot equivalent units (TEUs). Three main factors have combined to limit containerized trade growth: the decline in volumes on the head haul leg of the East Asia to Europe trade route (Table 1.2); the limited growth of the North–South trade owing to the impact of low commodity prices on the terms of trade and the purchasing power of commodity exporting countries; and the pressure on intra-Asian trade resulting from the slowdown in China. The distribution of containerized trade by trade route and region is set out in Figure 1.5.

Volumes on the mainlane east–west route (Figure 1.6) increased at a modest rate of about 1.2 per cent in 2015, taking the total to 52.5 million TEU. On the Asia–Europe route, growth was constrained by the negative performance (−2.2 per cent) on the peak leg of the Asia–Europe trade, which reflected weaker import demand in Europe, a weak euro, the negative impact of the unilateral coercive measure of international sanctions on import volumes into the Russian Federation, and adjustments in retail inventories.

Table 1.2 Estimated containerized cargo flows on major east–west container trade routes, 2014–2015 (millions of TEUs and percentage change)

	Transpacific		Europe Asia		Transatlantic	
	East Asia–North America	North America–East Asia	Asia–Europe	Europe–Asia	Europe–North America	North America–Europe
2014	15.8	7.4	15.2	6.8	3.9	2.8
2015	16.8	7.2	4.9	6.8	4.1	2.7
Percentage change 2014–2015	6.6%	−2.9%		0.0%	5.4%	−2.4%

SOURCE UNCTAD, based on MDS Transmodal, World Cargo Database, 16 June 2016

Figure 1.5 Distribution of global containerized trade by route, 2015 (percentage share of global trade in TEUs)

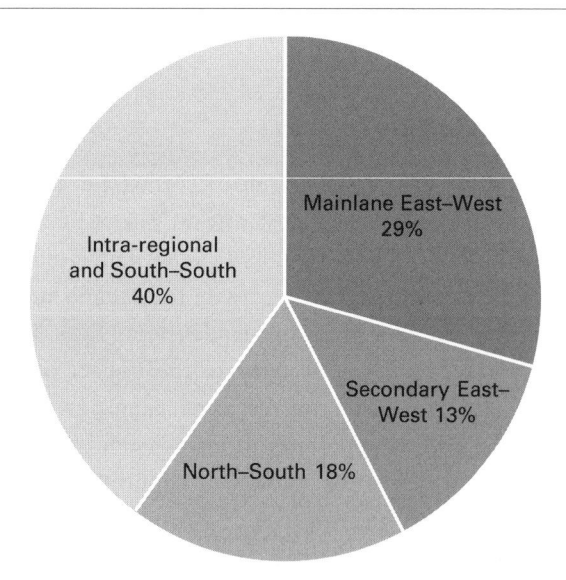

- Intra-regional and South–South 40%
- Mainlane East–West 29%
- Secondary East–West 13%
- North–South 18%

SOURCE UNCTAD *Review of Maritime Transport 2016*, based on Clarksons Research, *Container Intelligence Monthly* (2016)

On the Transpacific trade route, firm demand in the United States supported volumes with an overall growth of 3.6 per cent in 2015. A strong dollar and rising consumer spending boosted US imports from China and Vietnam.

Volumes on the North–South trade route increased at a moderate 1.4 per cent in 2015, taking the total to 30.8 million TEU. Limited growth reflected

Figure 1.6 Estimated containerized cargo flows on major east-west container trade routes (million TEUs), 1995–2015

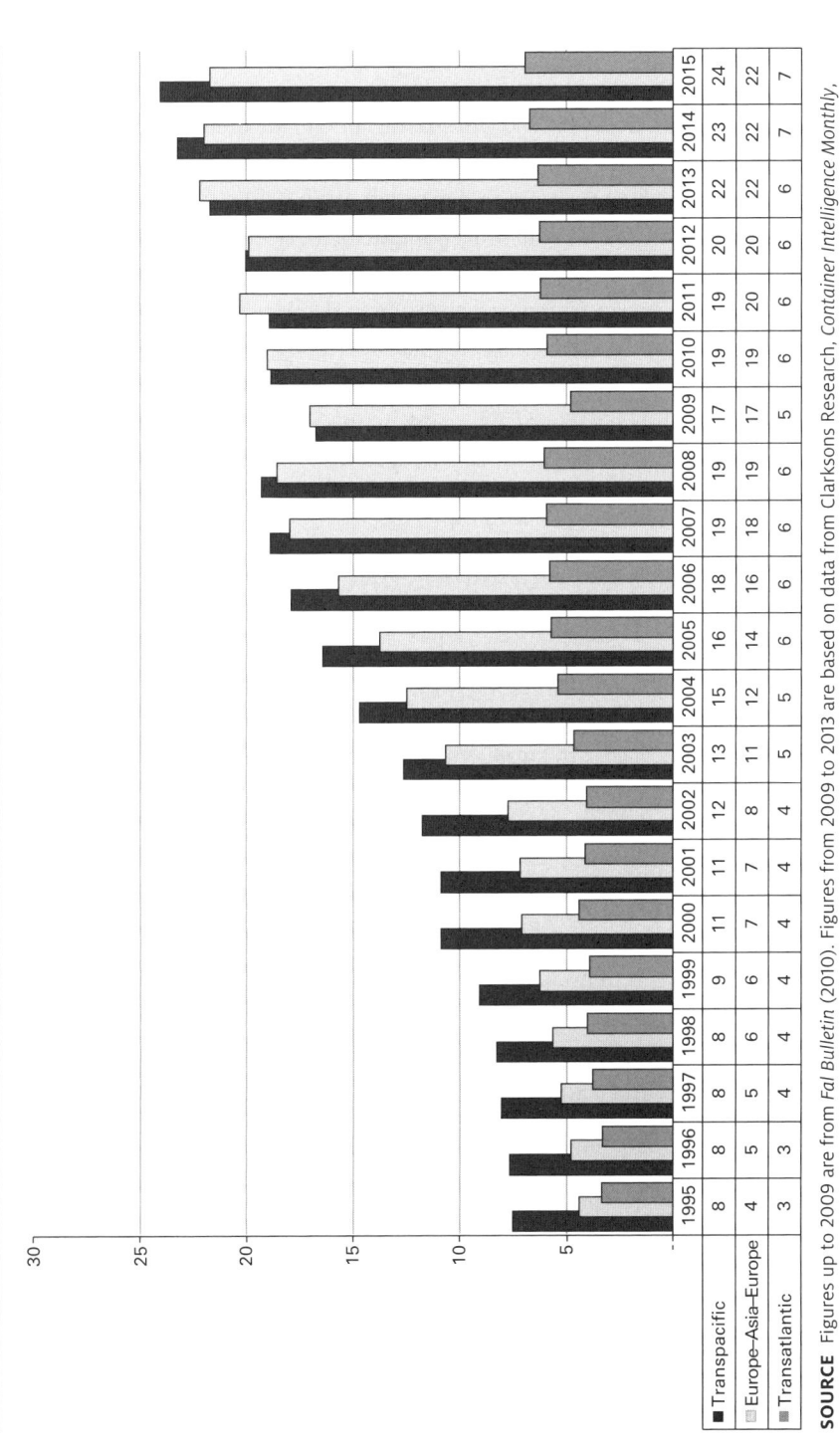

	1995	1996	1997	1998	1999	2000	2001	2002	2003	2004	2005	2006	2007	2008	2009	2010	2011	2012	2013	2014	2015
■ Transpacific	8	8	8	8	9	11	11	12	13	15	16	18	19	19	17	19	19	20	22	23	24
▨ Europe–Asia–Europe	4	5	5	6	6	7	7	8	11	12	14	16	18	19	17	19	20	20	22	22	22
■ Transatlantic	3	3	4	4	4	4	4	4	5	5	6	6	6	6	5	6	6	6	6	7	7

SOURCE Figures up to 2009 are from *Fal Bulletin* (2010). Figures from 2009 to 2013 are based on data from Clarksons Research, *Container Intelligence Monthly*, various issues

NOTE Figures for 2014 and 2015 are based on MDS Transmodal data

the weak container import demand in Africa and Latin America resulting from, among other factors, the political unrest in a number of North African countries, the recession in Brazil and the negative impact of the eroding terms of trade on the purchasing power of commodity-exporting developing economies in the two regions (Danish Ship Finance, 2016).

Intra-regional container trade expanded at an estimated 3.1 per cent in 2015. Intra-Asian trade, which accounted for over two-thirds of the total, expanded at the softer rate of 2.9 per cent, down from 6 per cent recorded in 2014. The situation in China and the import declines in other Asian economies such as Japan and Indonesia weighed down on growth. Intra-Asian trade continued to be supported, however, by relocating manufacturing centres from China to other parts of Asia and by increased imports into Vietnam, the Philippines and the Republic of Korea as well as the robust growth on the Asia and Indian Sub-Continent route (Clarksons Research, 2016a).

Infrastructure developments affecting demand and reshaping routes

In 2015, a number of infrastructure development and expansion projects were announced, launched or completed with a view to improving connectivity, enhancing access to suppliers and consumers and enabling trade and regional integration. These initiatives included the construction, expansion and improvement of logistics infrastructures and physical assets such as the Panama and Suez canals, as well as China's One Belt, One Road (OBOR) and the joint Japan and Asian Development Bank (ADB) initiative, 'Partnership for Quality Infrastructure', both of which are attracting attention due to their potential to stimulate growth, boost trade and drive up demand for transport and logistics services.

A landmark development in 2015 was the expansion of the Suez Canal. The US $8.2 billion expansion project was completed and the maritime passage opened for operations. Another milestone was reached in June 2016 when the expanded Panama Canal opened for operation to allow for the passage of larger neo-Panamax ships.

Another recent development with potentially significant implications for seaborne trade is China's OBOR initiative. Launched in 2013, OBOR aims to establish new trading routes, links and business opportunities by further connecting China, Asia, Europe, Africa and the transition economies along five routes. The implementation process was initiated in 2015, but the full implementation of OBOR across all countries involved is a long-term endeavour that will take many years (China-Britain Business Council, 2015).

In principle, should OBOR be fully implemented, the expected benefits are likely to be broad based and span a number of areas, countries and regions.

The success of OBOR rests heavily on the optimization of the transport infrastructure and services, including shipping and logistics, required to support the connectivity within China and beyond. In turn, the transport sector will benefit from the trade growth opportunities generated by OBOR and growth in volumes arising from reduced transport costs, greater market access, connectivity as well as infrastructure and industrial development. For shipping, these could provide the additional boost to lift volumes and reverse recent trends of weak demand and slow growing trade. It could help bring balance to the market which is currently plagued by a mismatch between demand and supply, facing continuing excess capacity.

Maritime connections linking China to the Piraeus Port through the Indian Ocean and the Suez Canal are expected to provide an alternative to Rotterdam, Antwerp or Hamburg while cutting 10 days from the journey to Central or Eastern Europe (Pong, 2015). In this respect, the expanded Suez Canal is likely to benefit from the new traffic to be generated by OBOR, the Iranian trade flows that will arise with the final removal of international sanctions, and the oil trade expected to result from the rise of the Indian refinery market (SAFETY4SEA, 2016).

Overland transport offers alternative logistics options for business and trade, especially for high value-added and time-sensitive goods (Pong, 2015). Several railways that already operate between China and Europe provide an advantage in terms of average number of travel days, which hovers around 15 days compared to 30–40 days by sea. Rail transport compares favourably with air transport in terms of shipping costs and constitutes a more environmentally friendly mode of transport. Today, the overall implications of OBOR for the modal split and the share of maritime transport in particular remain unclear.

Trade liberalization and e-commerce

While tackling the weakness in global demand caused largely by stagnant real wages is essential to boosting trade, a number of actions could potentially be envisaged to support a recovery in the global aggregate demand and support trade. These include, for example, a roll-back on restrictive measures and the implementation of the WTO trade facilitation agreement which could potentially increase trade by up to US $1 trillion (World Trade Organization, 2016). Efforts to further liberalize trade through regional agreements are being pursued. Some initiatives have the potential to create large markets and cover a large share of global GDP if and when fully implemented. A case in point is the Trans-Pacific Partnership (TPP), adopted in 2015, which brings together 12 countries. The TPP is expected to create a market of 800 million people with over 40 per cent of the world GDP (United Nations Department of Economic and Social Affairs, 2016).

Elsewhere, negotiations for the Regional Comprehensive Economic Partnership (RCEP), which would cover more than 3 billion people when completed are ongoing, together with the negotiations for the Transatlantic Trade and Investment Partnership (TTIP). Meanwhile, the ASEAN Economic Community (AEC) launched in December 2015 could generate a market worth US $2.6 trillion and cover over 622 million people (King, 2015).

According to UNCTAD, broad economic agreements among a group of countries that together have significant economic weight such as the TPP, TTIP and RCEP could have a major impact on investment patterns. The three regional groupings each account for a quarter or more of global foreign direct investment (FDI) flows (UNCTAD, 2014).

As part of the OBOR initiative, China is also planning to negotiate a free trade agreement with 65 countries. According to its Ministry of Commerce, by the end of 2015 China had established 53 economic cooperation zones in 18 countries along the OBOR routes, with associated investments of over US $14 billion, and had signed one free trade agreement with 11 countries and a bilateral investment agreement with 56 countries. China is also pursuing trade facilitation initiatives through Customs cooperation with neighbouring countries.

For developing countries, e-commerce offers potential business opportunities and gains as it alters consumption patterns and consumers' shopping behaviour and allows access to a wider selection of goods and brands at relatively reasonable cost. By boosting and reshaping consumption patterns and enabling small and medium-sized enterprises (SMEs) to reach new markets overseas, e-commerce is also generating greater trade volumes. While in principle these developments have the potential to generate higher demand for shipping, ports and logistics services, the precise impact on maritime transport is yet to be fully assessed, as e-commerce may pose some challenge to the shipping sector. For example, shipping may not be able to capture the full trade potential arising from e-commerce, as large retailers (eg Amazon and Wal-Mart) are increasingly optimizing travel distances, including by expanding their network of warehouses, positioning inventory and warehouse centres closer to consumption markets and developing their own ship carrying capacity to avoid the shipping costs of external shipping companies (Subramaniam, 2015).

Supply: the key players in international shipping

Different countries participate in different sectors of the shipping business, seizing opportunities to generate income and employment. The top five ship-owning countries in deadweight (dwt) in January 2016 are Greece, Japan, China, Germany and Singapore, while the top five countries by flag of registration are Panama, Liberia, Marshall Islands, Hong Kong China SAR and Singapore. The largest ship-building countries are China, the Republic of Korea and Japan, accounting for 91.4 per cent of gross tonnage constructed in 2015. Most demolitions take place in Asia. Four countries – Bangladesh, India, Pakistan and China – account for 95 per cent of ship scrapping gross tonnage in 2015. The largest suppliers of seafarers are China, the Philippines and Indonesia. As countries specialize in different maritime sub-sectors, the other side of the same coin is a process of concentration of the industry. When each maritime business locates in a smaller number of countries, most countries host a decreasing number of maritime businesses, albeit with growing market shares in these sub-sectors.

In spite of the uncertainties presented above, the long-term growth prospects for seaborne trade and the maritime businesses are positive. There are ample opportunities for developing countries to generate income and employment and help promote their foreign trade. Policy makers are well advised to identify and invest in maritime sectors where their countries may have a comparative advantage. It is no longer a policy choice to support 'the' maritime sector; the challenge is to identify and support selected maritime businesses. Policy makers need to carefully assess the competitive environment for each of the maritime sub-sectors they wish to develop. They need to consider the value added of a sector for the country's economy, including possible synergies and spill-over effects to other sectors – maritime and beyond. Policy makers should take into account that the port and shipping business is a key enabler of a country's foreign trade. Apart from possibly generating income and employment in the maritime sector, it is generally even more important to ensure that the country's traders have access to fast, reliable and cost-effective port and shipping services, whoever provides them.

Structure of the world fleet

In total, the world commercial fleet on 1 January 2016 consisted of 90, 917 vessels, with a combined tonnage of 1.8 billion dwt. The highest growth was recorded for gas carriers (+9.7 per cent), followed by container ships (+7.0 per cent) and ferries and passenger ships (+5.5 per cent). General cargo ships continued their long-term decline with the lowest growth rate of major vessel types. Their share of the world's tonnage today is only 4.2 per cent, down from 17 per cent in 1980.

The participation of developing countries in different maritime businesses

Throughout most of the 20th century, maritime business was concentrated in developed countries who had their own national fleets, which were built, owned, operated and manned by nationals of the country whose flag the ship flew. Today, only very few countries maintain a participation in all maritime businesses, but instead specialize in selected maritime sub-sectors. The process of specialization has also provided opportunities for developing countries, who are increasing their participation in practically all maritime businesses. Policy makers have an interest in identifying those maritime sectors where their countries participate at present, or might participate in future.

The following section discusses in more detail the participation of developing countries in ship owning, operation, registration, building and demolition as well as seafaring.

Ownership of the world fleet

Developed countries still account for almost 60 per cent of the world's ship-owning market, although the share of the developing countries has been increasing. The largest ship owners among the developing countries are in Asia, led by China and Singapore (Table 1.3). Of the top 35 ship-owning countries, 18 are in Asia, 13 in Europe and 4 in the Americas.

Going by sub-region, the largest ship-owning countries in South America are Brazil (15.8 million dwt), Venezuela and Chile. Angola (5.4 million dwt), Nigeria and Egypt are the largest ship owners in Africa. Among South Asian countries, India (21.7 million dwt) is the largest ship owner, followed by Bangladesh and Pakistan. In South East Asia, the largest ship-owning countries are Singapore (95.3 million dwt), Indonesia and Malaysia.

Liner shipping companies

Among different vessel types, container ships are most frequently deployed, ie used for the provision of regular liner shipping services, by companies that do not own the ship. Ship deployment and services are not decided by the ship owner, but by the liner shipping companies. These liner companies may charter the ships from the owners and managers. Charter owner companies such as V-ships, Anglo Eastern and NSB Niederelbe Schiffahrtsgesellschaft are often less well known to the public compared to the liner operators, such as Maersk or Evergreen, whose names are visible on the ships they operate and who offer their services to the traders (NSB, 2016). It is these liner companies that decide on the service patterns and vessel deployment, and the analysis of container shipping services thus needs to focus on the operators rather than on the owners.

At the end of July 2016, Maersk was the largest liner shipping company in terms of operated container ship capacity (TEU), with a market share of 15.1 per cent, followed by MSC (13.3 per cent), CMA CGM (9.2 per cent), China COSCO Shipping (7.8 per cent) and Hapag-Lloyd (4.8 per cent). Four of the top five carriers are European, while the majority of the remaining top 20 are based in Asia, and none is from the Americas or Africa, after the Chilean company CSAV was absorbed by Hapag-Lloyd from Germany.

A process of concentration among container ship operators continues to be observed. Recent and expected mergers include those between COSCO and China Shipping (both from China), between CMA CGM (France) and NOL (Singapore), and between Hapag-Lloyd (Germany) and UASC (Kuwait). In addition, the main operators continue to extend their collaboration in the form of alliances (Murphy, 2016; *Wall Street Journal*, 2016).

Container ship deployment and liner shipping connectivity

The trend towards industry consolidation is also reflected in the data on fleet deployment. The container ship sizes per country are going up, both average and maximum, while the number of companies providing services from and to the average country's seaports is going down.

The number of carriers competing for the average country's cargo has declined by 34 per cent in 12 years – from 21.1 in 2004 to 14.6 in 2016. While 14.6 companies per country usually suffice to guarantee a competitive market, the average hides a growing number of countries where there are only few providers offering container services, leading to potentially oligopolistic markets. In 2004, there were 44 countries with only five or fewer providers, against 56 such cases in 2016 – an increase of 27 per cent. During the same period, UNCTAD records a doubling in the number of countries with only one provider, increasing from five countries in 2004 to 10 countries in 2016 (Figure 1.7).

The overall position of a country within global container shipping networks is reflected through the UNCTAD Liner Shipping Connectivity Index (LSCI). In May 2016, the best-connected countries in East Asia are China and the Republic of Korea; Singapore and Malaysia have the highest LSCI in South East Asia; Sri Lanka and India in South Asia; Morocco, Egypt and South Africa in Africa, and Panama and Colombia in Latin America and the Caribbean.

Registration of ships

The tonnage registered under a foreign flag (ie where the nationality of the owner is different from the flag flown by the vessel) is 70.2 per cent of the world total. This system of open registries, ie where the owner of the ship and the flag the ship flies are from different countries, has shown to be an opportunity for many developing countries, including many Small Island Developing States (SIDS) such as the Marshall Islands, and Least Developed Countries (LDCs) such as Liberia, to provide the service of vessel registries. At the same time, the majority of ship owners are still in developed countries, and it is thanks to the system of open registries that they can remain competitive against fleets owned by companies based in developing countries. Under the flags of Panama, Liberia or the Marshall Islands, a German or Japanese owner can employ third-country seafarers, eg from the Philippines or Indonesia, who work for lower wages than their German or Japanese colleagues.

As of 1 January 2016, Panama, Liberia and the Marshall Islands continue to be the largest vessel registries. Together they account for a 41.8 per cent share of the world tonnage, with the Marshall Islands recording the highest growth among the major registries, at 12 per cent over 2015. The top 10 registries account for 76.8 per cent of the world fleet (dwt). More than 76 per cent of the world fleet is registered in developing countries, a further increase over 2015. This includes many open registries, that is registries where the owner does not need to be of the same nationality as the country where the ship is registered. Some of the nationally flagged fleets are also nationally owned. Notably in countries with long coasts, important cabotage and inter-island traffic, national legislation often limits the options of ship owners to flag out. Many of the ships flying the flags of China, India, Indonesia and the United States are deployed on cabotage services.

Figure 1.7 Presence of liner shipping companies: average number of companies per country, average of the average container-vessel size (TEU) per country, and average of largest ship (TEU) per country (2004–2016)

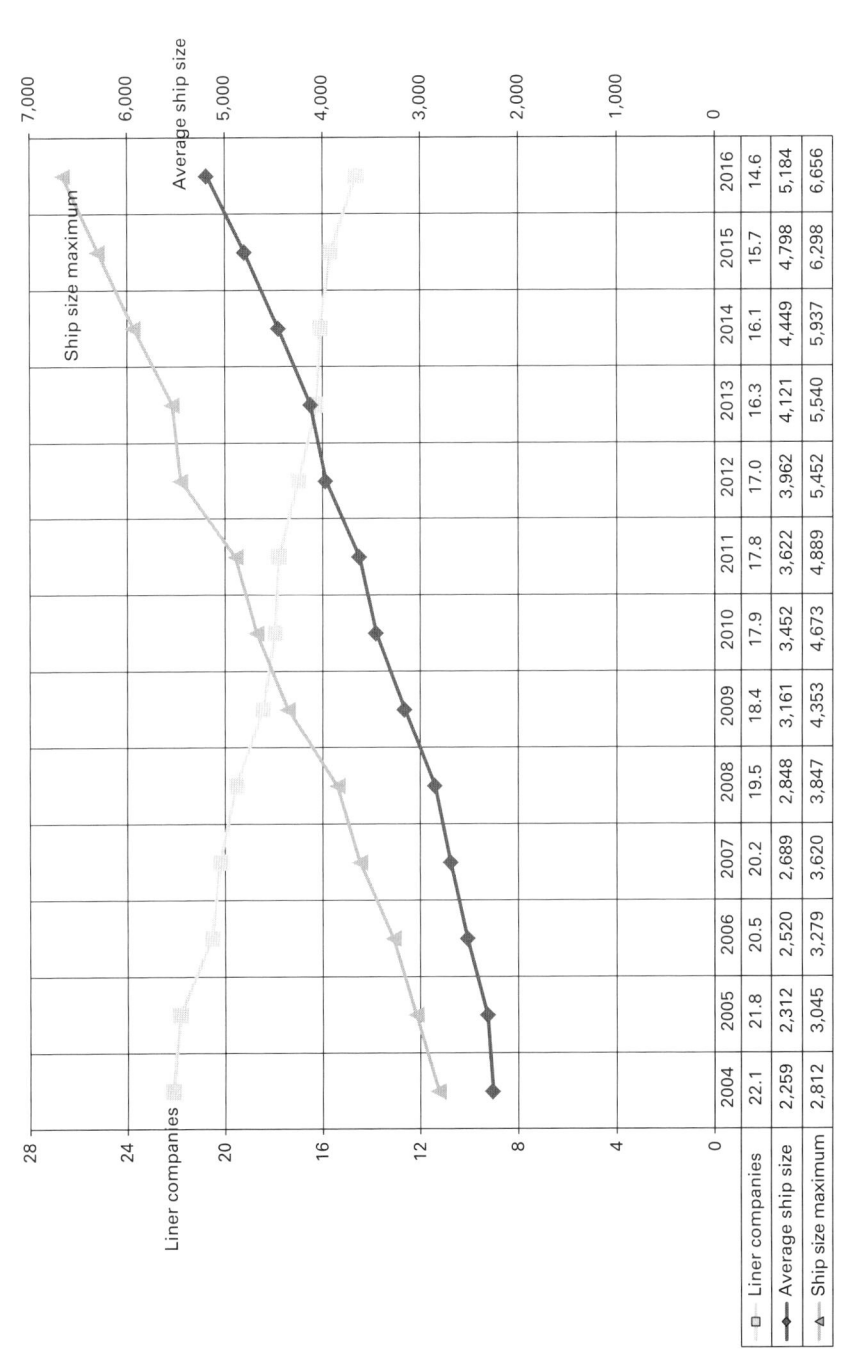

	2004	2005	2006	2007	2008	2009	2010	2011	2012	2013	2014	2015	2016
Liner companies	22.1	21.8	20.5	20.2	19.5	18.4	17.9	17.8	17.0	16.3	16.1	15.7	14.6
Average ship size	2,259	2,312	2,520	2,689	2,848	3,161	3,452	3,622	3,962	4,121	4,449	4,798	5,184
Ship size maximum	2,812	3,045	3,279	3,620	3,847	4,353	4,673	4,889	5,452	5,540	5,937	6,298	6,656

SOURCE UNCTAD *Review of Maritime Transport 2016* calculations, based on data supplied by Lloyd's List Intelligence. Data represents averages per country as per vessel deployment in 160 countries

Seafarers

The world's fleet provides approximately 1,545,000 jobs for seafarers in international shipping (BIMCO and ICS, 2016). Approximately 51 per cent of the positions are for officers, against 49 per cent for 'ratings', ie non-officer sailors such as able seaman or ordinary seaman. This is the first time in history that the proportion of officers is higher than that of ratings, reflecting technological advances and less demand for manual work on-board. In 2005, the ratio was still 45 per cent officers to 55 per cent ratings.

On-board employment is a vivid example of the importance of economies of scale in shipping. For a container ship or a dry bulk carrier of for example 10,000 GT, a crew of 14 or 15 seafarers is required. A ship 10 times larger, of 100,000 GT, will not require 10 times more seafarers, but can operate perfectly well with 19 or 20 seafarers.

Between 2005 and 2015, global demand for seafarers increased by 45 per cent, roughly in line with the growth of the world fleet during the same period. The largest numbers of seafarers are provided by China (243,635), followed by the Philippines (215,500), Indonesia (143,702), the Russian Federation (87,061), India (86,084) and Ukraine (69,000) (BIMCO-ICS, 2016). Taking into account population sizes, remittances from seafarers working abroad are significantly more important for the Philippines than for the other major suppliers (*Seafarer Times*, 2016). For example, as a share of the population, almost two out of every 1,000 Philippine nationals work on board a ship, compared to less than 1 out of every 10,000 from India (de Fries, 2011).

Countries also differ as regards the proportion of officers and ratings that work aboard ships. Nationals from Greece and Japan that work as seafarers, for example, largely do so as officers, while seafarers from the Philippines, Indonesia or Pakistan are much more likely to be employed as able seamen or ordinary seamen (UNCTAD calculations based on data from BIMCO-ICS, 2016).

Overall, the market for employment on board is increasingly separate from the country of ship ownership. Once a ship is registered in one of the major open registries, such as Panama, Liberia or the Marshall Islands, the ship owner is allowed to employ foreign nationals at wage levels that depend more on the seafarer's nationality than on the country of ownership or registration.

Ship building

In 2015, 91.3 per cent of ship building (GT) took place in just three countries: China (36.1 per cent); the Republic of Korea (34.3 per cent); and Japan

(20.9 per cent); these percentage shares are very similar to 2014, with a slight increase of the market share for China against a small decline for that of Japan. China had its largest shares in dry bulk carriers and general cargo ships; the Republic of Korea was strongest in container ships, gas carriers and oil tankers; and Japan mostly built dry bulk carriers. The rest of the world – including European ship builders – maintained a lead in the construction of ferries and passenger ships, including cruise ships. The Philippines established itself further in the market for container ships.

Ship scrapping

Most demolitions of old ships take place in Asia. Four countries – Bangladesh, India, Pakistan and China – accounted for approximately 95 per cent of known ship scrapping in 2015. Most tonnage (73 per cent of GT) that was demolished in 2015 was from dry bulk carriers. Among the other vessel types, Pakistan had the highest share of oil tankers, India demolished most container ships, and Bangladesh had the highest share in the offshore market.

The oversupply of container tonnage

Container ships have never been bigger than today and container freight rates have rarely been lower (see below, in the section on freight costs). In March 2016, the idle container ship fleet stood at 1.6 million TEU (Alphaliner, 2016). In June 2016, a shipper could pay less than US $800 to have his 40 ft container shipped from, for example, Shanghai to the West Coast of North America (Clarksons Research, 2016a, p14).

The oversupply of tonnage is the result of past investment decisions against slower than expected demand growth. Put differently, when the ships that enter the market today were ordered, the owners that placed the orders had expected the economy in 2016 to be in better shape than it became in reality. Individual carriers typically react to this situation by a) trying to reduce their costs, and b) growing their market share. From the company's perspective, this often means a) investing in modern large container ships to save fuel costs and achieve economies of scale, and b) seeking mergers to better control the market, which is necessary to fill the new large ships. This makes sense from the individual company's perspective, but it doesn't if we look at the big picture, and here are three reasons why not:

1 When replacing old ships with new ones, the old ones don't exit the market. The overcapacity usually stays on, unless scrapped, and most of

the container ship fleet is simply too young to be demolished. In the end, all carriers are confronted with the historically low freight rates. The overinvestment is not in the interest of the liner business.

2 The larger ships may cut unit costs for the carriers, but the total system costs are not reduced; in fact, they may actually go up. The costs of the megaships to the logistics system may overwhelm the benefits. The additional costs for ports, insurance companies, onward transport providers and the overall network structure (more transhipments with fewer direct services) will lead to higher total system costs as the vessel size goes up. This not only applies to those ports and routes which have to accommodate the largest ships, but due to the cascading effect it is also relevant in many smaller and developing countries' markets. The overinvestment is not in the interest of the carriers' logistics partners.

3 As ships get bigger they also need be filled with more cargo. As a result, there is space for fewer carriers in individual markets. We observe a continued process of concentration. While the lower freight rates may be good news for the shipper in the short term, there is a danger of more markets with oligopolistic market structures in the long term. The overinvestment is not in the long-term interest of shippers, at least in smaller markets.

The above-mentioned three reasons for not investing in more and larger container ships are not relevant for the individual carrier. As a commercial entity, it has to look at its own returns, and will not accept staying behind competitors. Still, for some carriers, diseconomies of scale have certainly been reached, as they cannot cover their fixed costs if ships are not reasonably full.

In the longer term, there is still scope for further consolidation. The logistics partners (ports, rail and trucking service providers) will do their best to adapt to growing vessel sizes, and the 'optimal' vessel size for the logistics system will be larger than today. In the meantime, the pressure on the maritime freight rates will continue, and the resulting low trade costs may help the global economy recover.

The recent insolvency of Hanjin Shipping reflects a new low in the troubled waters of container shipping. It is part of a longer story, with complex impacts, and we present three interrelated possible explanations for this situation, looking at the demand and supply curves in liner shipping.

First, there is less demand than expected. It takes time to plan, order and build ships. When today's container ship fleet was on the drawing board, everybody expected global trade to grow faster than it effectively did. As a result, the demand curve is more to the left than ship owners thought it would be when they constructed today's capacity for the short-term supply curve (Figure 1.8).

Second: expanding supply. In order to reduce their own company's unit costs, ship owners invest in new, bigger and more fuel-efficient ships. The problem is that the older capacity is not scrapped. It stays on the market, leading to an expanded capacity limit. The short-term supply curve moves to the right (Figure 1.9).

Figure 1.8 Lower than expected demand

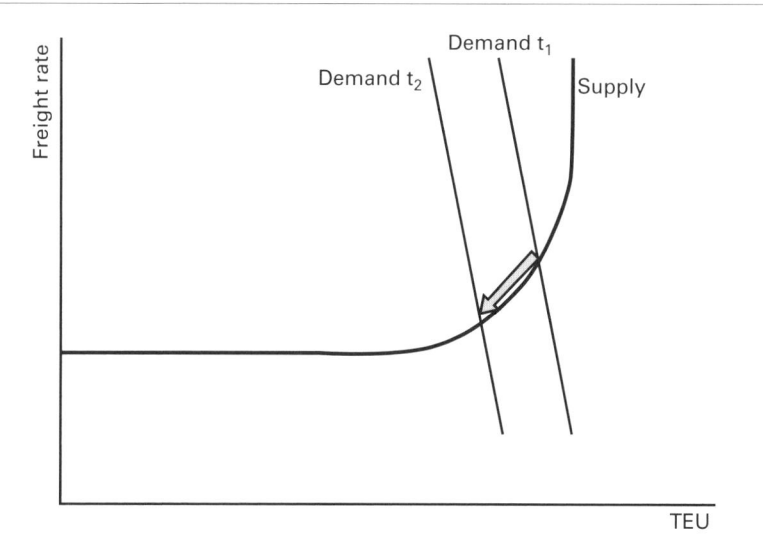

Figure 1.9 Expanding supply

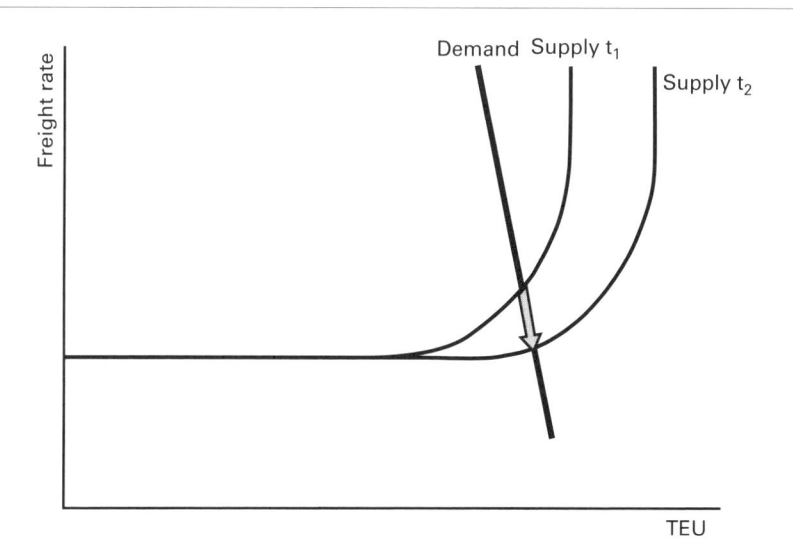

Figure 1.10 Technological change

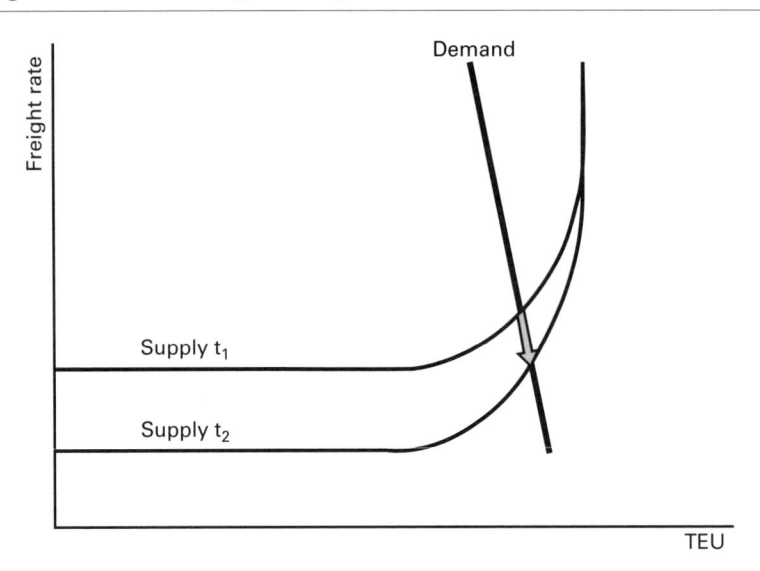

[Graph showing Freight rate vs TEU with Demand curve and two supply curves: Supply t₁ and Supply t₂, with Supply t₂ below Supply t₁]

Third: technological change. Last but not least, probably the most important development is technological change. With higher fixed costs (today's mega container ships cost about US $150 million), against lower variable costs (less fuel, communication and crewing costs per container), the short-term supply curve becomes steeper. The same change in demand leads to a higher change in the freight rate. Freight rates become more volatile. As long as a carrier can cover his variable costs, he will – in the short term – offer his services below his long-term average costs (Figure 1.10).

The typical shipping cycle over the last two centuries lasted between three-and-a-half and seven years. For more than a decade now, however, container ships have kept growing in size, which has encouraged ship owners to continue their investments in ever-bigger new ships for too long. The ever-steeper short-term supply curve has led to unsustainable low and volatile freight rates. Until we have reached a plateau in vessel sizes, we may see more cases like Hanjing Shipping.

Freight rates

In 2015, except for tankers, most shipping segments suffered historic low levels of freight rates and weak earnings, reflecting weak global demand and ship capacity oversupply. The tanker market remained strong, mainly on the back of continuing and exceptional fall in oil prices.

In the container segment, freight rates followed a downward trajectory, reaching record low levels as the market continued to struggle with a continuously weaker demand and ever-larger container vessels that entered the market in the course of 2015. In an effort to deal with low freight rate levels and to reduce losses, carriers continued looking at measures to improve efficiency and optimize operations. These included cascading, idling, slow steaming, and wider consolidation and integration as well as the restructuring of new alliances (Sanchez and Mouftier, 2016).

Similarly, the dry bulk freight market underperformed in 2015, owing to the substantial slowdown in seaborne dry bulk trade and excess tonnage influx. Rates fluctuated around or below vessel operating costs across all segments. Measures were also taken to mitigate the losses and alliances were reinforced, as illustrated by the emergence of the largest dry bulk alliance in February 2015.

In contrast, the 2015 market conditions in the tanker market were on the upside. Both the crude oil and oil product tanker markets enjoyed strong freight rates throughout the year. These were mainly triggered by a surge in seaborne oil trade and supported by a low supply of crude tanker fleet capacity.

Container freight rates

Reflecting weak growth in container trade volumes and an accelerated massive global expansion in container supply capacity (Figure 1.11), container freight rates dipped in 2015. At the heart of the container freight rates problem was the persistent global supply-and-demand imbalances and diverging trends (Table 1.3).

The oversupply of ship capacity resulted from the ever-larger vessels entering the market as carriers seek greater efficiency, economies of scale and market share. A record level of 211 new container ship deliveries entered the market in 2015 (almost half the 436 ships delivered in the peak year of 2008). These new ships added around 1.7 m TEU to the global fleet (with 87 per cent of this volume increase in the 8,000+ TEU sector) and have put freight rates under massive pressure (Clarksons Research, 2016b).

The high growth in fleet in 2015 proved to be difficult to manage, since the majority of trade lanes were already oversupplied with tonnage. The new megaships that entered service were deployed on the Far East and North Europe trade lane at a time when trade was slowing down. In addition, their entry into service resulted in a cascading effect, with larger vessels replacing smaller ships on routes that were already struggling with oversupply.

Figure 1.11 Growth of demand and supply in container shipping, 2000–2016 (annual growth rates)

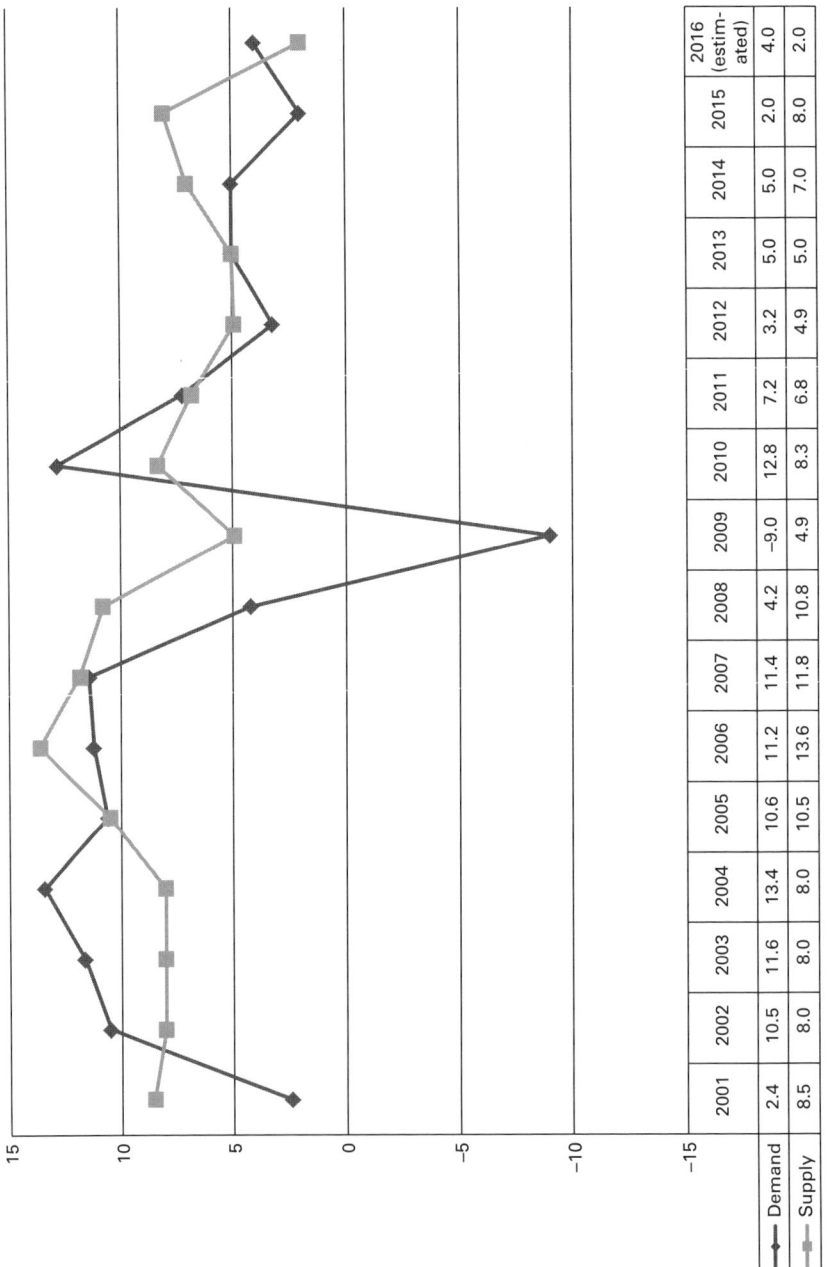

	2001	2002	2003	2004	2005	2006	2007	2008	2009	2010	2011	2012	2013	2014	2015	2016 (estimated)
Demand	2.4	10.5	11.6	13.4	10.6	11.2	11.4	4.2	-9.0	12.8	7.2	3.2	5.0	5.0	2.0	4.0
Supply	8.5	8.0	8.0	8.0	10.5	13.6	11.8	10.8	4.9	8.3	6.8	4.9	5.0	7.0	8.0	2.0

SOURCE *UNCTAD Review of Maritime Transport*, based on data from Clarksons Research, *Container Intelligence Monthly*, various issues
NOTES Supply data refer to total capacity of the container-carrying fleet, including multipurpose and other vessels with some container-carrying capacity. Demand growth is based on million TEU lifts. The data for 2016 are projected figures

Table 1.3 Container freight markets and rates

Freight markets	2009	2010	2011	2012	2013	2014	2015
Transpacific				($ per FEU)*			
Shanghai–United States West Coast	1,372	2,308	1,667	2,287	2,033	1,970	1,506
Percentage change		68.21	−27.77	37.19	−11.11	−3.10	−23.55
Shanghai–United States East Coast	2,367	3,499	3,008	3,416	3,290	3,720	3,182
Percentage change		47.84	−14.03	13.56	−3.7	13.07	−14.45
Far East–Europe				($ per TEU)			
Shanghai–Northern Europe	1,395	1,789	881	1,353	1,084	1,161	629
Percentage change		28.24	−50.75	53.58	−19.88	7.10	−45.82
Shanghai–Mediterranean	1,397	1,739	973	1,336	1,151	1,253	739
Percentage change		24.49	−44.05	37.31	−13.85	8.86	−41.02
North–South				($ per TEU)			
Shanghai–South America (Santos)	2,429	2,236	1,483	1,771	1,380	1,103	455
Percentage change		−7.95	−33.68	19.42	−22.08	−20.07	−58.75
Shanghai–Australia/New Zealand (Melbourne)	1,500	1,189	772	925	818	678	492
Percentage change		−20.73	−35.07	19.82	−11.57	−17.11	−27.43
Shanghai–West Africa (Lagos)	2,247	2,305	1,908	2,092	1,927	1,838	1,449
Percentage change		2.56	−17.22	9.64	−7.89	−4.62	−21.16

(Continued)

Table 1.3 (Continued)

Freight markets	2009	2010	2011	2012	2013	2014	2015
Shanghai–South Africa (Durban)	1,495	1,481	991	1,047	805	760	693
Percentage change		−0.96	−33.09	5.65	−23.11	−5.59	−8.82
Intra-Asian				($ per TEU)			
Shanghai–South East Asia (Singapore)		318	210	256	231	233	187
Percentage change			−33.96	21.84	−9.72	0.87	−19.74
Shanghai–East Japan		316	337	345	346	273	146
Percentage change			6.65	2.37	0.29	−21.10	−46.52
Shanghai–Republic of Korea		193	198	183	197	187	160
Percentage change			2.59	−7.58	7.65	−5.08	−14.44
Shanghai–Hong Kong (China)		116	155	131	85	65	56
Percentage change			33.62	−15.48	−35.11	−23.53	−13.85
Shanghai–Persian Gulf (Dubai)	639	922	838	981	771	820	525
Percentage change		44.33	−9.11	17.06	−21.41	6.36	−35.98

SOURCE Clarksons Research, *Container Intelligence Monthly*, various issues
NOTE Data based on yearly averages

Large container ships that formerly serviced the East Asia–North Europe route were, for instance, deployed into Transpacific trade route, and former Transpacific ships were reassigned to the Transatlantic route. Despite efforts to increase the idling of container ship capacity, which soared to 1.36 m TEU at the end of 2015, compared to only 0.23 m TEU at the beginning of the year, carriers were not able to absorb the new surplus capacity. Global idle container-ship capacity represented 6.8 per cent of the existing fleet capacity in 2015, a record high not seen since 2009 (when idle fleet reached 1.5 m TEU, ie 11.6 per cent of the fleet capacity) (Rogliano Salles, 2016).

In an attempt to also deal with supply and demand imbalance and low freight rate levels, carriers imposed several rounds of General Rate Increases (GRI) in 2015, all of which were unsuccessful. Slow steaming remained another key practice used by carriers to absorb excess tonnage (by increasing voyage times, reducing ship call frequency at a given port and optimizing the operations of larger vessels by increasing their occupancy rate), despite the low fuel price environment. Slow steaming is estimated to have absorbed around 2.5 m TEU of nominal capacity since the end of 2008 (Clarksons Research, 2016b). Furthermore, vessel scrapping has also helped to a certain extent in offsetting some of the influx of new tonnage by removing 201,000 TEU of older ships from the global fleet, representing only 11.7 per cent of the newbuilding deliveries (Rogliano Salles, 2016).

Meanwhile, the low bunker price allowed carriers to reduce their operating costs and cover some of the losses incurred from falling freight rates during 2015. Bunker prices averaged US $278 per tonne in 2015 (and reaching a 10-year low of US $140 per tonne in December 2015), corresponding to a 49 per cent drop to the average price of US $547 per tonne in 2014 (Rogliano Salles, 2016). However, the benefits gained from low bunker price, allowing carriers to maintain unit costs below unit revenue, were not sustainable given the persistent decline of freight rates in 2015. A case in point is Maersk Line, the world's largest container shipper, which saw an 82 per cent collapse in net profit to US $925 million in 2015 (Knowler, 2016). In addition, in August 2016, the largest bankruptcy ever to take place in container shipping unfolded, after the board of Hanjin Shipping voted unanimously to file for court receivership (van Marle, 2016).

Growing concentration and consolidation in the industry has failed to limit the severe market disorder and the plunge of freight rates witnessed in 2015. New rounds of alliances and restructuring may persist as market turbulence does not seem likely to stabilize in the near future.

Moreover, the arrival of mega-container ships is creating intense challenges on global shipping infrastructure. Ports' infrastructure and hinterland connectivity need to expand and adapt to the new requirements of larger ships. This would entail investing in infrastructure (such as bridge height, river width/depth, quay wall and space yard) and port equipment, as well as employing more highly skilled staff to operate and handle increasing volumes efficiently and safely. It has been estimated that transport costs related to mega-ships may increase by US $0.4 billion per year (one-third for extra equipment, one-third for dredging, and one-third for port infrastructure and hinterland costs) (International Transport Forum, 2015). This may suggest that cooperation and consolidation between carriers could be further reinforced, taking various forms in the future, including through vertically integrated activities such as joint investment in land, port and hinterland transport operations to optimize business and provide complete solutions to remain competitive. However, growing concentration may also squeeze out smaller carriers and result in an oligopolistic market structure in the long term.

At the same time, container ship charter rates also fluctuated and followed a downwards pattern. While charter rates increased at the start of 2015, the market plunged again near mid-year, affected by weak trade growth, the large quantities of chartered ships available and the increase in container ship idle capacity. As illustrated by the Hamburg Index for container ship time-charter rates (Figure 1.12), charter rates remained low in 2015 (averaging around 460 points) even when they appeared somehow to have improved from the previous yearly average (364 points). They continued to drop in the first half of 2016, reaching some of their lowest levels of the past five years and breaking below operating costs. The largest time-charter segments, Panamax and Sub-Panamax, have been hit particularly badly, falling by more than 50 per cent since May 2015. At the end of 2015, the one-year time-charter for a Panamax vessel could be fixed to US $6,000 per day (compared to US $10,150 per day at the end of 2014 and far from the US $15,000 per day as of mid-2015), whilst the one-year time-charter rate for a TEU Sub-Panamax vessel dropped to US $6,500 per day at the end of 2015 compared to US $8,000 per day at the end of 2014 (and far from the US $11,750 per day of mid-2015) (Clarksons Research, 2016b).

The chronic imbalance in demand and supply is expected to persist in 2016 and 2017 (where carriers with capacity up to 21,100 TEU will be in service). During 2015, and despite the weakening demand and low freight rates, carriers continued investing in larger vessels. Growth in global

Figure 1.12 New ConTex index, 2011–2016

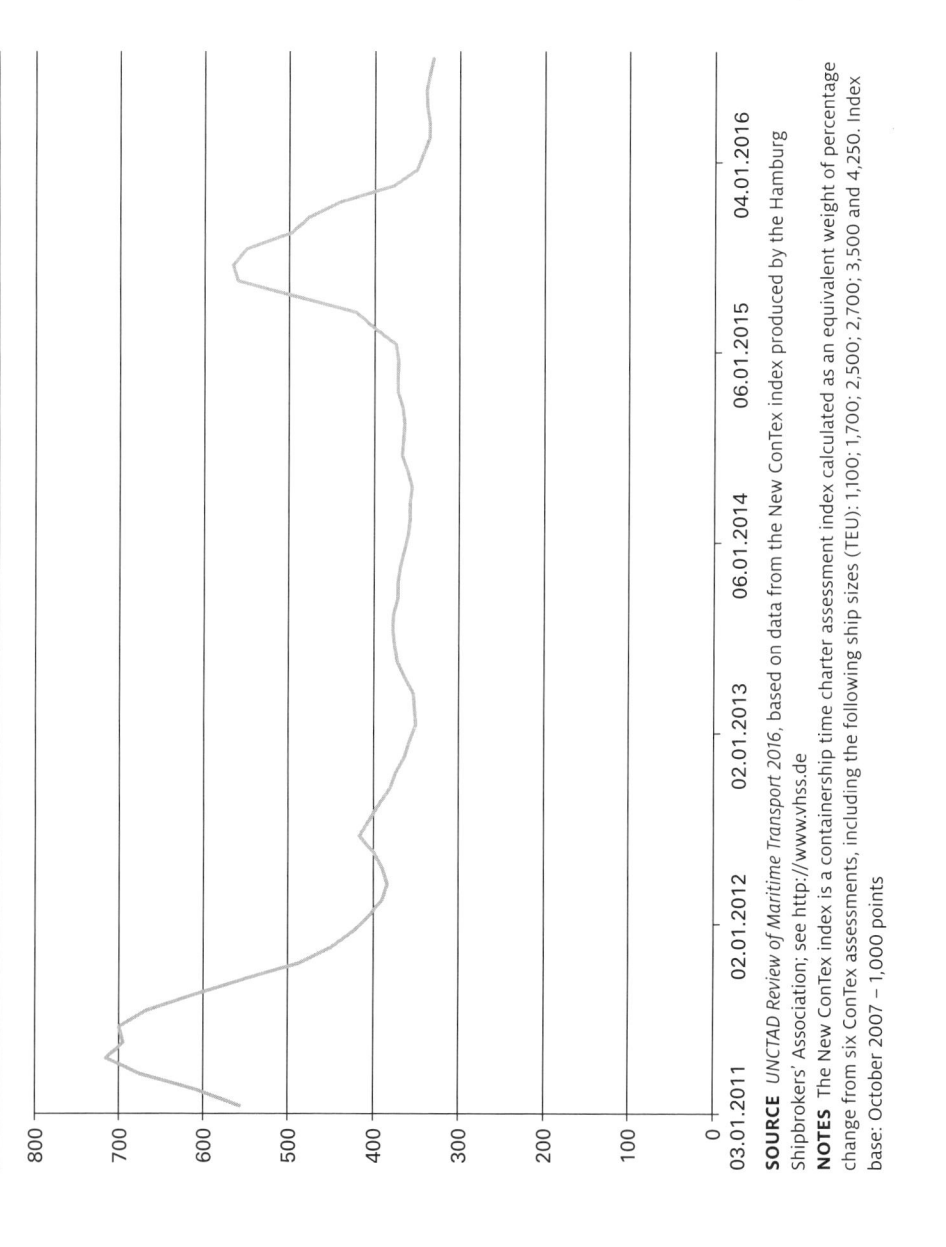

SOURCE *UNCTAD Review of Maritime Transport 2016*, based on data from the New ConTex index produced by the Hamburg Shipbrokers' Association; see http://www.vhss.de

NOTES The New ConTex index is a containership time charter assessment index calculated as an equivalent weight of percentage change from six ConTex assessments, including the following ship sizes (TEU): 1,100; 1,700; 2,500; 2,700; 3,500 and 4,250. Index base: October 2007 – 1,000 points

container ship fleet is projected to grow by 4.6 per cent in 2016 and another 5.6 per cent in 2017 (AlixPartners, 2016a), a rate that would also continue to outstrip growth in the global container demand and exacerbate the market's fundamentals. This in turn would challenge container ship market conditions and freight rates, especially on the mainlanes and in the short term (Clarksons Research, 2016b). Consequently, poor performance is also expected to persevere and may result in further consolidation and restructuring in the container shipping industry.

Dry bulk freight rates

In 2015, the dry bulk market witnessed one of its worst years since 2008. Dry bulk freight rates plunged to record lows as weakening demand and strong supply created a high imbalance in market fundamentals. The dry cargo market was mainly affected by the substantial slowdown in seaborne dry bulk trade.

On the other hand, the excess of supply-side tonnage remained high, although bulk carriers continued to cancel and push back newbuilding deliveries, while ship scrapping activities also surged to high levels. The increase in cancellation and scrapping activities helped to limit overall fleet growth to its slowest pace in 15 years (Clarksons Research, 2016b) but was enough to bridge the gap between supply and demand and bring the sector back into balance. Idling of vessels was also applied to limit supply but at a smaller scale (about 5 million dwt lying idle) (Danish Ship Finance, 2016).

Against these challenging market conditions, the Baltic Exchange Dry Index (BDI) reached several low levels. As noted in Figure 1.13, BDI dropped to an average of 519 points in December 2015, its lowest average level in the year, plunging by 43 per cent from its average level in December 2014. The dip continued in the early part of 2016, reaching an average of 319 points in February 2016.

In 2015, bulk carriers struggled with weak earnings and traded at rates fluctuating around or below vessel operating costs (Figure 1.14). Average bulk carrier earnings witnessed a decline of 28 per cent to reach US $7,123/day in 2015, the lowest level since 1999 (Clarksons Research, 2016b). The Capesize segment took the biggest drop, with average 4TC falling by almost 50 per cent in 2015, affected most acutely by the Chinese slowdown. The other segments also declined by around 30 per cent each in 2015, with Panamax 4TC reaching the lowest level, averaging US $3,450/day in December 2015. As rates continued to be under pressure with cost

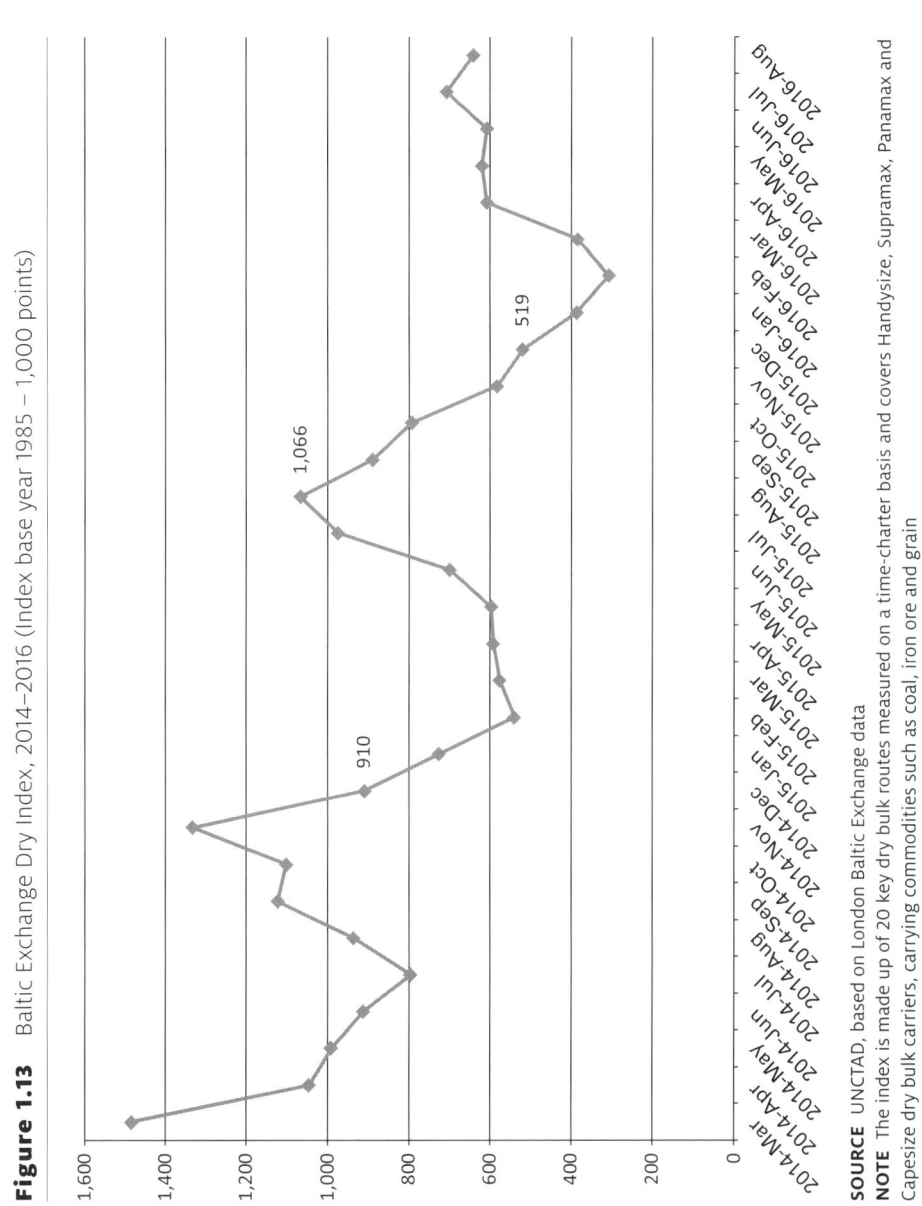

Figure 1.13 Baltic Exchange Dry Index, 2014–2016 (Index base year 1985 – 1,000 points)

SOURCE UNCTAD, based on London Baltic Exchange data
NOTE The index is made up of 20 key dry bulk routes measured on a time-charter basis and covers Handysize, Supramax, Panamax and Capesize dry bulk carriers, carrying commodities such as coal, iron ore and grain

of operations remaining high, many bulker carriers reported losses in 2015 and four companies filed for protection with many others seeking out-of-court restructurings (AlixPartners, 2016b).

As a reaction to the depressed rates, dry bulkers followed a similar approach to the alliances formed by the container shipping sector to reinforce collaboration, coordinate the chartering services, and improve market conditions. In this respect, Capesize Chartering Ltd, the largest dry bulk alliance, was formed in February 2015 between five ship owners (Bocimar International, CTM, Golden Union Shipping, Golden Ocean Group Limited, and Star Bulk Carriers), as a vehicle to share information and optimize fleet deployment with a view to reduce costs (AlixPartners, 2016b).

Going forward, the weak dry bulk demand outlook coupled with large vessel orders might delay the market recovery. At the same time, further industry consolidation along with vessel scrapping and vessel order cancellations will continue to be the likely response by bulk carriers to reduce imbalances and bring the market to more stable water.

Tanker freight rates

The tanker market recorded an exceptional performance in 2015. Both the crude oil tanker and oil product tanker markets enjoyed strong freight rates throughout 2015; the drop in oil prices since mid-2014 and a relatively low supply-side growth in 2015 underpinned this performance.

The progression of the Tanker Baltic Indices was relatively moderate. The average Dirty Tanker Index increased by 5.6 per cent to 821 points in 2015 compared to 777 points in 2014. The average Baltic Clean Tanker Index reached 638 points in 2015 compared to 607 in 2014, a 5 per cent progress compared to the 2014 annual average (Table 1.4).

All tanker segments performed well, benefiting from strong freight rates and low bunker price which resulted in strong tanker earnings. Worldscale (WS) rates observed a positive trend in most routes. For instance, the Persian Gulf–North-West Europe spot rates averaged WS59 points in December 2015, compared to WS32 in December 2014 (84 per cent increase). Persian Gulf–US Gulf spot rates (TD4) were equally firm and stood at WS49 points in December 2015, compared to WS34 in December 2014 (44 per cent), whereas Cross Med (TD6) rates averaged WS97 points in December 2015, compared to WS84 in December 2014. Clean tanker spot freight showed, on the other hand, a mixed performance. In 2015, the average clean tanker freight rates were significantly lower than the year before despite average monthly rates (Table 1.5).

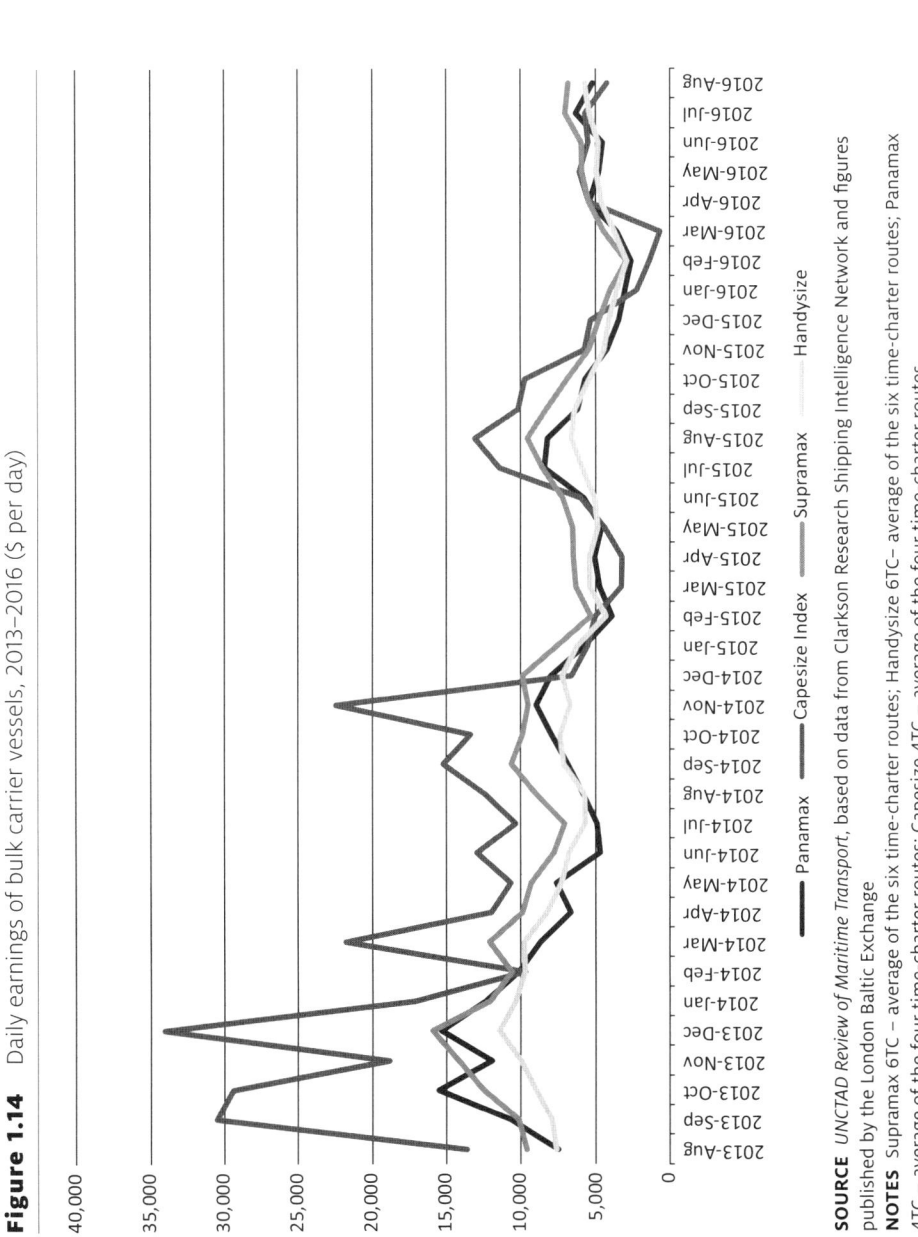

Figure 1.14 Daily earnings of bulk carrier vessels, 2013–2016 ($ per day)

—— Panamax   —— Capesize Index   —— Supramax   —— Handysize

SOURCE UNCTAD Review of Maritime Transport, based on data from Clarkson Research Shipping Intelligence Network and figures published by the London Baltic Exchange

NOTES Supramax 6TC – average of the six time-charter routes; Handysize 6TC – average of the six time-charter routes; Panamax 4TC – average of the four time-charter routes; Capesize 4TC – average of the four time-charter routes

Table 1.4 Baltic tanker indices

	2008	2009	2010	2011	2012	2013	2014	2015	Percentage change (2015/ 2014)	2016 (first half year)
Dirty Tanker Index	1,510	581	896	782	719	642	777	821	5.6	790
Clean Tanker Index	1,155	485	732	720	641	605	607	638	5	539

SOURCE Clarksons Research, Shipping Intelligence Network – Timeseries (Clarksons Research, 2016c)
NOTES The Baltic Dirty Tanker Index is an index of charter rates for crude oil tankers on selected routes published by the Baltic Exchange in London. The Baltic Clean Tanker Index is an index of charter rates for product tankers on selected routes published by the Baltic Exchange in London. Dirty tankers typically carry heavier oils, such as heavy fuel oils or crude oil. Clean tankers typically carry refined petroleum products such as gasoline, kerosene or jet fuels, or chemicals

Overall, average tanker earnings per vessel also increased to reach an average of US $31,036/day in 2015, an increase of 73 per cent from 2014, the highest level since 2008 (Clarksons Research, 2016b). The best and largest gains were observed in the VLCC segment, with average VLCC earnings more than doubling to reach US $64,846/day in 2015 and exceeding US $100,000/day in December, for the first time since mid-2008. Suezmax average earnings rose 68 per cent to US $46,713/day, while average Aframax earnings increased 54 per cent to US $37,954/day in 2015. Dirty Panamax earnings also improved, reaching an average of US $26,548/day in 2015, the highest level since 2008 (Clarksons Research, 2016b).

The product tankers also recorded some progress, reflecting an expansion in refinery capacity and demand growth (Clarksons Research, 2016b).

The 2016 scenario for the tanker markets and freight rates should remain the same as 2015. However, the 2016 projected moderated growth in tanker trade and the expected tanker deliveries may disturb the tanker market balance and put some downward pressure on freight rates.

Table 1.5 Tanker market summary – clean and dirty spot rates, 2010–2015 (worldscale)

Vessel type	Routes	2010 Dec	2011 Dec	2012 Dec	2013 Dec	2014 Dec	2015 Jan	Feb	Mar	Apr	May	Jun	Jul	Aug	Sept	Oct	Nov	Dec	Percentage change Dec 2015/Dec 2014
VLCC/ULCC (200,000 dwt+)																			
	Persian Gulf–Japan (TD3)	61	59	48	64	77	67	61	53	63	64	66	76	37	52	70	67	90	16.9
	Persian Gulf–Singapore (TD2)					71	69	68	54	61	66	66	59	36	56	71	66	83	16.9
	Persian Gulf–US Gulf (TD1)	36	37	28	37	34	39	31	27	61	38	35	35	22	30	37	42	49	44.1
	Persian Gulf–North-West Europe	57	59	26	–	32	38	33	27	27	46	40	40	27	35	54	39	59	84.4
	West Africa–US Gulf (TD4)	–	–	–	–	68	73	70	61	69	73	80	74	52	70	82	80	90	32.4
	West Africa–China (TD15)	–	58	47	61	63	59	57	52	5	65	65	66	45	54	68	69	77	22.2

(*Continued*)

Table 1.5 (Continued)

Vessel type	Routes	2010 Dec	2011 Dec	2012 Dec	2013 Dec	2014 Dec	2015 Jan	Feb	Mar	Apr	May	Jun	Jul	Aug	Sept	Oct	Nov	Dec	Percentage change Dec 2015/Dec 2014
Suezmax (120,000–200,000 dwt)																			
West Africa–North-West Europe (TD20)		118	86	70	102	76	86	86	91	73	90	91	83	69	63	81	89	80	5.3
West Africa–Caribbean/East Coast of North America (TD5)		103	83	65	97	79	86	72	93	77	94	87	74	67	65	80	91	81	2.5
Mediterranean–Mediterranean		113	86	67	99	84	94	94	102	85	99	124	84	64	81	84	101	97	15.5
Aframax (70,000–120,000 dwt)																			
North-West Europe–North-West Europe (TD7)		162	122	93	135	113	122	102	95	124	125	150	101	95	86	102	115	113	0.0
Caribbean–Caribbean/East Coast of North America (TD9)		146	112	91	155	108	135	159	168	126	111	155	111	115	103	115	175	130	20.4

Mediterranean–Mediterranean	138	130	85	100	106	113	137	116	106	118	134	97	101	74	91	112	97	−8.5
Mediterranean–North-West Europe	133	118	80	107	108	114	127	117	104	108	124	98	97	70	100	112	115	6.5
Indonesia–Far East	111	104	90	99	116	108	104	104	99	112	167	121	98	96	93	96	126	8.6

Panamax (40,000–70,000 dwt)

Mediterranean–Mediterranean	168	153	168	113	na	162	150	na	125	125	135	na	na	130	120	143	150	na
Mediterranean–Caribbean/East Coast of North America	146	121	160	105	130	–	153	125	115	120	135	158	na	87	90	150	na	na
North-West Europe–Caribbeean (TD12)	–	–	–	–	118	146	148	120	118	123	135	141	101	88	88	133	129	9.3
Caribbean–East Coast of North America (TD21)	–	–	–	–	113	–	159	148	126	111	149	151	109	94	115	163	160	41.6

(*Continued*)

Table 1.5 (Continued)

Vessel type	Routes	2010 Dec	2011 Dec	2012 Dec	2013 Dec	2014 Dec	2015 Jan	Feb	Mar	Apr	May	Jun	Jul	Aug	Sept	Oct	Nov	Dec	Percentage change Dec 2015/Dec 2014
All clean tankers																			
70,000–80,000 dwt	Persian Gulf–Japan (TC1)	–	–	–	81	102	90	100	103	95	104	125	148	166	84	78	72	90	−11.8
50,000–60,000 dwt	Persian Gulf–Japan (TC5)	–	–	–	93	110	118	106	117	107	119	140	162	148	108	79	83	94	−14.5
35,000–50,000 dwt	US Gulf–North-West-Europe (TC14)	–	–	–	–	142	92	72	129	93	104	117	125	93	104	74	94	105	−26.1
25,000–35,000 dwt	Singapore–East Asia	193	–	220	167	120	123	117	123	124	149	138	148	160	134	120	115	110	−8.3

SOURCE UNCTAD secretariat, based on Drewry Shipping Insight, various issues

NOTES The figures are indexed per tonne voyage charter rates for a 75,000 dwt tanker. The basis is the WS 100. VLCC: very large crude carrier; ULCC: ultra-large crude carrier

Outlook

The outlook for maritime transport, including in terms of demand, supply and freight rates, remains uncertain and subject to downside risks, including a weak global demand and investment, political and geopolitical uncertainties, further loss of momentum in developing economies, developments in energy markets and oil prices, and continued supply and demand mismatch with weaker trade being further challenged by an oversupply in ship capacity and rise in ship sizes.

All is not negative, however, despite it seeming that way; seaborne trade is still growing, with volumes exceeding 10 billion tonnes in 2015. Shipping continues to be the most important mode of transport for international trade, with a relatively low environmental impact when measured in per tonne-mile of transported cargo.

While a slowdown in China is bad news for shipping, developing countries other than China are increasingly arriving on the scene and have the potential to drive further growth. Post-sanctions recovery of the Islamic Republic of Iran is expected to stimulate crude oil trade as well as non-oil sectors. Also, while vertical specialization and production fragmentation involving China and the United States may have peaked, there remains scope to enhance the international division of labour by integrating the regions that have been at the margin of global supply chains, such as South Asia, Africa and South America. Developing countries could benefit by exploring the untapped potential and opportunities.

At the same time, and while South–South trade is gaining momentum and regional trade liberalization agreements are being negotiated or concluded, planned initiatives such as OBOR, the 'Partnership for Quality Infrastructure' and the expansion of transit passages and sea bridges such as the Panama Canal and the Suez Canal also present the potential to stimulate trade and reshape world shipping networks and trading routes as well as redefine hubs and multimodal networks. If fully implemented, OBOR, for example, could boost trade, drive up demand for maritime transport services, raise seaborne trade volumes, and provide opportunities for developing countries to strengthen their position both as users and providers. Already, developing countries account for 60 and 62 per cent of world goods loaded and unloaded respectively.

On the supply side, there is still scope for further consolidation in the industry. The logistics partners (ports, rail and trucking service providers) will aim to adapt to growing vessel sizes, and the 'optimal' vessel size for the logistics system will be larger than today. In the meantime, the pressure on the maritime freight rates will continue, and the resulting low trade costs may help the global economy recover.

In addition to demand and supply considerations, other factors including technology, innovation, data revolution and e-commerce can also transform and disrupt the shipping industry while generating both challenges and opportunities. These include efficiency gains, new business models, internet, digitization, efficient logistics, effective asset management and greater SME integration. Developing countries could leverage these trends to cut costs, raise productivity, develop capacity including skills and knowledge, and enable access to new businesses opportunities.

While the jury is still out as to whether and how these trends will materialize at a broader scale, it is nevertheless important that all countries, particularly in developing regions, bear these developments in mind, monitor their evolution, and assess the precise implications for their transport and logistics sectors and more broadly for their economies, societies and environments. An improved understanding of these trends and their implications will also help countries ensure that these are effectively integrated into relevant planning and investment decision processes and, more importantly, that they are also aligned with the 2030 Agenda and the global climate agenda.

References

AlixPartners (2016a) Container shipping outlook 2016: Overcapacity catches industry in undertow [online] http://www.alixpartners.com/en/Publications/AllArticles/tabid/635/articleType/ArticleView/articleId/1927/Container-Shipping-Outlook-2016.aspx#sthash.H8LjYIKw.dpbs [accessed 10 August 2016]

AlixPartners (2016b) Dry bulk shipping outlook: Already-troubled waters get rougher [online] https://www.alixpartners.com/en/LinkClick.aspx?fileticket=CcmHGpd3EQc%3D&tabid=635 [accessed 10 July 2016]

Alphaliner (2016) http://www.alphaliner.com [accessed 31 July 2016]

BIMCO and ICS (2016) *Manpower Report*, Maritime International Secretariat Services Limited, London

China-Britain Business Council (2015) One Belt One Road: A role for UK companies in developing China's new initiative: new opportunities in China and beyond [online] http://www.cbbc.org/sectors/one-belt,-one-road/ [accessed 10 August 2016]

Clarksons Research (2016a) *Container Intelligence Quarterly*, First Quarter

Clarksons Research (2016b) *Shipping Review and Outlook*, Spring

Clarksons Research (2016c) Shipping Intelligence Network – Timeseries [online] https://sin.clarksons.net/ [accessed 10 August 2016]

Container Intelligence Monthly (2016) **18** (5), May

Danish Ship Finance (2016) *Shipping Market Review*, May

De Fries, Saul (2011) Mobilizing the use of remittances towards poverty reduction and economic and social development through government initiatives: The Philippine experience. Study presented at UNCTAD: Single-year expert meeting on maximizing the development impact pf remittances, Geneva, 14–15 February

Drewry *Shipping Insight*: https://www.drewry.co.uk/maritime-research-products/shipping-insight-annual-subscription

FAL Bulletin (2010) International maritime transport in Latin America and the Caribbean in 2009 and projections for 2010, *ECLAC* [online] http://www.cepal.org/en/node/33845 [accessed 17 November 2016]

International Transport Forum (2015) The impact of mega-ships: Case specific policy analysis [online] http://www.itf-oecd.org/sites/default/files/docs/15cspa_mega-ships.pdf [accessed 10 August 2016]

King, Mike (2015) ASEAN Economic Community launch 'milestone event' – analyst, *Lloyd's Loading List*, 31 December

Knowler, Greg (2016) Maersk profit plunges on freight rate, oil price collapse, *Journal of Commerce*, Feb 10 [online] http://www.joc.com/maritime-news/maersk-profits-plunge-82-percent-freight-rate-oil-price-collapse_20160210.html [accessed 22 August 2016]

MDS Transmodal: http://www.mdst.co.uk/

Murphy, Alan (2016) M2 to become three, *Containerisation International*, July/August

NSB (2016) Presentation at European Marine Engineering – Amsterdam, Amsterdam, NSP Niederelbe Schiffahrtsgesellschaft mbH & Co. KG, April

Pong, Leung Kin (2015) 'One Belt One Road': Implications for the European Union, *European Union Academic Programme*, Hong Kong [online] http://euap.hkbu.edu.hk/main/one-belt-one-road-implications-for-the-european-union/ [accessed 17 November 2016]

Rogliano Salles, Barry (2016) 2016 Annual Review: Shipping and shipbuilding markets [online] http://www.brsbrokers.com/flipbook_en2016/files/downloads/BRS-ANNUAL-REVIEW.pdf [accessed 29 June 2016]

SAFETY4SEA (2016) New Suez Canal to benefit from 'one belt one road', 24 February [online] http://www.safety4sea.com/new-suez-canal-to-benefit-from-one-belt-one-road/ [accessed 29 August 2016]

Sanchez, Ricardo, and Mouftier, Lara (2016) The puzzle of shipping alliances, *PortEconomics* **29**, July [online] http://www.porteconomics.eu/2016/07/29/the-puzzle-of-shipping-alliances-in-july-2016/ [accessed 30 July 2016]

Seaborne Trade Monitor (2016) **3** (7), July

Seafarer Times (2016) Seafarers' 2015 remittances top US$5.8 billion, up 5.3% year-on year, Manila, 21 February [online] http://seafarertimes.com/2015-16/node/1826 [accessed 30 July 2016]

Subramaniam, Rajesh (2015) How will e-commerce transform the shipping industry? *Yale Insights*, 7 April

UNCTAD (2014) *World Investment Report*, New York and Geneva
UNCTAD (2016) *Review of Maritime Transport* [online] http://unctad.org/en/pages/publications/Review-of-Maritime-Transport-%28Series%29.aspx [accessed 20 November 2016]
UNDESA (2016) *World Economic Situation and Prospects*, January
Van Marle, G (2016) Alliance partners abandon ship as Hanjin applies for court receivership, *The Load Star* [online] https://theloadstar.co.uk/alliance-partners-abandon-ship-hanjin-applies-court-receivership/ [accessed 3 September 2016]
Wall Street Journal (2016) Hyundai Merchant Marine in talks to join 2M Alliance South Korean: Shipping line is $4.48 billion in debt, 23 June [online] http://www.wsj.com/articles/hyundai-merchant-marine-in-talks-to-join-2m-alliance-1466657851 [accessed 22 August 2016]
World Trade Organization (2016) Trade growth to remain subdued in 2016 as uncertainties weigh on global demand, PRESS/768, 7 April

Trade and customs procedures in international freight transport: requirements, issues and trends

02

ANDREW GRAINGER, Nottingham University Business School, UK

Introduction

At every port and border international freight operations are exposed to trade and customs procedures. In a typical international freight movement, exposure to trade and customs controls appear at least twice – once in the country of export and once in the country of import. Further procedures and controls may apply along the way when in transit. Without the clearance from authorities, goods may not continue on their journey. Thus, ports and border controls are an integral activity within global logistics operations (Figure 2.1). Ensuring compliance with applicable rules and procedures requires appropriate expertise and 'stuck at the port or border' is a common excuse for goods failing to arrive on time. In this chapter, we will explore that statement. While authorities offer an easy target for blame, good compliance practices and a commitment by policy makers towards

Figure 2.1 Ports and borders, an integral aspect of international freight operations

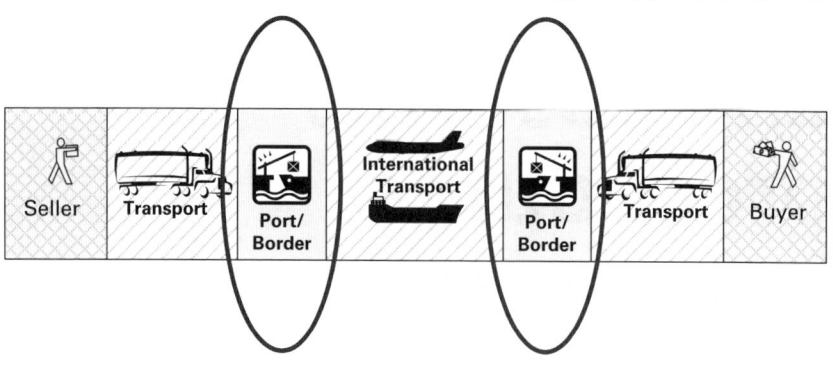

SOURCE Author

trade facilitation can significantly reduce the impact of trade and customs procedures upon the cost of international freight operations.

This chapter presents an overview of the applicable trade and customs procedures, considers to what extent procedures impact upon cost, and last but not least gives direction as to how the trade and customs environment can be improved. The latter point is particularly topical in light of ongoing global commitments towards reform, firmly placing the issues faced by logistics and transport operators at the heart of trade policy. For businesses who fail to be mindful of the regulatory requirements at ports and borders, consequences can be dire. In addition to delay, fines are likely. Where breaches are found to be deliberate, custodial sentences could apply. However, if managed well, concern for customs issues can help reduce costs, mitigate non-compliance risks, safeguard the company's good repute, and help underpin wider strategic capabilities that are reliant on cost-effective, reliable fast-track port and border clearance. Let us begin by considering what importers and exporters wishing to clear goods at the ports and borders need to know.

Trade and customs procedures

The range of trade and customs procedures can be broad. In the UK, for example, 60-plus regulatory regimes can be found (Grainger, 2008). Typically, they concern themselves with the goods moved, the vessels that carry the goods or the people that transport the goods. Their focus is: revenue collection, such as import and export taxes; safety and security, such as that of the supply chain, vehicles and staff; environment and health, such as quarantine controls; consumer protection, such as product testing and labelling; and trade policy, such as tariff quotas, quantitative restrictions and anti-dumping measures. The lead authority that can stop and hold goods at the ports and borders will usually be Customs, although institutional models do vary from country to country. Other government agencies, such as the Immigration and Quarantine Services or the Police and Border Guards, often have a visible presence too (Grainger, 2016).

The main function of Customs is usually to collect applicable duties (taxes) as well as to enforce trade-related prohibitions and restrictions. Customs may perform their function as a dedicated Customs Agency, a Ministerial Department (eg part of the Finance Ministry or Home Office), or from within a Revenue Authority (WCO, 2015b). Usually customs officers cooperate with other authorities, especially where the enforcement of prohibitions and restriction requires specialist expertise, such as in the case of veterinary checks (meat and other products of animal origin), phytosanitary checks (plants and other products of the soil), product standards (various product testing and safety agencies) and export controls (eg for goods with military application, toxic waste, certain chemicals that can be used in the manufacture of illegal drugs, and certain cultural goods) (Grainger, 2016).

The responsibility for complying with applicable rules and procedures depends on the commercial arrangements between the buyer and seller and their respective transport service providers, as well as any appointed intermediaries. For example, where goods are sold on a Free on Board (FOB) basis (ICC, 2010), the seller is responsible for export clearance while the buyer is responsible for import clearance. If it is sold on an ex-works (EXW) basis the buyer is responsible for the entire operation, whereas under Deliver Duty Paid (DDP) the seller would take care of everything. In many countries, customs declarants need to hold official licences, such as that of a customs broker. In other countries, the use of licensed customs professionals is voluntary or not required. In the UK, for example, there are no formal training or licensing requirements, although a quick glance at dedicated customs law books (eg for the EU: Lux, 2003; Lyons, 2008; Massimo, 2012; Witte and Wolffgang, 2012) will show how technical the topic can be. Failure to comply with applicable customs legislations can lead to fines and custodial sentences (eg BBC, 2012) (Grainger, 2016).

Customs-administered import taxes include import duties, usually a percentage figure based on the value of the goods, import-related value added tax (VAT), excise duties (eg on alcohol, tobacco and fuel), and other levies. In some countries export duties also apply. The procedures for declaring goods to customs administrations are usually based on international instruments, especially within the framework of the World Trade Organization's General Agreement on Tariffs and Trade (GATT, 1994) and the World Customs Organization's Kyoto [Customs] Convention (WCO, 1999). In many countries, customs declarations can be made electronically (ASYCUDA, 2016), but may still require supporting paper documents such as the import licence, origin declaration and copies of the commercial invoice.

Where transport routes involve several countries (eg to landlocked countries or via global logistics hubs) customs transit procedures come into play. These might be specific to the country or countries concerned, although there are efforts to simplify transit arrangements, including the TIR (Transports Internationaux Routiers) Convention for sealed vehicles and containers used in international shipments that have at least one leg by road (UNECE, 2014).

The assessment of customs duties is dependent on the correct tariff classification (WCO, 2016) and the country's (or Customs Union's) applicable customs tariff (eg European Commission, 2016; USITC, 2016). The majority of customs duties are assessed on an ad valorem basis, which is a percentage figure based on the value of the goods in accordance to the methods outlined in the WTO Valuation Agreement (WTO, 1994). Lower duty rates may be available where the country of origin benefits from preferential trade agreements. Of these there are many and the WTO counts 406 active regional trade agreements and lists a further 28 preferential agreements (WTO, 2016). The rules for determining the correct tariff classification, value and origin tend to be very technical and often require specialist training. Increasingly, businesses have the option of asking relevant authorities for support. Depending on the country concerned, advice may be available via a telephone helpline, in the form of a written opinion, or as a binding ruling (Grainger, 2016).

Usually, suitably authorized businesses can take advantage of special duty relief measures. These ensure that export-orientated manufactures are placed upon equal footing with competitors elsewhere in the world in instances where imported goods are incorporated into finished goods for export. Common duty relief procedures include inward processing relief (or duty drawback), manufacturing under customs control (or customs bond), export processing zones, temporary import (or admission) for re-exportation in the same state, and customs warehousing (Grainger, 2000; IFC, 2006). To give an example, Figure 2.2. highlights relevant procedures available to EU importers and exporters. Most modern customs administrations also

Figure 2.2 EU Customs import and export procedures with fiscal implications

Import
• **Import into Free Circulation** – customs duty and import VAT is paid and goods are removed from customs control; some goods may be subject to import licences and policy measures
• **Customs Warehousing** – enables goods to be stored without payment of import duty or VAT until released for free circulation or placed under another customs regime
• **Free Zones** – enable goods to be stored and processed without payment of import duty or VAT
• **Inward Processing Relief (IPR)** – suspension/drawback – allows conditional relief from duty on imported materials and components for use in manufacture of products for export; under IPR, suspension duty is suspended, while drawback duty is paid and later reclaimed
• **Processing under Customs Control** – allows specific dutiable components and materials to be imported without payment of duty, processed into finished products and released for free circulation at the duty rate of the finished good (this rate may be lower than the rate of the components and materials used in the production process)
• **Temporary Importation** – gives relief from duty for goods imported for a given period of time (maximum 24 months) and re-exported in the same state
• **Returned Goods Relief** – allows relief on re-importation of goods previously exported (eg rejected by customer)
• **End Use** – reduced/zero duty rates for goods intended for specified end use (eg aircraft, off-shore installations)
• **Other** – goods are re-exported, destroyed or otherwise disposed of without payment of duty
Export
• **Export** – goods leaving the EU may be subject to licensing requirements, export duties and commercial policy measures
• **Outward Processing Relief** – allows relief from duty on EU goods re-imported after repair or process abroad
• **Community Transit** – an EU customs procedure which controls and facilitates the movement of certain goods from one part of the EU to another – delaying duty and VAT payment
• **ATA Carnet** – may be used to simplify customs clearance of temporarily exported goods; the carnet replaces normal customs documents both at export and re-import
• **TIR Carnet** – subject to certain conditions, these allow goods to travel across national frontiers with the minimum of customs formalities

SOURCE 2913/92/EEC (1992); 2454/93/EEC (1993); Grainger (2000)

offer some form of operational concessions. These may, for example, permit suitably authorized traders to make declarations on a periodic basis (eg monthly), or clear goods at the importer's own premises with minimal – if any – interference by customs officers at the ports and borders. Again, access is usually subject to authorization (Grainger, 2016).

Increasingly, authorizations may also be tied to voluntary participation in customs partnership programmes that include additional supply

Figure 2.3 Overview of the EU's Authorised Economic Operator (AEO) programme

Eligible businesses

The AEO programme is open to all economic operators with import or export activities. These might be 'natural persons' or 'legal persons' (such as a company) who in the course of their business activities are involved in customs-related activities. Typically, economic operators are: manufacturers; exporters; freight forwarders; warehouse keepers; customs agents; carriers; importers; ports; secure freight parking operators; airport handling agents and others.

Types of AEO

Customs Simplifications (AEOC) – Provides for easier access to simplified customs procedures at the ports and borders, enabling inland (local) clearance, and simplified export procedures.

Security and Safety (AEOS) – Provides for operational benefits in the control and inspection of EU imports and exports with regard to safety and security. AEOS also provides the basis for mutual recognition with AEO-type programmes in certain non-EU countries.

Customs Simplifications/Security and Safety (**AEOF**) – a combination of the two above.

Key AEO benefits for businesses

The holder of the **AEOC** is entitled to: easier admittance to customs simplifications as the criteria which have already been examined when granting the AEOC will not be re-examined again; fewer physical and document-based customs controls than other economic operators, with the exception of those controls related to security and safety measures; priority treatment if selected for control; and possibility to request a specific place for such control.

The holder of the **AEOS** is entitled to: possibility of prior notification when selected for control; reduced data set for entry and exit summary declarations; fewer physical and document-based controls in respect of security and safety; priority treatment if selected for control; and possibility to request a specific place for such control.

The holder of an **AEOF** is entitled to both AEOC and AEOF benefits.

Additional benefits include: access to a designated contact point (or person) at the customs administration; use of the **AEO** logo in marketing and company literature.

In the near future, **additional benefits** will include: guarantee waivers for special customs procedures (as outlined in Figure 2.2), single authorization (enabling operators to draw on simplified customs procedures in more than one EU member state), self-assessment, and centralized (EU-wide) clearance.

Mutual recognition of AEOS with customs administrations in other countries

China, Japan, Norway, Switzerland and USA.

Linkages with other Accredited Operator Schemes (AOS)

Aviation Security: the AEO status should be taken into account by the competent authorities in the respective member states when applying for 'Know Consignor', 'Regulated Agent', or 'Account Consignor' status. Deeper integration between the AEO and the respective aviation security schemes is under consideration.

Fishing: AEOs dealing with fishery products and catch certificates (required for landing fish in the EU) may apply for the additional status of an 'Approved Economic Operator (APEO)', which confers simplified customs procedures for the import of fishery products into the EU.

Authorization conditions

Operators and applicants need to be 'in control' of their business and applicants need to show that they can influence their supply chain operations, implement appropriate organizational measures, have in place appropriate organizational controls, and be in a position to evaluate, adjust and refine their management systems.

The criteria for granting of an **AEOC** include: a record of compliance with customs requirements; satisfactory system of managing commercial and, where appropriate, transport records, which allows appropriate customs controls; and proven financial solvency.

The criteria for granting of AEOS include: a record of compliance with customs requirements; satisfactory system of managing commercial and, where appropriate, transport records, which allows appropriate customs controls. However, unlike an AEOC, an AEOS is not required to have a logistical system which distinguishes between Community and non-Community goods within their records, proven financial solvency, and appropriate security and safety standards.

The criteria for granting **AEOF**: must meet both the conditions for AEOC and AEOS.

SOURCE Edited extract from Annex 3, Widdowson *et al* (2014a)

chain security obligations (Widdowson *et al*, 2014a; 2014b). Examples of such programmes are the EU's Authorised Economic Operator (AEO) Scheme (Figure 2.3), the United States' Customs and Trade Partnership Against Terrorism (C-TPAT), and similar initiatives elsewhere (WCO, 2012; 2015). These programmes aim to develop deeper partnerships between the administration and business users in order to help foster greater commitment towards supply chain security as well as help reduce compliance costs. Harmonization of such programmes with an eye on paving the way for mutual recognition is sought through the WCO Safe Framework of Standards (WCO, 2015a). Efforts of alignment (and possible recognition) with related security programmes in aviation (ICAO, 2011) and maritime security (IMO, 2002; 2003) are under discussion (WCO, 2013; Widdowson *et al*, 2014a; 2014b; Grainger, 2016).

Depending on the type of control, officers during a physical examination may cross-check container seal numbers with the actual documentation, make x-rays and conduct other forms of external scanning, open consignments to visually verify contents, take samples for further testing, and conduct deep searches of the containers or vessel.

Physical customs inspections are normally guided by risk management principles that favour those businesses with a good compliance record (Widdowson, 2005; Han and Ireland, 2014). Other types of inspection, especially in the quarantine area, may be applied in a more broad-brush manner. They may even be subject to legislatively prescribed inspection quotas. For example, the EU Commission Decision 94/360/EC states that for beef and lamb the minimum number of consignments to be physically checked is 20 per cent, and for poultry, rabbit and game meats it is 50 per cent (Grainger, 2013; 2016).

Customs management practices

Recent research that looked at customs management practices in nine multinational companies from a cross-section of sectors (Grainger, 2016) suggests that customs managers are involved in a wide range of interdependent activities. These are summarized in Figure 2.4 and broadly fall into three categories: logistics support, which focuses on ensuring that goods are cleared without undue delay at minimal cost and that declaring parties have been instructed correctly; supply chain management, where activities can range from ensuring that supply chain partners meet their customs obligations to the modelling of customs duty liabilities in different types of supply

Figure 2.4 The activities of customs managers within multinational companies

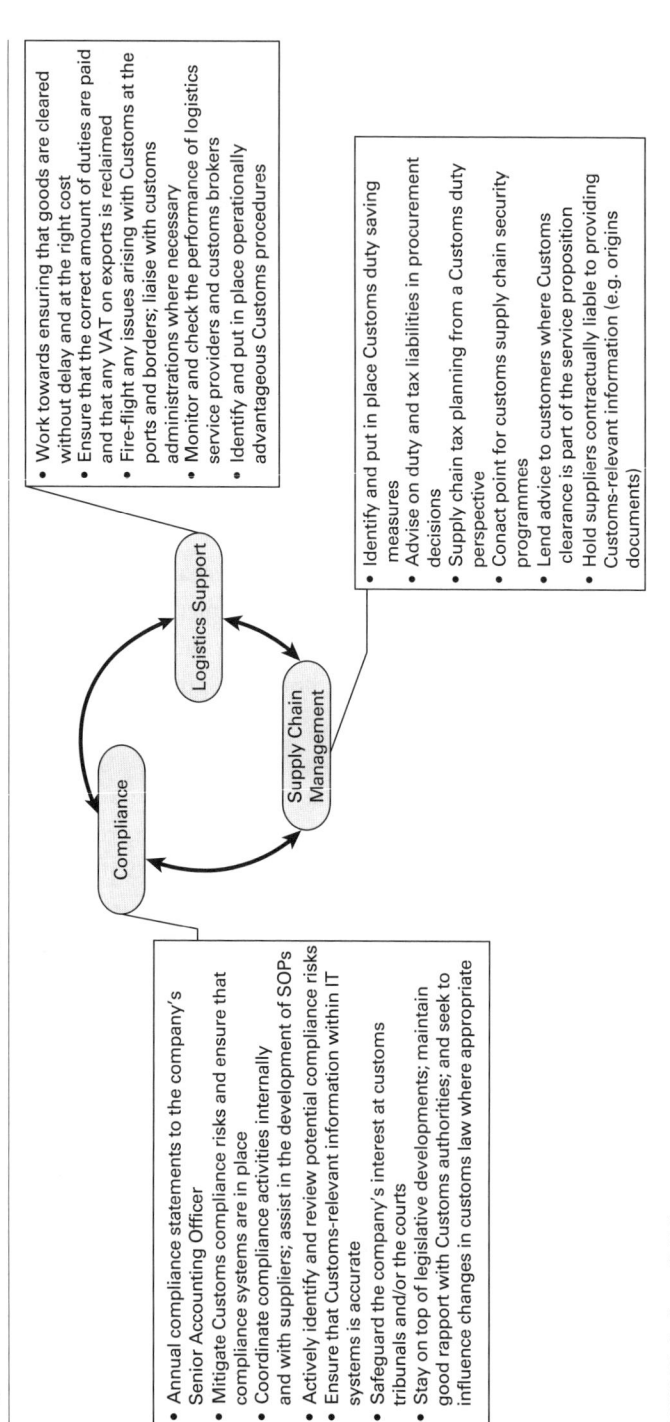

- Work towards ensuring that goods are cleared without delay and at the right cost
- Ensure that the correct amount of duties are paid and that any VAT on exports is reclaimed
- Fire-flight any issues arising with Customs at the ports and borders; liaise with customs administrations where necessary
- Monitor and check the performance of logistics service providers and customs brokers
- Identify and put in place operationally advantageous Customs procedures

- Identify and put in place Customs duty saving measures
- Advise on duty and tax liabilities in procurement decisions
- Supply chain tax planning from a Customs duty perspective
- Conact point for customs supply chain security programmes
- Lend advice to customers where Customs clearance is part of the service proposition
- Hold suppliers contractually liable to providing Customs-relevant information (e.g. origins documents)

Compliance ⇄ Logistics Support ⇄ Supply Chain Management

- Annual compliance statements to the company's Senior Accounting Officer
- Mitigate Customs compliance risks and ensure that compliance systems are in place
- Coordinate compliance activities internally and with suppliers; assist in the development of SOPs
- Actively identify and review potential compliance risks
- Ensure that Customs-relevant information within IT systems is accurate
- Safeguard the company's interest at customs tribunals and/or the courts
- Stay on top of legislative developments; maintain good rapport with Customs authorities; and seek to influence changes in customs law where appropriate

SOURCE Grainger (2016)

chain configurations (see Figure 2.5); and regulatory compliance, which is about safeguarding the company's good repute and minimizing risks of mistakes and illegal acts. The latter can extend to ensuring that staff do not pay bribes to customs officials, as this can expose the company to anti-corruption laws – such as the US's Foreign Corrupt Practices Act (enacted in 1977) and the UK's Anti-Bribery Act 2010.

Noteworthy is that most globally operating companies tend to outsource much, if not all, of their customs-related activities to third parties. These might be customs brokers, customs agents or freight forwarders. The advantage of subcontracting to specialists is that they benefit from economies of scale which can be passed on as a cost-effective service – especially in the day-to-day interaction with customs authorities. However, shippers still need to make sure that the appointed third parties are appropriately instructed and supervised. It is also not uncommon to rely on sophisticated electronic solutions. These are often integrated into wider Enterprise Resource Planning (ERP) systems (Appeals and Struye de Swielande, 1998; Hausman *et al*, 2010) and offer a high degree of automation. Indeed, the number of customs specialists within larger companies can be very small. Amongst the world's largest multinational manufacturing companies it is not uncommon to find less than 20 full-time specialists worldwide (Grainger, 2016).

It is also worth highlighting that within the 2016 Grainger study, several interviewed customs managers stated that their function is somewhat overlooked. Cost-saving customs measures may not be taken advantage of; risks may be taken that could easily be avoided – especially in instances where the customs-related activities of third parties are not robustly monitored. This suggests that there is considerable scope for improvement amongst many of the world's largest companies. However, the same study also highlighted that in some companies – especially those with a strong focus on customers' logistics service expectations, such as the fast parcel sector – the customs manager's function appears to be held in high regard. Their level of engagement in the company's wider operations is deep.

Figure 2.5 Example: import duties for roasted and unroasted coffee

In the European Union the import of roasted coffee, not decaffeinated (classified as 0901 21 0000) has an import duty rate of 7.5 per cent. The import of unroasted coffee, not decaffeinated (classified as 0901 11 0000) has an import duty rate of 0 per cent. In consideration of the higher duty rate for roasted coffee it may make sense to import unroasted coffee at 0 per cent and roast it in the EU.

Readers may wish to check for themselves by using the European Commission's TARIC Consultation Database (http://ec.europa.eu/taxation_customs/dds2/taric/taric_consultation.jsp) or by using the online customs tariff in any of the EU's Member States (for the UK go to https://www.gov.uk/trade-tariff).

The case for trade facilitation

Perceptions about the performance of specific customs and border agencies differ widely from one country to the next. In many places, such as in the UK, it is possible to clear goods within a matter of seconds providing that all declared information is in good order and without errors. Elsewhere, it can take days or weeks. Most logistics practitioners will have stories of where clearance took even longer. Much can go wrong and Figure 2.6 lists some of the frustrations that might arise.

In light of such frustrations, it is probably not surprising that numerous international organizations – such as the World Economic Forum (WEF, 2015), the Organisation for Economic Co-operation and Development (OECD, 2009) and the United Nations Conference on Trade and Development (UNCTAD, 2006a; 2006b), the World Bank (De Wulf and Sokol, 2005; McLinden et al, 2010), amongst others – are making strong cases for reform to help reduce the cost of trading across borders. Much of this work goes by the label of 'Trade Facilitation' (Grainger, 2011) and has manifested itself into mainstream trade policy in the form of the World Trade Organization's Trade Facilitation Agreement (WTO, 2014) as well as in many bilateral and

Figure 2.6 Negative experiences associated with poorly performing ports and borders

1) Excessive paperwork; multiple parties require documents that are similar or overlapping in content.
2) Long queues at the government offices responsible for stamping paperwork.
3) Checks at the border take too long.
4) The office hours kept by officials fail to coincide with when the goods arrive at the border.
5) Customs officers may be unnecessarily heavy handed in order to solicit payment for 'special' treatment.
6) Officers fail to appreciate how their actions impact on costs.
7) Published rules and procedures cannot be easily accessed or are out of date; compliance requirements are established through costly trial and error.
8) Officers at the ports and border interpret applicable rules and procedures differently, causing confusion and adding to cost.
9) The capacity of inspection facilities is constrained; significant backlogs and extended periods of delay result.
10) The various board agencies fail to coordinate their controls, resulting in duplication of control activity, delay and additional costs.
11) Paper documents go missing, especially when travelling with the goods (for example in the driver's cab).
12) Officials reject documents because of minor errors – for example; the number '8' can easily be confused with the letter 'B'; the letter 'I' and the number '1' look the same.
13) Correction and appeal mechanisms may not exist – or are very cumbersome unless facilitation monies have been paid.
14) The operational practices of one government agency contradict those of another.
15) Government agencies fail to take adequate advantage of modern technologies, thus adding to cost.

SOURCE Adapted from: Grainger and McLinden (2013)

regional trade agreements, signed or under negotiation (eg EU–Korea Free Trade Agreement, Transatlantic Trade and Investment Partnership, ASEAN Free Trade Area, Trans-Pacific Partnership Agreement).

As is highlighted in the WTO's World Trade Report 2015, significant benefits are to be had from trade facilitation (WTO, 2015). The OECD, for example, calculates that the WTO Trade Facilitation Agreement could reduce the worldwide cost for internationally trading businesses between 12.5 per cent and 17.5 per cent (OECD, 2015). Others have also made strong economic cases for trade facilitation (Wilson *et al*, 2005; Maur and Wilson, 2011; Mann, 2012).

What does compliance cost?

This is a difficult question, since it will inevitably depend on the specific nature of the shipment under consideration. There are several macro-level attempts that have helped support the case for trade facilitation (Walkenhorst and Yasui, 2003; Pomfret and Sourdin, 2010; Sourdin and Pomfret, 2012), though these do lack operational context. Inevitably, costs include the time, effort, and expense associated with preparing declarations to the relevant authorities. It also includes the costs of presenting cargo to the authorities, if selected for physical examination. Much of the necessary paperwork needs to be prepared months ahead, some of it days ahead, some of it on arrival, and some of it after arrival (Grainger, 2013).

Such direct costs may be measured, although the devil is in the detail. For example, in the UK (and elsewhere in the EU) customs authorities do not charge for their work. However, the authorities expect that cargo, when selected for examination, is made available for inspection at the dedicated inspection facility. This requires additional handling and dock-labour for which the port stevedore needs to be paid. Depending on the specific arrangements at the port, charges are levied, either as a flat-rate fee applicable to all port users, irrespective of whether their cargo is selected for inspection or not, or as an itemized bill that needs to be settled (eg by payment or through a credit facility) before goods are inspected (Grainger, 2014a). In addition, the shipping line may charge for demurrage (storage costs) and terminal handling because the cargo was not cleared through the port on time. At some ports, such demurrage and terminal handling fees can differ significantly from one shipping line to the next, irrespective of what the port may have charged the shipping line.

In addition to the directly experienced costs, there are also a wide range of indirect costs. These include costs resulting from poor performance, such as missed business opportunities, contractual penalties, additional demurrage and storage charges, inhibited competitiveness, and failure to take advantage of market opportunities (Grainger and McLinden, 2013). Further costs might result from hedging strategies, whereby companies hold additional buffer-stock (an inventory cost) to offset potential delay at the ports and borders. Operators may also choose to switch to more expensive transport modes (eg from shipping goods by sea to air or from rail to road) to offset – or even bypass – time penalties at the border. Business competitiveness is undermined.

Not to be forgotten are direct and indirect costs to governments. Direct costs here relate to the expense of enforcing trade and customs procedures. Indirect costs result from the misallocation of resources, reduced-revenue collection yields, vulnerabilities stemming from organized crime, denied access to trade and customs arrangements with key markets, inhibited economic growth, and a stunted tax base. Moreover, where inefficiency gives rise to corruption, the overall integrity of the governing institutions is severely undermined (Grainger and McLinden, 2013).

Fixes and reform

Trade facilitation champions have long advocated a series of recommendations about how to reduce costs in international trade. Much of this effort focuses on the simplification, standardization, harmonization, and modernization of trade and customs procedures. Some of the proposed solutions can be complex undertakings, such as the idea of the Single Window (UN/CEFACT, 2004; 2005). Its underlying idea is a solution whereby businesses deal with the various government agencies via one interface – a single window through which all documents can be passed for processing. Ideally that interface ought to be electronic and able to facilitate processing speeds within a matter of seconds. A prominent example of a single window infrastructure is Singapore's TradeNet system (see Applegate *et al*, 1993; 1995; Teo *et al*, 1997) which is often cited as a good example and links traders with 35 different government agencies (eg UN/CEFACT, 2005).

Other proposed trade facilitation ideas are far less technical, but can find wide application. For example, to avoid confusion about place names, there is an international effort to provide standardized location codes (UN/CEFACT, 2016). The result of this is that we all instantly recognize the LHR code as London Heathrow, LAX as Los Angeles, and GVA as Geneva – or

Genève in French, Genf in German, and Ginevra in Italian. There are many more ideas and initiatives (Figure 2.7) that have been sparked in the pursuit of trade facilitation. Topical areas include:

- the simplification and harmonization of applicable rules and procedures, which includes efforts aimed at harmonization, the avoidance of duplication and the accommodation of business practices;
- the modernization of trade compliance systems, such as by developing electronic systems, standardizing documents and information requirements, and sharing experiences;

Figure 2.7 The interdependent components of trade facilitation

The simplification and harmonization

i. Harmonization of procedures
   For example: the adoption of international conventions and instruments; the harmonization of controls applied by the various different government agencies.

ii. Avoidance of duplication
   For example: regional or bilateral agreements to recognize export controls in lieu of import control; shared inspection facilities, for instance for customs officers, veterinarians, plant health inspectors and health inspectors; the formal recognition of private sector controls (eg in the area of security or quality) in lieu of official checks.

iii. Accommodate business practices
   For example: to accept commercial documents (such as the invoice) in lieu of official documents; to allow goods to be cleared inland, away from the bottlenecks at ports and border-posts.

The modernization of trade

i. Solutions
   For example: use of electronic information systems, the Single Window concepts, electronic customs systems, port community systems, websites, and information portals.

ii. Standardization
   For example: electronic standards for the exchange of information between computers; paper document standards; barcode standards; document referencing conventions; standards for the description of locations.

iii. Sharing of experiences
   For example: training and awareness building; development of toolkits and implementation guides; collaborative and open source systems developments.

Administration practices

i. Service standards
   For example: public service level commitments; publish and make available applicable rules and procedures; produce plain language guides; develop online websites; keep the customs tariff up to date; provide for efficient appeal mechanisms.

ii. Management principles
   For example: enforcement of controls in proportion to the risk against which they seek to protect; selective (risk based) controls that reward compliant behaviour (eg preferential treatment at the border).

Institutional mechanisms and tools

   For example: establishing a national trade facilitation body; produce and publish whitepapers setting out reform ambitions and inviting stakeholder comments.

SOURCE Adapted from Grainger (2011)

- administration practices, including service standards and adherence to 'best practice' border management principles; and
- institutional mechanisms and tools, for example to monitor progress in trade facilitation, and work in partnership with the private sector.

In the context of the WTO Trade Facilitation Agreement, the focus is more specific (Grainger, 2014b; 2015). Many of the 13 articles are of an administrative nature, specifying: minimum benefits for trusted traders (reminiscent of the WCO's SAFE framework of Standards and its Authorised Economic Operator scheme; Article 7); advance customs rulings (for tariff classification and origin, but also recommended for customs value, duty relief, and quotas; Article 3); the right to appeal (Article 4); pre-arrival processing of customs declarations (Article 7); electronic payment of duties, taxes and fees (Article 7); the adherence to risk-based controls (Article 7); post-clearance audits by Customs (Article 7); the implementation of the special customs procedures, such as Inward Processing and Outward Processing Relief (Article 10); and expedited clearance for air cargo and perishable goods (Article 7).

Several of the Agreement's articles express the aim for authorities to cooperate with each other at home and internationally. This includes: common border procedures and uniform document requirements (Article 10); the adoption of the Single Window principle (enabling importers to submit all relevant information for declaration to the authorities via one single interface; Article 10); and mechanism for the exchange of information between customs administrations (eg copies of the import and export declaration as well as supporting documents such as the commercial invoice and shipping documents; Article 12). The agreement also states that WTO member states shall not introduce the mandatory use of customs brokers (Article 10). In countries where customs brokers are a licensed profession, applicable rules

Figure 2.8 Scope of WTO Trade Facilitation Agreement

1) Publication and availability of Information	7) Release and clearance of goods
2) Opportunity to comment, information before entry into force and consultation	8) Border agency cooperation
	9) Movement of goods under customs control intended for import
3) Advance rulings	10) Formalities connected with importation and exportation and transit
4) Appeal or review procedures	
5) Other measures to enhance impartiality, no-discrimination and transparency	11) Freedom of transit
	12) Customs cooperation
6) Disciplines on fees and charges imposed on or in connection with importation and exportation	13) Institutional arrangements (Art. 26)

SOURCE Adapted from WTO (2013)

governing their use must be transparent and objective. Likewise, the introduction of pre-shipment inspection requirements (a costly aspect of trade compliance in some developing countries) is to be discouraged (Article 10).

Apart from the WTO and WCO there are other international organizations with a strong interest in trade and customs policy. Indeed, many of them have helped set the groundwork for trade facilitation policy (Grainger, 2011). Noteworthy organizations are: the United Nations Centre for Trade Facilitation and Electronic Business (UN/CEFACT) which has produced a long list of trade facilitation recommendations (some dating back to the early 1960s); the United Economic Commission for Europe and the International Road Transport Union, who look after the TIR Road Transit Agreement; the International Chamber of Commerce, which has defined a widely used set of standard terms for how businesses trade with each other, the so-called Incoterms (ICC, 2010); the International Maritime Organization, International Air Transport Association and The International Civil Aviation Organization's efforts in supply chain and transport security amongst others.

Conclusion

Inevitably, trade and custom procedures have a direct impact on international freight operations and are a feature of the wider trade environment. While often highlighted as an obstacle to efficient international freight operations, one should not take the statement 'stuck at the port [or border]' for granted. Businesses who manage compliance requirements well are likely to have a significant advantage over others who do not. This chapter has provided a brief overview of what is required, although mastery, for those who want to apply themselves to this area, is advised. In some countries, training is available, as well as support by relevant professional bodies, such as those governing customs brokers and other freight professionals. In other countries, formal training is less readily available and is often 'on the job'. The International Network of Customs Universities might be a good starting point for identifying suitable educational providers.

Apart from the call for further awareness and training, there is also considerable scope for detailed research to help underpin ongoing trade facilitation efforts. This might, for example, focus on developing new ideas and solutions, or it might apply itself to evaluating and analysing current initiatives in order to make sure that current reform momentum is best applied. The topic of trade and customs procedures also offers an opportunity to extend how we view international freight and logistics operations. It is not just about physically moving goods from one place to the next. It is also about having concern for the wider regulatory environment within which that movement takes place. The requirements of customs and other border agencies are integral features within that operation.

It should also not be forgotten that regulation is dynamic in nature and can be influenced. Indeed, much of trade facilitation is about lending a voice to those involved in international freight operations and finding solutions that ensure that regulatory objectives are met without adding to costs. Indeed, many countries have recently set up dedicated trade facilitation bodies for this very purpose. The challenge is to ensure that requirements are appropriately articulated and communicated and the performance of border agencies is suitably monitored. The active support from practitioners and academics could go a long way.

References

2454/93/EEC (1993) Commission Regulation (EEC) No 2454/93 of 2 July 1993 laying down provisions for the implementation of Council Regulation (EEC) No 2913/92 establishing the Community Customs Code, *Official Journal of the European Union*, 36 (L253): 1–177

2913/92/EEC (1992) Council Regulation (EEC) No 2913/92 of 12 October 1992 establishing the Community Customs Code, *Official Journal of the European Union*, 35 (L302): 1–50

Appeals, T and H Struye de Swielande (1998) Rolling back the frontiers: the customs clearance revolution, *The International Journal of Logistics Management*, 9 (1): 111–118

Applegate, L M et al (1993) Singapore TradeNet: The tale continues, *Harvard Business School Cases*, 29 June

Applegate, L M et al (1995) Singapore TradeNet: Beyond TradeNet to the intelligent island, *Harvard Business School Cases*, 10 October

ASYCUDA (2016) About ASYCUDA, retrieved 18 February 2016 from http://www.asycuda.org/aboutas.asp

BBC (2012, 9 March) Ireland garlic scam: Paul Begley jailed for six years, retrieved 18 February 2016 from http://www.bbc.co.uk/news/world-europe-17320460

De Wulf, L and J B Sokol, eds (2005) *Customs Modernisation Handbook*, Washington, World Bank

European Commission (2016) TARIC Consultation, retrieved 10 February 2016 from http://ec.europa.eu/taxation_customs/dds2/taric/taric_consultation.jsp?Lang=en

GATT (1994) *The General Agreement on Tariffs and Trade*, WTO

Grainger, A (2000) Customs and international supply-chains issues, *Logistics & Transport Focus*, 2 (9): 40–43

Grainger, A (2008) Customs and trade facilitation: from concepts to implementation, *World Customs Journal*, 2 (1): 17–30

Grainger, A (2011) Trade facilitation: a conceptual review, *Journal of World Trade*, 45 (1): 39–62

Grainger, A (2013) Trade and customs procedures: The compliance costs for UK meat imports, *ePrints*, Nottingham, University of Nottingham: 50

Grainger, A (2014a) Trade and customs compliance costs at ports, *Maritime Economics & Logistics*, 16 (4): 467–83

Grainger, A (2014b) The WTO Trade Facilitation Agreement: Consulting the private sector, *Journal of World Trade*, 48 (6)

Grainger, A (2015) Customs issues falling under INTA's new remit, European Parliament, Brussels

Grainger, A (2016) Customs management in multinational companies, *World Customs Journal* (forthcoming)

Grainger, A and G McLinden (2013) Trade facilitation and development, in *Handbook of Trade Policy for Development*, ed A Lukauskas, R M Stern and G Zanini, Oxford, Oxford University Press

Han, C-R and R Ireland (2014) Performance measurement of the KCS customs selectivity system, *Risk Management,* 16 (1): 1460–3799

Hausman, W H *et al* (2010) A Process Analysis of Global Trade Management: an inductive approach, *Journal of Supply Chain Management,* 46 (2): 5–29

ICAO (2011) *Annex 17 to the Convention on International Civil Aviation* (9th edition, March 2011) Quebec, International Civil Aviation Organization

ICC (2010) *Incoterms 2010*, Paris, ICC

IFC (2006) *Reforming the Regulatory Procedures for Import and Export: Guide for practitioners*, Washington, The World Bank Group: 96–107

IMO (2002) *Amendments to the SOLAS (Safety of Life at Sea) Convention: Measures to enhance maritime security*, London, IMO

IMO (2003) *ISPS (The International Ship and Port Facility Security) Code,* 2003 Edition, London, IMO

Lux, M (2003) *Das Zollrecht der EG*, Bundesanzeiger Verlag

Lyons, T J (2008) *EC Customs Law*, Oxford, Oxford University Press

Mann, C L (2012) Supply chain logistics, trade facilitation and international trade: A macroeconomic policy view, *Journal of Supply Chain Management,* 48 (3): 7–14

Massimo, F (2012) *Customs Law of the European Union,* 4th Edition, Alphen aan den Rijn, Wolters Kluwer

Maur, J-C and J S Wilson (2011) *Trade Costs and Facilitation: Open trade and economic development*, Cheltenham, Edward Elgar

McLinden, G *et al*, eds (2010) *Border Management Modernization*, Washington, World Bank

OECD (2009) *Overcoming Border Bottlenecks: The costs and benefits of trade facilitation*, Paris, Organisation for Economic Co-operation and Development

OECD (2015) *Policy Brief: Implementation of the WTO Trade Facilitation Agreement: The potential impact on trade costs*, Paris, Organisation for Economic Co-operation and Development Trade and Agriculture Directorate

Pomfret, R and P Sourdin (2010) Trade facilitation and the measurement of trade costs, *Journal of International Commerce, Economics and Policy*, **1** (1): 145–63

Sourdin, P and R Pomfret (2012) *Trade Facilitation: Defining, measuring, explaining and reducing the cost of international trade*, Cheltenham, Edward Elgar

Teo, H-H et al (1997) Organisational transformation using electronic data interchange: The case of TradeNet in Singapore, *Journal of Management Information Systems*, **13** (4): 139–65

UN/CEFACT (2004) Recommendation No 33: Single Window Recommendation, CEFACT, Geneva, UN. ECE/TRADE/352: 37

UN/CEFACT (2005) *Case Studies on Implementing a Single Window to Enhance the Efficient Exchange of Information Between Trade and Government* [working draft], United Nations

UN/CEFACT (2016) UN/LOCODE, retrieved 18 May 2016 from http://www.unece.org/cefact/locode/welcome.html

UNCTAD (2006a) *Trade Facilitation Handbook Part I: National facilitation bodies; lessons from experience*, UNCTAD/SDTE/TLB/2005/1

UNCTAD (2006b) *Trade Facilitation Handbook Part II: technical notes on essential trade facilitation measures*, UNCTAD/SDTE/TLB/2005/2

UNECE (2014) *TIR Handbook; Customs convention on the international transport of goods under cover of TIR carnets (TIR Convention 1975)*, 10th Edition. Geneva, United Nations

USITC (2016) Harmonised Tariff Schedule, retrieved 18 February 2016, from http://hts.usitc.gov/

Walkenhorst, P and T Yasui (2003) *Quantitative Assessment of the Benefits of Trade Facilitation*, Working Party of the Trade Committee, Paris, OECD, TD/TC/WP(2003)31/Final

WCO (1999) *Revised Kyoto Convention: International convention on the simplifications and harmonisation of customs procedures*, Brussels, World Customs Organization

WCO (2012) *Compendium of Authorised Economic Operator Programmes*, 2012 edition, Brussels, World Customs Organization

WCO (2013) Establishment of tripartite cooperation between the WCO, ICAO and IMO to secure and facilitate trade, retrieved 18 May 2016 from http://www.wcoomd.org/en/media/newsroom/2013/july/establishment-of-tripartite-cooperation-between-the-wco-icao-and-imo-to-secure-and-facilitate-trade.aspx

WCO (2015a) *SAFE Framework of Standards: To secure and facilitate global trade*, Brussels, World Customs Organization, June

WCO (2015b) *World Customs Organization Annual report 2014-2015*, Brussels, World Customs Organization

WCO (2016) What is the Harmonised System (HS)? Retrieved 18 February 2016, from http://www.wcoomd.org/en/topics/nomenclature/overview/what-is-the-harmonized-system.aspx

WEF (2015) *Enabling Trade: Increasing the potential of trade reforms*, Geneva, World Economic Forum

Widdowson, D (2005) Managing risk in the customs context, in *Customs Modernisation Handbook*, ed L D Wulf and J B Sokol, Washington, World Bank: 91–99

Widdowson, D *et al* (2014a) *Review of Accredited Operator Schemes*, Centre for Customs and Excise Studies, Charles Sturt University

Widdowson, D *et al* (2014b) Review of accredited operator schemes: An Australian study, *World Customs Journal*, **8** (1): 17–34

Wilson, J S *et al* (2005) Assessing the benefits of trade facilitation: A global perspective, *World Economy* **28** (6): 841–71

Witte, P and H-M Wolffgang (2012) *Lehrbuch des Europäischen Zollrechts*, Herne, NWB Verlag

WTO (1994) *Agreement on Implementation of Article VII of the General Agreement on Tariffs and Trade 1994*, Geneva, World Trade Organization

WTO (2013) *Negotiating Group on Trade Facilitation: Draft consolidated negotiating text – Revision 16* [TN/TF/W/165/Rev.16] Geneva, World Trade Organization

WTO (2014) *Protocol Amending the Marrakesh Agreement Establishing the World Trade Organization*, Decision of 27 November 2014 (WT/L/940) General Council, Geneva, World Trade Organization

WTO (2015) *World Trade Report 2015; Speeding up trade: benefits and challenges of implementing the WTO Trade Facilitation Agreement*, Geneva, World Trade Organization

WTO (2016) Regional trade agreement, retrieved 18 February 2016 from https://www.wto.org/english/tratop_e/region_e/region_e.htm

PART TWO
International freight transport in practice

Multimodal transport solutions for grain exports from Kazakhstan

03

TIMUR BIMAGANBETOV, Ministry of Healthcare and Social Development, Republic of Kazakhstan
ANTHONY BERESFORD, Cardiff Business School, UK
STEPHEN PETTIT, Cardiff Business School, UK

Introduction

The purpose of this chapter is to evaluate multimodal transport developments in Kazakhstan, where operating conditions are complicated by historic connections to the former Soviet Union generating, for example, a bias in trade direction and in operating protocols. This chapter seeks to examine the trading methods and transport movements of grain exports from Kazakhstan, highlighting the unusual nature of both routing and carrying methods. Kazakhstan is a landlocked country and trade through neighbouring countries gives access to the sea either directly or indirectly, as several neighbouring states are themselves landlocked. The chapter explores existing and alternative routes available to Kazakh grain exporters. On these major trading routes, specific logistics and transportation problems, which are both soft (intangible) and hard (tangible), are highlighted. In order to best demonstrate the salient operational characteristics, an analysis of the movement of grain from Kokshetau (northern Kazakhstan) to Bandar Abbas (Iran) is conducted. An established multimodal transport time–cost model is used as a framework to evaluate the effectiveness of both existing and potential routes.

Kazakhstan, located in Central Asia, is one of the five landlocked countries in this sub region (along with Uzbekistan, Turkmenistan, Tajikistan and Kyrgyzstan). Each borders at least two of the others and they are double or even triple landlocked. The remoteness from sea ports and isolation from world markets leads to unstable trading conditions for Kazakhstan grain exporters to world markets. Long distances from the markets and additional border crossings increase the total expenditure for transport services. As a consequence, both export and import goods often transit through more than one neighbouring state, making transport complex (UNESCAP, 2003). Therefore, reliable and adequate transport and communications facilities play an essential role in the country's economic development. Rapid development of trade and globalization of the processes foster the necessity to invest in the transport sector. By 2015, the trade value between Asia and Europe had increased to US $1 trillion and the advantageous geographic position of Kazakhstan as a landbridge was being exploited. However, transit opportunities require modern transport infrastructure meeting international standards. The recent utilization of Aktau Port as a regional hub shows that reorganized logistics, and especially greater use of optimum combinations of multimodal transport, play a significant role in increasing Kazakhstan's trade competitiveness.

Increasing the number of markets places Kazakhstan under pressure to evaluate and revise its transport system. Kazakhstan, after gaining independence in 1991, inherited from the former Soviet Union a transport infrastructure which was built mainly to move the raw materials produced in Kazakhstan to Moscow. Overall, the transport infrastructure can be described as poor and there has been insufficient emphasis on the logistics sector, which is still immature. The recent economic downturn emphasizes the vulnerability of the transport sector and as a result steps are being taken to modernize the infrastructure. The levels of investment in the transport sector in 2014 reached US $18.8 billion (Sultangaliyeva, 2016; Rustrade.kz, 2016).

This chapter presents a review of multimodal transport developments in Kazakhstan in the context of grain export. As a severely landlocked country, Kazakhstan suffers from very high access costs for imports and similarly high distribution costs for exports. The location of Kazakhstan, south of Russia, west of China and north of, among others, Uzbekistan, Turkmenistan and Iran, presents a variety of challenges, especially in the form of route and mode selection. Of particular interest are the various routes and modes currently being utilized, or which could be utilized, for the movement of grain exports from the northern region Kokshetau to the port of Bandar Abbas located on the Persian Gulf in Iran.

Grain exports from Kazakhstan

Significant shifts in the geographic pattern of trade have been observed in the last decade. The key trading partners of Kazakhstan are China, Russia and the European Union and there has been growing Chinese influence. For example, China's share of imports in 2010 was 13 per cent or US $4.3 billion. This trend is not surprising, as China is becoming a major player in the markets of Central Asia, and Central and Eastern Europe. The relative importance of Russia has been declining, namely as a destination for Kazakhstan's exports (IMF, 2011).

In recent years, Kazakhstan has become one of the major players in the grain market. Kazakhstan is one of the 10 largest wheat producers and one of the five largest exporters of grain in the world. Its large land area and low production costs provide the prospect of moving up the value chain with development of wheat crops. In research carried out by OECD (2010) it has been reported that the low production costs create a key competitive advantage in the world grain market. As an example, wheat production costs in Kazakhstan in 2008 were only US $105 per tonne, while in the United States and France they were US $248 and US $202 per tonne respectively.

Wheat production in 2010 remained at around 10 to 12 million tonnes, which allowed Kazakhstan to meet domestic demand, and export up to 5 million tonnes of grain (ATF Bank, 2010). In 2011/2012 Kazakhstan grain yield rose to 27 million tonnes, including 22.7 million tonnes of wheat, which allowed the export of 15 million tonnes (July to July) (Sakenova, 2012). Since July 2012, Kazakhstan has exported about 7.5 million tonnes of grain annually, 34 per cent of this amount in the form of flour.

The geography of Kazakhstan grain markets comprises 25 countries, concentrated in the CIS countries, the European Union, the Middle East and North Africa. Traditional buyers of Kazakh grain are the countries of Central Asia. Geographical proximity, similarity of trading systems and the high-quality grain makes Kazakhstan an attractive supplier for these countries. Demand for grain from the Central Asian countries remains stable and less price-elastic, since the population of the region is characterized by constant growth with low levels of income (RFCA Ratings, 2010). As a further stabilization strategy, and to increase grain and flour exports, steps were taken to develop the following corridors:

1 Western corridor – through Aktau Port on the Caspian Sea in two directions – to the ports of Iran and to Baku in Azerbaijan: for effective use of the Caspian Sea route, in 2007 a grain terminal at Aktau Port was

upgraded, doubling its capacity. In the same year, a new grain terminal at the port of Baku was built, with a handling capacity of 350,000 tonnes per annum. The plant includes a grain terminal and flour mill complex, with five silos for temporary storage, each of which can accommodate up to 3,000 tonnes of grain, storage thus totals 15,000 tonnes.

2 Southern corridor – to Central Asian countries and Afghanistan: in 2010 the grain terminal in the port of Amirabad (Iran) was constructed with a throughput capacity of up to 700,000 tonnes of grain per annum. In 2009, at the Beineu station in the Mangistau region, grain silos were built with a storage capacity of 100,000 tonnes, which provides handling capacity for up to 1.5 million tonnes of grain for export to the Caspian region, Central Asia and Middle East.

3 Eastern corridor – to China: in order to facilitate the export of Kazakhstan's grain to the Chinese market, a new grain terminal was developed on the Chinese border between 2011 and 2013. This has an annual throughput of 500,000 tonnes of grain per annum, with a possible increase to 1 million tonnes with 25,000 tonnes of storage capacity at any one time (Turaeva, 2014).

Iran is one of the major importers of Kazakh wheat and is also used as a transit point for Middle and Far East countries with the port of Bandar Abbas. Iran and the Central Asian countries are becoming strategic partners for the export of grain, as Kazakhstan plans to diversify away somewhat from the Black Sea markets. The Iranian grain import market itself is of interest not only to Kazakhstan. Among the major suppliers of grain to Iran are Canada, Australia, Germany, Argentina, Russia and Ukraine, which supply wheat mainly to the southern regions. At the same time, the Iranian government generally supports freight delivery of grain. This is facilitated by the geography of the country: the north of Iran borders with the countries of the Caspian Sea region, to the west it has access to the Gulf countries, and to the south it has access to the open ocean through the Ottoman Gulf. In summary, flows into Iran are diverse and logistically price competitive.

The route for Kazakh grain to the Iranian grain market via the Caspian Sea was opened up in the mid-1990s. Up to 600,000 tonnes of grain per annum are handled through the Aktau Port terminal, which is a 100 per cent subsidiary of the JSC 'Food Contract Corporation' (FCC). FCC's mission is to ensure food security, stabilize the domestic grain market and promote the development of Kazakhstan's grain export potential through the effective management of resources and the promotion of grain export infrastructure in the grain industry. FCC buys grain from the farmers at a price of

US $134–140 and exports it overseas. FCC is the main operator in the Kazakhstan grain market and it operates on behalf of the state. Kazakhstan plans to expand grain exports to Iran to 700,000 tonnes per annum. For a landlocked country such as Kazakhstan, the movement of grain is a challenging issue. In Kazakhstan, due to the long distances, as a norm grain is transported mainly by rail but at the same time there is scope for multimodal solutions (Mazharova, 2011; Turaeva, 2014; Sultangaliyeva, 2016).

Principal grain routes

A routing analysis of the grain transport from Kokshetau, North Kazakhstan to Bandar Abbas, Iran is presented below. The main source of data was a series of interviews with Russian, Kazakh and Iranian transport companies (typically road hauliers), logistics service providers (LSPs) (offering tailored logistics packages, often including value addition), freight forwarders (agency services), public and private (usually specialist) grain traders. All data about transport costs and distances were retrieved using the real-time CIS Logistics software 'Rail Tariff' for Russia, Turkmenistan, Uzbekistan and Kazakhstan, and data regarding Iranian transport were obtained from Iranian LSPs, freight forwarders and transport companies. Current and up-to-date information regarding the grain market was collected with the help of 'Kazakh Zerno' Grain Information Agency. Secondary data about Kazakhstan were obtained from the National Library of the Republic of Kazakhstan and the Library of Railway Studies (Dedov and Froluva, 2015; Kazakhstan Railways, 2016).

Freight flows

When the crop is harvested, local farmers sell grain to the FCC or private traders. As mentioned earlier, the FCC buys the grain on behalf of the state for the established prices. During 2013–2014 the typical price was US $134–$140 per tonne. The FCC has grain bases and silos in several regions in Kazakhstan which are used for the storage of the grain and to bring it to standard conditions. Farmers, by means of their own capacity, or by contracting local freight forwarders, transport the grain by road to the nearest silos and transaction is completed by transferring the grain to the FCC bases. All transport costs incurred up to the grain base are borne by the farmer. The cost of movement by road varies from season to season and is usually negotiable. According to Ministry of Agriculture records these can vary between

Table 3.1 Routing alternatives for grain export, Kazakhstan–Iran

All rail	via Uzbekistan and Turkmenistan
	via Turkmenistan
Multimodal	Rail–sea–road via Aktau Port
	Rail–sea–road via Olya port
	Rail–sea–road via Astrakhan

US $0.5 and $26 per tonne. Grain is mostly transferred by Kamaz trucks with a capacity of between 20 and 25 tonnes. For the rail leg, grain wagons, covered wagons and gondola wagons are used (Kazdata.kz, 2016).

There are two main, high-volume routes which are currently in use by Kazakh grain exporters. The first route is through Uzbekistan and Turkmenistan to Iran by rail. The second route is via Aktau Port and onward to Bandar Abbas. Two additional routes are used by Kazakh private traders through the Russian ports, and also involve multimodal transport. A further route was recently opened up through Turkmenistan (Dedov and Frulova, 2015; Rustrade.kz, 2016). A summary of the all alternative routes and intermodal combinations is given in Table 3.1.

Grain is usually transported by rail through Uzbekistan and Turkmenistan to the Sarakhs station, which is located at the border between Turkmenistan and Iran. After this point Iranian merchants take over responsibility for the freight and use their own vehicles and warehouses to distribute the grain. On the route via Aktau Port, Iranian buyers load the cargo at the port on Free-on-Board (FOB) terms. Kazakhstan sells the grain mainly to Turkey and the UAE, and uses Iran as a transit country. Two routing options are available: through Russia and via the Black Sea to Turkey, and via the Caspian Sea through Iran to the UAE. In the latter case cargo reaches the port of Amirabad and is then moved to the port of Bandar Abbas in the Persian Gulf.

Kokshetau–Aktau Port –port Amirabad–port Bandar Abbas

This is the optimal route in terms of cost and because no middle country is involved in transit. It is the most competitive in terms of both rates and transit times. For grain exports, this route is viewed as a key alternative to the route through Uzbekistan (Sergeev, 2009), and is in regular use by Kazakh exporters. In Kokshetau, between 40 and 60 grain wagons are loaded in the linear silos per shipment. The capacity of the grain wagons can be 60, 65, 70 and 73 tonnes, and the average cost of loading is approximately

US $3 per tonne. After each wagon is sealed and all customs formalities completed, the certificate of export is issued and the grain transported to Aktau Port. The distance to Aktau Port is 2,260 km and the transit time is typically around 5 to 11 days. The route passes through main stations: Kostanai, Tobol, Altynsarin, Khromtau, Kandyagash, Sagyz, Kulsary, Beineu and Mangyshlak. As the grain is not moved on a Just-In-Time basis, rather as a continuous flow, the transport time between train loading and arrival at the export port is not especially critical. The main operator is JSC 'Kazakhstan Temir Zholy', which offers covered and gondola wagons to the private sector. Many freight forwarders also offer their service, but some private traders move their own cargo. An important point to note here is that in 2007 a new rail link connecting Altynsarin station to Khromtau was constructed. Prior to this date, all rail movements from North Kazakhstan to Aktau Port were operated through Russia. The new railway link reduced the distance to 1,500 km and saved up to 10 days' delivery time. At Mangyshlak station, JSC Kaskor-TransService takes over the wagons and is responsible for the final 15 km transit to Aktau Port. A typical cost for the rail leg is US $34 per tonne.

Aktau Port is the only port in Kazakhstan and it was built in 1963. From 1996 to 1999 it was reconstructed and now serves as a hub for the exports and imports of a wide range of goods to and from Kazakhstan. In 2002, for the specific purpose of the movement of grain, the Ak Bidai Grain Terminal was built with a throughput capacity of 600,000 tonnes per annum (Table 3.2). Currently the grain terminal provides transshipment of between 30,000 and 75,000 tonnes of grain per month depending on the volume of exports to the Caspian countries. This is the main problem, since the limited capacity of the grain terminal is the main bottleneck. The monthly demand from Iran is typically 350,000 tonnes a month and the terminal is often not able to meet this capacity requirement (Black Sea Grain, 2010).

Major transactions are processed on an FOB basis at Aktau Port. Vessels with a capacity of 3,000 to 5,000 tonnes are loaded over a period of three to four days. The grain loading speed at the terminal is 200 to 220 tonnes per hour, with the result that the vessel stays at the port for six days. The cost of the grain loading operation at the terminal is US $7 per tonne.

Table 3.2 Volume of grain shipped through JSC 'Ak Bidai Terminal'

Year	2005	2006	2007	2008	2009	2010	2011	2012
Volume ('000 tonnes)	36.2	125.9	180	260.4	557.5	403.8	307.7	500

SOURCE Alzhanova (2012)

Table 3.3 Kokshetau–Aktau Port–port Amirabad–port Bandar Abbas

Day	Leg	Mode	Transit time (days)	Distance (km)	Cost (USD) per tonne
1	Kokshetau (Loading)		1	0	3
2	Kokshetau–Aktau Port	Rail	8	2,260	34
	Port charges		4.5	0	23
			1.5	0	
15	Aktau Port–Port of Amirabad	Sea	2	785	35
	Port charges		5	0	32
	Port of Amirabad–Port of Bandar Abbas	Road	5	1,878	40
	Iran LSP Handling Charges Other Charges*		0	0	1.5
27	Port Bandar Abbas (Unloading)		1	0	10
28	**Total**		**28**	**4,923**	**178.5**

*Customs charges in Iran vary by up to 50 per cent depending on time of day, day of the week and season

With associated document charges, such as fumigation, certificate registration and port charges, overall port costs per tonne are around US $35 (Table 3.3).

The physical transport on this route is very reliable, and includes rail, sea and road transport to the port of Bandar Abbas. Rail freight represents 45.9 per cent of total journey and 19.75 per cent of total transport cost; the sea leg accounts for 15.9 per cent of the total journey and 18.7 per cent of the total transport cost. The road transport share is 38.14 per cent of the total journey time and a little over 32 per cent of total cost. The total transit time is 28 days. The road leg in Iran is very price competitive. Although Amirabad is the only port on the Caspian Sea which has a rail link with its hinterland, Iranian freight forwarders prefer road haulage, as it is fast, flexible, reliable and in this case also cheap. For example, the Khadem Group charges US $37 per tonne for trucking, plus $1.5 per tonne fees.

Sea freight rates on the Caspian fluctuate depending on the season from US $17 to $35 per tonne. The delivery time for 420 nautical miles is two days at an average speed of 10 knots. Sea freight is the most expensive, probably due to the short distance and the relatively small size of the vessels which, though perhaps around optimum size for the grain trade, are draught limited by shallow port approaches and depth alongside quays. The vessels are mostly under the Iranian flag, and shipments can be made to northern ports of Iran, such as Amirabad, Anzali and Noshahr, depending on need.

Delays are commonplace on this route and include: limited silo capacity; lack of long-term grain storage; inefficient loading-unloading equipment at Aktau Port; insufficient advance preparation of documentation; poor coordination between railway, port and ship; shortage of dry bulk fleet capacity; shortage of regular shipping lines and poor terminal facilities; and inefficient loading-unloading operations at the port of Amirabad (KTZH, 2012). If the delays along this route were to be eliminated, significant savings in shipping time and cost of transfer could be made. It takes 26 days at a cost of US $184 per tonne to move the grain to the port Bandar Abbas. The optimal option takes only 16 days and costs only US $159 for the same distance. A further option is shipment via the Aktau Port Ro-Ro ferry terminal, which gives an additional capacity of 500,000 tonnes per year. Table 3.4 details the movement and handling by container (TEU) via the ferry terminal.

This clearly demonstrates that the rail leg is cost competitive compared to shipping on the Caspian by sea. The rail leg accounts for 74.2 per cent of the total distance to the port of Amirabad, while the sea leg is 25.8 per cent. However, the cost share of the rail is only 32.6 per cent for 2,260 km, whereas the shipping leg represents 35.4 per cent of the total cost for only 875 km.

Currently two types of ferry are operated by the Azerbaijan State Caspian Shipping ferries, with capability to carry 28 or 52 wagons at a

Table 3.4 Cost per TEU container via ferry terminal of Aktau Port

Day	Leg	Mode	Transit time (days)	Distance (km)	Cost (USD)
1	Kokshetau (loading)		1	0	72
2	Kokshetau–Aktau Port	Rail	8	2,260	600
	Port charges		4.5	0	78
			1.5	0	438
16	Aktau Port–Port of Amirabad/Anzali/ Nousheher Other charges*	Sea	2	785	650
27	**Total**		17	3,045	1,838

*Customs charges in Iran vary by up to 50 per cent depending on time of day, day of the week and season

time. The ferry schedule is not published because of the expectations of the Azerbaijani loading teams of their optimum loading speed at the port of Baku, while in Aktau Port the loading rate is guaranteed. Depending on the season at the port, dozens – and sometimes hundreds – of wagons can be queued up prior to being loaded. In this regard, the national carrier of the JSC, Kazmortransflot, purchased four of its own ferry boats, and constructed a new ferry terminal (Sergeev, 2012). Total delivery time fluctuates from 16 to 25 days, and depends on various factors, such as availability of the vessels, port procedures, etc. Handling charges at Aktau Port for wagons are typically around US $16.72 per tonne. An additional $24.50 per tonne is charged for delay risk and security at the port. This option is usually used for transshipment to Azerbaijan, but some traders endeavour to use the ferry terminal to carry consignments to Iran. Sea freight to Azerbaijan is US $1,668 per wagon. However, most Kazakh traders are not aware of the option of using the ferry terminal or, for that matter, another alternative using bagged grain, an option not discussed in this chapter.

Kokshetau–Saryagash–Sarakhs–Bandar Abbas

This route is the oldest and, traditionally, has been used by grain exporters. The route bypasses Uzbekistan and Turkmenistan and is mostly used by private traders from Kazakhstan and Iranian freight forwarders. The transport cost of empty wagons back to Kazakhstan is already included in the tariffs. In 2001, Kazakhstan was transporting 100,000 tonnes of grain every month, around 1.2 million tonnes per year on this route. For several years, however, problems were experienced with Iran retaining grain wagons for between 40 and 60 days (Konyrova, 2012). According to the Farmers Union of Kazakhstan (2010), this route is the most challenging, congested and problematic route. Two serious constraints exist with this corridor: customs restrictions and problems with return of the wagons. Sitting at the border of Iran and Turkmenistan queuing Kazakh grain wagons is the result of customs processes in Turkmenistan. The unloading process of the wagons is very slow in Iran, and the average reverse flow of the returned wagons is about 20–24 empty grain wagons per day; this acts as a serious capacity constraint.

Such measures are also used by Uzbekistan as a competitive tool for the Iranian market to decrease the competitiveness at the Black Sea and Baltic areas (Farmers Union, 2010). All of these barriers, frequently imposed by Turkmenistan and Uzbekistan, seriously affect the grain trade and lower the priority of this route. The decision on granting and removing bans falls with the Central Board of Railway Transport, located in Moscow. The cost from

Kokshetau to Saryagash is around US $29.52 per tonne and delivery time varies from 4 to 11 days depending on the season and other factors. This route passes through major stations including Astana, Karaganda, Sary-Shagan, Shu, Lugovaya and Shymkent, and holding terminals and border crossings are frequent sources of delay.

The distance in Uzbekistan from Saryagash to Farap is 732 km and the cost estimated at around US $34.05 per tonne, with a delivery time of four days. The route follows a path through Tashkent, Kavast, Uluqbek and Buhara. The distance from Uzbekistan to Turkmenistan is 469 km and the cost is around US $21.40. The route proceeds via stations Mary and Altyn Sahra (Table 3.5).

Two chief options are available in this corridor: all-rail route from origin to destination and another with the split from rail to road at the Sarakhs border crossing. In the first option grain travels all the way from Kokshetau to Bandar Abbas by rail. In Iran, at Sarakhs, a break of gauge occurs at a cost

Table 3.5 Kokshetau–Saryagash–Farap–Sarakhs–Bandar Abbas

Day	Leg	Mode	Transit time (days)	Distance (km)	Cost (USD)
1	Kokshetau (loading)		1	0	3
2	Kokshetau–Saryagash	Rail	11	1,964	29.52
13	Saryagash–Farap	Rail	4	732	34.05
	Additional Charges ($8.77 per shipment)		0	0	0.1
	Military Convoy ($80.96 per wagon, compulsory)		0	0	1.34
17	Farap–Sarakhs	Rail	3	469	21.40
	Military Convoy ($ 33.77 per wagon)		0	0	0.56
	Brake of gauge charges ($203 per wagon)		1	0	3.38
20	Sarakhs–Bandar Abbas (by rail)	Rail	9	1,619	54
	(Sarakhs–Bandar Abbas)	**Road**	9	–	37
	Sarakhs charges		0		1.5
	LSP Handling charges		0		1.5
	Unloading charges at Bandar Abbas		1		10
	Other charges				
30	Total		(by rail)	30	4,784	160.35
			(by road)			142.97

penalty of US $203 per wagon before the grain can be delivered to its final destination. Hence, all rail routes are more expensive, and entail problems of wagon delay. In the second option, at the Iranian border, merchants unload the cargo into the nearest warehouse before loading it into trucks. Carriage by road within Iran is the main means of transport. Road haulage is popular, cheaper and faster, but the cost fluctuates from US $37 to $50 per tonne to reflect operating conditions. Usually Iran takes over the grain at Sarakhs and can resell it in the country, as demand for Kazakh grain is high and the selling price inside Iran is around US $290–300 per tonne, reflecting its high value.

There are some Iranian freight forwarders who offer services from Astana and Almaty to Bandar Abbas, and they charge US $250 and $210 per tonne respectively, but their capacity is limited. Delivery time from Astana to Bandar Abbas is 18–20 days and from Almaty 10–12 days. At the holding yards in Sarakhs, grain wagons are unloaded to the warehouses and the wagons are sent back to the holding yards in Kazakhstan. From Sarakhs to Bandar Abbas the carriage rate is US $50 per tonne by truck. Delivery to Sarakhs can take up to 25–30 days, but with tight control by the freight forwarders this can be decreased to 7–10 days. Border waiting procedures are the most time consuming, and can last up to 15 days. Changing between breaks of gauge is itself a quick process, but sometimes such procedures can take two days including administration and ancillary activities.

Uzbekistan, meanwhile, charges on average US $8.77 per shipment, regardless of the size of load and compulsory military security, or $80.96 per wagon. The cost of military security in Turkmenistan is US $33.77 per wagon, but this is not a compulsory charge. At the Turkmen–Iran border a further break of gauge takes place (1,520–1,435 mm) and an additional US $203 must be paid. Further charges include the Sarakhs border charge at US $1.5 per tonne and an LSP handling fee at $1.50 per tonne. At the port of Bandar Abbas, the unloading activities cost $10 per tonne. At peak season it is extremely difficult to acquire sufficient grain wagons for this route, and Kazakh private traders use covered wagons for transport. Two-door covered wagons are provided at an indicative price by Kazakhstan Temir Zholy (KTZH). Both doors are fully secured before grain is loaded. The gross weight of the wagon does not exceed 88 tonnes, with a net cargo capacity of 68 tonnes.

Uzen (Kazakhstan)–Bereket (Turkmenistan)– Gorgan (Iran)

This railway line, opened in 2014, links Kazakhstan to the Persian Gulf and the sea ports of Iran, and increased grain sales to the littoral states.

This route is one of the shortest, most cost-effective and fastest ways of connecting Europe and Central Asian states with the Gulf and Indian Ocean States, being three times shorter than the route via the Suez Canal. It is estimated that the operation of this route has enabled grain exports to Iran to reach 5 million tonnes per annum.

In May 2012, a new international railway entry point at Bolashak (Kazakhstan) and Serhetyaka (Turkmenistan) opened which connects Iran with Kazakhstan via Turkmenistan (Tengrinews, 2012). This was one stage of a major international project including the modernizing of the north–south route, and the construction of the Uzen–Gorgan railway line was one part of the project (MTK RK, 2012). The north–south project was implemented based on an agreement signed between Kazakhstan, Turkmenistan and Iran in 2007. The total distance of the route is 686 km, including 146 km within Kazakhstan, 470 km within Turkmenistan, and 70 km within Iran. Construction costs within Kazakhstan were around US $433 million. The route capacity is 12 million freight tonnes per annum. Initially 3–5 million tonnes of cargo were handled annually, but this figure is expected to increase to 10–12 million tonnes (MTK RK, 2009; Turkmenistan.ru, 2012).

In addition to supplementing existing routes via Aktau Port and through Uzbekistan, this corridor added an additional 3 million tonnes of capacity annually. According to the President of the Grain Union of Kazakhstan, with the completion of the railroad, shipping costs of Kazakh grain to Turkey dropped from US $135 to $41 per tonne and the market shifted from the Black Sea and Baltic Region to Iran, through Iran to Turkey and the Persian Gulf states, with an estimated consumption of 23 million tonnes annually. Although the performance of this route has not yet been analysed, according to Rail Tariff software, estimated transport costs from Kokshetau to Uzen station would be US $36.95 per tonne for a 2,435-km haul. With the remaining 146 km to the Turkmen border being charged at around $37–38, LSPs appraised the cost for the Turkmen haul at about $30–35 per tonne and the Iran leg at around $40 per tonne by road. With additional charges, the carriage to Bandar Abbas costs approximately $153 per tonne (updated from Sergeev, 2012).

Transport via Russia

A significant problem for Kazakhstan in the realization of its export potential is its land-locked continental location and neighbour position with two other major producers, Russia and Ukraine. All three countries are rather unstable producers of grain. Russia, with a yield of up to 30 million tonnes per annum, sometimes becomes a net importer of grain, and purchases large volumes from Kazakhstan. If, however, Russia's grain yield is more than 55 million tonnes, it virtually stops buying grain and becomes a major player in the export market. Thus, if the region has a large harvest, wheat prices significantly reduce, and, given the fact that Russia is a major importer of Kazakh grain, the drop in prices is worsened by decreased demand. In this situation, Kazakhstan producers have a very short period of time to seek new markets, using an aggressive marketing policy, which also has a negative impact on the selling price. Transport via Russia is the most expensive and often the most problematic. There are many sophisticated procedures and additional charges imposed by Russian Railways (RZD) and JSC RusAgroTrans (Shyntimirov, 2010).

For comparison, movement of the Kazakh grain from Bulaevo to the 'Seventh Continent' would cost US $31 per tonne for a distance of 90 km, while transport costs from Smirnovo (North Kazakhstan) to Saryagash (South Kazakhstan) are US $30 per tonne for 2,115 km, ie remarkably cheap. When transporting in Kazakh wagons, RZD insist on contracting LPTrans, which in turn charges an extra $10 per tonne (Shyntimirov, 2010). Research revealed that all the main Russian Caspian Sea ports are busy with the shipment of Russian grain, and shipments via the Astrakhan Grain Terminal and the grain terminal in Olya port for Kazakh grain are currently not possible. The capacity of the Olya grain terminal is limited and Russian grain is prioritized. A second phase of construction will expand the capacity to 1 million tonnes a year, possibly allowing this route to be utilized.

Olya port is located in the delta of the Volga River at the 67th km of Volga–Don–Caspian canal, close to the Caspian Sea. An advantageous geographical location creates conditions for year-round cargo transshipment, and provides access to the river, sea, road and rail lines. In 2012, a new grain terminal opened, with a throughput capacity of 500,000 tonnes per annum with 27,400 tonnes of storage capacity. This has performed well in the first few years of its operation.

The strategic location of Olya port on the Caspian Sea enables it to serve as a link between Europe and Asia, and some Kazakh private traders transport grain in containers from there. Each container is filled with 50 kg bags of grain and the net weight of each TEU is 24 tonnes. In certain circumstances this is a reasonably efficient system, as the bagged grain is 'unitized' early in the supply chain. From Kokshetau to Olya port, transfer is through Russia via Kartaly station. The total distance to Olya port is 2,717 km. The distance from Kokshetau to Kartaly is 649 km at a cost of US $234.1 per TEU. The remaining distance from Kartaly to Olya is 2,068 km at a cost of US $1954 per TEU. From Kartaly, wagons are moved by Russian Railways and leasing costs for containers and railway charges are included. Port charges are estimated at US $800 per tonne and time spent at the port is between 7 and 10 days. Sea freight is $1,700 per container with 2–3 days delivery time.

For this route, freight movement in 20-foot containers from Kokshetau to Bandar Abbas is via Olya port and Anzali port. Rail freight represents 36.5 per cent of the total transport cost and 48.5 per cent of the total journey, while the sea leg constitutes 25.6 per cent of the total cost and 17.8 per cent of the total journey. The road transport share of the total cost is 19.5 per cent, with 23 per cent of the route. Thus the sea leg, using only medium-sized ships is, surprisingly, the most expensive leg, since it is not sufficiently dominant to reap either economies of scale or economies of distance. The cost of rail transport in Russia is higher than for road due to the tariffs imposed by RZD. Only small traders use this route as an alternative because of high costs. The cost per tonne for this corridor is approximately US $276.50. Table 3.6 details approximate costs for each leg. It would appear that delays at border crossing points are mostly procedural, and the excessive waiting time can entail additional costs, deterioration of the grain and cancellation of the contract with Iranian merchants. Thus the route is not attractive for Kazakh grain traders and information for this corridor is therefore scarce.

Table 3.6 Kokshetau–Kartaly–Port Anzali–Port Bandar Abbas (per TEU)

Days	Route	Mode	Distance (km)	Transit time (Days)	Cost (USD)	Cost (%)	Distance (%)
1	Kokshetau–Kartaly	Rail	649	3	234.1	3.5	11.5
4	Kartaly–Olya Port	Rail	2,068	10	1,954	29.4	36.9
	Port charges		0	10	800	12.05	0
24	Olya Port–Port Anzali	Sea	1,000	3	1,700	25.6	17.8
	Port charges		0	5	650	9.8	0
31	Port Anzali–Port Bandar Abbas	Road	1,878	5	1,300	19.5	23.2
Total			5,595	36	6,638.1	100	100

Discussion and conclusion

In summary, Kazakh grain exporters use two main routes for grain shipments to Iran and hence onto world markets. The route via the port of Aktau (Aktau Port), although efficient and competitive in terms of time and cost, is constrained by capacity limitations, in particular the need for additional investment in both port infrastructure and grain terminal facilities. The routes through Uzbekistan and Turkmenistan face a range of problems including delays in the reverse flow of rail wagons, which in turn leads to transit restrictions by the neighbouring countries. The route through Russia is both very long and very time inefficient, and is often used as a route of last resort for a small number of traders.

The route via Aktau Port is the most advantageous and does not use a third country for transit purposes. Shipment through Uzbekistan and Turkmenistan is not reliable, although it is competitive in terms of price. Delay of the reverse flow of the wagons worsens the situation, with consequent shortages of grain wagons in Kazakhstan. Frequent bans imposed by transit countries decrease the attractiveness of this route. The route via Russia is the least competitive in terms of price, transit time and reliability, and only a few traders use it. Transport by road in Kazakhstan is expensive and is used only to carry the grain to the silos. The price by road varies by season according to volume and carrier and is also negotiable.

Although the Iranian rail network has access to ports, the cargo volume does not reflect the current demand. The ports of Bandar Abbas, Amirabad, Bandar Imam Khomeini and Khoramshahr have rail links, but their rail share is not significant. Other ports, including Anzali, Chabahar, Noshahr, Bushehr and Asaluyeh do not have rail connections. According to PMO statistics, out of 140 million tonnes of cargo shipped to and from ports, rail freight's share constitutes only 3.4 million tonnes, ie around 4 per cent (PMO News, 2011). There is a huge reliance placed on road transport, which accounts for over 90 per cent of Iranian freight and passenger traffic.

From this study, it was found that for a landlocked country such as Kazakhstan, the dominant leg for long distances should be rail (UNESCAP, 2003), reliance on this mode being created by lack of access to the sea and the poor condition of the road network. Road haulage, despite its flexibility, only serves as a feeder leg. Due to the volume/value ratio of the grain, transport by air is excluded. The distance of the sea leg on the Caspian is short and may therefore be regarded as short-sea shipping using medium-sized vessels which can barely compete with rail.

Solutions for Grain Exports from Kazakhstan

Of all the alternative routes between the Kokshetau grain region and Iran, routing via Aktau Port is the most cost competitive; it is reliable and achieves good transit times. This route is normally the fastest and no middle country is involved in the transshipment. Routes through Uzbekistan are cheaper, but there are problems with delay, and periodic bans imposed by Uzbekistan and Turkmenistan decrease the attractiveness of this corridor. It must also be noted that in reality, sea freight rates between Aktau Port and Amirabad are also adjusted to account for peak seasons. The freight rate fluctuates from US $18 to $35 and was the highest rate seen in this study. The rail transport to Aktau Port averages eight days, although it may take only five. All the transactions are usually made on FOB terms and accordingly Iranian buyers take over the cargo at Aktau Port and bear all onwards expense. The capacity of the grain terminal is limited to only 50–70,000 tonnes a month with an annual demand of 300,000–350,000 tonnes, which in turn creates the need to look for alternative routes and options. Kazakhstan grain traders suggest that expansion of port infrastructure and investment on building more grain terminals at Aktau Port will solve all the existing logistics and transport problems.

With the expansion of the capacity of the grain terminal at Aktau Port to 300,000 tonnes a month, the supply will be matched to the demand and the need to seek alternative routes will be eliminated. First, the Kazakh traders will solve the problem with grain wagons. Along with the 5,200 grain wagons, covered and gondola wagons are utilized for the shipment of bulk cargo. The need to rent extremely expensive grain wagons from RosAgroTrans will not be necessary and the utilization of three types of wagons from Kazakhstan Temir Zholy will be sufficient. The turnaround time of the wagons from Kokshetau to Aktau Port and vice versa will be only 11–12 days. Second, once the supply matches demand, the need for the alternative routes will be eliminated. Transshipment via Russian ports at the Caspian Sea is very expensive, since Kazakh exporters have to rent additional Russian wagons and containers and pay exploitation fees for Russian Railways. All the complicated procedures and excessive paperwork, along with the extra miles via Russian railways, will not be required.

Third, heavy investment in Aktau Port and expansion of trade agreements with China will increase the export of Kazakh grain. The quality of Kazakh grain is similar to that from Canada, and China can consider the substitution of Kazakh grain for Canadian, US and Australian grains. The lengthiest and most costly routes via Black Sea to Europe, Japan and Korea may not be important, and the US $40 per tonne state subsidy would be returned to the Kazakh treasury. Fourth, once capacity of the grain terminal at Aktau Port is increased, big bags and other alternate options may vanish. Big bags are expensive, and incur excessive port handling charges. With all the wagons being operated in Kazakhstan the existing problems of keeping and delaying the return of the wagons need to be resolved. The construction of the new railway from Uzen to Gorgan partly solved existing problems. With the opening of a new route via Gorgan, the problems of returning grain wagons, breaks of gauge and intermediate involvement of the transit country, Turkmenistan, still exist. However, this route only removed Uzbekistan from the corridor and may be considered as an alternative for transit through Iran to Persian Gulf states for grain and other commodities.

The route via Sarakhs is an alternative route and is used mostly by private traders. Only a few companies have a quota to use the Ak Bidai Terminal and it takes time-consuming paperwork to receive it. It is also a competitive route and half of the export via Iran is attributed to it. The problems with late delivery of the grain wagons and frequent conventional bans lower the attractiveness of this corridor. Most of the traders are not aware of another alternative via the Russian ports of Olya and Volga. But expensive rents of the wagons and containers, and expensive Russian railway tariffs, increase the usage via Sarakhs. The carriage of 1 TEU from Kokshetau to Amirabad will cost approximately US $5,000 per container. Overall charges per tonne/km for the three routes are shown in Table 3.7.

Multimodal transport development in Kazakhstan is in its initial stages and its importance and effectiveness are not fully explored. As Banomyong (2001) argues, multimodal transport corridors generate the economies of scale within transport systems and each mode is orchestrated in an efficient, productive manner. As the geographical pattern of trade expands, the transport system should meet all the requirements to comply with it. Strategies for freight transport should be employed and re-evaluated at government level. With the development of new modal, intermodal and node infrastructures in Kazakhstan, accessibility to international markets will grow to new levels. Smooth and interrelated reliable linkages between modes and infrastructure within transport system will be critical to service quality.

The route choice decision-making process in this case study is limited and for the private traders, routing via Sarakhs is the best option in terms of cost and transit time. One of the other suggestions would be the consideration of a port's capital structure change from fully state owned to half public owned by issuing an extra number of shares. In this case, the state would hold 70 per cent of total equity, while the remaining 30 per cent would be distributed among

Table 3.7 Cost of freight/km by modes of transport (in USD), freight unit per tonne

No	Route	Mode	Distance (km)	Cost/ tonne-km
1	Kokshetau–Aktau Port	Rail	2,260	0.01
	Aktau Port– port Amirabad	Sea	785	0.04
	Port Amirabad–Port Bandar Abbas			
	Total	Road	1,878	0.02
		Multimodal	4,923	0.07
2	Kokshetau–Saryagash	Rail	1,964	0.01
	Saryagash–Farap	Rail	732	0.04
	Farap–Sarakhs	Rail	463	0.04
	Sarakhs–Bandar Abbas	Rail	1,619	0.03
	Sarakhs–Bandar Abbas	Road	1,619	0.02
	Total (all rail)	Rail	4,778	0.12
	Total (intermodal)	Inetrmodal	4,778	0.11
3	Kokshetau–Kartaly	Rail	649	0.01
	Kartaly–Olya port	Rail	2,068	0.03
	Olya Port–port Anzali	Sea	1,000	0.07
	Port Anzali–port Bandar Abbas	Road	1,878	0.02
	Total	**Multimodal**	**5,595**	**0.13**

local and foreign investors. Funds generated by Initial Public Offerings (IPOs) could be invested in further development. Given the increasing demand for grain commodities around the world, the realization of this idea should not fail.

References

Alzhanova, M (2012) Export of the grain will rise, *Almaty: Central Asia Monitor*, [online] http://camonitor.com/archives/4580#facebook (In Russian)

ATF Bank (2010) *The Grain of Kazakhstan: Back to the top. Analytical Research*, Astana

Banomyong, R (2001) Assessing import channels for a land-locked country: The case of Lao PDR, *Asia Pacific Journal of Marketing and Logistics*, **16** (2), pp 62–81

Beresford, A K C (1999) Modelling freight transport costs: A case study of the UK–Greece Corridor, *International Journal of Logistics Research and Applications*, **2** (3), pp 229–46

Black Sea Grain (2010) New Iranian Grain Terminal will allow more Kazakh Imports, *Kiev: Black Sea Grain* [online] http://www.blackseagrain.net/agonews/new-iranian-grain-terminal-will-allow-more-kazakh-imports

Dedov, A N and Froluva, S O (2015) Current conditions and perspectives of the development of railway transport of Kazakhstan under the framework of the single economic area, *Trud Universiteta*, **3** (60), pp 62–65

Farmers Union (2010) About 900 thousand metric tons of wheat in danger, *Astana: The Farmers Union of Kazakhstan* [online] http://sfk.kz/index.php?id=8&kid=91 (In Russian)

IMF (2011) *Republic of Kazakhstan: Selected issues*, International Monetary Fund, Washington DC

Kazakhstan Railways (2016) Tariff Policy [online] http://www.railways.kz/node/7840

Kazdata.kz (2016) Marketing Directory, International Trade: Kazakhstan, Russia, Belarus, Armenia, Kyrgyzstan – EEU and customs union – who benefits – imports and exports of Kazakhstan [online] http://kazdata.kz/04/2016-03-eaes-ts-kazakhstan-tovgovye-otnosheniya.html

Konyrova, K (2012) The issue of the Grain Pool of Kazakhstan, Russia and Ukraine has been postponed, *Almaty: Mir Finansov* [online] http://www.wfin.kz/vopros-sozdaniya-zernovogo-pula-kazakhstana-rossii-i-ukrainy-poka-otlozhen

KTZH (2012) *Development of transport and logistics system of the Republic of Kazakhstan*, Temir Zholy, Astana, Kazakhstan

Mazharova, V (2011) *Transport in Kazakhstan: Current situation, problems and development prospects*, Kazakhstan Institute of Strategic Research under the President of Republic of Kazakhstan, Almaty

MTK RK (2009) *Kazakhstan: Presentations of the transport projects*, Ministry of Transport and Communications of Republic of Kazakhstan, Bishkek

OECD (2010) *Kazakhstan: Sector competitiveness strategy, key findings*, OECD, Competitiveness and Private Sector Development, Paris

PMO News (2011) Rail access to the port to be developed, *PMO News, Supplement to Port & Maritime Magazine*, Tehran, Iran, 12 December 2011, p 2

RFCA Ratings (2010) *The Analysis of the Crop of Kazakhstan*, RFCA Ratings Analytical Service, Almaty

Rustrade.kz (2016) Summary of the trade – economic collaboration between the Russian Federation and the Republic of Kazakhstan [online] http://www.Rustrade.kz

Sakenova, M (2012) The new reality of the world exporter, *Agro Zharshy*, 23 March (In Russian)

Sergeev, F (2009) Kazakhstan opens new routes for transporting grain to the south, bypassing Uzbekistan, *Petropavlovsk: Kazakh-Zerno* [online] http://www.kazakh-zerno.kz/index.php?option=com_content&view=article&id=7634&catid=14&Itemid=108 (In Russian)

Sergeev, F (2012) Will Kazakh grain leave exports from the Black Sea to the southern seas? *Petropavlovsk: Kazakh-Zerno* [online] http://www.kazakh-zerno.kz/index.php?option=com_content&task=view&id=62532 (In Russian)

Shyntimirov, M (2010) RZD have done everything to destroy grain exporters, *Petropavlovsk: Kazakh Zerno* [online] http://www.kazakh-zerno.kz/index.php?option=com_content&task=view&id=17308 (In Russian)

Sultangaliyeva, A (2016) *Kazakhstan and Neighbours: Opportunities and limitations*, The World Economics and Politics Institute, Almaty/Astana

Tengrinews (2012) Kazakhstan–Turkmenistan border will see new railway crossing, *Tengrinews.kz, Almaty* [online] http://en.tengrinews.kz/politics_sub/Kazakhstan-Turkmenistan-border-will-see-new-railway-crossing-10373/

Turaeva, M O (2014) Transport Infrastructure of the Central Asian countries under the conditions of modern regionalisation, *Moscow Economics Institute*

Turkmenistan.ru (2012) International Rail Station to be built on Turkmenistan-Kazakhstan Border, *Turkmenistan.ru* [online] http://www.turkmenistan.ru/en/articles/16303.html

UNESCAP (2003) *Transit Transport Issues in Land-locked and Transit Developing Countries*, ESCAP, Bangkok

The transport of oil and gas

04

HANCE D SMITH, Cardiff University (emeritus), UK
AZMATH JALEEL, Cardiff University, UK

Introduction

The transport of hydrocarbons is central to global transport on both land and sea, due to the primary role of crude oil and natural gas in the world energy budget, and the important place of hydrocarbon products in the supply of both fuels and materials for the petrochemical industry. This chapter begins by recounting the temporal patterns of development of transport of crude oil, natural gas and hydrocarbon products, and the basic elements and factors underlying this development, including the regional dimensions of this global transport system. The second theme focuses on the technology of transport, including tankers, pipelines and terminals. This is followed by consideration of environmental aspects, including geographical patterns of transport, routine operations and random shocks deriving especially from shipwrecks. The section on political economy deals with global patterns of demand and supply of hydrocarbon resources, the implications for shipping and pipelines, and geopolitical influences on the transport system, including war. Finally, there is a discussion of governance and management, including the roles of the industry and of the state system respectively in the development and regulation of transport of oil and gas. The conclusion briefly re-examines present patterns and suggests likely future trends.

Development

The transport of oil and gas had its origins in the development of the oil industry, and oil transport has had a strong maritime focus from the start.

The first truly commercial oil works based on oil shale was established at Bathgate in Scotland in 1851. The first commercial production of crude oil took place in Pennsylvania in 1859, with the first oil cargo shipped in 1861. To begin with, oil was shipped in barrels, soon to be replaced by metal cases – case oil. The first modern oil tanker was the Zoraster, which made her maiden voyage from Baku to Astrakhan in 1878 (LeVine, 2007). The first purpose-built ocean-going tankers entered service in the 1880s: in 1886 there were 12 tankers; by 1891 there were 90 operating in the Atlantic (Stopford, 2009). The oil companies pioneered the use of tankers. As well as the Atlantic trade exporting oil from the United States to Europe, the opening of the Suez Canal to tankers in 1892 permitted the rapid expansion of trade between the Caspian oilfields connected by pipeline from Baku to Batumi in the Black Sea, from where tankers voyaged to South and East Asia. By 1920 the global oil trade had reached 35 mt, and continued to expand to 182 mt by 1950. The main sources of supply during this first long stage of development included the United States, Mexico, Venezuela (Lake Maracaibo, another notable early development of production from the marine environment, entered production in the 1920s (Salas, 2009)), the Caspian Sea, the Middle East, Burma and Indonesia. The Great Depression of the 1930s marked the progressive ending of this phase, and was associated with a glut of oil together with mergers and acquisitions resulting in the emergence of the giant oil companies which dominated the oil industry in the 1950s. Also important were advances in the science and technology not only of oil production, but also of applications in fields such as road, marine and air transport, generation of electricity, and manufacture of petrochemicals.

The first part of the next long stage, from the 1950s until the 1970s, was associated with a huge expansion of the global economy, and a decisive shift from coal to oil and, to a more limited extent, natural gas for energy generation, transport, manufacturing industry and domestic consumption. Whereas the first long stage of development was characterized by refineries located in proximity to the resources, such as at Abadan in the Gulf, and Curaçao in the West Indies, the oil companies now located refineries close to markets. Thus the former predominance of relatively small product tankers was replaced by expansion of a global tanker fleet designed for the carriage of crude oil. Successive generations of tankers were associated with increases in size. The typical tanker size in 1950 was 17,000 dwt; the first VLCC (Very Large Crude Carrier) entered service in 1966, and the first ULCC (Ultra-Large Crude Carrier) in 1976. Economies of scale and sophisticated logistical planning of the tanker transport system were accompanied by restructuring of ownership, so that by the late 1960s the oil companies owned 36 per cent of the tanker fleet, while a further 52 per cent were time chartered by the oil companies on progressively longer time scales; the spot market accounted for the remaining 12 per cent of the fleet (Stopford, 2009).

On land the expansion of crude oil production required the development of long-distance pipelines, especially from Southwest Asia into European markets (Smith, 2014). Also significant was the growth of offshore production, with associated pipeline development and tanker operations, notably in the Gulf of Mexico, North Sea, The Gulf, and the South China Sea. Cumulatively, onshore and offshore production, together with the increasing size of tankers, led to construction of a large number of specialized oil and gas terminals, located either in existing ports or on green field sites. Meanwhile, the enormous expansion in the use of oil and gas was also associated on land with complex networks of pipelines, and road and rail distribution systems carrying both natural gas and oil products in the expanding urban industrial regions of the global economy.

The third and present phase commencing in the 1990s is notable for the continuing dominance of sea transport of crude oil. However, there has also been significant development of sea transport of liquefied natural gas (LNG) in dedicated LNG tankers. This requires large-scale, long-term investment which is difficult to set up. It also requires plentiful resources at prices competitive with other energy sources, and a market supplied with pipeline networks for distribution to both commercial and domestic users. Thus, economic and geopolitical stability is particularly desirable. A second important feature of the current system is the widespread use of a range of liquefied petroleum gas (LPG) tankers. These carry both petroleum gases and chemical gases, produced especially in the North Sea and Middle East regions both through extraction of gas from crude oil and as a refinery by-product. In Japan, LPG is mainly used as fuel, in contrast to Europe where it is used largely as feedstock in the petrochemical industry. A third element is the product tankers used to transport refined oil products. On land there has also been extensive development of pipeline networks, especially those supplying natural gas to the European markets. Meanwhile, there has also been continuing rapid expansion of offshore hydrocarbon resources, not only on the continental shelves, but also in deep water on the continental slopes, most notably in the Gulf of Mexico, offshore West Africa, and offshore Brazil (Smith and Thrupp, 2015). Crude oil and natural gas are transported from offshore by both pipelines (for large fields or groups of fields) and dedicated tankers (for small-scale developments).

Figure 4.1 Major oil and LNG tanker routes

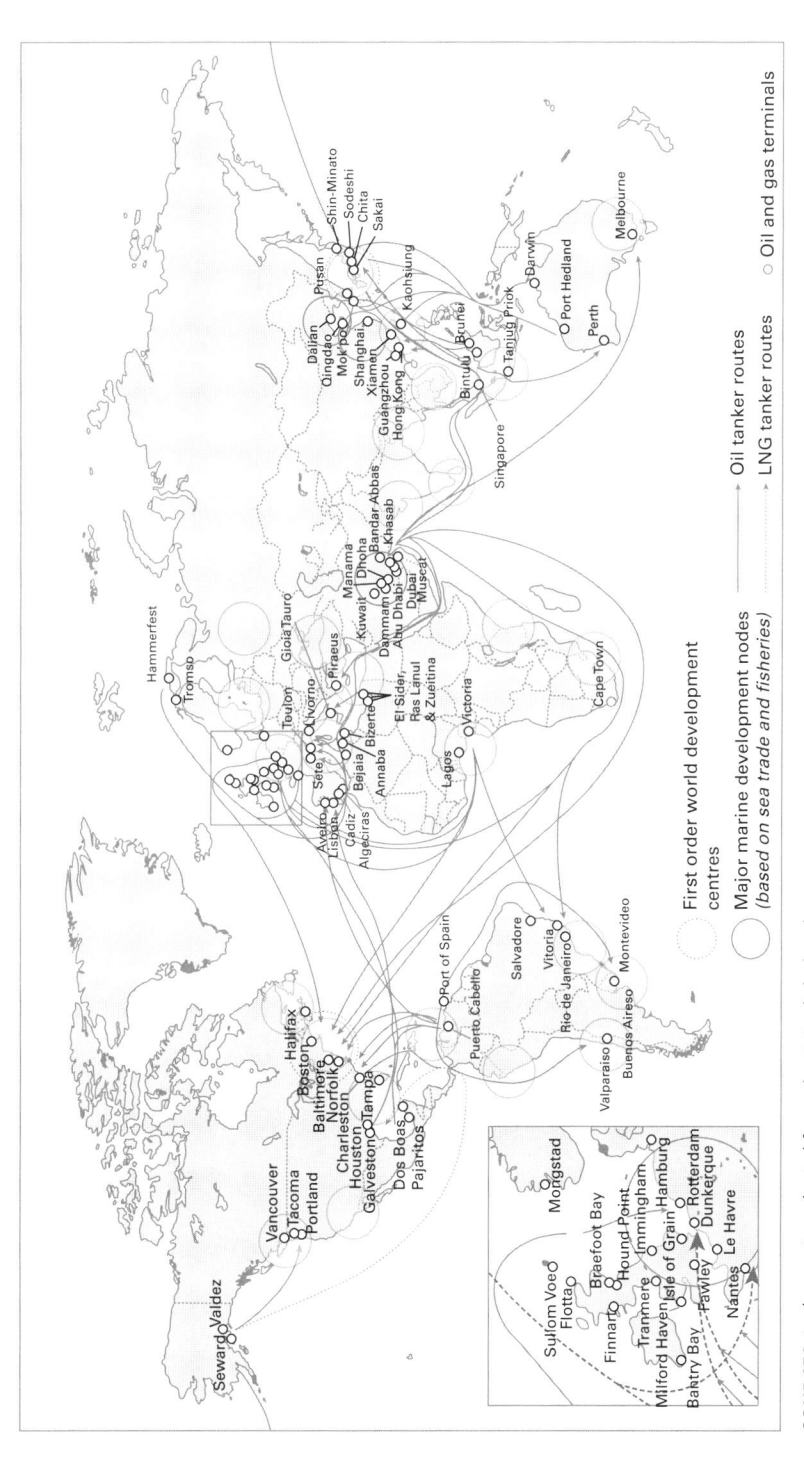

SOURCES tanker routes adapted from: 1) *BP Statistical Review 2016*
2) http://ckrhmt2008.weebly.com/transportation-routes.html; http://www.marine-knowledge.com/oil-tanker-routes/oil-tanker-routes1/
3) https://www.sec.gov/Archives/edgar/data/1627482/000119312515055485/d836806df1a.htm
4) http://www.apslng.com/solutions.html

Figure 4.2 Global oil and gas production, 2015

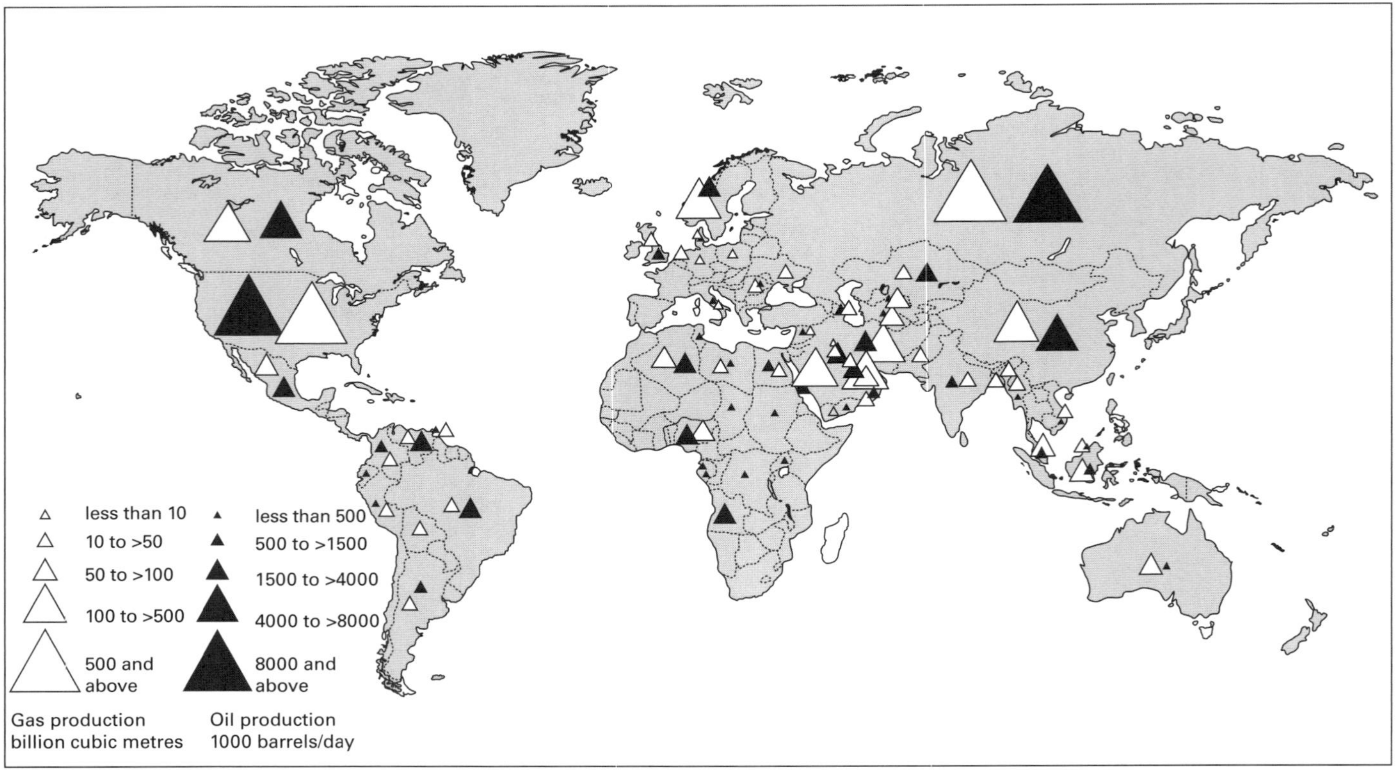

SOURCES *BP Statistical Review 2016*

The development of the oil and gas transport system clearly reflects both the stages of development first fully summarized by Rostow (1960) as well as the cyclical nature of maritime transport evolution on several temporal scales (Stopford, 2009). Although the transport of oil and gas is affected by short-term shipping cycles, the long-term development outlined above is strongly related to Kondratieff long-wave cycles. The transport system continues to be driven by demand for hydrocarbon products in world markets, as the global economy continues to industrialize. The supply of oil and gas resources responds to this market pressure, although it is notable that the distribution of these resources is significantly different from the geographical patterns of the principal urban industrial concentrations of the global economy. These patterns are summarized in Figures 4.1 and 4.2. Understanding the nature and operation of the transport system depends on assessment of the respective roles of technology, environment, political economy, and governance and management. The discussion which follows considers these factors in turn. The interplay between technology and environment on the one hand, and political economy on the other is central to the transport system for oil and gas. Thus technology is the first major theme to be considered.

Technology

The principal sources of demand for tankers and pipelines in the oil and gas industry derive from naturally occurring hydrocarbons. There exists a large group of compounds ranging from crude oil to natural gas, with innumerable combinations of the two. Crude oil containing natural gas requires stabilization through removal of the natural gas before it can be safely transported by tanker or pipeline. Natural gas from gas fields can be transported relatively easily by pipeline, but has to be liquefied for tanker transport. Relatively small quantities of natural gas contained in crude oil can also be liquefied to produce liquefied petroleum gas (LPG) which can be transported by purpose-built tankers, and used to produce olefins (including ethylene, the initial building block for plastics) and aromatics. As well as producing some LPG, refining crude oil produces a wide range of liquid fuels, lubricants, and naphtha which can be transported by sea in product tankers and on land by pipelines and road and rail tankers. The most important natural gases include methane, which can be used directly for domestic gas supply via gas grids. Ethane is used to produce ethylene, manufactured in ethylene cracker plants located at oil or gas terminals; propane and butane are used, for example, in the production of bottled gas.

The design and operation of tankers, as with other types of ship, involves a number of preliminary considerations (Stopford, 2009). These include how the ships will be traded, what types of cargo(es) will be transported, how the cargoes will be stowed, and how the cargoes will be handled. Also important are decisions on how big the tankers should be, what their normal operating speeds should be, and how flexible the ships should be in operation, for example, switching between trades, as in the case of oil-bulk-ore (OBO) ships.

Oil tankers constitute the largest single sector of the merchant ship fleet. By the mid-2000s this comprised over 6,000 vessels, some 37 per cent of the fleet (Clarkson Research Studies, 2006, quoted in Stopford, 2009). The tanker fleet is primarily classified in terms of size in deadweight tonnes by the Average Freight Rate Assessment (AFRA) system, established by Royal Dutch Shell in 1954 and overseen by the London Tanker Brokers Panel (Hamilton, 2014). The purpose of the system is to standardize contract terms, establish shipping costs, and to relate shipping operations to the geography of shipping routes including ports, canals and straits. The smaller general purpose and medium-range ships are used for shorter distances, such as between Europe and North America, commonly carrying refined products. The most common size is the long-range tanker transporting both hydrocarbon products and crude oil (Figure 4.3). These ships can access most large ports involved in the oil trade. As progressively larger ships were added to the fleet in the 1960s and 1970s, the classification was expanded to include especially Very Large Crude Carriers (VLCCs) and Ultra-Large Crude Carriers (ULCCs). Such ships are limited to specially constructed deep water terminals. An example is Bantry Bay in the Republic of Ireland (see Figure 4.1), completed in 1969 and used for transshipping cargoes into smaller consignments for onward shipment to European ports. Of particular importance are the maximum sizes of ships which can transit the Panama (Panamax) and Suez (Suezmax) Canals. The Suez Canal was deepened in 2009, and the Panama Canal's third set of locks was opened in 2016, thereby increasing the size of ship (New Panamax) which can be accommodated. An influential factor in the increase of tanker sizes was the closure of the Suez Canal, first in 1956, and more importantly in 1967, necessitating voyages from the principal oil fields in the Middle East via Cape Agulhas to Europe. The much larger tankers required achieved substantial economies of scale. A significant development in the closing decades of the 20th century was the limited development of the OBO ships, which could carry dry bulk cargoes such as iron ore, as well as crude oil. Since the Exxon Valdez disaster in 1979 (see below), single-hulled tankers

Figure 4.3 *Eagle Kinarut*

Vessel type: Crude Oil Tanker, Size: L x B: 244 m x 42 m, GT: 60,379, DWT: 107,481 t, Year built: 2011, Flag: Singapore
SOURCE https://www.flickr.com/photos/9300748@N08/6167683985/in/photolist-ap1Zz4-aFWKj2

have been phased out, and replaced by double hull tankers. This process was aided first by the US Oil Pollution Act of 1990 (OPA90) and further encouraged by the IMO Regulation 13F which required tankers ordered after 6 July 1993 to have double hulls; with a few local exceptions, all single hull tankers were to be phased out by 2010 (Stopford, 2009).

The development of LNG tankers began in the 1970s and levelled off in the 1980s, before expanding again in the 1990s as the present phase of global economic development got under way. As already noted, the development and transport of natural gas is based on a project approach with time scales in the order of 20 years, due to the enormous investments in ships, terminals and processing which are required. Thus shipping LNG is expensive. In an LNG tanker, the gas boiled off the liquefied cargo is used to power the ship (Figure 4.4).

The development of LPG tankers originated in the 1930s. There are three major components in the world LPG fleet. The smallest, short-haul vessels which constitute the greatest number of ships are mainly pressurized and carry petrochemical products on coastal trades in the major core areas of the global economy (Figure 4.5). The medium-sized tankers are mainly fully refrigerated and engaged in both long-haul trades and short sea trades. The largest class of LPG tankers, which comprise over half the fleet in terms of capacity, are fully refrigerated and ply long-haul trades, such as from the Middle East to Japan.

Figure 4.4 *Arctic Lady*

Vessel Type: LNG Tanker, L x B: 288 m × 49.04 m, GT: 121,597, DWT: 84,878 t, Year Built: 2006, Flag: Norway
SOURCE https://www.flickr.com/photos/68359921@N08/13272553913/in/photolist-meMDrv-2Y1AJC-mdRiSr

Figure 4.5 *Elisabeth*

Vessel Type: LPG Tanker, L x B: 97.24 m × 16.5 m, GT: 3,493, DWT: 3,990 t, Year built: 2009, Flag: Hong Kong
SOURCE https://pixabay.com/en/ship-ships-shipping-tanker-nok-286761

The transport of offshore oil and gas to shore terminals is concentrated in the major regions already noted above, especially the Gulf of Mexico and offshore North West Europe (Figure 4.6). There is a balance between the use of purpose-built tankers on the one hand, and pipelines on the other. Pipelines have high capital costs and relatively modest running costs over the lifetimes of fields, whereas for tankers the reverse is the case. Pipelines have the advantage of maintaining relatively uninterrupted flow of hydrocarbons, while transport by tanker inevitably means successive consignments, which are vulnerable to changing weather conditions: a tanker loading at sea is constrained by strong winds and heavy seas. While pipelines are necessarily limited in location to the shore terminals to which they are connected, tanker operations have a high degree of flexibility, being able to supply terminals in widely dispersed locations. In practice, pipelines are most economical for the development of large fields or groups of fields, while tankers are best suited to individual small fields in dispersed locations as well as for the early development stages of large fields, before pipeline installation. For such situations, a floating Spar may be used to store crude oil (Owen and Rice, 1999).

Land transport of oil and gas depends on pipelines, rail and road transport. The principal focus of this chapter is on crude oil and natural gas transported to refineries and gas processing plants, for which pipelines predominate although, notably in the United States, significant amounts are also transported by railroad. The transport of oil and gas products from processing to market also relies to a substantial extent on pipelines; however, large quantities of fuels in particular, such as petrol and diesel, are transported by road. Some two-thirds of all land pipelines are located in the United States (CIA, 2016), reflecting the primary role of oil and gas for energy generation both for the manufacturing industry, domestic use and for all modes of transport, together with the recent rapid expansion of the fracking industry for the production of natural gas. Of particular note in Europe is the role played by long-distance land pipelines which supply crude oil and natural gas (Figure 4.6) to markets in Western Europe. Such land pipelines often pass through extreme climatic zones such as drylands – some of which are also associated with earthquakes – and cold climates (Sweeney, 2005). Where possible, pipelines are buried on land, but this is not always possible. A good example is the Alaska pipeline, which has to withstand extremes of cold, and is built in large part above the land surface (Figure 4.7). Steel pipelines carrying crude oil or natural gas liquids (NGL) acquire internal deposits of hydrocarbon compounds which require periodic

Figure 4.6 Major European oil and gas pipelines

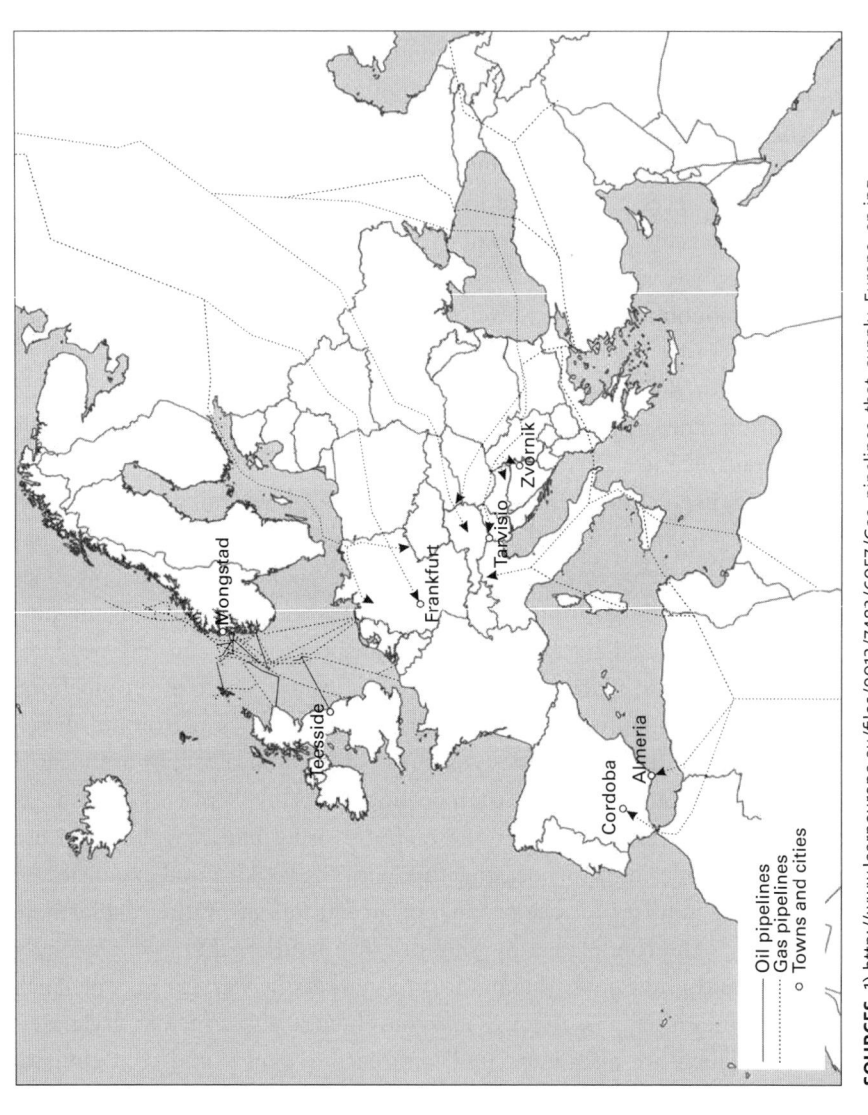

SOURCES 1) http://www.learneurope.eu/files/9013/7483/6057/Gas_pipelines_that_supply_Europe_en.jpg
2) http://marcon.com/index.cfm?SectionListsID=49&PageID=1876

Figure 4.7 Alaska oil pipeline

Source https://pixabay.com/en/winter-alaska-pipeline-oil-snow-681175/

removal using metal pigs which are run through the pipelines. They also require regular inspections to detect any damage by outside agency such as sandstorms and earthquakes, or internal stresses resulting in metal fatigue and possible pipeline failure.

Crude oil and natural gas terminals are of two kinds. First are those handling production. Crude oil terminals may be fitted with processing equipment to stabilize the crude by removal of gas. In limited quantities this gas may be flared off. Large-scale production of natural gas may be associated with the installation of an LPG plant as, for example, at Sullom Voe; or construction of an ethylene cracker plant, as at Braefoot Bay (Figure 4.1). Otherwise natural gas is transported by pipeline or LNG tanker to markets. Large-scale export of LNG requires a gas liquefaction plant at the terminal. Offshore fields are linked by pipeline or tanker transport to coastal terminals. The second type of terminal is constructed for the reception of crude oil by sea from distant sources of production. Many of these terminals are located in dedicated dock areas of large commercial ports, such as Rotterdam and Hamburg. Others have been built on green field sites with deep water access, such as Bantry Bay, already noted above, or Finnart on Loch Long (Figure 4.1).

Environment

The role of the environment includes both the influence of the environment upon oil and gas transport on sea and land respectively, and the environmental impact of transport operations on both sea and land. Transport operations for downstream products are focused on the major urban industrial regions of the developed world (Figure 4.1), in the form of dense networks of coastal tanker routes, and land-based pipelines, rail and road links. These regions are located in the northern hemisphere in a range of environments, including climates ranging from temperate to desert, and in monsoon lands. Much of the land surface is densely settled, and human impacts are of primary concern. These regions are not extensively considered in this chapter. Rather, attention is focused on the long-distance sea and land transport routes for crude oil and natural gas (Figures 4.1 and 4.6). In both marine and land environments, a distinction can be made between routine operations on the one hand, and catastrophic events such as shipwrecks and pipeline fractures on the other.

At sea, the main influences stem from the dynamic nature of the ocean-atmosphere system, and relate to the design and operation of tankers, pipelines and terminals. Tankers have to operate in widely varying weather and sea conditions. Those servicing fields cannot load crude in winds above Force 6 on the Beaufort scale. Pipelines are buried on the seabed and at pipeline landfalls as far as possible to avoid scour by currents on the seabed and damage by anchors and fishing gear. Terminal locations favour sheltered locations and deep water for handling tankers. On land, as already noted, pipelines have to be designed to cope with extremes of climate, ranging from the Arctic conditions of Alaska to the hot deserts of Southwest Asia. Routine operations include inspections for any damage caused by the environment. An additional consideration, especially for marine environments, is the medium-term implications of climate change associated with, for example, increased storm risk (Bowes-Larkin *et al*, in press).

The environmental impacts of routine operations centre round both construction of infrastructure such as terminals and pipelines, and the dangers of pollution inherent in transport operations. Both terminals and pipelines have substantial localized impacts, including modification of geomorphological characteristics of the coast, alterations to hydrology, and ecological impacts on both seabed and land. Pollution arises from small-scale leaks and spills from pipelines, terminal equipment and tankers. Most of these are readily contained. Occasionally more serious incidents arise.

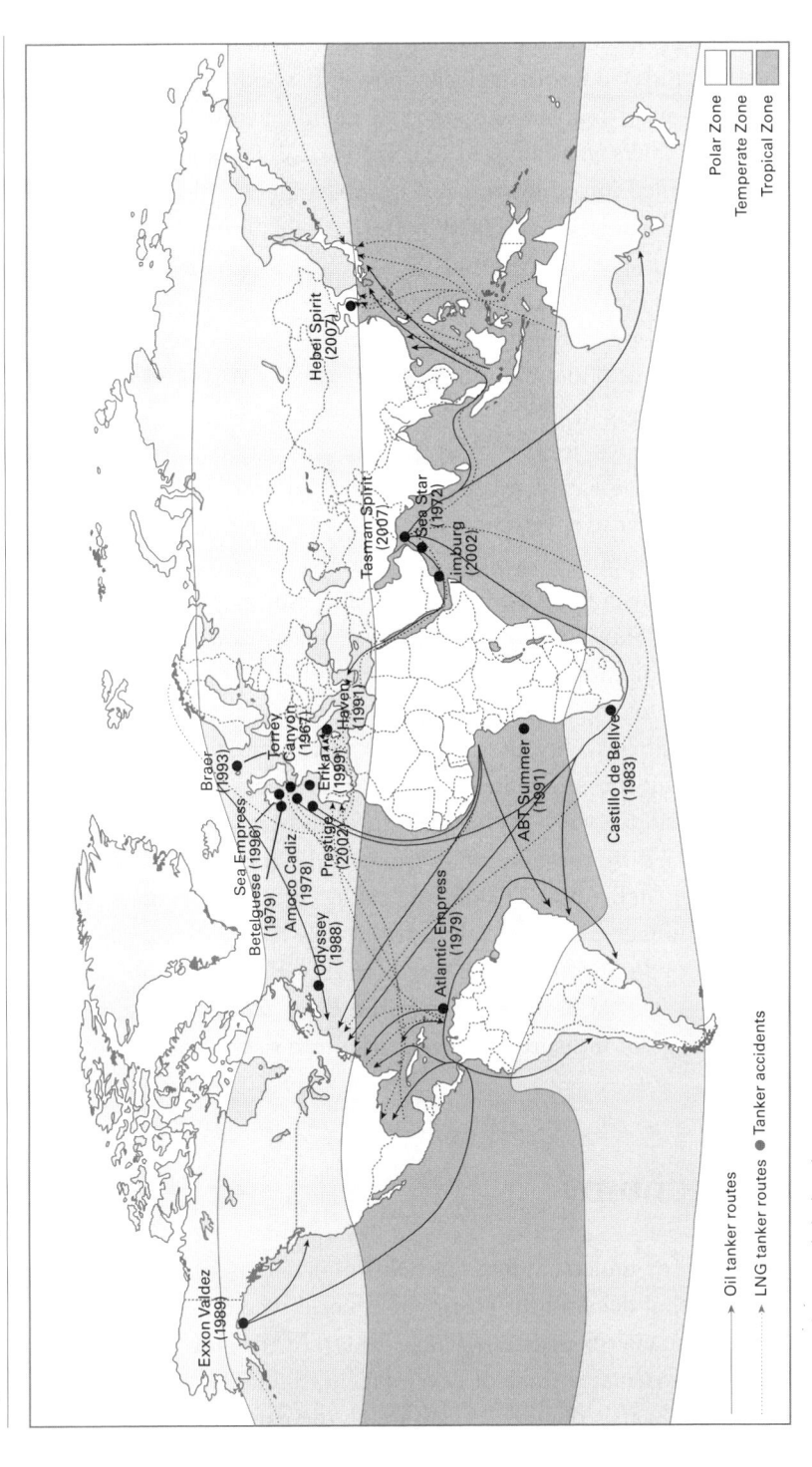

Figure 4.8 Major tanker accidents with tanker routes

SOURCES 1) *BP Statistical Review 2016*
2) http://ckrhmt2008.weebly.com/transportation-routes.html; http://www.marine-knowledge.com/oil-tanker-routes/oil-tanker-routes1/
3) https://www.sec.gov/Archives/edgar/data/1627482/000119312515050485/d836806df1a.htm
4) http://www.apslng.com/solutions.html
5) http://www.telegraph.co.uk/news/worldnews/australiaandthepacific/newzealand/8812598/10-largest-oil-spills-in-history.html
6) http://www.nationalgeographic.com.au/people/oil-tanker-disasters.aspx

One of the best documented was the case of the *Esso Bernicia* at Sullom Voe. The ship was being docked at the terminal when a fire in the engine room of one of the three tugs led to the tug losing power. In windy conditions, the two remaining tugs were unable to stop the ship colliding with the jetty. One of the ship's bunker tanks was damaged, and around 2,000 tonnes of Bunker C heavy fuel oil spilled into the sea, causing substantial short-term pollution and ecological damage, exacerbated by the partial failure of equipment designed to limit the impact of such spills (Ritchie and Kingham, 1991).

While catastrophic incidents involving substantial environmental damage do occur on land as, for example, the pollution of the Gulf as a direct result of the 1991 Gulf War, most interest attaches to the wrecks of tankers (Figure 4.8). Tanker accidents are generally well documented, and some have been associated with extensive follow-up studies of environmental impacts, such as the wrecks of the *Exxon Valdez* and *Braer*. Environmental damage has generally been extensive, resulting in widespread pollution of coastal regions, including substantial ecological repercussions for marine life, including fish, cetaceans and birds. In cold climates especially, such as that in the Prince William Sound incident in Alaska, impacts can last for many years (Wiens, 2013). Situations are complex and difficult to predict. In the case of the *Braer*, for example, the weather conditions included severe gales persisting for some three weeks after the wreck. The Gullfaks crude cargo was separated out by the environmental conditions: light fractions were dispersed by high winds over both adjacent land and sea; heavy fractions sank and were carried by the tide for substantial distances before ending up on the seabed (Ritchie and O'Sullivan, 1994). In all cases, an often-complex range of human factors has played a decisive role, with sometimes substantial long-term implications. The case of the *Exxon Valdez* ultimately led to the passing of OPA90; in the case of the *Braer*, a UK Government inquiry led to a range of measures to deal with future risk (Department of Transport, 1994).

Political economy

The starting point for understanding the political economy of oil and gas transport is the global demand for energy in a world where hydrocarbons remain the dominant energy resource (Odell, 2004). As the global economy embarks upon its next major stage of development, the long-term trend of energy demand is upwards (Figure 4.9), although the pattern of demand is subject to short-term fluctuations, notably in response to the business cycle,

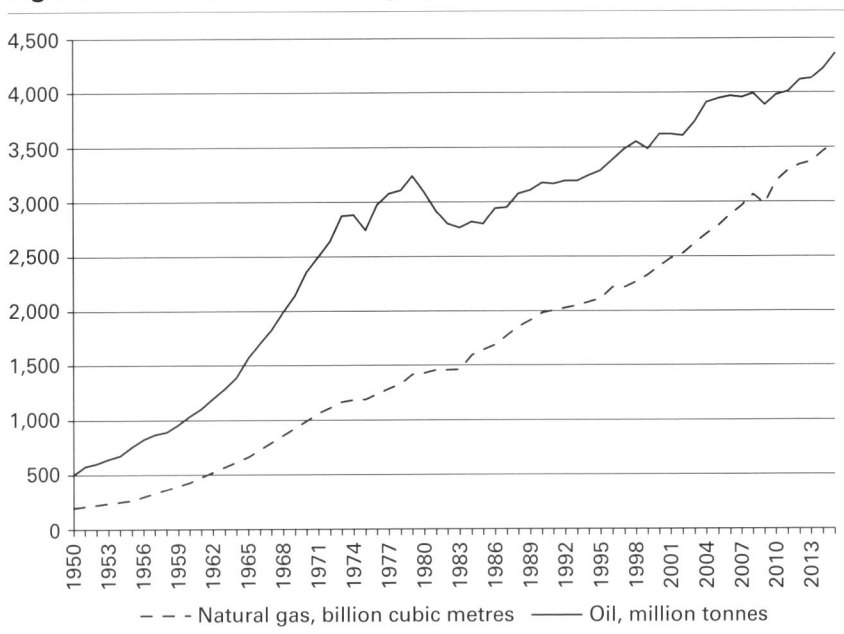

Figure 4.9 Global oil and natural gas production trends 1950–2015

‐ ‐ ‐ Natural gas, billion cubic metres ——— Oil, million tonnes

SOURCES For oil and gas, 1965–2015: *BP Statistical Review of World Energy* (series); For oil, 1950–1964: Worldwatch Institute from US Department of Defense and US Department of Energy data: http://www.earth-policy.org/datacenter/pdf/book_wote_energy_oil.pdf; For gas, 1950–1964: A review of green energy growth prospects: http://peakoil.com/alternative-energy/a-review-of-green-energy-growth-prospects
NOTE 1 billion cubic metres Natural Gas = 0.90 million tonnes oil equivalent

and seasonal variations due to changes in demand, the northern hemisphere winter in particular being associated with spikes in demand. There are also substantial regional variations in demand. Thus, the mature major industrial regions of Western Europe, North America and East Asia (Republic of Korea and Japan) exhibit relatively stable patterns of demand, while the world's major industrializing regions – especially China and India – are associated with the principal increases in demand. In the mid-2010s, the easing of demand in the global economy as a whole was principally due to the slowing of economic development in China.

On the supply side, the world economy is entering a period of fundamental long-term change, partly obscured by short-term developments, including the expansion of fracking to produce natural gas in the United States, the world's primary market for hydrocarbons. The United States is now self-sufficient in natural gas and has begun to export LPG gas. The response of the Middle East producers has been to maintain production levels, leading to a short-term glut in oil and gas markets, with consequent steep falls in prices. Beyond this, hydrocarbons are in long-term competition with other sources of energy, including coal, nuclear energy, hydroelectricity and other renewables including wind, solar, geothermal, biomass and waste. Further, there is a strong trend developing to replace coal and crude oil by natural gas, notably in power generation.

Supply of energy resources is also characterized by strong regional patterns. By 2015, oil's share of global energy consumption was 32.9 per cent (BP, 2016), with major production regions including the Russian Federation and Kazakhstan, Middle East and North Africa, Nigeria, Angola, United States, Mexico, Venezuela and offshore regions including the North Sea, United States, Indonesia, Angola and Brazil. Natural gas production is especially concentrated in the Russian Federation, Middle East, United States and the North Sea. The development of nuclear energy and renewables is concentrated in the developed worlds of North America, Europe and East Asia together with the industrializing economies of China, India and Brazil. The supply of oil and gas products remains largely in the refineries of the market regions.

Overall, pipelines carry approximately two-thirds of the trade in hydrocarbons, including crude oil, natural gas and products. This is a reflection of the vast networks of product pipelines in the world's urban industrial regions, together with long-distance pipelines linking European markets with sources of crude oil and natural gas in the Russian Federation, Kazakhstan and the Middle East (Figure 4.8). However, the Middle East, as the world's leading producer of crude oil, is also linked to major markets by tanker routes (Figure 4.1). This includes European markets served by both the Suez Canal and Cape routes, the latter especially used by VLCCs and ULCCs which are too big to transit the Canal. A notable short-term situation related to the mid-2010s low oil price and hence low price for bunker fuel, is that smaller tankers which normally transit the Suez Canal can voyage more economically around the Cape, thus avoiding Suez Canal charges. The second major tanker route is from the Middle East to East Asia, including Japan, Republic of Korea and China. The majority of tanker routes are served by the long-range tankers already noted (Figure 4.3). In 2014, 1.7 billion tonnes of crude oil accounted for 17 per cent of international seaborne trade, followed by petroleum products at 9 per cent and gas and chemicals at 6 per cent (UNCTAD, 2015).

In the mid-2010s, the rapidly increasing demand for natural gas was leading to the emergence of a fully integrated global market for LNG transport to replace the earlier separate markets focused respectively on the Pacific and Atlantic (Natgas Info, 2016). The LNG trade by sea was initially based on export of gas from Asia and the Middle East to the major industrial and industrializing economies of East and South East Asia. The Atlantic trades began with export of gas from North Africa to Western Europe. In the global market, the principal suppliers to European markets include the pipeline trades from the Russian Federation, North Africa and Norway, and the LNG tanker trade from the Middle East. Gas exports from the United States to Europe are just beginning. In the Pacific region, LNG tankers provide the principal links from the Middle East to South East Asia, China, Japan and the Republic of Korea.

The transport of oil and gas is also influenced in the long term by a number of factors beyond the present economics and geography of the industry. These influences are already in evidence, although the full implications are likely to become more apparent on the decadal time scales of the present long stage of global development, extending to the middle of the 21st century and beyond. In the realm of economic geography is the continued development of the global economy, with changing balances in economic influences among both the major and minor core regions (Figure 4.1). In this regard, considerable recent attention has been generated on the possible implications of major sea route changes. The most immediate of these is the plans for construction of a canal linking Lake Nicaragua with both the Pacific and Atlantic oceans, which would have the potential to greatly increase shipping traffic between these oceans. A second, probably longer-term influence, is the opening up of the Arctic Ocean which would result from the current climate warming trend, and which would dramatically increase the accessibility of European and East Asian core regions to each other at the expense of the Suez Canal and Cape sea routes.

More immediate geopolitical influences being played out in the 2010s demonstrate tensions both among producing regions, and between producing regions on the one hand and market regions on the other. Foremost among these has been and remains the political instability in the Middle East, resulting from time to time in open warfare. The successive closures of the Suez Canal – especially that of 1967 – had, apart from trade disruption, a major influence on the development of the tanker trade through the introduction of very large ships and the utilization of the Cape route. More recently, the Iran-Iraq war of 1979, the Gulf War of 1991, the subsequent Iraq war, the Libyan civil war, the recent diplomatic and economic isolation of Iran ending in 2016 and the ongoing Sunni-centred uprising, the Syrian civil war and the Yemeni civil war have caused varying degrees of destruction to infrastructure and disruption of the oil and gas trades. The mid-2010s battle for market share engendered by the US shale boom has created further global instability in the global oil and gas markets, producing steep falls in prices, despite its potential for decreasing dependence of the global economy on supplies of hydrocarbons from the Middle East and North Africa. Political instability in Nigeria continues to disrupt production and export of crude oil. Finally, Russia periodically threatens interruption of gas supplies to Ukraine and Western Europe, related to the seizure of Crimea and the war in the eastern Ukraine. All these issues create uncertainty in oil and gas markets, and thus to both sea and land transport of crude oil and natural gas.

Governance and management

The oil and gas transport industry operates within a complex system of governance and management. Major elements include respectively the roles of private sector industrial organizations, states, international state organizations, and the framework of international law. The major objectives of governance and management include the setting and maintenance of industry standards; the management of safety and risk; representation of industry interests; state regulation of the industry at both state and international levels; and environmental and social affairs.

Much of this activity is centred within the industry itself and also within the wider shipping industry. The major decision makers within the oil and gas transport industry include oil companies, commodity traders, ship owners and operators, pipeline owners and operators, shippers, charterers and banks, all working within frameworks set by regulatory authorities. The oil companies are concerned with the management of exploration and production of oil and gas natural resources, as well as downstream refining and distribution. As such they are significant participants in the ownership and operation of pipelines and tankers, although on a smaller scale than in the first two stages of development discussed at the beginning of this chapter. A small number of commodity traders also play an important role in the international trade in oil.

The oil tanker component of the industry plays a key role in management, including possession of its own trade association, the International Association of Independent Tanker Owners (INTERTANKO), established in 1970, which represents the independent tanker owners and operators of oil, chemical and gas tankers, that is non-oil companies and non-state controlled tanker owners – approximately half the global tanker fleet. The International Tanker Owners Pollution Federation (ITOPF) is a not-for-profit organization established in 1968 after the wreck of the *Torrey Canyon* to provide round-the-clock impartial advice and assistance in oil spill response, claims analysis and damage assessment, contingency planning, training and information. The International Oil Pollution Compensation Funds (IOPC Funds) were also set up in the wake of the *Torrey Canyon* disaster to provide financial compensation for oil pollution damage that occurs in member states resulting from spills of persistent oil from tankers, since when they have been involved in 149 incidents of varying impact around the world.

The management of risk is handled by organizations in the wider shipping industry. The central roles are played by marine insurance companies, Protection and Indemnity (P&I) Clubs and classification societies. Marine insurance companies provide insurance on measurable risks, such as hull and machinery insurance for ship owners, while P&I Clubs deal with wider, indeterminate risks such as environmental pollution and war risk. The foundations of marine insurance are provided by the classification societies which provide survey and certification services for ships, necessary for the provision of marine insurance (IACS). A specialist service of note is provided by the International Maritime Bureau (IMB), a specialized division of the International Chamber of Commerce. The IMB Piracy Reporting Centre provides the first point of contact for shipmasters to report actual or attempted piracy attacks or suspicious movements, thereby initiating a response process.

The oil and gas transport industry as part of the wider shipping industry is also served by national and international trade associations, such as the UK Chamber of Shipping and BIMCO. These trade associations provide policy expertise and networks to liaise with national and international governmental organizations (BIMCO). Finally, key roles are played by research and advisory organizations such as Drewrys and Clarkson Research Services, and information providers such as Lloyd's List and IHS Fairplay.

The role of individual states is central to the regulation of shipping, including tankers, and pipelines. This centrality is well illustrated by the passing of the US federal Oil Pollution Act of 1990 (OPA90), in the wake of the *Exxon Valdez* disaster which, among other things restricted entry of tankers into Prince William Sound, and hastened the global provision of double-hulled tankers and corresponding phasing out of single hull tankers by the 2010s. Negotiation of international pipeline wayleaves and company organization to build and operate pipelines is a complex process vulnerable to geopolitical influences, not least in the European region (Figure 4.8).

Apart from the construction and operation of international land pipelines, the role of states acting together is best illustrated by the advent of

Port State Control (PSC) in the wake of the *Amoco Cadiz* wreck in 1978. PSC inspections are designed to ensure compliance with international conventions such as SOLAS, MARPOL, STCW and the MLC, covering respectively safety at sea, marine pollution, training and certification of seafarers, and maritime labour. These originated with the 1982 Paris Memorandum covering European states, and now consist of nine regionally based Memorandums of Understanding (MOUs). The United States is not a member of any MOU – the US Coastguard fulfils the same function.

At international level, the primary regulatory agencies are the International Maritime Organization (IMO) and, to a lesser extent, the International Labour Organization (ILO). The ILO was originally established in 1919 and became the first specialized agency of the United Nations in 1946, being concerned with the establishment and maintenance of labour standards. Established in 1948, the IMO is a specialized maritime agency of the United Nations concerned with the safety, security and environmental performance of international shipping (IMO). Both agencies operate through implementation of international conventions. A significant role is also played by the United Nations Conference on Trade and Development (UNCTAD), which is concerned with supporting developing countries to access the benefits of a global economy more fairly and effectively. This includes production of an annual review of maritime transport.

Finally, the oil and gas transport industry is subject to the full range of international conventions, most notably the Law of the Sea Convention, which provides the framework for the governance and management of the world ocean in which the industry operates, including the role of states, the uses of the sea, and dispute resolution procedures. The industry is also increasingly concerned with the Framework Convention on Climate Change, with its implications for air pollution from ships.

Conclusion

The shipping industry can lay claim to be the first truly globalized industry, and this remains especially true for the oil and gas transport industry, both with regard to shipping and land- and sea-based pipelines. As part of the evolving world economy, it also is entering a new 'long wave' stage of development which is likely to extend to the middle of the 21st century. As well as continued industrialization, this will be associated with the continued importance of hydrocarbons as the primary energy resource for the global economy. However, the period will also be important for the large-scale replacement of coal and, to a lesser extent, crude oil by natural gas and renewables, especially in the most advanced industrial regions. Technological development in shipping and terminals is still trending towards increasing automation, even if not reaching as far as the crewless ship. The risks posed, especially to the marine and atmospheric environments from both routine operations and accidents, remain considerable, but are being tackled at legislative and organizational levels, although the results may take decades to emerge. The political economy of oil and gas transport at the economic level is such that tankers and pipelines will remain central for the next several decades, but geopolitical stresses of a developing state-based multi-polar global power structure will also remain very important. Thus the complex industry-state system of governance and management will continue to evolve to meet the challenges involved. For this, ever-closer cooperation among all the decision makers will be required.

References and resources

BIMCO (2016) https://www.bimco.org/About-us-and-our-members [accessed 30 September 2016]

Bowes-Larkin, A, Wrobel, P, Bucknall, R, Smith, T (eds) (forthcoming) Shipping in Changing Climates, *Marine Policy* Special Issue

BP (2016) *BP Statistical Review of World Energy 2016* [online] https://www.bp.com/content/dam/bp/pdf/energy-economics/statistical-review-2016/bp-statistical-review-of-world-energy-2016-full-report.pdf [accessed 30 September 2016]

Central Intelligence Agency (CIA) *World Factbook* [online] www.cia.gov [accessed 28 September 2016]

Clarkson Research Studies (2006) *Tanker Register*, London, Clarksons

Department of Transport (1994) *Safer Ships, Cleaner Seas: Report of Lord Donaldson's inquiry into the prevention of pollution from merchant shipping*, London, Stationery Office Books

Hamilton, T M (2014) Oil tanker sizes range from general purpose to ultra-large crude carriers on AFRA scale, *US Energy Information Administration* [online] http://www.eia.gov/todayinenergy/detail.cfm?id=17991 [accessed 26 September 2016]

ILO (2016) www.ilo.org/global/about-the-ilo/lang-en/index.htm [accessed 30 September 2016]

IMB (2016) http://www.iccwb.org/products-and-services/fighting-commercial-crime/imb-piracy-reporting-centre/ [accessed 30 September 2016]

IMO (2016) http://www.imo.org/en/About/Pages/Default.aspx [accessed 30 September 2016]

International Association of Classification Societies (IACS) (2016) Classification Societies – what, why and how? [online] www.iacs.org.uk [accessed 30 September 2016]

INTERTANKO (2016) http://www.intertanko.com/About-Us/ [accessed 30 September 2016]

IOPC Funds (2016) http://www.iopcfunds.org/about-us/ [accessed 30 September 2016]

ITOPF (2016) http://www.itopf.com/about-us/ [accessed 30 September 2016]

LeVine, S (2007) *The Oil and the Glory: The pursuit of empire and fortune in the Caspian Sea*, New York, Random House

Natgas Info (2016) International Gas Trade [online] http://www.natgas.info/gas-information/what-is-natural-gas/international-gas-trade [accessed 30 September 2016]

Odell, P R (2004) *Why Carbon Fuels Will Dominate the 21st Century's Global Energy Economy*, Brentwood, Multi-science Publishing

Owen, P and Rice, T (1999) *Decommissioning the Brent Spar*, London, E & F Spon

Ritchie, W and Kingham, L (1991) The Esso Bernicia oil spill, Shetland, 1978–79: experiences and lessons, *AAPG Data Pages Inc* [online] www.searchanddiscovery.com/abstracts/html/1991/annual/abstracts/0662c.htm [accessed 28 September 2016]

Ritchie, W and O'Sullivan, M (1994) *The Environmental Impact of the Wreck of the Braer*, Edinburgh, The Scottish Office

Rostow, W (1960) *The Stages of Economic Growth: A non-communist manifesto*, Cambridge, Cambridge University Press

Salas, M T (2009) *The Enduring Legacy: Oil, Culture and Society in Venezuela*, Durham and London, Duke University Press

Smith, H D (2014) Persian Gulf: oil and energy, in Mick Ashworth, Philip Parker (eds) *The Times History of the World in Maps: The rise and fall of empires, countries and cities*, Glasgow, HarperCollins Publishers, pp 200–01

Smith, H D and Thrupp, T (2015) Oil and gas, Chapter 18 in Hance D Smith, Juan Suarez de Vivero, Tundi Agardy (eds) *Routledge Handbook of Ocean Resources and Management*, London and New York, Routledge, pp 269–82

Stopford, M (2009) *Maritime Economics*, third edition, London, Routledge

Sweeney, M (ed) (2005) *Terrain and Geohazard Challenges Facing Onshore Oil and Gas Pipelines: Evaluation, routing, design, construction and operation*, London, Thomas Telford

UNCTAD (2015) *UNCTAD Review of Maritime Transport 2015*, Geneva, United Nations

Wiens, A (ed) (2013) *Oil in the Environment: Legacies and lessons of the Exxon Valdez oil spill*, Cambridge, Cambridge University Press

Global container transport

05

ROLF NEISE, International School of Management, Germany

Introduction

Container shipping celebrated its 60th birthday in 2016. The 26th of April 1956 was one of those days which changed the world, when a refitted World War II oil tanker, the *Ideal-X*, carried 58 shipping containers from Newark to Houston in the United States – the first ever transport of the modern shipping container. Although it was a modest beginning, container shipping has developed into a huge industry which has, due to the sharp reduction of transport costs, made globalized trade cost efficient.

The container is seen as the 'work horse' of international trade (Rodrigue and Slack, 2013). Today around 70 per cent of all globally transported non-bulk cargo is in containerized form (UNCTAD, 2015). The construction of container vessels and the economies of scale introduced by ever-larger ships have offered massive reductions in the cost of transporting goods. Containerization enabled the standardization of port handling equipment which increased the speed of cargo handling. It led to the establishment of global liner networks and enabled intermodal transport between different modes. Cargo security improved at the same time. All of this has massively changed the way that both manufactured and preliminary goods are shipped around the world.

Today consumers are connected with the lowest-cost production locations. The global outsourcing boom is based on containerization as well as multi-location processing. All in all, containerization has been one of the greatest facilitators of change in the world economy in the last few decades. This chapter begins with an examination of the development of container shipping. Current and future global trade perspectives looking forward to

2030 are explained, together with shipping networks and a discussion of the key origins and destinations, main routes and service types. The main actors and their interactions with each other in the Maritime Container Transportation Chain (MCTC) are described. A presentation of the latest technology developments in terms of vessels, handling equipment but also IT tool support completes this comprehensive overview of global container transport.

History of containerization

The early years

The idea of using a 'Box' to keep goods in during a transport instead of loading them separately has a long history. Wooden covering boxes were used in England for combined rail- and horse-drawn transport in the 18th century (Ripley, 1993). In several countries in the 19th and early 20th century, early container forms existed which were used in rail freight transport. In the 1920s, the first kind of standard for rail containers had already been developed by the Railway Clearing House (RCH) in Britain, so that there could be better cross-use between the different railway companies (Hendrickson, 2015). These containers were either 5 or 10 feet long. During World War II, the US Army used small standard-sized containers, which proved to be a good means of quickly and efficiently loading and unloading.

The birth story of the modern container, however, is connected to Malcom P McLean, a trucking entrepreneur from North Carolina, United States (World Shipping Council, 2016). In 1955 he bought a steamship company with the idea of transporting entire truck trailers with their cargo still inside. He realized it would be much simpler and quicker to have one container that could be lifted from a vehicle directly on to a ship without first having to unload its contents. This idea led to a revolution in cargo transportation and subsequently international trade – one container, with the same cargo, can be transported with minimum interruption between ships, trucks and trains.

The adoption of the container into transport chains took years and has required significant investment. Not only have ships, trucks and trains had to be adapted to carry containers, but so too have the terminals to handle them. The container business has also displaced many thousands of dock workers around the world who formerly handled break bulk cargo. In 1965, dock labour could move only 1.7 tonnes per hour onto a cargo ship; five years later they could load 30 tonnes in an hour (*Economist*, 2013). A cost comparison of container transport relative to bulk shipping has shown that the transport costs were reduced considerably, by about 20 times (Rodrigue and Slack, 2013).

The 'Box' and its breakthrough

Containers as rectangular closed boxes with doors fitted at one end and plywood floors are either made of corrugated weathering steel – most common (see Figure 5.1) – or aluminium. The importance of standardizing the sizes of containers was recognized early in the 1960s.

In 1961, the International Organization for Standardization (ISO) set standard sizes. The two most important, and most commonly used sizes even today, are the 20-foot and 40-foot lengths. The 20-foot container, referred to as a Twenty-foot Equivalent Unit (TEU), became the industry standard reference with cargo volume and vessel capacity now measured in TEUs. The 40-foot length container – literally two TEUs – became known as the Forty-foot Equivalent Unit (FEU) and is the most frequently used

Figure 5.1 40-foot containers at Terminal Augsburg

SOURCE Author, available at https://commons.wikimedia.org/w/index.php?curid=1923693

Table 5.1 Container weight and dimensions (according to ISO 668)

Type	Gross (kg)	Tare (kg)*	Net (kg)*	Length (m)	Width (m)	Height (m)	Capacity (m³)
20 ft	30,480	2,200	28,280	6.058	2.438	2.591	33.1
40 ft	30,480	3,800	26,680	12.192	2.438	2.591	67.5
40 ft high cube	30,480	3,900	26,580	12.192	2.438	2.896	75.3

SOURCE Author, based on ISO 668 (2013)
* is not determined by the standards, but by the container's construction (example here: popular steel container)

container today. A further variation of the 40-foot container is the 40-foot High Cube Container which has a greater height (see Table 5.1).

This standardization paved the way for container ships to be used to transport goods between countries. The first international voyage of a container ship took place in April 1966 as Sea-Land's *Fairland* sailed from Port Elizabeth in the United States to Rotterdam in the Netherlands with 236 containers. The breakthrough to persuade the world of the container's potential took place in the late 1960s as the US forces in Vietnam were supplied with containers (World Shipping Council, 2016). 1968 and 1969 were the Baby Boomer years for container shipping; more container ships were built with continuously increasing capacity. The first container ships with a capacity of more than 3,000 TEU were completed in 1972 by the Howaldtwerke Shipyard in Germany. From those days onwards an entire industry emerged. Ships, chassis for transport on trucks and trains and terminals to handle the units were built, based on the standardized container size. Corresponding information technology was also developed to manage the complex logistics processes.

Global container trade

The boom years

From the 1970s onwards, the container shipping industry grew exponentially. Connections between Japan and the US west coast, and Europe and the US east coast were established. The first consortia (a group of carriers sharing space on ships) were founded in the early 1970s on the Europe–Asia route.

By the end of the 1970s, global shipping was largely containerized, with the exception of the Middle East, the Indian sub-Continent, and East and West Africa. But it took only a further four years before they also arrived there.

In 2008, the international seaborne trade by container ships was more than 12 times higher than in 1980 (see Figure 5.2) with an average growth rate of 9 per cent up until 1995, followed by an average growth rate of 10.6 per cent until the end of 2007. During the same period, total seaborne trade grew by an average of 3.9 per cent (UNCTAD, 2014). The global recession in 2008/2009 led to an overall reduction for the industry which was resolved around 2010. Since then an average increase of more than 5 per cent has been observed.

Meanwhile, leading scientists are of the opinion that container and container shipping are largely responsible for the growth of global trade and that the effects of containerization on global trade are much larger than those of free trade agreements (Bernhofen *et al*, 2012). Their estimates suggest that containerization not only stimulated trade in products that could be containerized (eg auto parts) but also had complementary effects on products considered to be less appropriate for containerization (like automobiles) (*Economist*, 2013).

Outlook

The current global economy is characterized by a slowdown in large, emerging developing economies like China and a slow-moving and uneven recovery in the advanced economies (UNCTAD, 2015). In 2015, the world gross domestic product (GDP) increased by 2.4 per cent, compared to 2.5 per cent in 2014. According to the OECD Outlook from June 2016 (OECD, 2016a) the growth in 2016 was projected to be about the same as in 2015, with 2017 only marginally stronger. In a projection to 2030, the World Economic Forum is suggesting an annual global growth rate for the GDP of 2.8 per cent (World Economic Forum, 2016) whereas the OECD is projecting an average of 3.0 per cent per annum until 2060 (OECD, 2012).

Seaborne trade is closely associated with changes in GDP. According to the OECD a 1 per cent increase in real GDP corresponds with a 1.1 per cent growth in seaborne trade (measured in tonnes) (OECD, 2016b). On that basis, seaborne trade is expected to grow annually by around 4.0 per cent to 2030. The OECD expects the long-term growth in container traffic to be at least in line with that for total seaborne trade (OECD, 2016c). The latest estimation for 2016 of Clarksons Research is in line with this assumption projecting a 4.1 per cent increase (Lloyd's List, 2016).

Figure 5.2 International seaborne trade carried by container ships (1980–2014) in million tonnes loaded

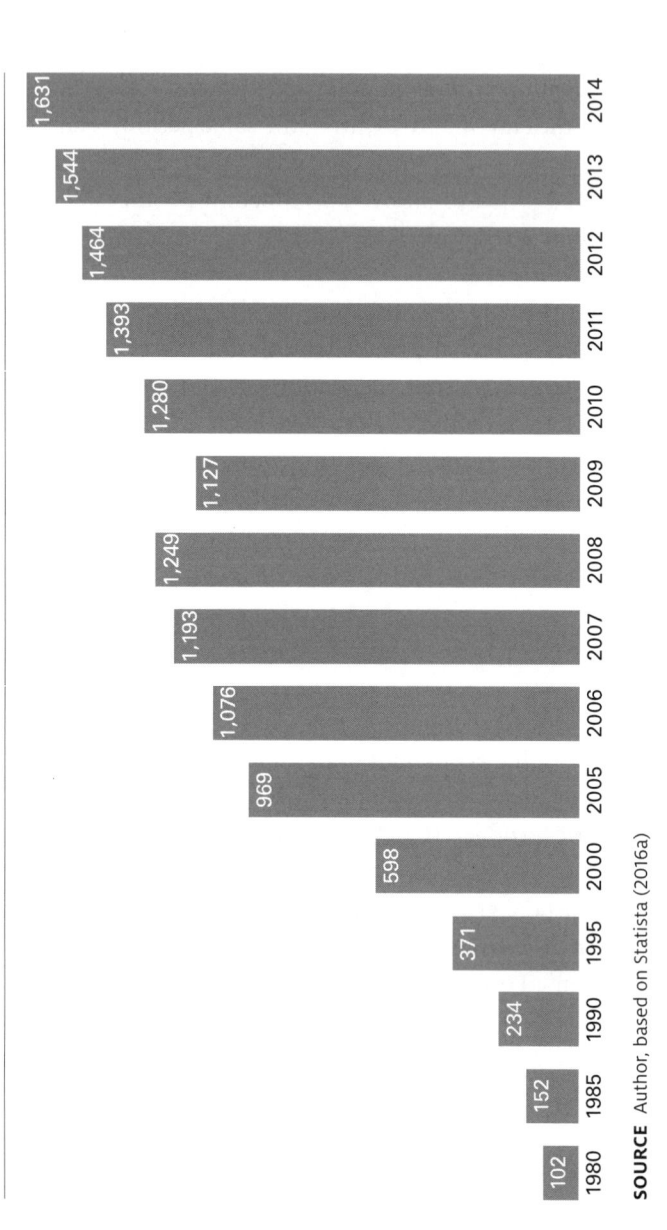

Year	Million tonnes
1980	102
1985	152
1990	234
1995	371
2000	598
2005	969
2006	1,076
2007	1,193
2008	1,249
2009	1,127
2010	1,280
2011	1,393
2012	1,464
2013	1,544
2014	1,631

SOURCE Author, based on Statista (2016a)

Major container trade routes today and in future

Container shipping routes can be divided into three main groups:

(1) East–West trades, which link the major industrial centres of North America, Western Europe and Asia in the northern hemisphere. These routes are by far the biggest globally, dominating container trade (see Table 5.2). The major routes here are Asia–North America and Asia–North Europe.

(2) North–South trades, which link the major production and consumption centres of Europe, Asia and North America with developing countries in the southern hemisphere such as Asia or North America–East Coast South America.

(3) Intraregional trades operating in shorter hauls and with smaller ships. Asia has the biggest interregional container trade.

An illustration of these flows is shown in Figure 5.3.

Table 5.2 Major trade routes (TEU shipped) in 2013

Route	West Bound	East Bound	North Bound	South Bound	Total
Asia–North America	7,739,000	15,386,000			23,125,000
Asia–North Europe	9,187,000	4,519,000			13,706,000
Asia–Mediterranean	4,678,000	2,061,000			6,739,000
Asia–Middle East	3,700,000	1,314,000			5,014,000
North Europe–North America	2,636,000	2,074,000			4,710,000
Australia–Far East			1,072,016	1,851,263	2,923,279
Asia–East Coast South America			621,000	1,510,000	2,131,000
North Europe/Mediterranean–East Coast South America			795,000	885,000	1,680,000
North America–East Coast South America			656,000	650,000	1,306,000

SOURCE Author, based on World Shipping Council (2013)

Figure 5.3 Estimated containerized cargo flows on major container trade routes 2014, by trade route (in million TEU)

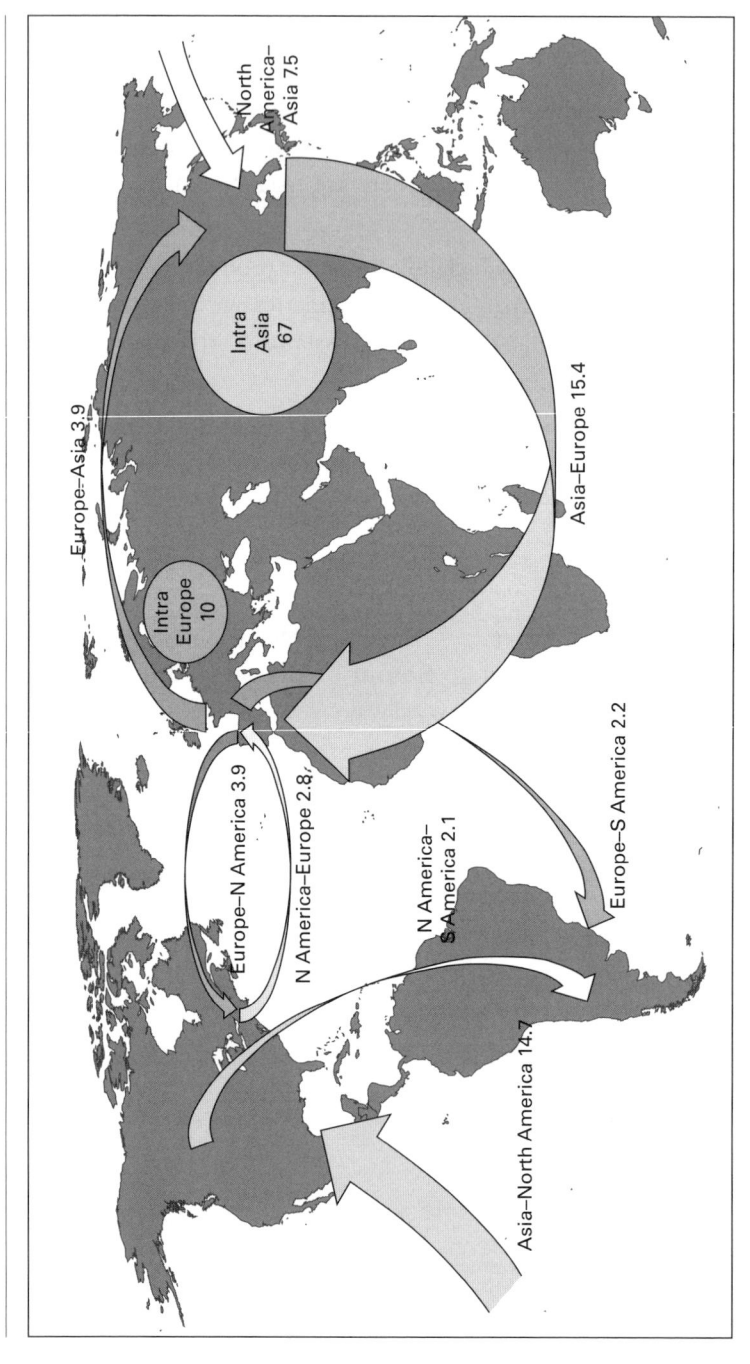

SOURCE Author, based on Statista (2016b)

According to the Global Marine Trend 2030 Report (Lloyd's Register *et al*, 2013), market power will shift towards emerging economies, mainly driven by Asia Pacific. Therefore, the greatest growth in container trade until 2030 will take place between the Far East and the Middle East as well as in the intra-regional trade within Asia-Pacific. The developing Asian economies have benefited from growth fuelled by exports to developed economies, but as they become wealthier they are expected to consume more and consequently trade more with each other.

Therefore, the largest container transshipment destination globally will still be South East Asia in 2030, with China in the leading position. China, as a resource-hungry country, has already established new trade routes with emerging countries in Africa as well as being one of Brazil's biggest trading partners today. Europe, the current second-largest transshipment destination, will face a much slower growth, as will North America. The consulting company PwC predicts that by 2030 new transport corridors will emerge, especially between Asia and Africa, and Asia and South America (PricewaterhouseCoopers, 2010). The areas of Africa, South America and the Indian sub-continent have been traditionally under-served by the container shipping industry. However, they have growing economies and populations. This will lead to a significant increase in demand on transportation infrastructure, particularly modern port facilities and container handling capability, in the future (APM Terminals, 2010).

Maritime Container Transportation Chain (MCTC)

The objective of the MCTC is to organize door-to-door transportation. The overall management of these activities is either done by the shipper/consignee, the shipping line or the sea freight forwarder. The main actors in the MCTC are described accordingly and Figure 5.4. illustrates a simplified MCTC.

The actors

Container equipment owners

The ownership of marine (ISO) containers is mainly shared between shipping lines (56.6 per cent) and container leasing companies (43.4 per cent) (UNCTAD, 2011). Container leasing companies' business is to lease containers to shipping lines. These are globally operating companies; the biggest five

Figure 5.4 The Maritime Container Transportation Chain

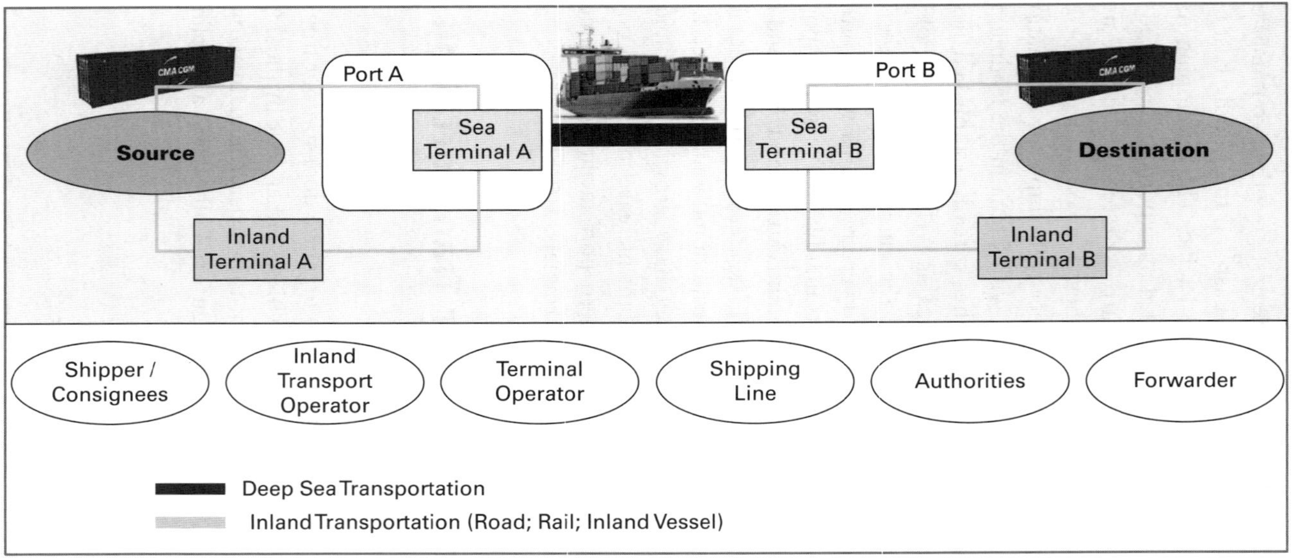

SOURCE Author

control about 60 per cent of the leasable container equipment. They have to provide a certain flexibility in the management of containerized assets in terms of the temporal and geographical dynamics of demand. Differences between leasing contracts mainly relate to the arrangement's duration, responsibilities for repositioning and for maintenance and repair of containers. Crucial conditions are the locations to drop off and to pick up the container. Master leases, long- or dry-term leases and short-term leases exist.

Normally a newly built container is leased by long-term or dry lease (five to eight years). The lessor purchases the containers, but the shipping line performs all the management activities. Master leases are short-to-medium term, where fleet management responsibilities are completely covered by the lessor. Since the economic crisis in 2009, leasing companies have increased their share of containers globally while shipping lines have maintained their absolute container numbers. This was different before the crisis, as ocean carriers had launched common projects with the container manufacturing industry. Beside the vertical integration, this was due to the increase in cost of new containers, the repositioning of empties and, in part, very low freight rates. As a consequence, the container leasing business became less profitable.

Sea freight forwarders

Sea freight forwarders manage the entire MCTC or parts of it on behalf of the shipper (based on the Incoterms DDP or CIF, or for consignees FOB or EXW). This service is also called merchant's haulage. Forwarders are logistic service providers and are often 'capacity brokers' in a rather asset-free business. They manage approximately 35 per cent of the global sea freight market volume (Roland Berger Strategy Consultants, 2013). This model is mainly applicable for shippers/consignees who have outsourced their logistics activities or who do not have full knowledge of sea freight operations. It is also often used for more complex supply chains with less-than-container loads (LCL), where value-added services are required.

Thus, the sea freight forwarders offer all kinds of related services, such as cost calculation, customs clearance and provision of required documents. In the last couple of years there has been an increasing demand to offer additional value-adding services such as Track and Trace, quality controls, etc. Transport, transshipment and other required logistics activities are either purchased by the shipper/consignee, by the forwarders or the forwarder itself contracts in its own name as a carrier. The top 10 sea freight forwarders in 2014 (measured in TEUs) are shown in Figure 5.5.

This market segment is expected to grow further as shippers are more and more focusing on their core business activities, letting third-party

Figure 5.5 Top 10 sea freight forwarders in 2014, based on ocean freight TEUs (000s)

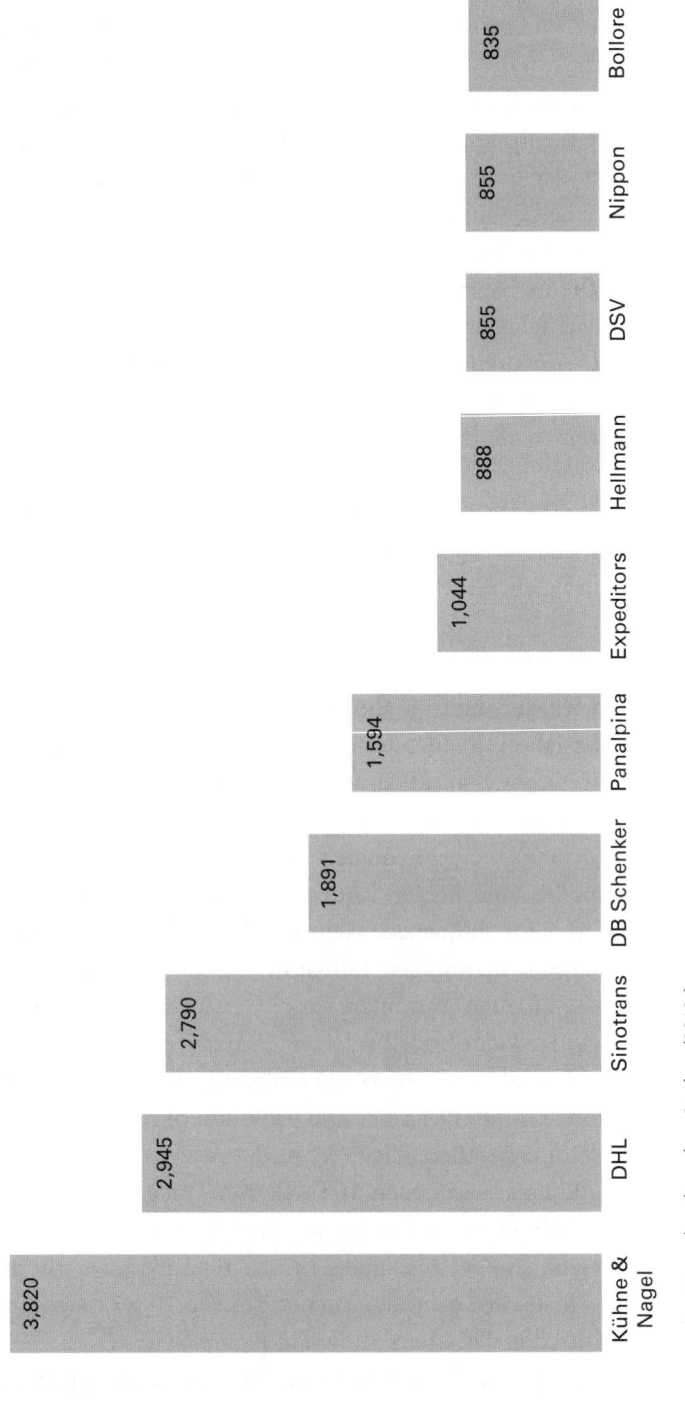

Company	TEUs (000s)
Kühne & Nagel	3,820
DHL	2,945
Sinotrans	2,790
DB Schenker	1,891
Panalpina	1,594
Expeditors	1,044
Hellmann	888
DSV	855
Nippon	855
Bollore	835

SOURCE Author, based on Statista (2016c)

providers manage more of their logistics. In addition, there is a shift away from airfreight towards sea freight, mainly due to cost advantages for shippers. On the other hand, the forwarding business model has relatively low margins (1–4 per cent) (Roland Berger Strategy Consultants, 2013) and is highly sensitive to declines in volume and gross profit.

The sea freight market dynamics, with high/volatile freight rates and increasing cost pressure from shipping lines and shippers combined with sea freight forwarding business characteristics, result in some challenges for forwarders. Nowadays, freight forwarders' operating models need to ensure compatibility with the emerging e-commerce systems, with EDI requirements and with cloud-based supply chain solutions. According to Roland Berger, a more active participation in the sea freight value chain bears potential for revenue diversification for freight forwarders. The use (or the development) of e-commerce platforms is essential. The market leader Kühne & Nagel, for example, has developed an in-house transport management system for its forwarding activities (SALog). In addition to e-commerce activities, sea freight forwarders have to offer multimodal end-to-end solutions to their customers, including all required elements of the MCTC.

Shipping lines

Shipping lines provide maritime transportation services and transport freight between ports via waterways. Shipping lines crossing oceans are also called ocean carriers. In container shipping the shipping lines offer liner services with own and/or chartered vessels. The container shipping lines offer at least pier-to-pier transportation. In recent years, additional services have been offered, such as inland transportation or door-to-door logistics services. This is done in order to become independent of sea freight forwarders and to access customers at the source of freight (Grig, 2012), as well as increase control over the transport chain (Araujo de Souza *et al*, 2003). Due to this vertical or intermodal integration, shipping lines are involved for instance in operating terminals, depots, etc. Some of the largest container shipping lines are also engaged in horizontal cooperation and form strategic alliances. These enable them to reduce operating costs without sacrificing frequency of service, while retaining their independence (Talley, 2009). If, with regard to the organization of the MCTC, the ocean carrier organizes the pre- and on-carriage in addition to the maritime leg, a door-to-door MCTC, it is called *carrier's haulage*.

In recent years, much consolidation in the shipping line industry has occurred, resulting in a concentration of purchasing power with strong bargaining position vis-à-vis terminal and inland transport operations

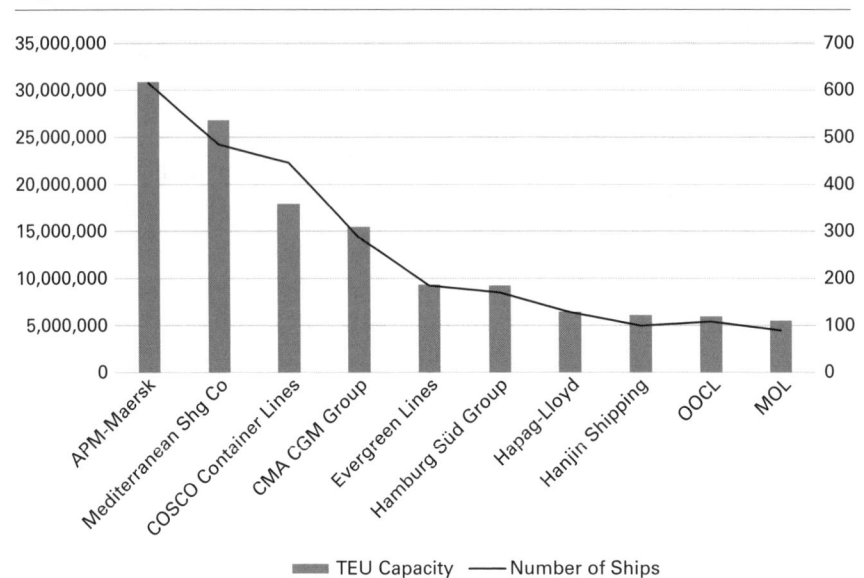

Figure 5.6 Top 10 sea freight carriers in 2016

[Bar and line chart showing TEU Capacity (bars) and Number of Ships (line) for: APM-Maersk, Mediterranean Shg Co, COSCO Container Lines, CMA CGM Group, Evergreen Lines, Hamburg Süd Group, Hapag-Lloyd, Hanjin Shipping, OOCL, MOL. Left axis 0–35,000,000 TEU; right axis 0–700 ships.]

SOURCE Author, based on Alphaliner (2016)

(Araujo de Souza *et al*, 2003). The ocean carrier market can be called oligopolistic as, in 2015, the three big ocean carriers (APM-Maersk, Mediterranean Shipping Company (MSC) and CMA CGM Group) together had almost a 35 per cent share of the world total container-carrying capacity (UNCTAD, 2015). Moreover, the top 10 ocean carriers accounted for nearly 66 per cent of world maritime shipping (Figure 5.6).

Cooperation, mergers and acquisitions

Cooperation and integration have become increasingly important over the last few years. This is mainly due to the strong decline of profitability in the industry in recent years, with huge overcapacities and volatile freight rates. The attempt to realize economies of scale and to decrease unit cost per TEU mile can only be achieved without destructive competition by combining the deployment of bigger vessels with an organizational scale increase (Chinnery, 1999). Horizontal integration in liner shipping comes in three forms (Notteboom, 2004):

1 trade agreements such as liner conferences;
2 strategic alliances; and
3 mergers and acquisitions (M&A).

The past few decades have been mainly influenced by M&A activities. In 1980, the top 20 carriers controlled 26 per cent of the global container fleet compared to 82 per cent in 2015 (UNCTAD, 2015). The main reasons for mergers and acquisitions are size, growth, economies of scale, market share and market power. The concentration in the liner shipping industry has continued with the mergers of CSAV and Hapag Lloyd, and Compañía Chilena de Navegación Interoceánica and Hamburg Süd, both in 2014. Recently a new 'shipping giant' was launched in China by a state-driven merger of the former rivals China Ocean Shipping Group Company (COSCO) and the China Shipping Group (CNSHI) (Reuters, 2016). In addition, the acquisition of Neptune Oriental Lines (NOL) and its APL ocean carrier from Singapore by CMA CGM, a French shipping company, was approved by the European Union (European Commission, 2016). Once completed, this deal would be the largest consolidation in the history of liner shipping – in terms of capacity – overtaking Maersk's acquisition of P&O Nedlloyd in 2005 (Wackett, 2015). Further M&A activities are already on the radar (JOC Consultants, 2015a).

A further approach to reduce costs and to maximize capacity utilization in the industry is the formation of strategic alliances (Table 5.3). Carriers remain operationally independent, but negotiate operating agreements such as vessel sharing agreements or slot chartering agreements. In 2015, 16 of the world's largest container shipping lines had consolidated their routes and services, accounting for 95 per cent of container cargo volumes moving in the dominant east–west trade routes (JOC Consultants, 2015b).

Table 5.3 Container ship industry alliances, as of March 2015

Alliance name	Alliance participating companies	Characteristics
2M	Maersk Line, MSC	A 10-year vessel-sharing agreement on the Asia–Europe and transatlantic routes
Ocean Three	CMA CGM, CSCL, UASC	Key container routes between Asia and Europe, as well as Asia and North America
CKYHE Alliance	COSCO, K Line, Yang Ming, Hanjin, Evergreen	Vessel-sharing agreement. Future dependent on Ocean Alliance
G6	APL, MOL, Hyundai, OOCL, NYK Line, Hapag-Lloyd	The G6 Alliance will cease operation in 2017 as its members enter new agreements

Membership of the alliances will change over a period of time and is also related to M&A activities. The merger of NOL with CMA CGM is, for example, dependent on APL leaving the G6 liner shipping alliance. Currently in discussion are further alliances, such as the Ocean Alliance led by CMA CGM SA and China's COSCO Group (Page, 2016). These alliances are expected to shift the industry towards the use of larger, more efficient and eco-efficient ships, particularly on Asia–Europe routes (UNCTAD, 2015).

Container ports

A port, as a place on a waterway with facilities for loading and unloading ships, is a node in a transport network. Ports which require substantial infrastructure investments can be classified into two categories, according to the ownership and provision of facilities and services: the comprehensive port and the landlord port (Cullinane and Song, 2002). The comprehensive port implies that the public port authority provides and maintains direct responsibility for the management and operation of all port services and facilities without any private activities. In contrast to this model, the port authority in a landlord port is limited to providing and maintaining the basic infrastructure and essential services (eg fire or security services). All other facilities and services are provided by independent private or public companies. Landlord port authorities lease the land to private port operators on the basis of long-term concession agreements.

In terms of container throughput, two-thirds globally is handled in ports in emerging markets. Table 5.4 shows the world's 20 leading container ports in 2014. The top 20 container ports accounted for approximately 45.7 per cent of world container port throughput in 2014 and have shown a 4.5 per cent increase in throughput compared to 2013 (UNCTAD, 2015). The list includes 16 ports from developing economies, all of which are in Asia and mainly in China; the remaining four ports are from developed countries, three of which are located in Europe and one in North America. All the top 10 ports continue to be located in Asia, signifying the importance of the region as a manufacturing hub. The port of Ningbo in China has achieved the highest growth, at 12 per cent.

Table 5.4 Top 20 container ports globally

Rank 2014	Port	Country	2014 Throughput (Million TEU)	2013 Throughput (Million TEU)	TEU Difference in %
1	Shanghai	China	35.29	33.62	4.97
2	Singapore	Singapore	33.87	32.58	3.96
3	Shenzhen	China	24.04	23.28	3.26
4	Hong Kong	China	22.23	22.35	−0.54
5	Ningbo	China	19.45	17.35	12.10
6	Busan	South Korea	18.68	17.69	5.60
7	Guangzhou	China	16.63	15.50	7.29
8	Qingdao	China	16.62	15.52	7.09
9	Dubai	UAE	15.25	13.64	11.80
10	Los Angeles	USA	15.16	14.60	3.84
11	Tianjin	China	14.05	13.01	7.99
12	Rotterdam	Netherlands	12.30	11.62	5.85
13	Port Klang	Malaysia	10.95	10.35	5.80
14	Kaohsiung	Taiwan	10.56	9.94	6.24
15	Dalian	China	10.13	10.02	1.10
16	Hamburg	Germany	9.78	9.30	5.16
17	Antwerp	Belgium	8.98	8.58	4.66
18	Xiamen	China	8.57	8.01	6.99
19	Tanjung Pelepas	Malaysia	8.52	7.63	11.66
20	Laem Chabang	Thailand	6.58	6.04	8.94
Total			**317.64**	**300.63**	**5.66**

SOURCE Author, based on Alphaliner (2015)

Sea terminal operators

The main actors in a port beside the Port Authorities are sea and inland terminal operators. The sea terminal operator is responsible for the organization and physical handling of loading and unloading ships. Depending on the port's size and functions, one or several terminals can be sited in a port. Operators are either the port authority, specialized terminal operators, or a shipping line (or an alliance of several shipping lines). This industry has expanded substantially in recent years, with global annual growth rates of up to 8 per cent. Drewry predicts an average global container port demand growth of 4.5 per cent per annum through to 2019 (Drewry, 2015a). This equates to an additional 168 million TEU of port traffic, bringing the global total to nearly 850 million TEU. Asia accounts for over 60 per cent of the forecast global demand growth.

In recent years, two concepts have been established in the market: transnational terminal operating companies that offer their services to multi-users, and shipping line-affiliated terminal operators with carrier-dedicated terminals (Grig, 2012). Vertical integration has been pursued in recent years by terminal operators to increase their influence along the MCTC. They offer further services around container handling (eg stuffing/stripping, repair, etc.) and are becoming more involved in hinterland transportation and inland terminals. If a sea terminal operator is acting in multiple locations and can handle more than 1 million TEUs a year it is called a Global Terminal Operator (GTO). In 2014, 23 companies were categorized by Drewry as GTOs (Drewry, 2015b). In general, GTOs are best placed to meet the high capital requirements to cover initial investments in a terminal of a reasonable scale.

The total world throughput in container handling reached 677.9 m TEU in 2014, a rise of 5.5 per cent compared to 2013. By equity TEU measure (throughput of each terminal is pro rata based on stake held) the top five players accounted for around 30 per cent of global throughput in 2014 (Table 5.5.). By total throughput in TEUs it was around 60 per cent compared to 32 per cent in 2001, which reflects strong consolidation over the years. GTOs have established a truly global presence, nowadays controlling large multinational portfolios of terminal assets. An average utilization band of 75–85 per cent was reached by the GTOs across their portfolios in 2014 (Drewry, 2015b).

Owning and operating container terminals on an international basis remains a very profitable business. Drewry estimates the EBITDA margins for GTOs to be in a range of 20–45 per cent (Drewry, 2015b). However, the industry is facing significant challenges ahead.

Table 5.5 Top 5 global terminal operators' equity based throughput 2014

Company	Country/ owner	2014 TEU	Global market share	Prediction 2019
PSA International	Singapore	55.1 m TEU	8.1%	+24 m TEU
Hutchison Port Holdings	Hong Kong, China	45.9 m TEU	6.7%	+14 m TEU
APM Terminals	Maersk	37.0 m TEU	5.4%	+15 m TEU
DP World	Dubai	35.8 m TEU	5.3%	+15 m TEU
China Merchants Holding	China	25.8 m TEU	3.8%	+4 m TEU

SOURCE Author, based on Drewry (2015b)

The emergence of international terminal networks

In response to the concentration trend that has taken place in container shipping, a number of terminal operators have opted for scale increases – specifically since the increase in privatization of port activities during the 2000s. Most of the time these activities ended up in mergers or acquisitions (Notteboom and Winkelmans, 2002), mainly between the years 2001 and 2008. Forms of operational cooperation in the market are only rarely happening. Overall, the expansion strategy is a mix of organic growth (new terminals) and acquisitions. The primary expansion focus of all GTOs is therefore green field developments in emerging market locations. Three types of GTOs with different expansion strategies exist.

Stevedores are terminal operators that expand through direct investment, often in line with their home port development. By expanding into new markets, they replicate their expertise in terminal operations and diversify their revenue geographically. The Port of Singapore Authority (PSA) is the largest GTO developed from a stevedore background. In parallel to the rapid expansion of its container operations in Singapore, PSA also embarked on a series of corporate developments. In 2002 they bought majority stakes in the Belgium operator Hesse-Noord Natie. Today they operate in 16 countries on three continents with a focus on Asia. PSA continues to expand its presence globally. The second-biggest GTO, Hutchison Port Holdings (HPH), also has a stevedore background. The main focus of operations for HPH is China, and their global presence comprises 25 countries on five continents. Both companies are connected, as PSA has held a 20 per cent stake in HPH's global terminal portfolio since 2006.

Maritime shipping companies invested in port terminal facilities to help support their core maritime shipping business. The terminal facilities can be operated on a single-user dedicated base or can alternatively be open to third shipping lines. APM Terminals, a sister company of Maersk Line, is the largest GTO developed from a maritime shipping background. Its network has a presence in 38 countries on five continents. Other shipping lines, such as MSC and CMA CGM, are also very active in this field, and will continue their activities.

Some **financial holdings** (eg investment banks, retirement funds etc) are attracted by the port terminal sector as an asset class with revenue generation potential. They normally follow an indirect management approach and leave the existing operator to take care of the operations, or they will manage the terminal assets directly through a parent company. Dubai Ports World (DPW), a branch of the Dubai World sovereign wealth fund, is the largest GTO developed from a financial background. DPW, in the GTOs top five since 2006, is a 'front-runner' in acquiring other companies, such as GSX World Terminals (2005) and P&O Ports (2006). Today, DPW is the most geographically diverse GTO, with a network in 40 countries spanning six continents.

Currently, discussion surrounds whether the consolidation process that has rapidly taken place in recent years may have reached it limits. Few large companies or terminal assets remain to be acquired, and in addition, GTOs already have a presence in most of the globally important ports. They also try to keep a competitive edge by building barriers to prevent competitors entering their domains. With that in mind, it can be expected that the top four players (PSA, APM Terminals, HPH and DP World) will maintain their lead over the other operators for a number of years to come. However, there are several aggressive and fast-growing companies on the market with ambitious plans, such as Ports America, Yilport and Gulftainer. Further consolidation may also be restricted by institutional factors, particularly the policies of national competition authorities who closely monitor the risks of having dominant actors in local/regional container markets. This can already be observed in the EU, where competition regulations have affected Hutchison's expansion plans within North Europe.

Sea terminal operators are well aware of the fact that the transport chain is viewed as a totally integrated system. The leading terminal operating companies have therefore developed diverging strategies towards the control of larger parts of the supply chain or the offer of value-adding services. The recent focus of Hutchison on inland logistics in China is an example (Hutchison Port Holdings Limited, 2015). Another example is Germany, where the German terminal operators are often directly involved in intermodal rail transport, eg Eurogate with its Hannibal Railway express to connect the ports in the north of Germany with the south and Italy (Eurokai, 2015). Some terminal operators have set up road haulage companies or operate their own feeder services. Finally, many terminal operators have integrated inland terminals in their logistics networks.

Outlook

The industry is confronted with larger and fewer shipping lines demanding better service at a lower cost, as well as increasing demand and the deployment of ultra-large container ships. This is leading to significant investments in additional capacity but also in innovative technologies, where terminal automation is gathering pace, and a highly specialized workforce.

Inland terminal operator

Inland terminal operators provide transshipment between road and rail and/or barge in the hinterland of the port. Beyond transshipment they usually offer other services (eg storage, container maintenance and repair, customs services, and road haulage to their customers). Operators are mainly specialized inland terminal operators, rail operators, shipping lines and alliances (Grig, 2012), or sometimes sea terminal operators and port authorities.

Multimodal transport in ports

As the shipping industry is already dominated by large vessels, mergers/acquisitions and strategic alliances, further cost savings have to be elaborated. A big portion of cost is related to inland transport; depending on the specific route, inland costs in the total costs of container shipping would range from 40 per cent to 80 per cent (Notteboom, 2004). These increasingly complex distribution requirements from customers create significant opportunities for shipping lines. It is not only about the transportation of goods from one point to another; the customers are seeking integrated supply chain solutions with door-to-door movements.

However, the carriers are confronted with new business solutions in addition to some challenges to further improve inland logistics. Landside operations are management intensive and generally require a high proportion of buy-in services. Inland movements also generate work-intense activities such as the repositioning of empty units, network control and tracking. Other challenges relate to volume and equipment-type imbalances, unforeseen delays in ports and the inland transport leg, as well as the uncertainty of forecasts. Carriers are using IT solutions to face the challenges of inland logistics and to manage global container flows, taking into account the effects of global trade imbalances. They also use chassis pools and master leases to lessen equipment surpluses/deficits and interchange equipment among liner conference members or members of the same strategic alliance. The formation of strategic alliances has had further positive effects on inland logistics, as members are sharing inland logistics information, techniques and resources as well as negotiating collectively with suppliers (eg terminals, rail operators, feeders, barge operators, etc).

Meanwhile, most of the ocean carriers are offering end-to-end solutions to their customers either via their own sister companies or via ad hoc coordination with independent logistics service providers. Maersk Sealand, one of the first carriers investing in these solutions, can still be seen as the only 'fully integrated' carrier in the MCTC offering integrated logistic packages (Damco) and also managing the container terminal operations (APM Terminals).

The equipment

Containerships

Since the beginning of containerization in the mid-1950s, container ships have undergone several changes, mainly in terms of size driven by economies of scale. The larger the number of containers being carried, the lower the costs per TEU. Drewry calculated for the trans-Pacific route potential cost differences of around 50 per cent between a Panamax unit of 4,000 TEU and a mega post-Panamax unit of 10,000 TEUs (Drewry Shipping Consultants, 2001). Other authors came to similar conclusions (Cullinane *et al*, 1999). But the bigger the ships become the more challenging it is for the corresponding port infrastructure and handling equipment. Substantial capital investment is required to accommodate larger containerships. Today we are confronted with a shrinking number of harbours able to handle the huge vessels. The different containership generations can be classified into five classes (Rodrigue and Slack, 2013) (see also Figure 5.7):

A Early containerships. These ships were based on modified bulk vessels or tankers that could transport up to 1,000 TEUs. They carried onboard cranes since most port terminals were not equipped to handle containers. At the beginning of the 1970s, the first fully cellular container ships (FCC; second generation) were constructed. These ships were composed of cells lodging containers in stacks of different height. The whole ship was used to stack containers, including below deck. Cranes were removed from the

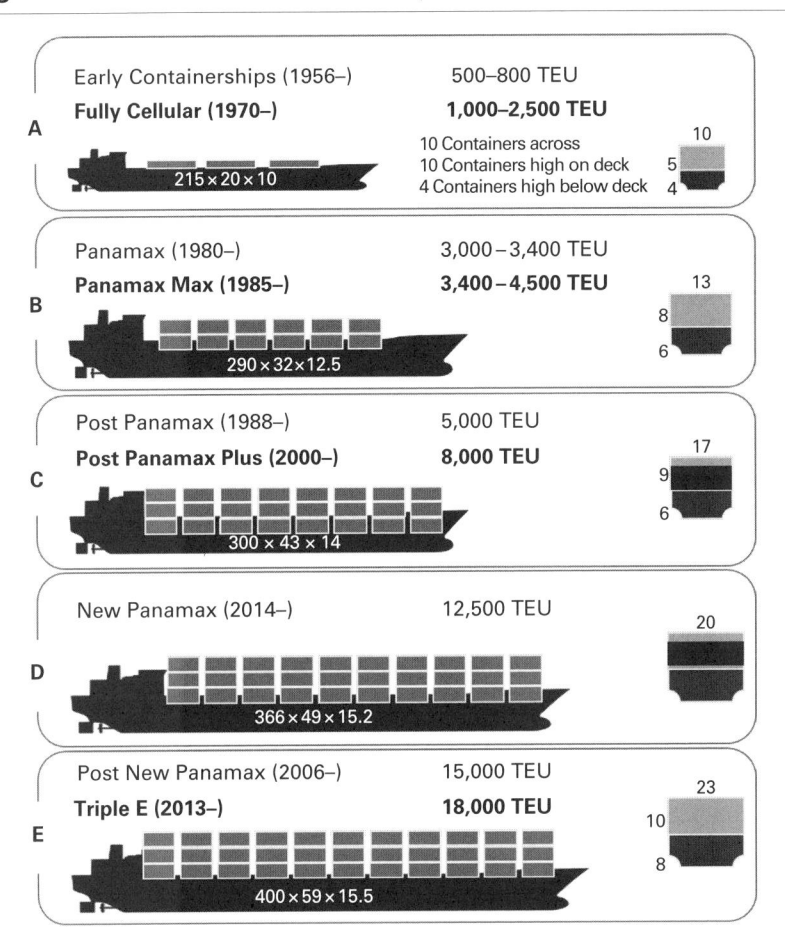

Figure 5.7 The evolution of containerships

A Early Containerships (1956–) — 500–800 TEU
Fully Cellular (1970–) — 1,000–2,500 TEU
215 × 20 × 10
10 Containers across
10 Containers high on deck
4 Containers high below deck
10 / 5 / 4

B Panamax (1980–) — 3,000–3,400 TEU
Panamax Max (1985–) — 3,400–4,500 TEU
290 × 32 × 12.5
13 / 8 / 6

C Post Panamax (1988–) — 5,000 TEU
Post Panamax Plus (2000–) — 8,000 TEU
300 × 43 × 14
17 / 9 / 6

D New Panamax (2014–) — 12,500 TEU
366 × 49 × 15.2
20

E Post New Panamax (2006–) — 15,000 TEU
Triple E (2013–) — 18,000 TEU
400 × 59 × 15.5
23 / 10 / 8

SOURCE Author, based on Ashar and Rodrigue (2012) (all dimensions are in metres)

ships, which led to the first specialized container terminals. They were also faster, with speeds of 20–24 knots, which would become the speed of reference in containerized shipping.

B Panamax. The size limit of the Panama Canal has defined this standard with a capacity of about 4,000 TEUs.

C Post-Panamax I and II. This containership class was the first one to exceed the 32.2 m width limit of the Panama Canal (Post-Panamax I). But the growth of size continues with the ongoing increase of container demand. Once the Panamax threshold was breached, ship size quickly increased, with capacities reaching 8,000 TEUs in the late 1990s (Post-Panamax II). These ships require deep-water ports with at least 13 m of draught and highly efficient container handling terminals.

D New-Panamax, or Neo-Panamax (NPX). These ships are designed to fit exactly in the locks of the expanded Panama Canal, which opened in June 2016, with a capacity of about 12,500 TEU.

E Post-Panamax III and Triple E. In 2006, a further generation of container ships was introduced by Maersk, with a capacity in the range of 11,000 to 14,500 TEUs; eg the *Emma Maersk*. A further extension led to the introduction of 'Triple E' class ships, also called Ultra-Large Container Vessels (ULCV) of about 18,000 TEUs in 2013, mainly used for routes between Asia and Europe.

Outlook

Beside the tremendous investments into port infrastructure and handling equipment, even for bigger containerships, there are further bottlenecks that exist in the size and the draught of the Panama Canal, the Suez Canal and the Strait of Malacca. Furthermore, limits to economies of scale exist, as the amount of cargo has to be commercially sustainable, specifically as the shipper demands frequent services with weekly schedules. In addition, a high utilization of the available slot capacity on bigger vessels is desired by the carrier to reach the full benefits of economies of scale. Currently under discussion is the 'Malacca Max' class that could carry about 27,000–30,000 TEU, but they are not expected to be constructed within the next decade.

Containership speeds have peaked at an average of 20–25 knots and it is unlikely that speeds will increase due to energy consumption; nowadays many shipping lines are opting for slow steaming to cope with higher bunker fuel prices and overcapacity.

Empty container logistics

The necessity for empty container logistics is inherent in the container transport system. Customers who want to export their goods by containerized transportation need the provision of an empty container at their site. Customers who import containerized cargo for their commercial activities receive a loaded container, which becomes empty after unloading (Olivo *et al*, 2005). Thus empty container logistics ensures that empty containers are available at the right place, at the right time, in the right quality, in the right condition, for the right customer and at the right cost (Hüttmann, 2013). As commercial traffic is never in balance (see, for example, Figure 5.3 and 5.8), with imbalances between the Far East and Europe and the Far East/United States, the repositioning of empty containers represents an essential

Figure 5.8 Full and empty container handling and empty container incidence worldwide 2005–2011 (in million TEU)

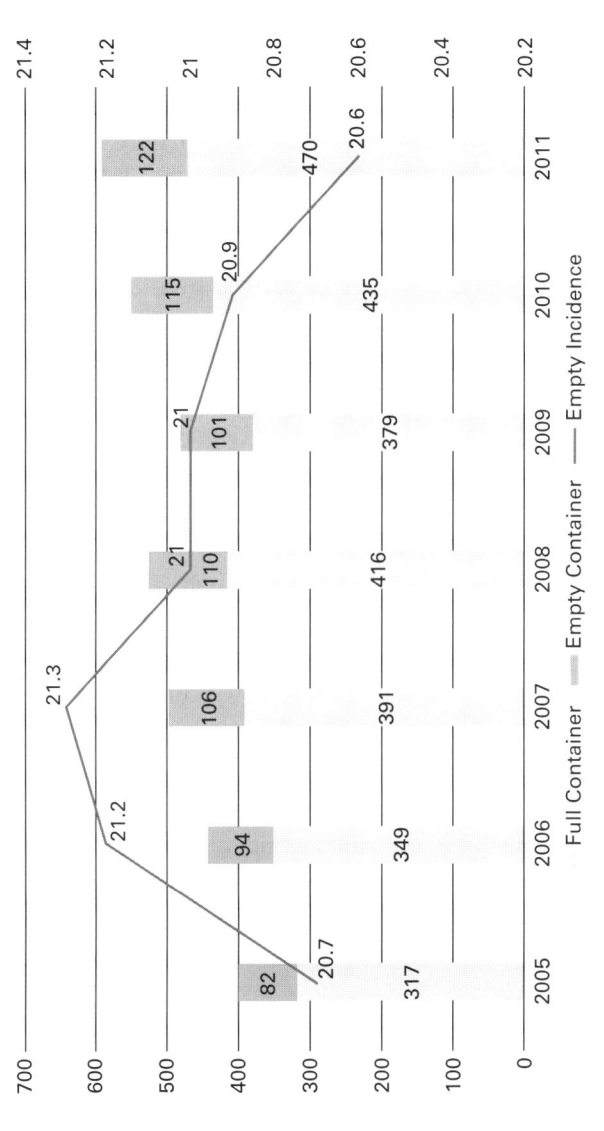

Year	Full Container	Empty Container	Empty Incidence
2005	317	82	20.7
2006	349	94	21.2
2007	391	106	21.3
2008	416	110	21
2009	379	101	21
2010	435	115	20.9
2011	470	122	20.6

SOURCE Author, based on Drewry Shipping Consultants Ltd (2012)

task which is, according to Notteboom and Rodrigue (2008), one of the most complex problems concerning global freight distribution. Beside this global imbalance, seasonal effects (eg agricultural products) have an impact on the flow of cargo and the flow of empty containers (Konings and Thijs, 2001). Though worldwide transported container volumes (empty and loaded) have increased consistently, empty container incidence has been almost stable at between 20 per cent and 21 per cent in recent years (see Figure 5.8). The share of landside empty containers is even higher and estimated to be around 40 per cent of all containers transported (Konings and Thijs, 2001).

Repositioning takes place between areas with a shortage of containers (the demand area) and areas with an excess of empty containers (the surplus area). The need for repositioning thereby occurs on a global, interregional or regional/local level. It can be performed by all modes of transportation. Shipping lines optimize their empty container logistics on a global scale, and there are tools available to support these activities. The consulting group BCG, as an example, is facilitating a global marketplace 'xChange' through which industry players can redress carrier-specific imbalances by sharing empty containers (Sanders *et al*, 2015).

At a local level, port authorities often develop an empty container logistics strategy for the port region with the participation of the major stakeholder groups, such as the HHLA in Hamburg with the 'Virtual Depot' project. This project aims to avoid empty container trips to the container depots by exchanging information between import and export service providers via a cloud-based IT system. The export service provider can reserve available empty containers from an import service provider which are to be returned to a depot (Fehrs, 2016). The movement of empty containers impacts on the operational costs of shipping companies. According to Rodrigue (2013) it is estimated that shipping companies spend on average €110 billion per year in the management of their container assets (purchase, maintenance, repairs), of which €16 billion is for the repositioning of empty ones. This means that this repositioning accounts for 15 per cent of the operational costs related to container assets.

Information and communication technology (ICT)

The role of ICT in optimizing maritime logistics chains is still underestimated (ISL, 2014). It cannot be ignored that despite the development in ICT and in trade data-exchange standards, most of the processes in many ports remain predominantly paper based (Dimitrios and Athanasios, 2013). The network infrastructures at many ports were installed around a decade ago and often are not adequate for the high bandwidth and secure protocols required by new IT applications (Economist Intelligence Unit, 2015). The main components of managing and optimizing the MCTC are now discussed.

Port community systems

Collaboration within the MCTC has evolved, and ITC systems are more and more present in the daily activities of the shipping industry. Actors that had a competitive status in the past are now collaborating via the use of communication platforms to exchange information.

A port community system (PCS) is a modular electronic platform which connects the multiple communication systems of each of its members in the port (see Figure 5.9). There are a wide range of PCS setups existing and each has its own characteristics. Most of these systems are developed independently in the various ports around the world. Carlan *et al* (2015) distinguish between four main functionalities of a PCS: Logistics, Navigation, Dangerous Cargo Declaration and Customs. Only few system cover the whole range of applications; examples include Portnet in Singapore as a private service port or DAKOSY in Hamburg and APCS in Antwerp as landlord ports.

Figure 5.9 Port community systems

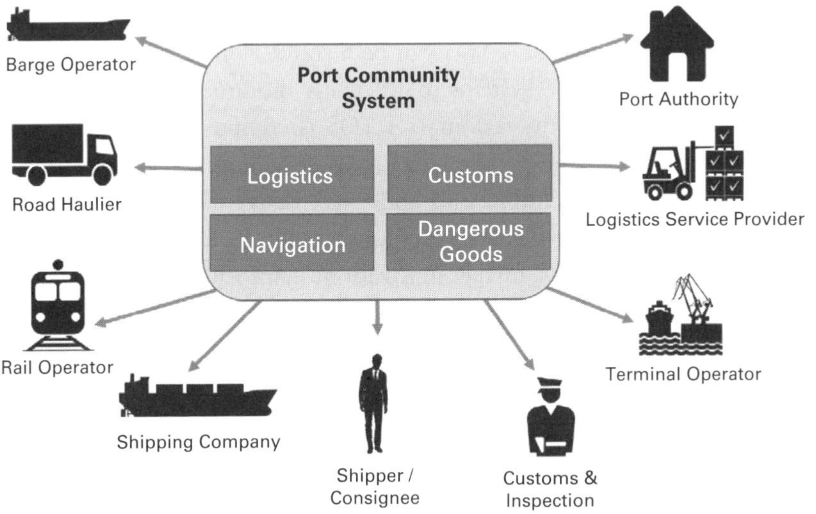

SOURCE Author

These systems are a significant step forward for communication between the actors in the MCTC. The main benefits are:

- to connect the various actors in a port;
- to optimize the flows of information (efficiency and effectiveness);
- to improve the efficiency of internal operations;
- to optimize, manage and automate port and logistics processes through a single submission of data;
- to better control the import/export activity by customs services.

There is also a wide range of IT solutions to manage port operations. Integrated systems, designed for real-time planning, to link maritime transport with hinterland transport as well as with all other actors in the MCTC are therefore the focus, such as Terminal Operating Systems (TOS). To receive real-time data these systems can be linked with Vessel Traffic Service (VTS) systems, a marine traffic monitoring system, and/or radar or GPS systems.

Terminal operating systems

Nowadays, a growing number of terminals are using higher levels of automation to improve their competitiveness. The IT basis for all these activities is a Terminal Operating System (TOS). The TOS controls the movement and storage of different types of cargo in and around a container terminal. It enables terminals to make better use of their assets, labour and equipment, plan workloads and get up-to-the-minute information to make timely and cost-effective decisions. A TOS can be a stand-alone system, but often it is linked with other ITC systems to efficiently monitor the flow of products in, out and around the terminal. A TOS is composed of sub-systems for administration, planning, scheduling, executing and reporting parts. A multimodal approach including rail and truck deliveries is normally also included. Major planning activities are illustrated in Figure 5.10.

Beside these IT solutions, further innovations in information and communication technology will have an impact on the MCTC (Blecker *et al*, 2011).

Robotics and automation

There has been a steady increase in automation in ports since the first automated stacking cranes were installed at the European Container Terminals in Rotterdam in 1990. Automated terminals have a clear advantage in

Figure 5.10   Terminal operating systems – planning functions

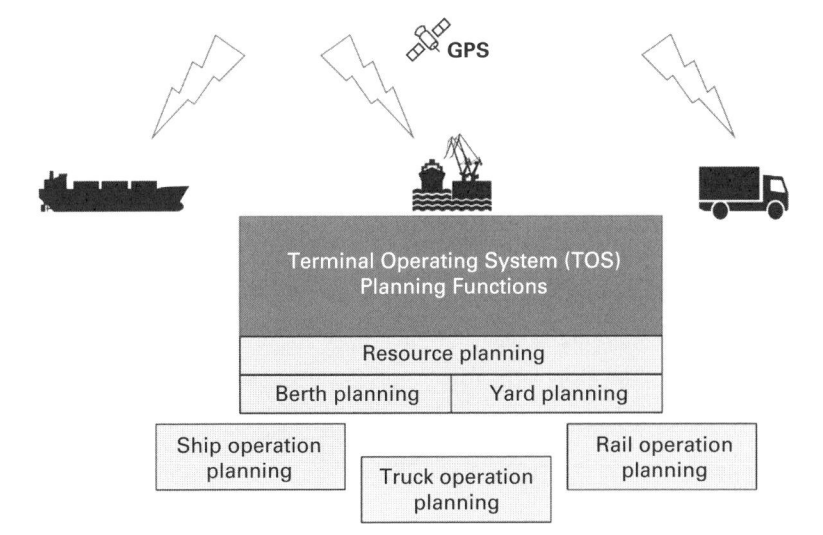

```
                            GPS

   [ship]              [terminal]                    [truck]

            ┌─────────────────────────────────┐
            │  Terminal Operating System (TOS)│
            │        Planning Functions       │
            ├─────────────────────────────────┤
            │        Resource planning        │
            ├───────────────┬─────────────────┤
            │ Berth planning│  Yard planning  │
            └───────────────┴─────────────────┘
   ┌──────────────┐                   ┌──────────────┐
   │Ship operation│                   │Rail operation│
   │   planning   │  ┌─────────────┐  │   planning   │
   └──────────────┘  │Truck operation│ └──────────────┘
                     │   planning   │
                     └─────────────┘
```

SOURCE   Author, based on Kim and Lee (2015)

terms of greater and more efficient loading and unloading capabilities. Automation makes most sense in ports where the cost of local labour and land is high and where there is a competitive need to efficiently handle larger ships. Shanghai, the world's busiest container port, is almost entirely manual, while Rotterdam's Maasvlakte II terminal, which opened in April 2015, has no personnel inside its cargo-handling section.

Beyond container handling, companies are looking to automate other parts of the supply chain by leveraging the latest innovations in robotics (DP World Report, 2015), such as autonomous vehicles within ports to move containers. Besides cost savings, another driver is the continued growth of e-commerce and changes in consumer preferences such as same-day deliveries.

Drone ships

A lot of attention is currently given to the development of unmanned ships. Studies are under way, including the European Commission-funded Maritime Unmanned Navigation through Intelligence in Networks (MUNIN) project (http://www.unmanned-ship.org/munin/). According to Rolls-Royce (Tovy, 2016), heading a consortium to develop the technology, remote-controlled 'drone ships' will be plying the sea lanes without crews on board by the end of this decade. Sensors such as radar, lasers and computer programs will allow the ships to pilot themselves. Land-based control centres using surveillance drones to monitor what is happening both on board and around the ship will remotely monitor and control the unmanned ships of the future, taking over if there is a problem or for complex docking procedures.

By eliminating crew-related infrastructure, Rolls-Royce estimates that the ships will be safer, cheaper and more environmentally friendly as they could reduce fuel consumption (and hence emissions) by up to 20 per cent. However, drone ships are facing significant challenges. One is regulatory, as international maritime conventions set minimum crew requirements. In addition, it is unclear when autonomous ships will be able to adequately cope with the challenges of weather, obstacles and in-trip repair. But even if it takes longer to develop fully autonomous ships, partial automation, with much-reduced crew numbers, is likely to be an intermediate step.

3D printing

Further structural changes might come from other IT developments, such as 3D printing to synthesize a three-dimensional object. If this trend gains recognition, the balance between transportation and labour cost may change. Part of the global production may shift back to wealthy countries with local 3D production centres supplying products on demand. This would lead to decreased shipping volumes of goods between Asia and other continents, at the same time increasing the shipping volumes of raw materials between continents to produce the prints. In research conducted by PwC (Tipping and Schmahl, 2015) it was found that as much as 37 per cent of the ocean container business is at risk because of 3D printing. Footwear, toys, ceramic products, electronics and plastics have, according to this analysis, the highest potential for disruption. While this innovation is difficult to predict, there are likely to be consequences for the shipping industry in the future.

Conclusion

The Global Container transport industry has been, and is, going through a turbulent period. 2015 was the fifth consecutive year of crisis, with falling revenues and declining profit margins. In 2016, Drewry expects industry-wide losses of more than US $5 bn, with record-low freight prices (KPMG Transport Tracker, 2016). The unbalanced supply and demand situation, with even larger vessels in the order books of the carriers, will further widen this imbalance and put the freight rates under pressure in future. The distinct impact of new developments, such as 3D printing or near-shoring as a consequence of increasing labour rates in Asia on the shipping industry cannot been foreseen in detail yet, but they will further influence the industry.

The container industry's merger and aquisition activities, and cooperation through strategic alliances, represent a first step towards recovery. Further comprehensive transformations that address technical issues with an intense use of IT applications and optimization software have to follow, as well as organizational adaptation. These future challenges will only be met if the mindset in this traditionally oriented industry changes and accepts more innovative solutions.

References

Alphaliner (2015) *Weekly Newsletter*, (19), available at <http://www.alphaliner.com/get_public_newsletter.php?file=2015/no19/Alphaliner%20Newsletter%20no%2019%20-%202015.pdf>

Alphaliner (2016) Top 100 Operated fleets as per 13 June 2016, available at <http://www.alphaliner.com/top100/>

APM Terminals (2010) Press Release 21 Oct 2010: 2/3 of global container throughput handled in ports in emerging markets, available at <http://www.apmterminals.com/~/media/Files/Corporate/News/Press%20Releases/2012/12/192%20101021_Port_Finance_Conference.ashx>

Araujo de Souza, G, Beresford, A and Pettit, S (2003) Liner shipping companies and terminal operators: Internationalisation or globalisation? *Maritime Economics & Logistics*, **5** (4), pp 393–412

Ashar, A and Rodrigue, J-P (2012) The evolution of containerships: The geography of transport systems, available at < https://people.hofstra.edu/geotrans/eng/ch3en/conc3en/containerships.html>

Bernhofen, D, El-Sahil, Z and Kneller, R (2012) Estimating the effects of the container revolution on world trade, University of Nottingham research paper, 3 February

Blecker, T, Jahn, C and Kersten, W (2011) *Maritime Logistics in the Global Economy: Current trends and approaches*, Eul Verlag, Köln

Carlan, V, Sys, C and Vanelslander, T (2015) Port Community Systems costs and benefits: from competition to collaboration within the supply chain, available at <http://imet.gr/Portals/0/Intranet/Proceedings/SIGA2/carlan_sys_vanelslander[1].pdf>

Chinnery, K (1999) Global alliances in container shipping and their potential effects on ports, *Ports and Harbors*, **44**, pp 20–22

Cullinane, K and Song, D-W (2002) Port privatization policy and practice, *Transport Reviews*, **22** (1), pp 55–75

Cullinane, K, Khanna, M and Song, D-W (1999) How big is beautiful: economies of scale and the optimal size of containership, *Liner shipping: what's next?* Proceedings of the IAME conference, Halifax, pp 108–40

Dimitrios, T and Athanasios, B (2013) Port Community Systems: Requirements, functionalities and implementation complications, 13th World Conference on Transport Research, Rio de Janeiro, July, available at <http://www.wctrs-society.com/wp/wp-content/uploads/abstracts/rio/selected/2024.pdf.>

DP World Report (2015) Annual Report and Accounts, available at <http://web.dpworld.com/wp-content/uploads/2014/05/2016_04_07_DPWorld_AR15_Web.pdf>

Drewry (2015a) Global Container Terminal Operators Annual Report 2015, available at <http://www.drewry.co.uk/news.php?id=395>

Drewry (2015b) Press release 24 August 2015: Rising demand & big ships driving container port investment boom, available at <http://www.drewry.co.uk/news.php?id=395>

Drewry Shipping Consultants (2001) *Post-Panamax Containerships – The Next Generation*, Drewry, London

Drewry Shipping Consultants Ltd (2012) *Container market – 2012/13: Annual review and forecast, incorporating the Container Forecaster – 3Q12*, Drewry Publishing, London

Economist (2013) Why have containers boosted trade so much? Press release, 21 May, available at <http://www.economist.com/blogs/economist-explains/2013/05/economist-explains-14>

Economist Intelligence Unit (2015) A turning point: The potential role of ICT innovations in ports and logistics, *DP World*, available at <http://web.dpworld.com/wp-content/uploads/2015/11/ICT-innovations-DP-World_Eng.pdf>

Eurokai (2015) Jahresbericht 2015, available at <http://www.eurokai.de/Investor-Relations/Finanzberichte>

European Commission (2016) Press release 29 April 2016: Mergers: Commission approves container liner shipping merger between CMA CGM and NOL, subject to conditions, available at < http://europa.eu/rapid/press-release_IP-16-1631_en.htm>

Fehrs, I (2016) Pilot project 'Virtual Depot' – virtual exchange – real success: Presentation held at the TOC Europe Container Supply Chain Conference in Hamburg, 15 June

Grig, R (2012) *Governance-Strukturen in der maritimen Transportkette: Agentenbasierte modellierung des akteursverhaltens im extended gate*, Universitäts-Verlag, Berlin

Hendrickson, K E (2015) *The Encyclopaedia of the Industrial Revolution in World History Vol. 3*, 3rd edn, Rowmann & Littlefield

Hutchison Port Holdings Limited (2015) The World of Hutchison Port Holdings Limited: Company overview 2015, available at <https://www.hph.com/files/contentdoc/1442376130_HPH%20Flyer%202015%20Eng.pdf>

Hüttmann, B K (2013) Empty container logistics in the maritime economy, in *Schriftenreihe Volkswirtschaftliche Forschungsergebnisse Vol. 188*, Hamburg, Kovač

ISL (2014) ICT: Next game changer for future efficient and secure maritime logistic chains, *European Maritime Day 2014*, available at <https://www.isl.org/en/news/successful-workshop-european-maritime-day-2014>

ISO 668 (2013) Series 1 freight containers – Classification, dimensions and ratings, available at <http://www.iso.org/iso/catalogue_detail.htm?csnumber=59673>

JOC Consultants (2015a) Press release 9 Nov 2015: Container shipping industry faces potential wave of consolidation, available at <http://www.joc.com/maritime-news/container-lines/container-shipping-industry-faces-potential-wave-consolidation_20151109.html>

JOC Consultants (2015b) Press release 7 Jan 2015 by Leach, P: Shippers, regulators will be watching closely as alliances launch services, available at <http://www.joc.com/maritime-news/container-lines/ocean-three/shippers-regulators-will-be-watching-closely-alliances-launch-services_20150107.html>

Kim, K H and Lee, H (2015) Container terminal operation: Current trends and future challenges, in *Handbook of Ocean Container Transport Logistics*, Springer International Publishing, Switzerland, pp 43–73

Konings, R and Thijs, R (2001) Foldable containers: A new perspective on reducing container-repositioning costs. Technological, logistic and economic issues, *European Journal of Transport and Infrastructure Research*, **1** (4), pp 333–52

KPMG Transport Tracker (2016) Global transport: Market trends and views, kpmg.com, February/March, available at <https://www.kpmg.com/BE/en/IssuesAndInsights/ArticlesPublications/Documents/kpmg-transport-tracker_042016.pdf>

Lloyd's List (2016) Press Release 5 April 2016: Global box trade forecast to grow 4.1% in 2016, available at <https://www.lloydslist.com/ll/sector/containers/article521375.ece>

Lloyd's Register, QinetiQ and University of Strathclyde (2013) Global Marine Trends 2030, available at <http://www.futurenautics.com/wp-content/uploads/2013/10/GlobalMarineTrends2030Report.pdf>

Notteboom, T E (2004) Container shipping and ports: An overview, *Review of Network Economics*, **3** (2), June, available at <http://www.vliz.be/imisdocs/publications/278392.pdf>

Notteboom, T E and Rodrigue, J-P (2008) Containerisation, box logistics and global supply chains: The integration of ports and liner shipping networks, *Maritime Economics and Logistics*, **10** (1/2), pp 152–74

Notteboom, T E and Winkelmans, W (2002) Stakeholder Relations Management in ports: Dealing with the interplay of forces among stakeholders in a changing competitive environment, paper presented at IAME Conference, Panama City, Panama, November 2002

OECD (2012) *Looking to 2060: A global vision of long-term growth*, OECD Economics Department Policy Notes, No 15, November 2012, available at <https://www.oecd.org/eco/outlook/2060policynote.pdf>

OECD (2016a) *The Ocean Economy in 2030*, OECD Publishing, Paris, available at <http://dx.doi.org/10.1787/9789264251724-en>

OECD (2016b) Capacity to grow: Transport infrastructure needs for future trade growth, Paris 2016, *International Transport Forum*, available at <http://www.itf-oecd.org/capacity-grow-transport-infrastructure-needs-future-trade-growth-0>

OECD (2016c) *Economic Outlook 2016 Issue 2 Chapter 1: General assessment of the macroeconomic situation*, available at <http://www.oecd.org/eco/economicoutlook.htm>

Olivo, A, Zuddas, P, Di Francesco, M and Manca, A (2005) An operational model for empty container management, *Maritime Economics and Logistics*, 7 (3), pp 199–222

Page, P (2016) Shipping lines prepare new global alliance, Wall Street Journal, available at <http://www.wsj.com/articles/shipping-lines-prepare-new-global-alliance-1462909188>

PricewaterhouseCoopers (2010) *Transportation and Logistics 2030, Volume 3: Emerging Markets – new hubs, new spokes, new industry leaders?*, available at <http://www.pwc.com/gx/en/transportation-logistics/tl2030/emerging-markets/pdf/tl2030_vol3_final.pdf>

Reuters (2016) Press release 18 Feb 2016: China launches new shipping giant to battle downturn, available at <http://www.reuters.com/article/us-china-shipping-cosco-idUSKCN0VR0AK>

Ripley, D (1993) *The Little Eaton Gangway and Derby Canal*, 2nd edn, Oakwood Press

Rodrigue, J-P (2013) The repositioning of empty containers, in *The Geography of Transport Systems*, Hofstra University, Department of Global Studies and Geography, available at <https://people.hofstra.edu/geotrans/eng/ch5en/appl5en/ch5a3en.html>

Rodrigue, J-P and Slack, B (2013) Intermodal Transportation and Containerization, in *The Geography of Transport Systems*, Hofstra University, Department of Global Studies and Geography, available at <https://people.hofstra.edu/geotrans/eng/ch3en/conc3en/ch3c6en.html>

Roland Berger Strategy Consultants (2013) Seafreight forwarding – business model under pressure? p 25, available at <http://www.rolandberger.ch/media/pdf/Roland_Berger_Challenges_in_sea_freight_forwarding_20130514.pdf>

Sanders, U, Riedl, J, Kloppsteck, L, Christian Roeloffs, C and Schlingmeier, J (2015) Think outside your boxes: Solving the global container-repositioning puzzle, *BGC Perspectives*, 17 November, available at <https://www.bcgperspectives.com/content/articles/transportation-travel-logistics-think-outside-your-boxes-solving-global-container-repositioning-puzzle/>

Statista (2016a) International seaborne trade carried by container ships from 1980 to 2014 (in million tons loaded), available at <http://www.statista.com/statistics/253987/international-seaborne-trade-carried-by-containers/>

Statista (2016b) Estimated container cargo flows on major container trade routes in 2015, by trade route (in TEUs), available at <http://www.statista.com/statistics/253988/estimated-containerized-cargo-flows-on-major-container-trade-routes/>

Statista (2016c) The world's leading ocean freight forwarders in 2015, based on ocean freight TEUs (in 1000s), available at <http://www.statista.com/statistics/254936/leading-ocean-freight-forwarders-worldwide-based-on-market-share/>

Talley, W K (2009) *Port Economics*, London, Routledge, p 14

Tipping, A and Schmahl, A (2015) Commercial Transportation Trends, *Strategy&*, available at <http://www.strategyand.pwc.com/perspectives/2015-commercial-transportation-trends>

Tovy, A (2016) Crewless 'drone ships' will be sailing the seas by 2020, *Telegraph*, 11 April, available at <http://www.telegraph.co.uk/business/2016/04/09/crewless-drone-ships-will-be-sailing-the-seas-by-2020/>

UNCTAD (2011) *Review of Maritime Transport 2011*, Geneva, United Nations, p 40

UNCTAD (2014) *Review of Maritime Transport 2014*, Geneva, United Nations, p 5

UNCTAD (2015) *Review of Maritime Transport 2015*, Geneva, United Nations, p 7

Wackett, M (2015) CMA CGM $2.4bn offer for APL accepted in deal to create third-biggest box carrier, *Loadstar*, available at <http://theloadstar.co.uk/cma-cgm-2-4bn-offer-apl-accepted-deal-create-third-biggest-box-carrier/>

World Economic Forum (2016) What will global GDP look like in 2030? Available at <https://www.weforum.org/agenda/2016/02/what-will-global-gdp-look-like-in-2030/>

World Shipping Council (2013) Major Routes, available at <http://www.worldshipping.org/about-the-industry/global-trade/trade-routes>

World Shipping Council (2016) The history of containerisation, available at <http://www.worldshipping.org/about-the-industry/history-of-containerization>

Car shipping 06

PAUL NIEUWENHUIS, Cardiff Business School, UK

Introduction: the car shipment market

Cars have always been a globally traded product, although for many years those flows involved very small numbers of complete units, or – as in the case of Ford's Model T, for example – built-up chassis or even kits of components for local assembly at branch plants (Casey, 2008). This approach saved money, as boxes of components are cheaper to ship than fully built-up cars. In any case, these cars were built with a separate body and chassis, allowing chassis to be shipped separately from bodies, which in the case of Ford's Model T were outsourced (Nieuwenhuis and Wells, 2007; Casey, 2008). In addition, countries such as Australia banned the import of – then usually wooden – bodies for both environmental and political reasons and only imported running chassis, which then received locally built bodies (Birney, 1985: 21). This practice was indeed common around the world, as a car was understood as consisting of a running chassis; the body was seen as quite separate, not the responsibility of the vehicle producer, but to be ordered and built separately to the taste and budget of the owner by independent coach builders. With the advent of the all-steel body and mass production during the 1920s and 1930s, such concerns faded and restrictions could be eased, although the trade in kits (CKD or SKD) continues to this day with Tesla's facility in Tilburg, Netherlands, a recent example (Williams, 2015a).

Things really changed when larger flows of fully built, mass-produced steel cars began to emerge, as with the shipping of Volkswagens from Germany to the United States, from the 1950s onwards. From the 1960s, much larger flows of finished cars from Japan started. When markets for Japanese cars opened up in developed countries such as the United States, Europe and Australia, larger shipments of cars became necessary. This led to the development of ships dedicated to this trade, initially the PCC (Pure Car Carrier) and more recently the more flexible PCTC (Pure Car and Truck

Carrier), which features movable deck sections to accommodate 'high and heavies', namely larger and heavier vehicles than the standard passenger car, such as earth-moving equipment and cranes. However, other types of ships are also used to ship cars, with many more valuable cars being containerized and therefore forming part of the container shipping sub-sector. Reefers have also been used, as with the flows of Japanese used cars to New Zealand, whereby these can serve as a return load for ships carrying agricultural products from New Zealand to East Asia (Beresford *et al*, 2002).

The PCTC is effectively a large box featuring usually between five and seven decks where cars and other vehicles can be parked in tight formation with minimal wasted space. Cars are one of the few cargoes that can move themselves, so no specific handling equipment is needed other than skilled drivers and skilled loading staff. However, lead times are such that large areas are needed – sometimes multi-storey car parks – to hold a steadily accumulating number of cars before it constitutes a full load for the typical deep-sea car carrier. Similarly, at the receiving port, sufficient space needs to be available to unload the cargo in a timely manner, from which the vehicles can then gradually be dispersed to dealers or national sales company sites. Such ocean-going car carrier ships are typically capable of taking 5,000 to 7,000 cars or 'Car-Equivalent Units' (CEUs) as one load.

With several ports of call for each vessel, it is essential that vehicles are loaded such that those for the first destination port can be unloaded first, those for the second port next, etc. This can be challenging, as cargoes also need to be loaded for maximum stability for ocean crossings. That this process does sometimes go wrong is illustrated by the capsize or sinking of car carriers with cargoes of cars on board. In January 2015, the car carrier *Höegh Osaka* listed and grounded outside the Port of Southampton in the UK. The subsequent investigation by the UK Marine Accident Investigation Branch concluded that:

> The cargo loading plan had not been adjusted for a change in the ship's usual journey pattern and the number of vehicles due to be loaded according to the pre-stowage plan was significantly different from that of the final tally.
> (Williams, 2016a)

Due to local holidays, the vessel called at Southampton first, instead of Bremerhaven and Hamburg, where it would also normally have refuelled. By reversing that order, the vessel ended up going to sea top heavy, with the vehicles for Southampton unloaded before the vehicles destined for Germany, which were on a higher deck. With less bunker fuel on board as well, the centre of gravity had become too high, thus causing the capsize. In January 2016, the ERL carrier Modern Express was abandoned in the Bay of Biscay after listing and taking on water. ERL has two car carriers and specializes in shipping to West Africa from Antwerp and Le Havre. The vessel was on a return journey with a cargo of construction machinery and timber as a back-haul (Williams, 2016b). On 3 February it was successfully towed into the port of Bilbao (Wright, 2016). Ro-ro car carriers are not the most stable vessels in any case, and minor factors can be critical, making them particularly vulnerable.

Although these specialized ships have developed and grown into their role over decades, one legacy remains, and that is the unit of measurement used, the CEU, which is still based on a 1966 Toyota Corolla, despite the fact that cars have increased in size considerably since then. In fact, while the average car at that time would fit into an imaginary 10,200-litre box (total length × total width × total height), by 1995 this 'box' had grown to 11,100 litres (Nieuwenhuis, 2006a, b). The first generation 1966 Corolla measured 3850 mm × 1490 mm × 1380 mm and around half the first few generations of Corolla were exported, amounting to some 5.4 million between 1966 and 1984 (Ruiz, 1986). Since then, volumes of cars shipped have also increased significantly, with additional flows from South Korea and to a lesser extent from Malaysia and Thailand being added. Increased flows from China can be expected over the next decade or so, as the home market becomes saturated and the local product more internationally competitive. More localized, regional flows add further shipping volume.

The shipping of finished cars is one of the truly global parts of the vehicle logistics system; other flows are strictly national or regional (Coia, 2014a). Car manufacturers thus rely very heavily on shipping for global trade. Purpose-designed car carriers carry between 2,000 and 7,000 tightly-packed cars across the seas. The smaller-capacity vessels are largely used for shorter haul and coastal routes, while the larger 4,000 to 7,000-car vessels are used on intercontinental deep-sea routes, with even larger vessels now being launched as outlined below. Not surprisingly, several carmakers, such as Nissan and Hyundai, became directly involved in the shipping themselves. Some still have close links with fleets of car carrying vessels, with several plants – especially in Japan and Korea – located on the quayside for direct loading. Others subcontract to specialized shipping firms such as MOL or Wallenius Wilhelmsen Logistics (WWL). As cars require little to no handling equipment for the loading/unloading process, dedicated roll-on, roll-off (Ro-Ro) car carriers can be used.

Figure 6.1 Japanese Car exports 1975–1995 (000s)

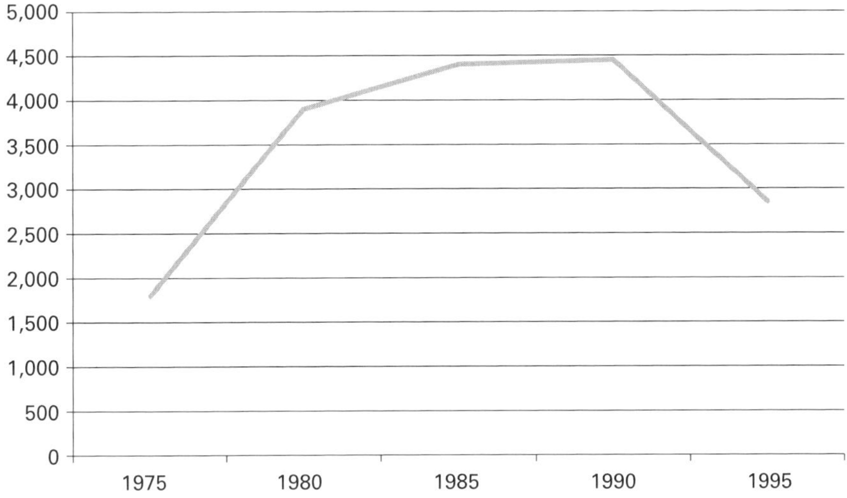

[Line chart showing Japanese car exports rising from about 1,800 in 1975 to about 3,900 in 1980, plateauing near 4,500 from 1985 to 1990, then declining to about 2,900 by 1995.]

SOURCE Author, compiled from JAN (several years)

In terms of value, the European Union is the largest exporter of cars, followed by Japan, the United States and Canada, and South Korea, with Mexico sixth (Eurostat, 2013). The United States is the largest importer by some margin, with EU and China vying for a distant second place. Clearly this pattern of trade, with major exporters and markets separated by oceans, promotes the need for shipping to fulfil such flows, as a result of which – despite increasing localization of production – global shipping of cars continues to be important. It is, however, a dynamic picture, with some flows growing, then shrinking as export country producers localize production near target markets (see Figure 6.1). Other flows then emerge to compensate to some extent for the loss in overall volume, although the actual routes and destinations often change in the process, while events such as the 2008–2009 recession can depress demand in many markets at the same time, causing pressure on overall shipping demand.

Moves to more localized and regional flows

Whilst shipments from Japan and South Korea have traditionally been quite one-sided, with exports vastly exceeding imports, recent shifts to more local routes can result in similarly unbalanced flows. Coia (2014b) notes, for example, that increased exports from Spain, combined with a still depressed local market, have resulted in three cars shipped out for each car shipped into Spanish ports. Spain has seen a general shift of production from plants further north, such as Ford's Genk plant in Belgium, which closed, while GM is now sourcing more vehicles from Spain instead of South Korea, which again affects the volumes shipped from the Far East to Europe. Other flows that are growing include exports from Turkey and both imports to and exports from production facilities and markets in North Africa (Coia, 2014b). The latter are often served using Gioa Tauro in Italy and Vigo in Spain as hubs. Such an approach allows faster transit times for deep-sea carriers, which call at fewer ports, from which smaller flows using smaller Ro-Ro vessels then serve local hub ports, and from there to spoke ports such as the Turkish port of Derince. Demand in Turkey is particularly volatile, making import volumes unpredictable, whereas exports, which are driven by more stable demand in, for example, West and Central Europe, have shown steady growth; exports currently amount to around 800,000 cars and commercial vehicles a year. This, of course, creates a degree of imbalance in shipments (Coia, 2014c). As demand changes, such hub-and-spoke approaches can be changed again to allow the larger vessels to work closer to capacity by calling at more, smaller ports while sailing slower to save fuel, and hence cost. At such times, the smaller ports are also less congested, making for more efficient operating conditions and a faster turnaround for the larger vessels.

For larger countries, such as India, China or the United States, it can be worthwhile to use coastal shipping to move cars from manufacturing locations to more distant national markets. In India, this is a relatively recent development. Hyundai started using a link from Chennai, near its main Indian manufacturing base, to Pipavav in the northwest. Such moves are supported by government policy, which is encouraging a move away from road-based transport to rail and sea. As many vehicle assembly facilities are based in the south, serving North India, as well as local regions, the need for moving cars is growing. However, ports are often slow to adapt with suitable facilities and appropriate fees and port charges (Cross, 2016), while Indian Railways are positioning themselves as key competitors in this trade (*Automotive Logistics*, 2016). In the United States, rail has mostly been successful in competing against shipping for finished vehicle transport.

Such local flows become very dependent on specific markets and can therefore easily become affected by local market fluctuations. With the rapid decline in the Russian car market, for example, as a result of falling oil and gas prices, local shipping flows of cars, as well as car components, reduced. Such developments can make such smaller regional routes suddenly unviable (Vorotnikov, 2015). However, there is a long history of using local and coastal shipping to move cars around areas such as Europe, the Caribbean, the Middle East and East and West Africa. Hyundai-Kia has recently started shipping products from its Czech and Slovak facilities to Spain via the Slovenian port of Koper to Tarragona using the Adriatic and Mediterranean route, for example. This replaces a previous land-based service (Williams, 2016c). Such smaller ports have an increasingly important role to play in these regional flows, although vehicle movements through Koper have grown rapidly to move it to a position only just outside the top ten European vehicle ports (Table 6.1).

Table 6.1 Top ten car ports in Europe, 2013

Rank	Port	Country	Main car makers using port	Units handled (000s)
1	Bremerhaven	Germany	BMW, Mercedes-Benz, VAG	2,180
2	Zeebrugge	Belgium	Mitsubishi, GM, Toyota	1,940
3	Emden	Germany	VAG	1,220
4	Grimsby, Immingham & Killingholme	UK	BMW, Toyota, VAG	950
5	Antwerp	Belgium	Fiat, Ford, Mazda	760
6	Southampton	UK	BMW, Honda, JLR	744
7	Tyne	UK	JLR, Nissan, Volvo	644
8	London	UK	BMW, Ford, JLR	545
9	Vigo	Spain	PSA, Renault-Nissan, Toyota	495
10	Barcelona	Spain	Renault-Nissan, VAG	488

SOURCE Adapted from Coia (2014b)

Industry developments

There are a number of companies of varying size involved in the finished vehicle trade employing PCTCs. While some are familiar names in shipping, engaged in other activities such as container shipping, some are specialist car shipping companies. This is due in part to the need for dedicated vessels, but also to the unique demands of the automotive sector, with a number of these firms engaged in more value-added activities up and down the automotive value chain. These activities include production line clearing, whereby the finished vehicle logistics provider itself handles some of the final stages of vehicle manufacturing on the production line, such as fluid filling and water testing. Many will also then move the vehicles to the port. At the importing end, some firms have PDI (pre-delivery inspection) centres and even fit some 'dealer fitted' options such as alloy wheels before final delivery to the client.

Although the industry was affected by the global downturn from 2008 to 2012, which occurred when quite a few new vessels were under construction, the time lag in such new builds has allowed demand to catch up in recent years. The widening of the Panama Canal prompted several orders for Panamax or post-Panamax-size car carriers with a capacity of up to 8,000 CEU (Coia and Ludwig, 2013). The world's largest car carrier, the *Höegh Target*, the first of its 'New Horizon' class of carriers, has a capacity of 8,500 CEU; it made its maiden voyage in August 2015 and was the first of six such vessels commissioned by Höegh (Hogg, 2015); the second of these vessels, the *Höegh Trigger*, was delivered in November 2015 (Williams, 2015b). WWL took delivery of two 8,000 vehicle capacity 'High Efficiency Ro-Ro' (HERO) vessels in 2015, with another six put into service by 2018 (Hogg, 2015). At the same time, however, the recovery has been accompanied by the greater fragmentation of routes outlined above. These two trends combined are likely to lead to more use of these larger vessels over simple long routes with few stopping points, with an increased use of smaller vessels and hub-and-spoke ports for these new regional flows. The current challenge, then, is to optimize vessel deployment and port calls for these more fragmented flows, which themselves are more prone to short-term disruption, as highlighted earlier.

The new generation of larger vessels is aimed primarily at the traditional routes of major flows from East Asia to Europe and North America. However, such traditional one-way flows with very little back-haul are increasingly unfeasible due to cost, adding a further driver to the more diverse and localized routing approaches outlined earlier. Fortunately, in recent years, flows of luxury cars from Europe to the Far East have provided some balance in terms of back-haul, while at the same time volumes from Japan and Korea have reduced due to increases in local transplant production in Europe and North America.

In many cases now and increasingly, the Asia–Europe route is therefore the back-haul for the flow of luxury cars from Europe to the Far East, especially China, prompting K-Line, for example, to use its first post-Panamax vessel on this route (Drewry, 2012; Coia, 2014d). At the same time, such transplants can themselves create new flows. With plants becoming increasingly specialized in one or two models, this brings about a need to ship different models around the world in order to offer a full product portfolio in all markets; thus BMW has shipped some 2 million vehicles from its plant in South Carolina, many of which were shipped to EU markets, including Germany (Williams, 2016d), thereby also balancing out somewhat the more dominant flows from the EU to North America.

Coia and Ludwig (2013) and Coia (2014d) quote shipbroker RS Platou as defining full-capacity utilization in car carriers as 90 per cent. They calculate that for 2013, for example, that rate was 86 per cent and for 2014 84 per cent, thus suggesting overcapacity of 4 to 6 per cent against this suggested projected maximum and a 14 to 16 per cent shortfall against the theoretical maximum of 100 per cent, although this varies year on year and the situation eased somewhat during 2015. Precise figures are not always available and there are regional differences. Clearly ways have to be developed to balance the different vehicle flows between global and regional/local. A flexible and dynamic approach to allocating capacity to major ocean routes on the one hand and hub-and-spoke ports using smaller vessels on the other has to be developed, whereby changes in such patterns at short notice have to be expected in future in order to optimize capacity provision and utilization, and flexibility.

Although the industry is still adding capacity, as indicated by the data presented in Table 6.2, with several more vessels under construction, at the same time, many older vessels are due to be decommissioned over the next few years (Coia and Ludwig, 2013). This will also allow them to be replaced with cleaner, more efficient vessels (see below). Another measure to manage capacity is the practice of chartering vessels when demand increases. Although this implies the availability of charter capacity at any given time, such situations often arise when a particular shipper receives a new contract, or when a new vehicle, or model, proves more popular in particular markets than originally planned – both not uncommon in the automotive industry, and usually affecting only one or two finished vehicle logistics providers at any one time.

Table 6.2 Car shipping operators' ranking (CEU capacity-estimates)

Ranking	Operator	Principal routes	CEU capacity (2013)	CEU capacity (2014)
1	NYK	Deep sea	630,000	630,000
2	MOL	Deep sea	590,000	580,000
3	EuKor	Deep sea	450,000	455,000
4	K Line	Deep sea	420,000	450,000
5	WWL	Deep sea	405,000	400,000
6	Höegh AL	Deep sea	325,000	320,000
7	Grimaldi	Short sea	180,000	180,000
8	Glovis	Deep sea	175,000	350,000
9	Cido	Short sea	100,000	100,000
10	CSAV	Short sea	60,000	40,000
11	Toyofuji	Short sea	60,000	60,000
12	ARC	Short sea	40,000	40,000
13	ECL	Short sea	30,000	30,000
	Others	Various	350,000	280,000
Total			**3,815,000**	**3,915,000**

SOURCE Author, compiled from WWL, Seaweb, Lloyd's, *Automotive Logistics*
CEU = Car Equivalent Unit

Automotive clients on the whole prefer smaller, more frequent deliveries as these provide greater flexibility and enhanced ability to respond to short-term changes in market demand. Carmakers also need accuracy so that they can predict when vehicles will appear within the national distribution networks. For this reason, some firms, such as Eukor and MOL have a mix of vessels of different size on order. Another option is to move older, smaller vessels from deep-sea to short-sea duty; this has led to an increase in capacity of such short-sea vessels in recent years, to typically around 4,500 CEUs in areas such as the Mediterranean (Coia and Ludwig, 2013). In container shipping the move towards ever-larger ships is also increasingly being questioned, as the resulting loss of flexibility is recognized as an issue, which is best addressed through a more diverse mix of vessels of different size (Lloyd's List, 2016).

As well as localizing production in developed mature markets such as Europe and North America, Japanese and Korean producers are also increasingly moving production to ASEAN countries. This ensures a lower risk of disruption – such as from the 2011 Tohoku earthquake and tsunami – as well as lower production costs derived from reduced labour costs. Malaysia, Thailand and Indonesia have become significant players in the region. Localized production in China and India is at present primarily serving these home markets, but is also increasingly used to feed other markets, with Hyundai exporting from India and GM, for example, sourcing cars for the US market from China (Coia, 2014d). At the same time, GM's decision to end shipping of Chevrolet-badged cars from Korea to Europe reduced that flow by some 200,000 a year from 2016 (Coia and Ludwig, 2013). Similarly, the cessation of local manufacturing in Australia from 2017–18 will end the flow of vehicles from there, while increasing demand for imports. In response, Ro-Ro facilities at the port of Melbourne are enjoying a major expansion, and by January 2018 will be able to handle 1,000,000 units annually (Hogg, 2016). The Ro-Ro terminal will handle vehicles sourced from all major car production regions.

Another major growth area for vehicle production is Mexico, where Audi, Honda, Nissan and Mazda have all added capacity. This increases demand for shipping capacity to the US east and west coasts from Mexican ports such as Veracruz, although in view of the relatively short distances, rail is seen as a major competitor here. Rail can also be competitive in other areas; in 2016, BMW started a new rail route from the Bavarian city of Regensburg to Chengdu in China. China is mainly served through ports on its east coast, but logistics from there into central or western provinces is still inefficient due to inadequate infrastructure, as well as the sheer size of the country. Thus, a more direct route into non-coastal areas is attractive, while the speed, at 17 days compared with 55 days on average by sea, is also appealing (Williams, 2016e). BMW previously started using rail to ship CKD kits to China, while the rail link from Chengdu in China into Russia and then Europe is already well established.

Environmental impacts

Despite the fact that, at the time of writing, fuel costs have eased, the advent of oil price volatility will make fuel costs less predictable in future. Add to this the increasing pressure on emissions, especially of Sulphur Oxide (SOx) and costs are likely to rise over time. Sulphur emissions are a real problem and, in the transport context, are now primarily associated with the shipping sector; oceangoing ships contribute 5–8 per cent of the global total, as well as around 15 per cent of nitrogen oxides (NOx) (Corbett *et al*, 2007). At the Paris Climate Summit in 2015, both shipping and aircraft were identified as 'the elephants in the room' by NGOs, being major carbon dioxide emitters with little regulation and limited discussion of their role in climate change at the summit. In 2008 a UN study recalculated the CO_2 emissions from shipping and concluded that rather than the 1.8 per cent of the global total attributed to the sector up until then, it was in fact responsible for more than double that at 4.5 per cent (Vidal, 2008), with the prediction that this will increase further (EC, 2016). This figure is roughly comparable with that derived from oil refining worldwide. More recent vessels are designed with CO_2 reduction in mind and the Höegh Target, for example, launched in 2015, is estimated by its operator to emit 50 per cent lower CO_2 emissions per car carried than existing carriers (Hogg, 2015). The vessel is used on the East Asia to Europe route.

More serious, according to some, are the NOx, PM and SOx emissions from shipping. The latter in particular are a real problem due to the fact that while vehicle fuel has benefited from steadily decreasing sulphur content, shipping bunker fuel can contain up to 45,000 ppm and has been estimated to be responsible as a result for around 60,000 deaths a year (Corbett *et al*, 2007). In response, MARPOL Annex VI was put in place to limit such emissions. In addition, a number of jurisdictions have introduced Sulphur Emissions Control Areas (SECAs) where much lower limits apply of a maximum of 0.1 per cent sulphur content in emissions; more similar to road vehicles. Examples of such SECAs are around the Port of Long Beach in Southern California and the North Sea and Baltic in Northern Europe. An increasing number of shippers mention the advent of SECAs as having the potential to affect their business, particularly in terms of adding cost (Coia, 2014d). Not only is the fuel itself more expensive – leading many to reserve it for use in SECAs and other port areas only – but various types of after-treatment technology may be needed. Alternative fuels such as LNG are also under consideration and trial. To some extent this is a new development in shipping, which – in terms of environmental regulation – has been /lagging somewhat behind the automotive sector.

At the same time, the automotive industry itself is increasingly forced to take a more holistic approach to its environmental impact. Gone are the days when a mere focus on meeting toxic emissions regulation was sufficient to trade as a viable, responsible business. The environmental impact of manufacturing plants has had to be reduced significantly, particularly in Europe and North America, leading to the widespread introduction of water-based paint plants, for example, while similar standards have been rolled out to suppliers. Within the automotive sector, environmental considerations have long played a pivotal role, with tailpipe emissions controls dating back to the early 1960s. Since then, the attention of both legislators and NGOs, as well as consumers, has seen a broader range of environmental impacts under scrutiny. A significant part of the environmental impact of the manufacturing phase involves moving vehicles, raw materials and components around – the transport aspect of the logistics function. Many plants, particularly in Germany, traditionally rely on rail access, while some – such as PSA with the Rhine from its Mulhouse plant – use inland waterways to ship out finished cars. Despite increasing localization of production through transplant production near recipient markets, many cars are still shipped and this is forecast to grow.

While deep-sea shipping has a number of environmental advantages over land transport, with the cleaning up of truck emissions, shipping is beginning to emerge as a significant source of pollution in its own right. Although the effect of maritime emissions tends to be away from urban areas, ports and many inland waterways are close to or run through urban areas, so the effect of shipping will be felt in densely populated urban areas. In terms of their carbon dioxide (CO_2) emissions, ships can contribute markedly to global figures. In overall terms, ships contribute around 5–8 per cent of global SOx emissions, 15 per cent of global NOx emissions and around 2.5 per cent of global CO_2 emissions (Corbett *et al*, 2007; EC, 2016). Other sectors, notably air transport, also have a significant impact and yet, like shipping, they are still largely unregulated or in an earlier phase of regulation. Developing early regulation in such sectors allows the 'low-hanging fruit' to be tackled in the first or second phase of emissions regulation and this can invariably be done at lower cost and with greater environmental benefit than further regulation in sectors with more mature regulatory regimes, such as the car and truck sector. The analysis by Nieuwenhuis *et al* (2012) shows that transporting cars over longer, intercontinental distances is always going to generate relatively high levels of CO_2 emissions, even using modes that have a low level of impact per tonne/km travelled, such as shipping. However, conversely, when each mode is used over optimum distances, multimodal supply chains could well be developed that deliver relatively low overall CO_2 emissions per unit carried. One area to consider is to encourage shipping within regions such as the Far East or Europe, rather than between them.

The future car carrier

In this context, the presentation in 2005 of a concept ship in the form of an environmentally optimized car carrier by leading shipping firm WWL was significant. The vessel, named *E/S Orcelle* (E/S for Environmentally Sound Ship), after an endangered species of dolphin, would use energy sources readily available at sea for propulsion, notably solar power, wind power and wave power. It would therefore have a zero emissions potential, although WWL themselves acknowledge that various technological developments are needed before the ship can be turned into reality. The shipping firm expects this to be possible by about 2025 (Schilperoord, 2006). To design the concept, WWL assembled a team of naval architects, environmental experts and industrial designers. The ship is designed to carry around 10,000 cars – significantly more than today's vessels – despite having a similar vessel weight to current ships. This is achieved through the use of advanced lightweight materials, such as aluminium and composites, while the designers have also eliminated the need for ballast water tanks by incorporating greater stability into the basic design. The vessel would be on a par with or slightly larger than the largest car carriers of today at 250 m length, 30–40 m height and a draft of 9 m. It would achieve a maximum speed of 27 knots (Schilperoord, 2006).

The ship features three sail-like structures on top which are covered in solar panels. At the same time, they can be used as sails, thus harnessing wind power. Wave power is harnessed via a series of 12 lateral fins. The systems can be used in a combination of hydrogen, direct electric power or mechanical energy to propel the ship and power its on-board services. The fins can double as propulsion units, in conjunction with two conventional propellers, which are electrically driven. Around half the energy will be provided by hydrogen fuel cells. The elimination of the need to take on ballast water is a novel feature and a significant contribution to the concept's environmental credentials. Released ballast water can often contain contaminants or alien marine organisms which are then dumped at sea. The stability in both empty and laden conditions is provided by the hull which combines a narrow central hull with four supporting stabilizing structures; this design is known as a pentamaran. The design also dispenses with the conventional propeller and rudder at the stern by the use of the movable propeller pods outlined above.

Conclusions

The vehicle shipping sector is subject to a number of pressures. Some of these are linked to global shifts in production locations and markets. These include the increasing use of transplant production to serve local markets, while at the same time such facilities can specialize in the production of specific models for which there is global demand. Add to this the growth of newly emerging markets, and the traditional flows of vehicles from East Asia to Europe and North America, and those from Europe to North America, no longer dominate. Instead, a much more fragmented pattern of flows between and within regions has been emerging, calling for a more complex approach from shippers and a more diversified fleet of vessels of different size, calling at ports of varying size, with vessels deployed, and the ports used subject to change at short notice. In all this, the issue of demand forecasting has emerged as a weakness in the sector generally (Ward, 2016). The need to improve forecasts is increasingly being addressed with more sophisticated modelling methods, although the industry has not always been willing to adopt these (Park *et al*, 2008).

At the same time, new pressures have emerged to reduce the environmental impact of shipping. While the shipping industry has historically been subject to self-regulation steered by the IMO, now there is a new wave of legislation restricting access to certain areas – notably SECAs – while setting specific limits on certain emissions, which means the use of higher-cost fuels and investment in after-treatment technologies. In all this, it is likely to be the better resourced, as well as the more agile operators who are likely to survive. At the same time, however, overall global demand for car shipping is still growing and likely to continue to do so for the foreseeable future, suggesting profitable niches are continually emerging and they are there to be exploited.

With the *E/S Orcelle*, Wallenius Wilhelmsen set a stake in the ground; the company is determined to move towards more environmentally sound vessels and is expecting its competitors to follow. This could make a significant contribution to further cleaning up the automotive supply chain in an area that is often overlooked. MOL's *Emerald Ace*, launched in 2012, was probably the first car carrier to begin to introduce such technologies; it features lithium-ion batteries that are charged at sea by solar power. This power can be used in port, avoiding the use of the engine (Coia and Ludwig, 2013). Other predicted developments include the possibility of autonomous car carriers. It is argued that the automotive industry, with its interest in autonomous cars and a rapidly developing ability to deliver such technologies, may be one of the main drivers, as a shipping client, towards autonomous ships (Hogg, 2014).

References

Automotive Logistics (2016) Indian Railways launches auto rail hub in Chennai as part of wider rail freight plans, *Automotive Logistics*, 2 March

Beresford, A, Marlow, P, Nieuwenhuis, P and Wells, P (2002) *Shipping Air: The global distribution of new and used Cars*, Cardiff: CAIR

Birney, S (1985) *Australia's Own; The history of Holden*, Sydney: Golden Press

Casey, R (2008) *The Model T: A centennial history*, Baltimore: The Johns Hopkins University Press

Coia, A (2014a) NYK not afraid to go local for logistics, *Automotive Logistics*, 11 February

Coia, A (2014b) European vehicle ports sail into the light, *Automotive Logistics*, 17 March

Coia, A (2014c) Big movements needed at Turkish ports, *Automotive Logistics*, 4 June

Coia, A (2014d) Shipping focus: Capacity in balance, *Automotive Logistics*, 17 December

Coia, A and Ludwig, C (2013) Global ro-ro report: Moving with the trade winds, *Automotive Logistics*, 17 December

Corbett, J, Winebrake, J, Green, E, Kasibhatla, P, Eyring, V and Lauer, A (2007) Mortality from ship emissions: a global assessment, *Environmental Science and Technology*, **41**, pp 8512–18

Cross, B (2016) Hyundai opts for Indian coastal service but ro-ro rates are prohibitive, *Automotive Logistics*, 23 February

Drewry (1999) *Market Outlook for Car Carriers: New opportunities in a new millennium*, London: Drewry Shipping Consultants Ltd

Drewry (2012) *Car Carriers 2012*, London: Drewry Maritime Research

EC (2016) Reducing emissions from the shipping sector, *Climate Action* [online] ec.europa.eu/clima/policies/transport/shipping/index_en.htm [accessed 18 April 2016]

Eurostat (2013) International trade in motor cars [online] ec.europa.eu/Eurostat/statistics-explained/index.php/International_trade_in_motor_cars

Hogg, R (2014) Shipping focus: The ghosts of future shipping, *Automotive Logistics*, 17 December

Hogg, R (2015) Post-Panamax car carrier – Höegh Target – docks in UK, *Automotive Logistics*, 28 August

Hogg, R (2016) Australia's biggest automotive terminal opens in Melbourne, *Automotive Logistics*, 11 April

Lloyd's List (2016) Mega boxships lose their appeal as trade fundamentals shift, *Lloyd's List Daily Briefing*, 2 March

Nieuwenhuis, P (2006a) The miraculous growing car (I), *AWK Automotive Environment Analyst*, **130**, May

Nieuwenhuis P (2006b) The miraculous growing car (II), *AWK Automotive Environment Analyst*, **130**, May

Nieuwenhuis, P, Beresford, A and Choi, K-Y (2012) Shipping or local production? CO_2 impact of a strategic decision: an automotive industry case study, *International Journal of Production Economics*, **140** (1), November

Nieuwenhuis, P and Wells, P (2007) The all-steel body as a cornerstone to the foundations of the mass production car industry, *Industrial and Corporate Change*, **16** (2), pp 183–211

Park, B-J, Choi, H-R, Kim, H-S and Jung, J-U (2008) Maritime transportation planning support system for car shipping company, *Journal of Navigation and Port Research, International Edition*, **32** (4), pp 295–304

Ruiz, M (1986) *The Complete History of the Japanese Car: 1907 to the present*, Sparkford: Haynes

Schilperoord, P (2006) *Future Tech: Innovations in transportation*, London: Black Dog

Vidal, J (2008) True scale of CO_2 emissions from shipping revealed, *Guardian*, 13 February, p 1

Vorotnikov, V (2015) Baltic seaports hit by fall in vehicle and parts imports to Russia, *Automotive Logistics*, 21 April

Ward, J (2016) Trying to tie down demand, *Automotive Logistics*, 17 January

Williams, M (2015a) Tesla now in production at Tilburg for European customers, *Automotive Logistics*, 5 October

Williams, M. (2015b) Höegh takes delivery of second post-Panamax vessel, *Automotive Logistics*, 17 November

Williams, M (2016a) MAIB: Stability issues to blame for Höegh Osaka grounding, *Automotive Logistics*, 21 March

Williams, M (2016b) ERL ro-ro vessel abandoned in Bay of Biscay, *Automotive Logistics*, 27 January

Williams, M (2016c) Glovis Europe goes short-sea for Hyundai and Kia exports to Spain, *Automotive Logistics*, 22 March

Williams, M (2016d) BMW hits 2m export milestone at port of Charleston, *Automotive Logistics*, 22 March

Williams, M (2016e) Gefco supports BMW with Silk Road rail shipments, *Automotive Logistics*, 23 March

Wright, P (2016) Abandoned cargo ship *Modern Express* successfully dragged into port after rescue operation, *IBTimes* [online] www.ibtimes.co.uk/abandoned-cargo-ship-modern-express-successfully-dragged-into-port-after-rescue-operation-1541939

PART THREE
Trading regions

International freight logistics in South East Asia: The Indonesia–Malaysia–Thailand Growth Triangle (IMT-GT)

07

RUTH BANOMYONG, Thammasat University, Thailand

Introduction

The Indonesia–Malaysia–Thailand Growth Triangle (IMT-GT) is a sub-regional cooperation initiative formed in 1993 by the governments of Indonesia, Malaysia, and Thailand to accelerate economic transformation in less-developed provinces (ADB, 2008a). The private sector has played, and will continue to play, a key role in promoting economic cooperation in the IMT-GT. Since its formation, the IMT-GT has grown in geographic scope and activities to encompass more than 70 million people. It is now composed of 14 provinces in Southern Thailand, eight states of Peninsular Malaysia, and the 10 provinces of Sumatra in Indonesia.

The IMT-GT idea was initiated by the former Prime Minister of Malaysia, HE Tun Dr Mahathir Mohamad, and in 1993, the former President of Indonesia, HE Suharto, and the Prime Minister of Thailand, HE Chuan

Leekpai, also endorsed the establishment of the IMT-GT in Langkawi, Malaysia. The IMT-GT provides a sub-regional framework for accelerating economic cooperation and integration of the member states and provinces in the three countries (Banomyong, 2014). The IMT-GT promotes private-sector-led economic growth and facilitates the development of the sub-region as a whole by exploiting the underlying complementarities and comparative advantages of the member countries. To date, the IMT-GT has a geographic scope of 32 provinces and states:

- ten provinces in the island of Sumatra in Indonesia (Aceh, North Sumatra, West Sumatra, Riau, Jambi, South Sumatra, Bengkulu, Bangka-Belitung, Riau Island, Lampung);
- eight states in Peninsular Malaysia (Perlis, Kedah, Pulau Pinang, Perak, Selangor, Kelantan, Melaka, Negeri Sembilan);
- fourteen provinces in Southern Thailand (Yala, Pattani, Songkhla, Narathiwat, Satun, Trang, Phattalung, Nakhon Si Thammarat, Chumphon, Ranong, Surat Thani).

The member states and provinces in this sub-region form a natural bloc for economic cooperation given their many complementarities, geographical proximity, and close historical, cultural and linguistic ties. The extensive land area, a dynamic private sector, abundant supply of labour at a competitive price and a large internal market of more than 70 million people, plus potential markets in neighbouring sub-regions, offer a vast potential for economic development to be enhanced in this area (ADB, 2008a).

The Asian Development Bank (ADB) has been involved in the IMT-GT programme since its inception, and has been a Regional Development Partner since 2007 (ADB, 2010). The IMT-GT distinguishes itself from other regional cooperation initiatives supported by ADB in that:

- it is a grouping of sub-national entities;
- the private sector participates as an equal member;
- it has a permanent secretariat, the Centre for IMT-GT Sub-Regional Cooperation (CIMT) funded by its members;
- it focuses on fostering not only overland trade and transport, but rather a full array of multimodal freight logistics links.

The IMT-GT Road Map identified five economic corridors as key to strengthening regional infrastructure to support increased intra- and extra-regional trade, investment and tourism (IMT-GT, 2007). These are:

1 the Extended Songkhla–Penang–Medan Economic Corridor;
2 the Straits of Melaka Economic Corridor;
3 the Banda Aceh–Medan–Pekanbaru–Palembang Economic Corridor;
4 the Melaka–Dumai Economic Corridor; and
5 the Ranong–Phuket–Bandah Aceh Economic Corridor.

The economic corridor approach has been identified as a core strategy for accelerated development of the IMT-GT, and the development of these economic corridors was declared a Flagship Project of IMT-GT at the 13th Ministerial Meeting of IMT-GT in Selangor in September 2006:

> For IMT-GT, the corridor approach will (i) provide focus and serve as a catalyst to the development and growth of ancillary activities and areas within and around the economic corridors, (ii) generate investment opportunities in terms of commercial activities and infrastructure support services, (iii) achieve synergy through clustering of projects within and around the economic corridors. (IMT-GT Roadmap of Development, 2007)

However, for economic corridors to be successful as drivers of development, freight logistics capability within these corridors will need to be enhanced as in the case of the North–South Economic Corridor in the Greater Mekong Sub-region (ADB, 2007; Banomyong, 2008a). It is therefore of great importance that regional linkages among neighbouring countries are understood in the Indonesia–Malaysia–Thailand Growth Triangle (IMT-GT) in order to further support trade, enhance regional economic integration and improve freight logistics for better access into the 'global' market.

A number of major infrastructure investments are already being undertaken by IMT-GT countries and more are planned. The physical connectivity between neighbouring countries will be significantly improved upon the completion of these infrastructural investments. The improving infrastructure, coupled with expanded cross-border cooperation among the IMT-GT countries, will accelerate the process of integrating the sub-region's economic corridors into the rest of the world and the 'global' market. To reap the substantial potential benefits of integrated economic corridors, IMT-GT countries need to have a clearer understanding of the opportunities and challenges that will arise from this economic integration process. Adequate transport and communications facilities are considered major determinants of trade performance and of the costs and profitability of trading internationally (ESCAP, 2000). Efficient freight logistics corridors can play an important role in increasing the sub-region's trade competitiveness.

The main purpose of this chapter is to provide a freight logistics analysis of corridors in the IMT-GT based on empirical data gathered in the field and to propose policy recommendations to increase freight efficiency and effectiveness. The chapter will cover four issues related to freight logistics in the IMT-GT:

- IMT-GT trade flows;
- the methodology used for the freight logistics analysis;
- the description of each corridor's freight logistics capability within the IMT-GT; and
- proposed policy recommendations.

IMT-GT trade flows

The following section provides a brief description of trade patterns in the IMT-GT. The biggest problem with the available trade statistics is that countries mostly provide trade value and not trade volume (Jacyna, 2013). Another issue is the lack of specific IMT-GT trade data and trade volumes are often estimated based on the 'field' knowledge of local authorities, but these estimations are likely to be somewhat arbitrary. The island of Sumatra in Indonesia was relatively less problematic, as official statistics provide import and export volumes. However, with regard to IMT-GT trade statistics, it is difficult to acquire trade statistics specifically for trade within the sub-region. While the direction of trade can be found with relevant IMT-GT countries being included it is difficult to identify specific IMT-GT origins and destinations. Nonetheless, the available data does provide some indication of trade patterns within the sub-region itself.

Thailand–Malaysia

Thailand mostly exports agricultural products while Malaysia exports industrial goods to Thailand. Thailand exports more than it imports via Malaysia, with rubber products being the main commodity. The rubber products that are exported from Songkhla, in Southern Thailand, are loaded onto seagoing vessels in Penang (Malaysia) for their final destination. Malaysia plays an important role as a transit country for Thai export goods from the south of Thailand.

In comparison to Thai exports, Malaysian exports to Thailand are quite small in terms of value, with most goods being heavy industrial equipment utilized locally in Southern Thailand. Among the Association of Southeast Asian Nations (ASEAN) countries, Malaysia is the second-biggest trading partner for Thailand behind Singapore and has the highest ratio of border trade in terms of value compared to other neighbouring countries such as Myanmar, Lao PDR or Cambodia.

Malaysia–Indonesia (Sumatra Island)

Malaysia is an important trading partner for Sumatra Island. This is particularly true for the import of consumer products and industrial goods to Sumatra. Malaysia is the top ASEAN exporter into Sumatra but not the top destination for Sumatra's export. Barter trade between both countries is important but barter trade data is not easily available. Malaysia mostly exports general goods, some agricultural products and used goods while exports from Sumatra range from seafood to agricultural products to timber (Asia Survey and Services, 2004).

Exports from Sumatra are mostly destined for the Far East and North America. Sumatra's exports are mostly composed of mineral fuel, oil products, chemicals and fertilizers. Singapore does play a role as a transshipment platform for goods originating from or destined for Sumatra. Sumatra's export trade with other IMT-GT countries is minimal compared to its total export volume.

Thailand–Indonesia (Sumatra Island)

Direct trade between Southern Thailand and Sumatra Island is almost non-existent. There are trade flows between Thailand and Sumatra, with fertilizers being one of the main exports from Sumatra, but the data does not show the precise destination location. Import from Thailand to Sumatra is again minimal. However, this lack of data and of volume may represent an opportunity for trade as there is demand for Thai products in Sumatra and Southern Thailand does need Sumatra's traditional export commodities such as mineral fuel and fertilizers.

In the IMT-GT countries, Malaysia has substantial trade with both Thailand and Sumatra. There is quite an important flow of goods between Thailand and Malaysia. This trade is bilateral, cross-border and transit, with a number of goods from Southern Thailand utilizing Penang port as port of loading to other markets. There are also strong trade levels between Malaysia and Sumatra, with Port Klang playing an important role. However, trade between Thailand and Sumatra is not very developed, as Thailand only plays a marginal role in the island export and import trade. This trade linkage between Southern Thailand and Sumatra must be further encouraged. It is interesting to note that Malaysia's role in the IMT-GT is very central in the flow of trade within the sub-region. Thai exporters from the south of the country use Malaysia as a transit platform, while Sumatra also sees Malaysia as a very important trading partner. However, Singapore is shown to compete to a certain extent with Malaysia with regards to transit goods.

IMT-GT economic hubs can be determined based on their local economic activity as well as on export/import trade value and volume. These preliminary criteria can help in the identification of potential IMT-GT economic hubs. In Thailand, potential economic hubs for the five IMT-GT corridors, based on these criteria, are Hat Yai/Songkhla, Trang, and Phuket. In Malaysia, the potential economic hubs are Penang, Port Klang and Malacca, while in Sumatra the potential economic hubs are Bandah Aceh, Medan, Dumai, and Palembang.

Analytical framework

In order to formulate adequate and relevant IMT-GT freight logistics policies, a specific methodology is needed. The purpose of the methodology is first to describe the current freight logistics situation also known as the 'AS IS' situation within the IMT-GT and then explore possible policies that may lead to the best 'TO BE' situation (Banomyong *et al*, 2008). A national or regional logistics system scorecard is based on the four dimensions of a logistics system. These four dimensions can be utilized as a starting point in terms of a framework needed for macro-evaluation purposes. The four components of a macro-logistics system are infrastructure, institutional framework, service providers and traders, as represented in Figure 7.1.

This macro assessment is based on empirical and secondary data for the four dimensions in the IMT-GT. A number of key performance indicators have been identified to compare and contrast the logistics capability of IMT-GT member countries. The assessment provides an overall picture of IMT-GT member countries' freight logistics capability based on these four distinct dimensions. However, there is also a need to be able to analyse the logistics capability of the five proposed economic corridors, as the macro assessment cannot provide corridor-level details. This is the rationale behind the development of the freight logistics assessment framework for corridors.

Figure 7.1 Macro logistics assessment framework

```
                    ┌──────────────────┐
                    │  Infrastructure  │
                    └──────────────────┘
                           ↕
   ┌──────────────┐     ┌──────────┐     ┌──────────────┐
   │   Service    │ ↔   │ Logistics│ ↔   │ Institutional│
   │  Providers   │     │  System  │     │  Framework   │
   └──────────────┘     └──────────┘     └──────────────┘
                           ↕
                    ┌──────────────────┐
                    │Shippers/Consignees│
                    └──────────────────┘
```

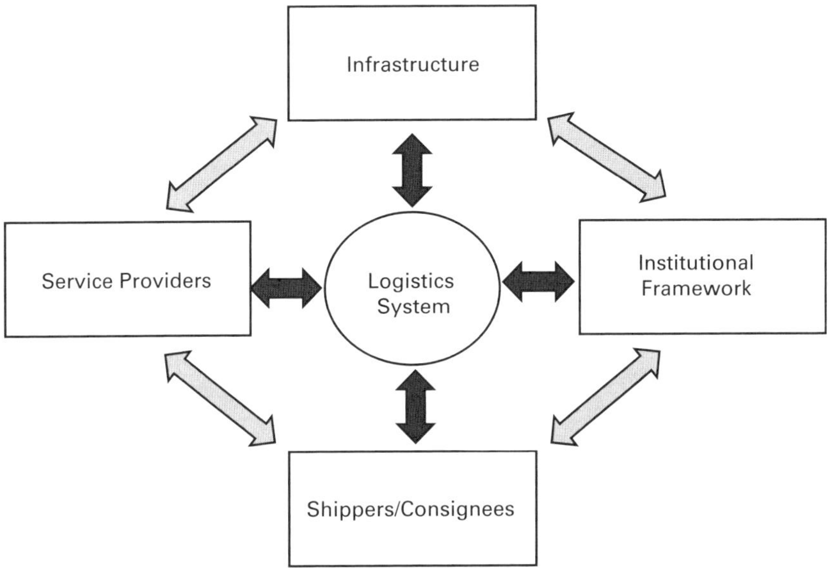

SOURCE Adapted from Banomyong (2008b)

Freight logistics assessment framework for corridors

After the chosen corridor has been assessed based on the cost and time dimension, it is then necessary to clarify the freight corridor's integration level, as shown in Table 7.1. This clarification enables policy makers to better understand the corridor they are dealing with and what should be priorities in terms of development. The objective is to reach Level 4 which is a fully fledged economic corridor, but Level 3 would be acceptable, as the corridor will be considered as a logistics corridor.

This integration level framework will be used in the assessment of the five main corridors in the IMT-GT. The different level of corridor integration will provide the basis for classification of these corridors.

The purpose of this section was to introduce an overall methodology to support the formulation of logistics development policies. The methodology is based on an in-depth understanding of the 'as is' situation of the logistics system of a country or a region. This 'as is' situation can be measured based on a macro-logistics scorecard that is based on the performance of four logistics components: (1) Shippers and Consignees; (2) Logistics Service Providers; (3) Institutional Framework; and (4) Infrastructure. However, the data for this logistics scorecard may not fully describe particular freight logistics activities within corridors. This is particularly true when data is not easily available.

Table 7.1 A typology of corridor development

Stage	Corridor	Definition
Level 1	Transport Corridor	Corridor that physically links an area or region.
Level 2	Multimodal Transport Corridor	Corridor that physically links an area or region through the integration of various modes of transport.
Level 3	Logistics Corridor	Corridor that not only physically links an area or a region but also harmonizes the corridor institutional framework to facilitate the efficient movement and storage of freight, people and related information.
Level 4	Economic Corridor	Corridor that is able to attract investment and generate economic activities along the less-developed area or region. Physical linkages and logistics facilitation must be in place in the corridor as a prerequisite.

SOURCE Author

An analysis of freight logistics in IMT-GT's corridors

The purpose of this section is twofold. The first objective is to provide an overview of the macro-logistics framework, while the second objective relates to the description of freight logistics in the five IMT-GT corridors.

Macro-logistics assessment

The macro-logistics system can be assessed based on four dimensions. However, there are still some dimensions that overlap, such as the institutional framework and the cost as well as the time related to export and import procedures. Logistics service providers operate based on the existing infrastructure (hardware) and institutional framework (software).

Infrastructure

The logistics infrastructure in the IMT-GT is considered adequate for the present volume of freight and vehicles moving along the main economic corridor, with some reservation for the Sumatra domestic corridor. However, this does not mask the reality that infrastructure in certain segments of the

IMT-GT is still lacking. Infrastructure will need to be harmonized to facilitate the movement of goods and people along the corridor (Price, 2006; Thai, 2008). Table 7.2 presents an overall assessment of the infrastructure in the IMT-GT based on existing infrastructure characteristics.

Institutional framework and shippers/consignees

The three IMT-GT countries are part of the ASEAN Economic Community (AEC) which is a regional single market and production base. It is expected that trade rules and procedures to and from the three countries should in theory not be so different. This is clearly not the case, as illustrated in these comparative tables of export and import cost of the three IMT-GT countries. The described export and import cost does not include the cost of freight.

The amount of time taken and cost involved are clearly an important burden for the shippers/consignees (Bookbinder and Tan, 2003). This directly affects their competitiveness, not only in connecting to regional IMT-GT or ASEAN markets but also to the global market. The cost and

Table 7.2 IMT-GT logistics infrastructure characteristics

	Road	Port	IWT	Airport	Railway
Malaysia	Good	Fair/Good	Fair	Good/Fair	Good
Thailand	Good/Fair	Fair	Fair	Good/Fair	Fair/Poor
Indonesia	Fair	Fair	Fair	Fair	Fair/Poor

SOURCE Author, based on stakeholders' views

Table 7.3 IMT-GT export cost and time comparison per TEU (2016)

Country	Nature of export procedure	Hours	Cost (US$)
Indonesia	Border compliance	36	250
	Documentary compliance	72	170
Indonesia export total		**108**	**420**
Malaysia	Border compliance	20	321
	Documentary compliance	10	45
Malaysia export total		**30**	**366**
Thailand	Border compliance	51	223
	Documentary compliance	11	97
Thailand export total		**62**	**330**

SOURCE Author, adapted from www.doingbusiness.org, accessed May 2016

time represented in Tables 7.3, 7.4 and 7.5 are also a reflection of complicated and cumbersome procedures as well as, in certain places, weak infrastructure (Grainger, 2007). Document preparation is the most time-consuming activity as well as the most expensive. The longer it takes, the more expensive it becomes for the shipper/consignee. This in turn affects the competitiveness of countries in the IMT-GT as well as that of the region.

Loading and unloading will usually take longer than crossing a land border per se. In fact, the Thailand–Malaysia land border crossing performance should be taken as an example, especially for imports into Thailand, of best practice in terms of efficiency and cost even though improvement is possible. Imports into Indonesia are characterized by long lead time; exports are somewhat shorter and should reduce the strong imbalance between actual transport time and non-transport activity if the study explored the traffic of the various IMT-GT corridors from an Indonesian export perspective. Countries in the IMT-GT sub-region facilitate export more than import, and that is reflected in their import procedures.

These discrepancies in trading and customs procedures between IMT-GT countries are one of the major obstacles to the integration of the sub-region. Malaysia seems to be the most open economy followed by Thailand and Indonesia. This perception is also confirmed in the analysis of the specific IMT-GT corridors, where the Malaysian context is the most conducive for trade facilitation followed by Southern Thailand and Sumatra. Harmonization and simplification is needed to enhance the integration of the sub-region.

Table 7.4 IMT-GT import cost comparison per TEU (2016)

Country	Nature of import procedure	Hours	Cost (US$)
Indonesia	Border compliance	80	384
	Documentary compliance	144	160
Indonesia import total		**224**	**544**
Malaysia	Border compliance	24	321
	Documentary compliance	10	60
Malaysia import total		**34**	**381**
Thailand	Border compliance	50	233
	Documentary compliance	4	43
Thailand import total		**54**	**276**

SOURCE Author, adapted from www.doingbusiness.org, accessed May 2016

Table 7.5 Logistics services provided in IMT-GT countries

Logistics services	Indonesia	Malaysia	Thailand
Provision of Domestic Containers	Yes	Yes	Yes
Track & Trace capability	Partial	Partial	Yes
Distribution centres	Partial	Partial	Partial
Cross-docking facilities	Yes	Partial	Partial
National booking centres	Partial	No	No
Standard Service Contract	Partial	Partial	Partial
House Bill of Lading	Yes	Yes	Partial
Multimodal Transport Document	Yes	Yes	Partial
Forwarding Industry concentration	Partial	No	No
Concentration of foreign LSPs	Yes	Partial	Partial
Trucking industry concentration	Yes	Partial	No
Truck leasing	Yes	Partial	No

SOURCE Banomyong (2008b)

Logistics service providers

Local logistics service providers in the IMT-GT are small and medium enterprises (SMEs) with limited capital and know-how. These local providers are under much competition from major courier companies as well as from local manufacturers who prefer to in-house their own logistics. Currently there are still gaps in logistical services provided within the Asia-Pacific region as a whole (Lieb, 2007).

It is interesting to note that if all the infrastructure as well as the regulatory framework was in place then there would be more entry opportunities for foreign global service providers, as local firms do not have the capital, or the networks, to compete with these global companies. The strong trait of the local service provider industry is its flexibility capability at a localized scale, which is consistent with other service providers in South East Asia (Andersson and Banomyong, 2010).

Freight logistics corridor analysis

The following section is a description of the five IMT-GT corridors based on a freight logistics perspective. The costs and times are based on quotes and estimates provided by local service providers and shippers/consignees plying their trade within the IMT-GT. These numbers and figures are solely for illustrative purposes to support intellectual discussions on IMT-GT issues and to pinpoint where the bottlenecks are.

Songkhla–Penang–Medan corridor

The Songkhla to Penang corridor is very important for Thai exporters located in the south of the kingdom. This is particularly true for those exporters who are exporting rubber-related products as well as those in the agro-industry. Exporters and manufacturers are well served by numerous local logistics service providers. Many of their local shippers/consignees are traders located in Hat Yai that export rubber and para wood via Penang in Malaysia. Not only are Thai logistics companies providing services up to Penang port but they are also acting as shipping agents for certain shipping lines based in Penang. This enables them to get access to empty containers in Penang and move them to the south of Thailand for stuffing and re-export via Penang port. Their biggest complaints are currently the high price of fuel, especially compared to Malaysian prices, and the lack of opportunities for Thais to invest and operate in Malaysia, especially in logistics-related services. The Thai excise department also forbids Thai trucks to refuel in Malaysia. There are still some minor operational problems for border crossings but many issues have been resolved. Customs facilities may need to be expanded, as peak-hour congestion is becoming an issue as delays become inevitable.

Local entrepreneurs feel that they are being left to their own devices. This is particularly true when national leaders meet and come up with grand statements, then the implementation is left to permanent government officials and business leaders from the IMT-GT countries. It takes around 1 to 1.5 hours to go from Hat Yai to Dan Nok. Both borders are used for the transit of freight but the most favoured route is currently via Dan Nok and Changloon, while the more traditional border crossing is the one at Padang Besar. According to local sources, most Thai trucks arrive at the border in the morning in order to be cleared into Malaysia in the afternoon.

In Penang, it was confirmed that traditionally, the export of Thai rubber and para wood from the south of Thailand is done via Penang port. However, their current biggest worry is competition from Port Klang in attracting the said Thai cargo. The Prai terminal is specifically dedicated to 'barter trade' with cargo to and from Sumatra and Myanmar. Wan Hai Line is currently one of the biggest movers of containers for Thai southern exporters. The demand from Southern Thailand is so strong that there is a strong imbalance, with many empty containers being carried from Penang port into Thailand for stuffing and re-export. The IMT-GT is not currently considered as a major driver of growth for local Thai businesses, as the focus is solely on the Hat Yai to Penang linkage with third countries. Cargo flows within the IMT-GT region are mostly concentrated between Southern Thailand and North Malaysia, while minimal with Sumatra. The estimate is that around 12 per cent of Penang cargo throughput originates from or is destined for the Penang area but Penang port is still congested and not well managed from the perspective of some users.

Belawan port, near Medan in Sumatra, is one of the biggest concerns. The access road to and from the port is in a poor state and cannot cope with the number of trucks. Another worrying issue is the number of overlapping agencies with jurisdiction over export and import cargo (which also depends on the type of commodity). It is not uncommon to find up to 12 overlapping agencies with jurisdiction over a particular commodity. The container terminal in Belawan caters both for domestic and international freight, and the ratio is currently estimated at 50 per cent for each. Most of the international freight is transport via Singapore, while Port Klang only represents 2 to 5 per cent. There is only one weekly feeder service between Belawan and Penang. It is interesting to note that the port operator in Belawan was unable to identify the feeder link with Penang. However, most of the direct traffic is done via small wooden boats that use the bulk (Prai) terminal. These small boats have a natural advantage, as pilotage is not compulsory for them.

There used to be many wooden vessels providing such a service but now the fleet has been greatly reduced. Most of the commodities being moved are cabbages/coffee and animal feed from Belawan to Penang, and from Penang to Belawan it is mostly consumer products, and some shallots from northern Thailand (seasonal products). There also used to be a roll-on, roll-off operator between Belawan and Penang but this now has moved to Aceh due to insufficient demand. On average, at Belawan, it takes a day to stuff or un-stuff a container at the Container Freight Station (CFS). The trucking cost between Belawan and Medan has been quoted at US $100 per TEU with an average transit time of one hour.

However, it is not unusual for the trucking time to be more than two hours between Belawan and Medan because of transportation problems such as traffic jams and the truck's own bad condition. Export and import procedures from Belawan port are still expensive and complicated, with missing documents creating delay in the process itself. The export process usually takes two to three days until the commodities can leave Belawan port and can be as expensive as US $170 per container (or US $250 if fumigation is needed). The data shown in Tables 7.3 and 7.4 is for Jakarta only so discrepancies exist with Belawan port.

The cost to actually transport a container between Belawan and Medan is less than the actual cost of processing the entry of the imported goods. The most important non-transport-related cost is the Customs licence. If the goods need to be quarantined, then non-transport-related cost can be as high as twice the transport cost. Speed money or 'tips' do not seem so high compared to all the other related costs. Import cost is usually much more expensive than export cost at an average of US $250 to $300.

Table 7.6 provides a description of the cost and time increases within the Hat Yai to Medan corridor. Strangely enough, the cost of transport by sea is higher than the cost of transport by road. This is probably due to the

Table 7.6 Cost and time data on the Hat Yai–Medan corridor

Location/Activity	Transport mode	Cost ($/tonne)	Time (hours)	Distance (km)
Hat Yai to Sadao	Road	2.25	1.5	60
Sadao • Export processing fee		1.83	0.5	N/A
Bukit Hitam • Import processing fee • Transloading		2.22 1.83	0.5	N/A
Bukit Hitam to Penang port		2.90	3.5	150
Local Malay toll fee		0.45	N/A	N/A
Penang-Prai terminal • General charge • Wharfage handling charge • Surcharge for loose cargo		0.46 1.16 0.15	6	N/A
Penang to Belawan	Sea	20.00	15	260
Belawan port • Unloading/loading • Import processing fee		2.42 4.63	8 48	
Belawan port to Medan	Road	5.55	1	11
Total		**45.85**	**85**	**481**

SOURCE Author, compiled from industry sources

limited number of sailings between Belawan and Penang port; there is only one weekly service. The cost between Penang and Belawan is even higher by over US $100/TEU than the cost between Port Klang and Belawan. This poses a dilemma, as it seems that it would be preferable to utilize the Port Klang–Belawan link instead.

It is interesting to note that the cost of border crossing represents almost 23 per cent of the door-to-door cost, while physical transport is around 67 per cent. The longest delay is at the port of Belawan due to relatively long import procedures. Border crossing time at the Thai–Malay border is seen as more seamless even though there are limitations.

The overall impression from following the Songkhla–Penang–Medan corridor is that there are two distinct levels of corridor integration. The linkages between Songkhla and Penang are quite well developed while on the other hand the links between Penang and Medan are more on a traditional basis or 'archaic'. This does not mean that there is no freight logistics linkage, it only means that the type of logistics available is a reflection of the type of trade between Penang and Sumatra. The direct linkage between Southern Thailand and Sumatra is almost non-existent or has to be done via Penang or Port Klang. Table 7.7 assesses the development level of the Hat Yai to Medan corridor and provides a description of the corridor level. This table is quite interesting as the overall assessment is only equivalent to a Level 2 corridor, which is a multimodal transport corridor. The weakest point in this corridor is the weak physical linkage between Penang and Belawan port. This seriously hinders the integration of this IMT-GT corridor, even though within each respective IMT-GT country there are domestic corridors that are at a logistics, and almost an economic, corridor development level.

Table 7.7 Hat Yai to Medan corridor development level

From	To	Level
Hat Yai	Sadao	3
Sadao	Bukit Hitam	2/3
Bukit Hitam	Penang	3/4
Penang	Belawan	2
Belawan	Medan	3
	Overall level	**2**

SOURCE Author

Trang–Satun–Perlis–Penang–Port Klang–Malacca corridor

The building of physical connectivity has been the central means for promoting closer economic and social linkages in the IMT-GT. The efforts along this particular corridor have been multimodal, with land as well as coastal linkages. The development of road and bridge networks between Thailand and Malaysia has facilitated better movement of goods and people across the border. Furthermore, supporting infrastructure such as border posts with integrated CIQs along the Thailand and Malaysia border have also been upgraded to facilitate more movement of goods and passengers. There has also been much progress in enhancing sea transport linkages between Southern Thailand and northern Malaysia. Traffic growth between Kantang port in Trang Province in Thailand and Penang port in Malaysia has averaged 37 per cent per year since Trang Province became a member of IMT-GT in 2004. Plans for new port construction and expansion will help boost regional economic growth in the southern part of Thailand.

Cross-border trade and investment flow between Southern Thailand and Malaysia has been traditionally strong, particularly in agriculture where joint ventures for commercial production have been set up to tap economic complementarities. Thailand has established an ad hoc special development zone enjoying tax holidays, freer labour mobility and nearly zero fees to enhance the investment climate in its three southernmost provinces. Kantang port has played a key role in bridging the connection between Trang Province and Penang, and in particular Penang port. This has offered a modal alternative for shippers based in Trang for access to mainline vessels in Penang. The Kantang express provides vessels of up to 160 TEU between Kantang and Penang on a twice-weekly service basis. Table 7.8 shows in detail the cost and time components of this particular corridor.

Transportation cost has a ratio of 74 per cent of the total cost, with sea transport between Kantang to Penang taking up to 45 per cent of the total transport cost. In terms of distances, sea transport is quite expensive but this is also a reflection of the limited traffic that exists between Kantang and Penang. It is true that there are more and more containers moving between both ports but there is no critical mass yet. The longest delay occurs at Kantang port in Thailand, because the port is not fully containerized and does not have all the necessary equipment for the efficient loading/unloading of containers.

The Malaysian part of this corridor mirrors the Malaysian Northern Corridor Economic Region (NCER) development project. The Malaysian Government will provide an environment conducive to economic development, by combining both physical infrastructure, such as irrigation, utilities

Table 7.8 Cost and time data between Trang and Malacca

Location/Activity	Transport mode	Cost ($/tonne)	Time (hours)	Distance (km)
Trang to Kantang port	Road	2.25	1	18
Kantang port unloading/loading		1.50	24	N/A
Thai export processing fee		1.83	0.5	N/A
Kantang to Penang	Sea	12.00	24	225
Penang port loading/unloading • General transshipment charge • Wharfage		 0.20 1.00	 6	 N/A
Import processing fee		2.22	0.5	N/A
Penang to Malacca	Road	5.40	8	420
Total		**26.40**	**64**	**663**

SOURCE Author, compiled from industry sources

and transportation, as well as soft infrastructure such as human capital, funding, incentives and an improved public service delivery system. The focus will be on improving national and regional connectivity; strengthening the utilities infrastructure to support economic growth; providing targeted, competitive incentives to encourage businesses to invest in the promoted areas; and establishing a dedicated organization to drive and coordinate the implementation. This is similar to the concepts proposed by the ADB.

Container haulage fees in Malaysia are higher than in Thailand but the operating cost may be different as the fuel price is subsidized in Malaysia, while in Thailand, fuel is based on the market prices. It is interesting to note that Malaysian truckers consider that the Thai government supports the Thai trucking industry, while the Thai truckers believe that the Malaysian government is constantly helping the Malaysian trucking industry. There is a clear lack of information and understanding on both sides of the border. Table 7.9 is an analysis of the corridor development level on the Trang to Malacca corridor. There is a high corridor development level in Southern Thailand and northern Malaysia, but the weakest link in this corridor is the Kantang to Penang sea link, which could be improved in terms of frequency and efficiency.

This does not mean that the Kantang to Penang is a 'bad' or 'weak' link. It only means that based on the existing freight volume between both ports, there is sufficient level of service but not yet enough integration to move to a higher corridor development level.

Table 7.9 Trang to Malacca corridor development level

From	To	Level
Trang	Kantang	3
Kantang	Penang	1
Penang	Malacca	3/4
	Overall level	1

SOURCE Author

Malacca–Dumai corridor

This corridor is the shortest corridor within the IMT-GT. There are no regular cargo vessels plying their trade on this particular route. However, there are some small wooden boat operators that provide some freight services. Goods from Dumai are mostly vegetables or fish, while goods from Malacca are mostly sugar, flour and other consumer products. From a logistics perspective the integration is very limited for freight activities, as there are no real major commodity flows between the locations. There is, however, a constant flow of passenger traffic between them, with at least daily ferries. Table 7.10 provides cost and time information between Malacca and Dumai.

The major activity along this corridor is the movement of people between Dumai and Malacca. Ferries operate from Port Klang, Port Dickson and Malacca in Malaysia. Table 7.11 is an analysis of the corridor development level between Malacca and Dumai. Currently there is just a physical sea linkage between both ports; there is no scheduled shipping line and the port of Malacca is not adequately equipped to handle containers.

Table 7.10 Cost and time data between Malacca and Dumai

Location/Activity	Transport mode	Cost ($/tonne)	Time (hours)	Distance (km)
Malacca port • General charge • Wharfage handling charge • Surcharge for loose cargo		0.46 1.16 0.15	6	
Malacca to Dumai port	Sea	12	6	106
Lhokseumawe port • Unloading/loading • Import processing fee		2.42 4.63	8 48	
Total		**20.82**	**68**	**106**

SOURCE Author, compiled from industry sources

Table 7.11 Malacca to Dumai corridor integration level

From	To	Level
Malacca	Dumai	1
	Overall level	**1**

SOURCE Author

Aceh–Medan–Dumai–Jambi–Palembang corridor

The Bandah Aceh to Palembang corridor is the only domestic corridor in the IMT-GT. However, this does not mean that there is actually freight moving between Bandah Aceh and Palembang. Freight flows are concentrated between Bandah Aceh and Medan; Medan is the main trading hub for the north Sumatra region. Most of the imported goods from foreign countries transit via the port of Belawan, as ports in Aceh have limited capability for containerized freight. This corridor is characterized by the poor conditions of the roads in certain areas and is in need of rehabilitation and upgrading.

The cost and time data (Table 7.12) obtained are based on quotes provided by local freight forwarders. These forwarders acknowledged that cost and time may vary depending on the commodity carried as well as the volume. These service providers were also the first to explain that there is no traffic flow between Aceh and Palembang. They stated that traffic moves over shorter distances; eg Medan to Aceh, and Dumai to Pekan Baru, which is the provincial capital of Riau province. The time data does not take into account the waiting time at each location.

Table 7.13 is an analysis of the corridor development level between Bandah Aceh and Palembang. Currently there is just a road link within this corridor. There is no railway connection and the road infrastructure in

Table 7.12 Cost and time data between Aceh and Palembang

From	To	Mode	Cost (US$)/tonne	Time (hours)	Distance (km)
Aceh	Medan	Road	53	12	627
Medan	Dumai	Road	56	11	595
Dumai	Jambi	Road	41	9	438
Jambi	Palembang	Road	30	8	317
Total			(average) 45	40	1,977

SOURCE Author: compiled from industry sources

Table 7.13 Aceh to Palembang corridor integration level

From	To	Level
Banda Aceh	Medan	3
Medan	Dumai	3
Dumai	Jambi	3
Jambi	Palembang	3
	Overall level	3

SOURCE Author

certain sections is lacking. However, since this is a domestic corridor, there is no issue related to import and export regulations. The development level of the corridor is therefore higher than that of the other international corridors but this does not mean that this is the most advanced or developed corridor. It means that there is physical linkage within the corridor as well as a common institutional framework that regulates the movement of freight.

Ranong–Phuket–Aceh corridor

This corridor is the latest economic corridor identified within the IMT-GT. Currently there are no cargo movements linking Ranong province in Thailand to Aceh in Sumatra via Phuket. However, there is interest from the private sector to provide some maritime connections between Phuket and Aceh based on barges/lighters. The maritime links are not yet settled, as Sabang port north of Aceh is positioning itself as a key transshipment hub with the support of Dublin port.

Trucking operators providing services between Ranong and Phuket are scarce, as commodity flows between both provinces are limited. The estimated current logistics cost and time details from Ranong to Phuket are shown in Table 7.14, with figures based on estimates provided by industry. Theoretically it is possible for vessels to provide services between Phuket and Sabang port but since Sabang port is currently being earmarked as a deep-sea port with investment coming in from Dublin port, it is preferable to consider the port of Lhokseumawe instead. The port of Lhokseumawe is more geared towards regional freight.

The border crossing is still one of the main bottlenecks to the integration of the Ranong to Bandah Aceh corridor. A common feature of all the international corridors is that export is easier and less time consuming than import. Table 7.15 is an analysis of the corridor development level between Ranong and Bandah Aceh. Currently there is no traffic between the

Table 7.14 Cost and time data between Ranong and Aceh

Location/Activity	Transport mode	Cost ($/tonne)	Time (hours)	Distance (km)
Ranong to Phuket (via Takaopa–Kaolak–Tublom–Kokegloy)	Road	16	4	280
Phuket port charges		2	6	
Phuket export customs		1.83	0.5	
Phuket to Aceh Province (Lhokseumawe)	Sea	14	26	315
Lhokseumawe port • Unloading/Loading • Import processing fee		2.42 4.63	8 48	
Lhokseumawe port to Banda Aceh	Road	17.35	4	205
Total		**58.23**	**96.5**	**800**

SOURCE Author, compiled from industry sources

Table 7.15 Ranong to Bandah Aceh corridor development level

From	To	Level
Ranong	Phuket	3
Phuket	Lhokseumawe	1
Lhokseumawe	Bandah Aceh	3
	Overall level	**1**

SOURCE Author

locations but it is hoped that in the future there will be. The missing link is a maritime link between Phuket and Bandah Aceh. If there is sufficient traffic, then there might be operators, but this is not the case at the present moment.

Even if there is a physical sea link between Phuket and Lhokseumawe, there is currently no traffic between the ports. This corridor is only as strong as its weakest link and its weakest link is the maritime leg. Tables 7.16 and 7.17 provide an overall summary of cost and time comparison within these five IMT-GT corridors.

From the benchmark tables, preliminary investigation indicates that direct transport cost ratios in the IMT-GT are higher than for non-transport cost activities. The case of the Aceh–Palembang corridor is somewhat of

Table 7.16 IMT-GT Cost comparison

Route	Physical transportation (%)	Non-transport activity (%)
IMT-GT: Hat Yai–Medan	67	33
IMT-GT: Trang–Malacca	74	26
IMT-GT: Malacca–Dumai	57	43
IMT-GT: Aceh–Palembang	100	0
IMT-GT: Ranong–Aceh	82	18

SOURCE Author

Table 7.17 NSEC/EWEC/IMT-GT time comparison

Route	Physical transportation (%)	Non-transport activity (%)
IMT-GT: Hat Yai–Medan	25	75
IMT-GT: Trang–Malacca	51	49
IMT-GT: Malacca–Dumai	8	92
IMT-GT: Aceh–Palembang	100	0
IMT-GT: Ranong–Aceh	35	65

SOURCE Author

an outlier as it is the only domestic corridor that is within the scope of the study. Comparatively speaking, this means that formalities and other fees are less than in the other non-IMT-GT corridors. In terms of direct transport time, the IMT-GT corridors do not seem to be very efficient. A lot more time is taken during loading/unloading, administrative and customs formalities. It must not be forgotten that one of the main characteristics of the IMT-GT corridors is that short-sea shipping is a mode of transport that depends very much on outbound and inbound port capability. It is important for the IMT-GT to have increased and enhanced cooperation. This is particularly true at border crossings when delays are the norm. Trade and transport facilitation can play a role in supporting economic growth within the sub-region. However, it is important for all member countries to gain benefits from freight logistics enhancement within each economic corridor.

Conclusion

The study of freight logistics with a view to implementing improvements is a relatively new agenda for IMT-GT integration. It is acknowledged by local stakeholders that having an efficient freight logistics system in the IMT-GT sub-region can help support existing corridors' integration and evolution into economic corridors. Infrastructure is not considered as a major issue, especially between Thailand and Malaysia, as there are already numerous projects in place. Infrastructure rehabilitation within Sumatra is still an important component of improved logistics in this area. The linkages between Sumatra and the other IMT-GT areas also need to be accelerated in order to gain the benefits from such a growth triangle.

Penang and Port Klang can play a crucial role in becoming key freight logistics platforms for the IMT-GT sub-region with its strong connection with Southern Thailand and North Sumatra. The overall observation from empirical evidence is that there are two distinct levels of integration in the IMT-GT. The linkages between Southern Thailand and North Malaysia are quite well developed and the various corridors that link both countries can be considered as Level 3 corridors, almost ready to be Level 4, with the various industrial development projects that are currently being put into place.

However, there are still specific issues that need to be resolved, in particular those related to the current existing institutional framework. Trade, transport rules and regulations should be further relaxed in order to promote efficient cross-border logistics and transportation (Banomyong and Beresford, 2001). This can be carried out by abolishing transportation quotas between Thailand and Malaysia, particularly on perishable goods, and eliminating required upload and download practices at the cross-border areas, through mutual recognition of road vehicle registration, transport operating licences, vehicle inspection certificates as well as vehicle insurance across the border.

The links between Malaysia and Sumatra are more traditional or 'archaic', as there seem to be only Level 2 corridors linking these areas. This does not mean that there is no logistics linkage, only that the type of logistics services available is a reflection of the type of trade between Malaysia and Sumatra. The specificity of 'barter trade' in Penang for trade with Myanmar or Sumatra is a good illustration. Direct linkage between Southern Thailand and Sumatra is non-existent or has to be done via Penang or Port Klang in Malaysia.

From a freight logistics perspective, the challenge will be how to increase the integration of Sumatra within the existing logistics linkages between

Thailand and Malaysia. This can only be done if intra-IMT-GT trade is supported and facilitated. It is important not to forget that freight logistics is a derived demand that supports local, border, regional and international trade. The provision of reinforcing border trade as a means to accelerate logistics integration in the IMT-GT, especially in the various border areas, should be explored. Special measures to facilitate border trade such as bilateral payment arrangement schemes should be intensively promoted, as many local traders are relying upon less-formalized means of payment.

More intra-regional investment should also be emphasized, especially at the SME level. However, most local SMEs have limited funding to participate in related IMT-GT activities and this reduces their trading opportunities with other IMT-GT partners. In fact, there is a common perception that Thailand and Malaysia gain much more than Sumatra from the IMT-GT, due to the different levels of integration between IMT-GT countries.

Activities within the IMT-GT need to foster closer public and private collaboration as well as advance the role of provincial and state governments. Coordination and support among provincial and central agencies in the IMT-GT is critical, as there are still 'gaps' in the understanding and implementation of related IMT-GT agreements. Maybe it is also a question of capacity building from governmental officials' perspectives. They need more support in order to better understand how to implement the various IMT-GT agreements. Provincial governors should not solely focus on provincial issues but must be able to have the vision of linking their provinces within the IMT-GT sub-region.

From a freight corridor perspective, there should be more institutional support for the enhanced integration of Sumatra into the IMT-GT. This enhanced integration and cooperation is important for trade between Sumatra and Malaysia but even more for trade between Sumatra and Southern Thailand. There is great potential for trade and investment but the flows are minimal and need to transit via Malaysia. Each proposed policy measure is based on specific findings and issues highlighted from the data described in this chapter. Table 7.18 shows the relationship between the proposed support policies and key IMT-GT freight logistics issues.

The lack of standardized and harmonized border and transit trade procedures in the IMT-GT, as well as weak infrastructure linkages, especially between Sumatra and the rest of the sub-region, is currently hindering the development of IMT-GT freight logistics. The purpose of enhanced freight logistics is to be able to meet customers' requirement while controlling or even lowering all costs involved. This is not the case yet in the IMT-GT.

Table 7.18 Proposed IMT-GT freight logistics policy

IMT-GT freight logistics issues	Proposed projects
Trade and Transport Facilitation	• Pilot implementation of trade and transport facilitation measures between Hat Yai and Medan • Expansion of bilateral exchange of traffic rights arrangements between Thailand and Malaysia • Promotion of inter-provincial and district cooperation and coordination mechanisms (logistics facilitation) • Establishment of mechanisms to improve coordination between and among central, provincial and border area officials
Infrastructure Development	• Improving road connections within Sumatra
Infrastructure Maintenance	• Provision of maintenance funds for roads in Sumatra
Capacity Building	• Developing logistics capacity in the IMT-GT for public and private sector
Further Development Studies	• Study on the establishment of IMT-GT logistics platforms/centres within the IMT-GT • Study on the establishment of IMT-GT logistics standard information system

SOURCE Author

Infrastructure linkages are the backbone of freight logistics development in the IMT-GT but this upgrade in infrastructure must be done in conjunction with the facilitation of trade, transit and transport services to create an effective and efficient integrated freight logistics system within the IMT-GT itself.

An integrated approach is needed in order to solve these problems (Goh and Ang, 2000). This integrated approach should combine solutions to the 'hardware' infrastructure aspect with the solutions to the 'software' rules and regulation aspect (Razzaque, 1997). Most of the problems involved in the development of freight logistics for cross-border and transit trade are related to the import/export processes of countries in the IMT-GT. Infrastructure is considered a key constraint, especially in Sumatra, but the impact may seem less important due to the relatively low volumes involved as well as a commitment by member countries to physically and institutionally link freight corridors.

This reality may be true for now but with the establishment of the ASEAN Economic Community (AEC) on 31 December 2015, the situation is starting to change and the emergence and implementation of logistics and economic corridors could be finally in place for the near future. However, the challenge remains around how to transform these freight corridors into fully-fledged economic corridors that can attract investment and generate economic activities in remote areas of the corridor such as border crossings and certain areas located far from the sub-regional economic hubs.

References

ADB (2007) *Logistics Development Study of the GMS North South Economic Corridor*, Manila, Philippines: The Asian Development Bank

ADB (2008a) *Logistics Development Study of the Indonesia–Malaysia–Thailand Growth Triangle (IMT-GT)*, Manila, Philippines: The Asian Development Bank

ADB (2008b) *The East West Economic Corridor Logistics Benchmark Study*, Manila, Philippines: The Asian Development Bank

ADB (2010) *The Greater Mekong Subregion Logistics Development Strategy*, Manila, Philippines: The Asian Development Bank

Andersson, A and Banomyong, R (2010) The implications of deregulation and liberalization on the logistics service industry in Lao PDR, *International Journal of Production Economics*, **128** (1), pp 68–76

Asia Survey and Services (2004) *A Study to Identify Barter Trade Opportunities in the IMT Development Cooperation*, unpublished report

Banomyong, R (2014) Comparing corridor development in the Greater Mekong Subregion and the Indonesia–Malaysia–Thailand Growth Triangle, in *Transnational Dynamics in Southeast Asia*, ed. N Fau, S Khonthapane and C Taillard, ISEAS, Singapore, Chapter 4, pp 84–104

Banomyong, R (2008a) Logistics development in the Greater Mekong subregion: A study of the north–south economic corridor, *Journal of Greater Mekong Subregion Development Studies*, **4**, December 2008, pp 43–58

Banomyong, R (2008b) Logistics development study of the Indonesia–Malaysia–Thailand growth triangle (IMT-GT), Centre for Logistics Research Faculty of Commerce & Accountancy Thammasat University, 71 pp, available at <http://www.imtgt.org/Documents/Studies/Logistics-Development-Study.pdf>

Banomyong, R and Beresford, A K C (2001) Multimodal transport: The case of Laotian garment exporters, *International Journal of Physical Distribution and Logistics Management*, **31** (9), pp 663–85

Banomyong, R, Cook, P and Kent, P (2008) Formulating regional logistics development policy: The case of ASEAN, *International Journal of Logistics Research & Applications*, **11** (5), pp 359–79

Bookbinder, J H and Tan, C S (2003) Comparison of Asian and European logistics system, *International Journal of Physical Distribution and Logistics Management*, **33** (1), pp 36–58

ESCAP (2000) *An Asia-Pacific Perspective for Integrating Developing Countries and Economies in Transition into the International Trading System on a Fair and Equitable Basis*, United Nations, New York

Goh, M and Ang, A (2000) Some logistics realities in Indochina, *International Journal of Physical Distribution and Logistics Management*, **30** (10), pp 887–911

Grainger, A (2007) Government actors in international supply chain operations: Assessing requirements for skills and capabilities, Logistics Research Network Conference, Hull, England

IMT-GT (2007) IMT-GT: Building a dynamic future: a roadmap for development 2007–2011, IMT-GT Secretariat and Asian Development Bank, 41 pp, available at <http://www.imtgt.org/Documents/Books/roadmap-development.pdf>

Jacyna, M (2013) Cargo flow distribution on the transportation network of the national logistic system, *International Journal of Logistics Systems and Management*, **15** (2), pp197–218

Lieb, R (2007) The year 2007 survey: Provider CEO perspectives on the current status and future prospects of the third-party logistics industry in the Asia-Pacific region, *International Journal of Physical Distribution and Logistics Management*, **38** (6), pp 495–512

Price, P M (2006) A model for logistics management in a post-Soviet Central Asian transitional economy, *Journal of Business Logistics*, **27** (2), pp 301–31

Razzaque, M A (1997) Challenges to logistics development: The case of a Third World country – Bangladesh, *International Journal of Physical Distribution and Logistics Management*, **27** (1), pp 18–38

Thai, V V (2008) Service quality in maritime transport: Conceptual model and empirical evidence, *Asia Pacific Journal of Marketing and Logistics*, **20** (4), pp 493–518

North America's evolving international freight transport: challenges and responses

08

MICHAEL IRCHA, University of New Brunswick, Canada

Introduction

With relatively sparse populations and immense distances between major urban centres, Canada and the United States depend on an efficient transportation network. The 19th century Confederation of Canada was predicated on joining several separate British colonies with an east–west transcontinental railway. This key rail link opened the country's interior to global trade by sending resources to distant coastal ports for onward shipping. Developing Canada's east–west transportation corridor continued into the 20th century with Trans-Canada Airlines (now Air Canada), the Trans-Canada Highway and the Trans-Canada pipeline. Similarly, in the United States, extensive rail networks and the inter-state highway system opened the country for settlement and trade.

North America has an integrated continental transportation network supporting significant trade between Canada, the United States and Mexico. Although the network is integrated, freight movement between each country is not as frictionless as found within the European Union. There are many impediments to the free flow of transportation in North America despite free trade agreements and other reciprocal arrangements. These impediments are usually defined as technical non-tariff barriers and include cabotage restrictions, differing regulations and border crossing friction (Brooks, 2008).

The three North American countries are each other's major trading partners. Trade dependency was reinforced with the 1965–2001 Canada–US Automotive Products Agreement (Auto-Pact), removing tariffs from vehicles and parts while guaranteeing American automobile production in Canada, the 1988 Canada–US Free Trade Agreement (FTA), phasing out trade restrictions over a ten-year period, and the subsequent 1994 North American Free Trade Agreement (NAFTA) which included Mexico and replaced the FTA.

Continental free trade generated by NAFTA has created a significant North American trading bloc. In 2014, NAFTA countries exported 13.1 per cent of the world's merchandise trade and imported 17.2 per cent (World Trade Organization, 2015). The three countries generated this significant share of world trade with only 6.6 per cent of the world's population (Worldometers, 2016).

More recently, the NAFTA countries are reaching out globally to establish numerous bilateral free trade agreements. For example, Canada has completed or is in negotiation with 53 countries, including the European Union, in the Comprehensive Economic and Trade Agreement (CETA) and the Trans-Pacific Partnership (TPP). The United States and Mexico are similarly establishing bilateral free trade agreements, including with the EU and the TPP. These agreements will inevitably lead to increased commodity flows through North American gateway ports and in their supporting trade corridors.

This chapter reviews international freight transportation in North America. International freight moves globally, generally by sea, and continentally among the three NAFTA countries primarily by land – road, rail and pipeline. Global transportation and trade trends are examined on how they affect commodity movements both within NAFTA and internationally. Given the transportation friction generated by technical non-tariff barriers, the chapter considers gateways and trade corridors, regulatory challenges and system liberalization. The chapter concludes by considering the 2016 Canada Transportation Act Review's recommendations to improve Canadian and North American international freight transportation.

Integrated global transportation

Maritime trade underpins the global economy. Today, ships carry almost four-fifths of the world's merchandise trade by volume and 70 per cent by value (Premti, 2016). Seaports play a key role in transferring trade goods to and from ships to landside intermodal carriers. North America is fortunate in having many deep-water, natural ports around its many coastlines, coupled with the world's longest marine corridor, the Great Lakes and St Lawrence River, serving the continent's industrial heartland. International trade development depends on efficient intermodal transportation to move landed goods and material to inland destinations. North America's integrated transportation network provides efficient equipment and infrastructure to support NAFTA's international freight movement requirements.

International freight transportation is forecast to continue growing. In its October 2014 Global Economy Watch, PwC predicted that the world's Gross Domestic Product (GDP) will grow at an annual rate of about 3.2 per cent through to 2030 (Boxshall *et al*, 2014). World seaborne trade is expected to almost double from 10 billion tonnes in 2014 to 19–24 billion by 2030. Global population will also increase by over 1 billion in the same period, generating additional trade growth (QinetiQ *et al*, 2013). By 2030, the US population is forecast to grow by 38 million, while Canada expects an additional 5.6 million people (United States Census Bureau, 2015; Statistics Canada, 2015a).

Increasingly, national economies have gone global as private firms and industries seek international sources for inexpensive raw materials and lower-cost manufacturing opportunities. The 'container revolution' underpinned global economic growth. The rapid rise of containerized shipping over the past several decades led to incredible reductions in international freight rates which in turn fuelled the growth of the global economy, making 'the world smaller and the world economy bigger' (Levinson, 2006). For example, today, shipping goods is so inexpensive that it makes financial sense to send Scottish cod to China for filleting and then ship it back to Scotland for retail sale rather than pay Scottish fish workers (George, 2013). Complementing the rapid rise of international trade in high-value containerized commodities has been the growth of shipping raw materials and resources in support of the global distribution of manufacturing operations.

Many larger North American container ports are distribution hubs. For example, retail distribution centres have been established in various locations along the coasts to ensure continuity of continental logistics supply chains. Shippers want to ensure their imported commodities continue to be shipped despite occasional disruptions caused by labour strife in specific ports or natural and man-made calamities. The World Bank has recognized each country's relatively high level of logistics performance. In 2014, the World Bank's Logistics Performance Index ranked the United States 9th in the world, Canada 12th and Mexico 50th (World Bank, 2015).

International freight transport in North America depends on foreign flag vessels, due to high labour costs and restrictive national regulations. For example, Canadian ship owners involved in international shipping activities prefer foreign registries for their ships. In 2015, the Canadian fleet had 64.6 per cent by dead weight tonnes (dwt) registered under a foreign flag. The use of foreign flag registries in the US fleet was higher, at 85.5 per cent (UNCTAD, 2015). The remainder of the Canadian and US fleets were used for restricted domestic marine trade. Foreign flag vessels are able to operate in each of the three NAFTA countries provided they conform to national cabotage regulations. These vessels cannot carry cargoes from one domestic port to another; all moves must be international. This generally results in a single port call per country schedule. More than one port call requires inefficient ballast legs where the ship remains empty or partly empty travelling between domestic ports.

Ships travel on well-defined international sea routes. Today, traditional maritime routes are subject to change as the Panama Canal has been expanded to carry larger vessels, a considerably larger canal is being proposed through Nicaragua and the Suez Canal has been widened. These changes will inevitably affect sea routes and ports as shipping lines seek to shorten travel distances. For example, many US East Coast ports have invested considerable capital in dredging and modern cargo-handling facilities to serve the larger ships that are expected to traverse the expanded Panama Canal (Atkins, 2016).

As trade has grown, so have ships. Indeed, the increasing size of ships and their growing specialization continue to challenge ports and landside intermodal transportation in efficiently serving these behemoths. For example, container ships have grown to gigantic proportions, carrying up to almost 20,000 TEUs (twenty-foot equivalent container units). These Ultra-Large Container Vessels (ULCVs) are bigger than aircraft carriers. Their increased length, beam and draught limit their ability to service many of the world's ports (eg *MSC Oscar*: length 395.4 m; beam 59 m; draught 16 m). To continue to handle ULCCs, major hub container ports are being forced to dredge deeper, raise bridge heights, acquire new, higher and longer outreach quayside gantry cranes, and increase the size of container yards to store increased throughput generated by them. Their arrival at a container terminal causes a 'spike' in container handling activities. In many cases, this has led to increased traffic congestion on urban streets, as more trucks are used to handle the peak flow. Railways have to be able to supply additional container railcars (typically double-stack in Canada and the United States) to deal with the peak load.

Today's ULCVs are too large to traverse even the expanded Panama Canal, where the largest container ships are expected to carry about 13,000 TEU. At the moment, this is not a concern as ULCVs have been designed primarily for the Asia–Europe route as North American ports are not yet equipped to handle them efficiently. Despite this, some ULCVs will be deployed on the Pacific routes to North American ports. Recently, CMA CGM's *Benjamin Franklin*, an 18,000 TEU vessel, called at Los Angeles and Oakland to test the ports' readiness to handle larger ships (Meyer, 2016). The success of the test voyages led the shipping line determined to use ULCVs in its Pacific schedule (Drewry, 2016). The introduction of ULCVs into the world's container fleet has led to cascading older large 10,000 TEU container ships into other routes, in turn leading to further capital investment requirements in medium-sized ports.

The growth in container ship size reflects the continued quest by shipping lines for economies of scale. The larger the vessel, the lower the unit cost of transporting each container. Unfortunately, the world's container fleet expansion with larger vessels has come at a time of global economic slowdown. This has led to surplus shipping capacity with the resultant lower freight rates and significant financial challenges for shipping lines.

This same trend towards larger and more specialized ships occurred in the bulk trades, leading again to current overcapacity with economic slowdown and lower freight rates. For example, the Baltic Dry Index, a measure of the price of moving raw material by sea on bulk carriers, recently declined to a historic low, reflecting both the lower bulk shipping freight rates and excess tonnage capacity (Saul, 2016).

Continental international transportation

Despite the significant role of marine transport in carrying goods globally, on the North American continent land modes predominate in moving cargo across the extensive US land borders. For example, in 2013 Canada's international trade by value both globally and continentally included: road 43.6 per cent; marine 21.7 per cent; rail 12.4 per cent; air 11.8 per cent; and other (primarily pipeline) 10.5 per cent (IBI Group, 2015).

North American countries are major trading nations. In particular, Canada and Mexico are highly dependent on international trade. In 2014, Mexico and Canada were the fourth and fifth largest exporters in the G20, with exports amounting to 32 per cent of each country's GDP. While US exports represent a smaller proportion of GDP (13 per cent), the total amount of the country's exports dwarfs those of the other two NAFTA nations (World Bank, 2016). Manufactured exports predominate in Mexico's international exports (75 per cent) and are major components of exports from the United States (71 per cent) and Canada (45 per cent). Canada predominates with the export of resources such as fuels and minerals (33 per cent) and agricultural products (14 per cent), with Mexico and the United States shipping proportionately less (World Trade Organization, 2014a).

Given North America's extensive landmass, transportation has a major economic role. In Canada, commercial transportation services amount to 4.2 per cent of GDP, compared to 2.5 per cent in the United States (Statistics Canada, 2015b; US Department of Transportation, 2015). Given the extent of trade among the three NAFTA countries, it is not surprising that land transportation predominates. As shown in Table 8.1, the majority of international freight by value between Canada, the United States and Mexico is carried by truck and rail rather than by air or marine.

As shown in Table 8.2, in 2013, Canadian exports to the United States amounted to 75 per cent of total international exports. Canadian exports to the third NAFTA country, Mexico, were a mere one per cent. Canada

Table 8.1 NAFTA trade by mode of transport 2014

Mode	Canada–US By value (%)	Canada–US By weight (%)	US–Mexico By value (%)	US–Mexico By weight (%)	Canada–Mexico By value (%)	Canada–Mexico By weight (%)
Road	62	31	69	25	69	29
Rail	18	18	13	15	17	17
Air	6	1	4	0	8	2
Marine	3	18	12	60	65	45
Pipeline and other	11	32	1	0	0	7
Total NAFTA	60	71	38	27	2	2

SOURCE Based on Brooks (2008)

Table 8.2 North American international trade 2013

| Major export trading partners (percentage of total exports) |||||||
From\To	Canada	US	Mexico	European Union	China & Japan	Rest of the world
Canada		75	1	7	7	10
US	19		14	17	12	38
Mexico	3	80		5	2	10

| Major import trading partners (percentage of total imports) |||||||
To\From	Canada	US	Mexico	European Union	China & Japan	Rest of the world
Canada		51	6	11	14	18
US	20		12	17	26	25
Mexico	3	49		9	21	18

SOURCE Based on World Trade Organization (2013); World's Richest Countries (2015)

was the major destination for US exports, with 19 per cent heading north. Mexico was a close second, capturing 14 per cent of total US exports. In 2013, Canada imported more than half of its goods from the United States (51 per cent), 6 per cent from Mexico and 14 per cent from China and Japan. The United States received most of its imported goods from China and Japan (26 per cent), with Canada second at 20 per cent. Similar to Canada, Mexico received almost half of its imports from the United States (49 per cent) and a significant amount from China and Japan (21 per cent).

Table 8.2 reflects the significance of continental international trade in North America. In the case of Canada and Mexico, most international freight transportation is continental rather than offshore. In Canada's case, imports and exports to the United States and Mexico amount to almost 67 per cent of total trade, while Mexico's NAFTA imports and exports are about 68 per cent of total trade. US NAFTA trade is about half that of its continental partners at 33 per cent of total trade. Offshore international freight transportation is very significant for the United States. Indeed, from a global perspective, in 2014, NAFTA's international merchandise trade was more than 20 per cent of the world total with the United States handling 16 per cent, Canada 2.6 per cent and Mexico 2.2 per cent (World Trade Organization, 2014b).

Canada's gateways and trade corridors

The 1994 North American Free Trade Agreement (NAFTA) impacted Canada's traditional east–west international trade corridor by redirecting a significant portion of the country's international trade north–south into the United States. By 2014, predominant north–south intermodal railway traffic accounted for more than 27 per cent of total Canadian rail car movements (RAC, 2015). CN's railway acquisitions reflected this north–south shift, providing access through the central United States to the Gulf Coast and northern Mexico. CP Rail followed suit with similar northern US railroad acquisitions.

NAFTA's north–south trade orientation led many trade-oriented groups in Canada and the United States to support designating continental trade corridors for international freight transport. As a result, governments at all levels focused on trade corridors by encouraging significant public and private investment in transportation infrastructure and related economic development to facilitate international trade and stimulate economic growth. Many proposed north–south trade corridors linked US Interstate Highways with their Canadian counterparts. In 1991, the United States envisioned an integrated system of superhighways supported by the Intermodal Surface Transportation Efficiency Act (ISTEA). However, politics soon intervened, with congressional members adding their favoured routes to designated high-priority corridors in subsequent legislation such that these corridors now cross the country in a maze of routings in all directions. Other than some improvements to selected border crossings, little has been achieved. A coherent, rational integrated North American highway system has yet to be realized (Blank, 2008).

In Canada, trade corridor development benefited from its major trade routes lying east–west across the country, supplemented by NAFTA's north–south orientation in the continental heartland. Canada's traditional east–west corridor serves most of the country's population that lives in a linear band within 200 kilometres of the US border. As shown in Figure 8.1, Canada has unidirectional east–west trade routes while the United States has a multi-directional road and rail network with potential trade corridors branching in many directions.

Over the past several decades, efficient and low-cost transportation enabled Canadian trade to become increasingly international through sourcing and manufacturing components and products in lower-cost countries, particularly in Asia. Such economic globalization led Canadian trade

Figure 8.1 Main North American trade corridors, gateways and inland freight clusters

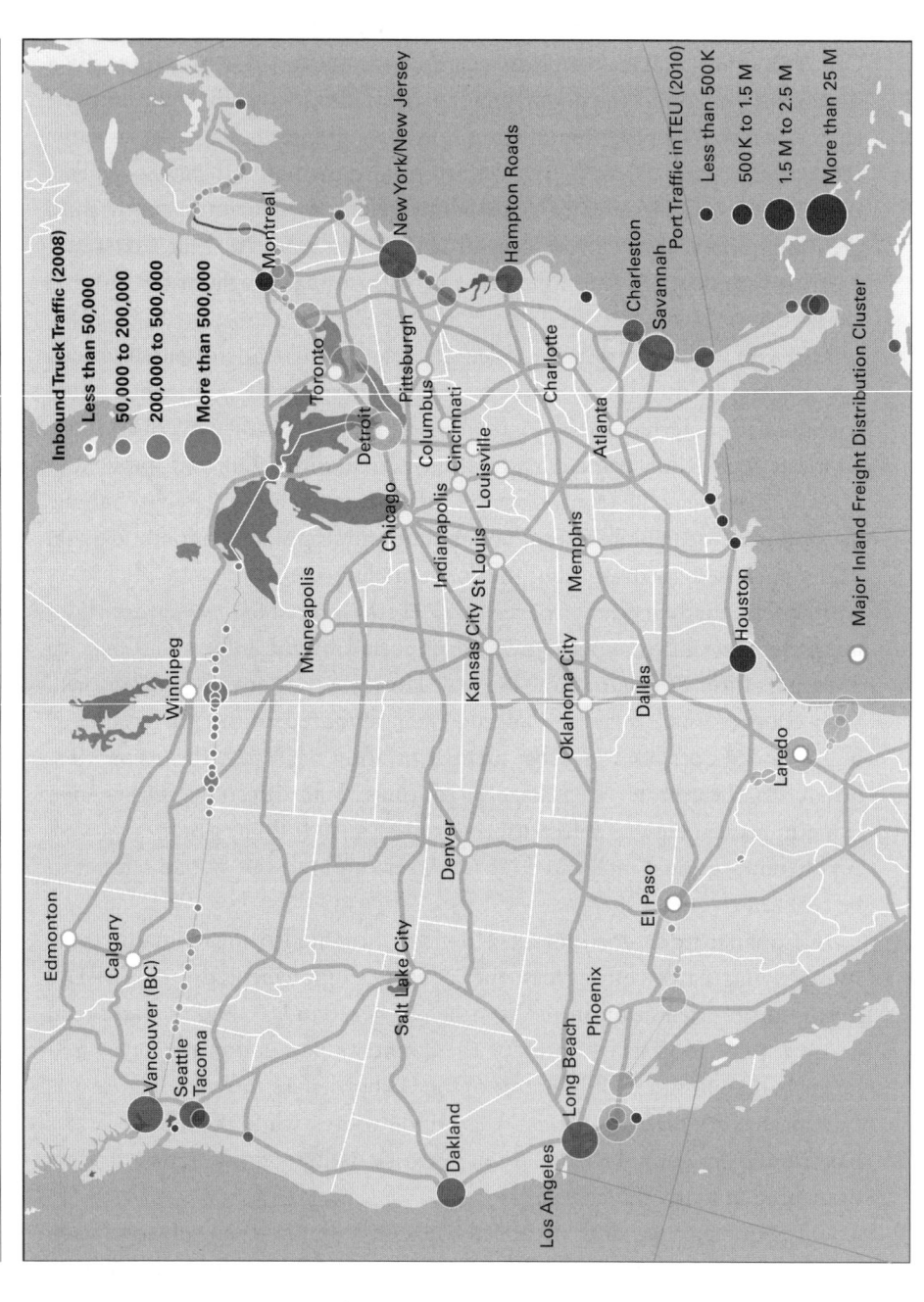

Source Rodrigue et al (2013)

Figure 8.2 Canada's Gateways: aligning transport and international trade

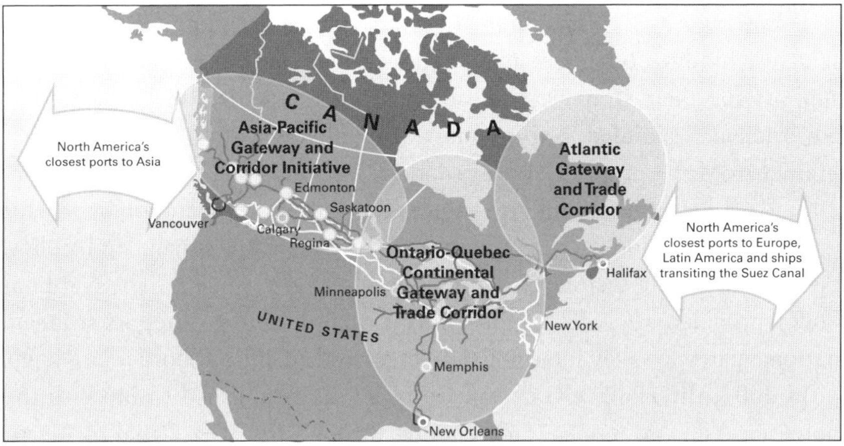

[Map showing Canada's gateways: North America's closest ports to Asia (Vancouver); Asia-Pacific Gateway and Corridor Initiative (Edmonton, Saskatoon, Calgary, Regina); Ontario-Quebec Continental Gateway and Trade Corridor (Minneapolis); Atlantic Gateway and Trade Corridor (Halifax); North America's closest ports to Europe, Latin America and ships transiting the Suez Canal; New York, Memphis, New Orleans]

SOURCE Canada's Gateways (2016)

corridor proponents to designate major ports as key 'gateways' connecting the corridors to the global marketplace (Figure 8.2).

In Western Canada, a coalition of private and public sector transportation interests collaborated to establish the Vancouver Gateway Council in 1994. Its aim was to rationalize transportation infrastructure services and investments to meet growing Asian trade demands. This coalition evolved into Canada's first successful trade corridor and gateway when the federal government launched the Asia-Pacific Gateway and Corridor Initiative (APGCI) in October 2006. A key factor in the federal government's support for the APGCI 'was the extent to which a stakeholder-driven consensus had taken shape over a number of years' (Transport Canada, 2007: 12). APGCI's aim was to reduce congestion and ease the flow of goods in and out of the major Canadian ports of Vancouver and Prince Rupert. Together with its public and private sector partners, the Government of Canada invested approximately CA $1.4 billion to support a wide range of public and private sector projects valued in total at CA $3.5 billion to enhance the reliability, efficiency and competitiveness of the transportation system. The APGCI focus on relieving logistics bottlenecks led to rail/highway crossing grade separations, road and bridge widening, terminal expansions, and short sea shipping (Transport Canada, 2015). As part of APGCI's rationalization strategy, in 2008 the federal government amalgamated three Vancouver-area port authorities (Vancouver, Fraser River and North Fraser River) into one unit, now known as Port Metro Vancouver

(Houston, 2008). Amalgamation was aimed at making effective and efficient use of Vancouver's port resources on land and water.

Following APGCI's success in attracting substantial transportation infrastructure funding, other Canadian regions sought similar public and private support for their strategic gateways and corridors. In 2007, the federal government responded to this countrywide interest with a National Policy Framework for Strategic Gateways and Trade Corridors (Transport Canada, 2007: 1). A key criterion for government support was: 'integration on several levels – across modes of transportation, between investment and policy, public and private sectors, and among levels of government.' The National Policy provided a CA $2.1 billion infrastructure fund to support strategic national gateways, key intermodal linkages and significant border crossings.

In 2004, the Halifax Gateway Council was established to tap into the potential Asian container trade coming through the Suez Canal to North America's East Coast. Subsequently, the Halifax Gateway Council was broadened into the Atlantic Gateway. A 2007 federal–provincial memorandum of understanding (MOU) led to the Atlantic Gateway and Trade Corridor. In the same year, a similar MOU established the Ontario–Quebec Continental Gateway and Trade Corridor, including major St Lawrence and Great Lakes ports. The Continental Gateway's focus was integrating the region's strategic ports, marine corridors and road and rail infrastructure with Canada's other two gateways and corridors. Montreal has positioned itself for significant growth in container throughput as part of the Continental Gateway strategy (Szakonyi, 2015).

Essentially, Canada's gateway and trade corridor strategies focused on multimodal transportation and served as a basis for effective international marketing and promotion of their regions' logistics performance and geographic advantages. As pointed out in the 2015 Canada Transportation Act Review report: 'Collectively the three strategies represented a significant effort to strengthen Canada's competitiveness in global trade... They all had a prominent focus on the inflow of containerized goods' (CTARC, 2015:38). Although the current gateway and trade corridor strategies deal with container imports, subsequent corridor renewal will need to consider bulk and container exports. The overlapping boundaries of Canada's three major transportation corridors with their north–south rail and road connections to the United States reflect an emerging, dual-pronged, national and international transportation strategy (Ircha, 2011).

Canada's approach to the promotion of trade corridors and gateways encourages enhanced integration, collaboration and cooperation in infrastructure investments by private and public partners. Private sector transportation operators, terminal managers and their clients are key to setting priorities for essential transportation infrastructure to overcome bottlenecks and expedite service. As Transport Canada pointed out: 'A key factor in gaining knowledge and gathering relevant information is consultation and collaboration with the private sector – owners, operators and users of the transportation system in Canada' (Transport Canada, 2012).

Regulatory challenges

Many challenges face North America's continental transportation system, including differing rules, regulations, and taxation regimes among Canada's provinces and US states. Canada, the United States and Mexico are federal governments with transportation regulatory authority divided between the federal and provincial/state governments in a variety of ways. For example, Canada's repatriated Constitution Act of 1982 assigns the federal and provincial governments with specific powers allocated to each level. Similar divisions of power apply in the United States and Mexico. Sections 91 (federal jurisdiction) and 92 (provincial jurisdiction) in Canada's Constitution Act list each government's ability to enact legislation. From a transportation perspective, the Canadian government has jurisdiction over inter-provincial and international activities such as air travel, marine shipping and ports, border crossings, national railways, inter-provincial trade and support for the National Highway system. On the other hand, provinces have jurisdiction over intra-provincial transportation including highways and short-line railways. To add to this jurisdictional mix, municipalities along with private operators, shippers and other users have varied interests in freight transportation. Similar jurisdictional transportation differences arise in the United States and Mexico as federal institutions.

Since Canada's Confederation in 1867, provincial transportation initiatives have varied across the country, leading to a myriad of differing standards, rules, regulations and fiscal regimes. Canadian provinces have different truck weights and dimensions, varied taxes on cross-province trucking and rail movements, and subsidy levels (such as assessment rules on property tax). The United States has a similar mix of state transportation rules, regulations and fiscal regimes. In transporting goods internationally, inter-provincially and inter-state, trucking firms must meet the lowest set of standards for the route. This reduces efficiencies in optimizing truck haul volumes and weights.

To further complicate matters, Canada's federal government handles its transportation systems differently from the United States. For example, on the marine side, Canadian Port Authorities (CPA) are required to contribute an annual stipend to the federal government based on their gross revenues along with the payment of property taxes to their host municipalities. In the United States, port authorities either pay little tax or have taxing authority to generate tax revenues from their host municipalities. US ports can raise capital funds by issuing tax-exempt revenue bonds while Canadian ports are expected to borrow capital funds from private financial institutions and were initially prohibited from accessing federal funding (Ircha, 2001a). Amendments to the Canada Marine Act in 2007 allowed CPAs to seek federal funds for specific capital needs related to infrastructure, security and environmental sustainability. Despite this renewed funding source, the CPAs' financial flexibility is still a long way from the broad-based fundraising abilities of their competing US counterparts.

A major problem stemming from Canada's divided jurisdiction is the lack of a cohesive approach to multimodal transport. Provincial governments, with their key transportation responsibility being roads and highways, tend to give short shrift to the needs of other transport modes (as these are considered to be federal concerns) (McMillan, 2006). Over time these challenges are beginning to be tackled. The Council of Ministers and Deputy Ministers Responsible for Transportation and Highway Safety has considered multi-jurisdictional issues aimed at achieving a rational, national approach. For example, the Council encouraged the collaboration and coordination of the many players and jurisdictions in the national system in their *Vision for Transportation in Canada* (Council of Ministers of Transportation, 2013). The Council also has a long-standing Task Force on Vehicle Weights and Dimensions Policy. A recent output of this Task Force is *Harmonization of Transportation Policies and Regulations: Context, progress and initiatives in the motor carrier sector* (Council of Ministers of Transportation, 2008).

Beyond the border

Canada and the United States have had a lengthy history of joint cross-border cooperation and collaboration. These include the longstanding 1909 International Joint Commission managing boundary waters, the joint development and management of the St Lawrence Seaway, North American Aerospace Defense Command (NORAD) and so forth. The terrorist attack on the World Trade Center towers in New York in 2001 led to a 'thickening' of the US borders for security reasons. In turn, increased security generated further border friction for commercial carriers, leading to longer wait times for customs and immigration clearance.

In order to begin 'thinning' the Canada–US border, in 2011 President Obama and Prime Minister Harper issued *Beyond the Border: A shared vision for perimeter security and economic competitiveness (BYB)*. The aim of the BYB, as it became known, was to 'enhance our security and accelerate the legitimate flow of people, goods and services' (Canada's Economic Action Plan, 2015). Among other goals, the BYB initiative also focused on security, trade facilitation and economic growth. In addition, the BYB created a Canada–US Regulatory Cooperation Council to better align the two countries' regulatory approaches.

The BYB led to increased cooperation and harmonization between the US Customs and Border Protection and Canada Border Services Agency, including steps to speed legitimate international shipments across the border. A key step was the introduction of an integrated cargo security strategy through a harmonized approach to screening and clearing imported international cargo. The aim was to increase security at the continent's perimeter and reduce the level of re-examination of imported containers crossing the US–Canada border – 'cleared once, accepted twice'. Pilot projects were initiated at the ports of Prince Rupert on the West Coast and Montreal in the St Lawrence, where CBSA conducted examinations on US-bound containers on behalf of the US CBP. The success of these pilot projects is expected to lead to improved border clearance procedures. The BYB led to several other successful initiatives including tamper-evident technology for container seals, standardizing regulations on wood packaging materials, harmonized trusted trader programmes and electronic single window data transfer initiatives (Stolarik, 2014).

Cabotage

Despite the extraordinary international cooperation between Canada and the United States, non-tariff frictions remain, such as cabotage. This is normally used by nation states to protect their domestic coastal trade for their own domestic carriers. For example, in Canada and the United States, short sea shipping is restricted to a national flagged vessel if more than one domestic port is being served. In other words, a Canadian flag vessel is required if cargo is being carried from one domestic port to another.

North American cabotage applies in varying degrees in the air, land and marine modes. In the air mode, Canada and the United States reached an 'Open Skies' agreement in 2005. This agreement extended fifth freedom rights to Canadian and US cargo and passenger carriers and seventh freedom rights to all-cargo services (Brooks, 2008). Fifth freedom includes the right to fly between two foreign countries on a flight originating or ending in one's own country, while seventh freedom is the right to fly between two foreign countries while not offering flights to one's own country (ICAO, 2005). Although these freedoms liberalized the air mode, they do not include full open skies as would be found under broadest ninth freedom rights.

North American land modes including trucking and rail also face cabotage restrictions. The NAFTA did not alter cabotage restrictions but did open national markets for international point-to-point traffic. This means a Canadian truck can transport cargo to a US destination and then carry a back-haul load. International truckers are also permitted 'incidental haulage' in moving their empty trailers from one domestic site to another, but cannot haul cargo within the other country. Reciprocal cabotage restrictions in Canada and the United States led trucking firms to arrange triangular routes, such as shipping goods from Canada's Atlantic provinces to a US destination, picking up back-haul cargo from the US to Ontario or Quebec, and then transporting Canadian cargo to their point of origin (Brooks, 2008).

Canada–US cabotage in the rail environment is less restrictive by providing entry and exit through various border crossings, routing freedom and greater flexibility in accessing cargo. However, immigration restrictions still apply with regards to rail crew changes at or near the border. Following earlier railway deregulation both in the United States and Canada, Canada's two national rail lines, CN and CP have made significant inroads into the United States through the acquisitions and bilateral agreements with American rail companies. US rail companies have not taken similar steps in acquiring Canadian railways (Brooks, 2008).

Cabotage restrictions in the marine mode hampered the development of international short sea shipping in North America. Unlike the European Union's extensive use of short sea shipping for goods transport, NAFTA did not remove marine cabotage in North America. In particular, during the NAFTA negotiations and subsequent bilateral discussions, US marine interests strongly lobbied against any relaxation of marine cabotage.

In the United States, the 'Jones Act' (Merchant Marine Act of 1920) restricts the movement of cargo and passengers between two American ports to ships that are US flagged, US owned and crewed by US citizens or permanent residents. Similarly, Canada's Coasting Trade Act of 1992 restricts cargo movement between any two Canadian ports to ships that are Canadian flagged, owned and crewed. In the Canadian case, a temporary Coasting Trade licence can be used to allow the entry of foreign-flagged vessels into the cabotage-protected trades if there is no Canadian-flagged ship suitable or available. There is no equivalent licence available in the US coastal trades. Cabotage restrictions are intended to protect national marine commerce as well as other safety, security and defence objectives. However, given the high level of cooperation and collaboration between Canada and the United States, there seems to be little need for cabotage restrictions for security reasons.

Short sea shipping

In 2003, Canada, the United States and Mexico signed a Memorandum of Cooperation on Sharing Short Sea Shipping Information and Experience to support the development of short sea shipping services as a means of shifting land transport to the marine mode (Brooks and Frost, 2004). The three governments recommitted their support of short sea shipping in a Vancouver Declaration in 2006. Developing an effective bi-national short sea shipping regime by eliminating cabotage requirements would help to reduce highway congestion, lower greenhouse gas emissions and other environmental pollutants and support container transshipment from major hub ports to feeder ports and the Great Lakes.

Short sea shipping has never really been well developed in North America. Flying a Canadian or US flag means considerably higher shipping costs. For example, a Canadian ship must carry crews holding Canadian certificates that are limited to Canadian citizens and permanent residents. Ships must be built in Canada or, if built offshore, be refitted to meet higher and more costly Canadian safety standards. US cabotage restrictions under the 'Jones Act' are even more onerous. Vessels serving more than one US port must be built in the United States and be crewed and owned by American citizens with no provision for bringing foreign-built or foreign-crewed ships into the US domestic trade. At an operational level, both Canadian and US seafarers are also expensive to employ.

The NAFTA and its predecessor, the FTA, failed to include provisions for the elimination or relaxation of cabotage provisions. Under NAFTA, Canada and Mexico liberalized cabotage rules with each other, but the United States choose to remain outside this arrangement. Cabotage hampers the development of a short sea shipping regime in the Great Lakes and North American coasts. For example, it is unlikely that an international operator would mount a one-port-per-country short sea shuttle service in the St Lawrence and Great Lakes system competitively with existing overland intermodal services.

Examples of North American short sea shipping do however exist. Oceanex's successful short sea service to Newfoundland from Montreal and Halifax has been in place for many years. Oceanex operates Canadian-flagged ships and provides transshipment services for domestic and international containers and trailers. Similarly, US flag carriers provide short sea shipping from the mainland to Puerto Rico, Hawaii and Alaska.

From a Canadian perspective, there are two significant impediments to developing a viable international short sea shipping regime: US cabotage restrictions embodied in the Merchant Marine Act of 1920 (Jones Act) and the application of the US Harbor Maintenance Tax (HMT) on imported cargo, including Canadian. Given the fierce resistance of US shipping lines to any relaxation of the Jones Act, it is doubtful cabotage changes will occur in the foreseeable future. For example, Senator John McCain has led a persistent but unsuccessful challenge to the Jones Act in recent years (Schuler, 2016). The HMT also serves as an impediment as cross-lake short sea shipping services would compete with trucks. The latter operate year-round, while shipping is curtailed by ice in winter months. Further, inbound trucked commodities do not pay HMT while shipped cargoes do. An extreme example of HMT's disincentive is the Detroit–Windsor Truck Ferry. It is normally fully loaded on the Detroit–Windsor run but empty on the return. This imbalance occurs despite the long wait time trucks experience at the Ambassador Bridge crossing into the United States (Edmonson, 2005).

Liberalizing the transportation system

North American transportation systems, particularly air and rail, have been undergoing a steady evolution of deregulation and movement towards commercialization and privatization.

On the airside, Canada, the United States and Mexico have entered into an open skies agreement permitting origin and destination flights between countries. In 2005, the United States and Canada reached an open skies agreement to further liberalize services (but not fully open skies such as the removal of cabotage restrictions). A 2005 article in *Airports* claimed the agreement 'largely opened up routes between Canada and the US but fell short of liberalizing express cargo services' (*Airports*, 2005). The volume of Canadian and Mexican air cargo is considerably less than in the United States. However, as pointed out by Brooks (2008), 'The Air cargo industry in North America is more mature in comparison to elsewhere in the world. As a result, the major players in North America have well-established networks…'.

There has also been ongoing airport liberalization in Canada and the United States. In the Canadian context, the devolution of airports from Transport Canada to non-profit locally based corporations began in the mid-1980s with the establishment of Local Airport Authorities (LAA) in Canada's major airports of Vancouver, Edmonton, Toronto and Montreal. The experience gained from the LAA model led a modified liberalization approach in the mid-1990s with the establishment of the National Airports System (NAS). The NAS shifted airport operations from Transport Canada to local authorities, leaving the federal government with a regulatory role. This major shift resulted from the federal government's quest to reduce annual budget deficits by reducing programmes and cutting staff.

The NAS comprises the four LAAs and a further 22 significant airports across the country as Canadian Airport Authorities (CAA). All other smaller airports were devolved to municipal or private operators. The airport devolution has been successful, as passenger and cargo throughput traffic has grown as LAAs and CAAs have invested in significant capital enhancements to their terminals and airside facilities as well as marketing and promoting airports seeking additional flights and services. Earlier, Canada had privatized its national air carrier, Air Canada in 1989.

North American rail liberalization initially emerged in the United States with the passage of the Staggers Act in 1980. This Act 'represented a significant withdrawal of federal involvement in the United States rail governance and an increase in market liberalization' (Davis, 2016). Canada followed suit, taking deregulatory steps with respect to its railways. A major step was fully privatizing Canadian National Railway in 1995 with the sale of this federal asset to financial underwriters for CA $2.2 billion. At the time, this was the largest initial public offering (IPO) in Canada's history (Bruce, 1997). Canada now has two private national railways, CN and CP, with both operating across the country and into the United States. The Association of American Railroads classifies CN and CP within the top nine North American railroads (Association of American Railroads, 2014).

On the marine side, Canadian ports were also liberalized to a degree in the mid-1990s under the federal government's deficit-cutting agenda. The Canada Marine Act of 1998 established a National Ports System comprising 18 Canada Port Authorities (CPA). The CPAs were established as commercialized semi-independent federal agencies with a mandate to promote and support Canada's international and domestic marine trade. Canada's major ports actively compete with each other and with their US counterparts for commodity throughput. In the US, ports are not federal but rather they come under the jurisdiction of state or municipal authorities (with the notable exception of the bi-state Port Authority of New York–New Jersey). Despite liberalization initiatives, Canadian and US ports function more as public enterprises than private operations (Ircha, 2001b).

Private operation has always been the approach taken in the North American trucking industry. Governments, typically at the state or provincial level, regulate truck safety and standards. Operational regulations include cabotage restrictions on domestic carriage of goods.

In summary, the North American transportation industry has evolved to the use of market forces and liberalization. In some cases, this commercialization shift has led to privatization (such as with Air Canada and CN). As discussed in the following section, the recent Canada Transportation Act Review recommends continued transportation liberalization.

Canada Transportation Act review

In her 2008 seminal text, *North American Freight Transportation: The road to security and prosperity*, Mary Brooks provided a comprehensive review of continental and international freight transportation in the post-NAFTA era (Brooks, 2008). Recently she stated her research findings are still applicable 'as very little has changed in the intervening years' (Brooks, 2016).

However, in the Canadian context, change may be coming as the Canada Transportation Act Review Committee (CTARC) recently submitted its report, *Pathways: Connecting Canada's transportation system to the world* to the newly elected federal government. The Minister of Transport Marc Garneau released the CTARC report in March 2016 for public review and consultations. CTARC was established by the then Minister of Transport Lisa Raitt in June 2014 with a distinguished panel of transportation experts with the broad mandate of reviewing not only the Canada Transportation Act but also all acts of Parliament related to transportation while explicitly considering the country's economic health and competitiveness. CTARC was also asked to consider current issues and a 30-year outlook to devise a pathway, primarily focused on economic concerns for an enlightened transportation system development, critical steps to improve trade-enabling infrastructure and other approaches to support Canada's future success. As stated by CTARC, 'in a world of massive and complex webs of interconnectedness, the quality of transportation and logistics systems may be the single greatest contributor to a country's economic performance' (CTARC, 2016a: 4).

In his opening remarks, CTARC's chair, the Honourable David Emerson stated that:

> A recurring theme in the Report is the inseparable relationship between Canada's international trade performance and the quality of the transportation and logistics systems... Access to a globally competitive transportation system

is vital to the prosperity of the country, the competitiveness of industry, the sustainability of communities and the ease with which Canadians can travel. (CTARC, 2016a: 2)

Over an 18-month period CTARC received 280 written submissions and held over 480 meetings and round-table discussions with the transportation and related sectors across Canada. Further, CTARC commissioned 36 targeted research projects to support their analysis, ensuring their findings reflected the current and projected situation in Canada's transportation and logistics industry.

This section outlines how CTARC recommendations address international freight transportation concerns raised earlier in this chapter. The federal government has established previous reviews of the Canada Transportation Act, the most recent in 2001. The recommendations in earlier reviews inevitably led to legislative changes to improve Canada's transportation system. Undoubtedly the CTARC report will yield similar positive change enhancing Canada's international freight transportation system's efficiency and effectiveness.

CTARC found the country's transportation system to be divided amongst myriad government departments and agencies – at times working at cross-purposes. For example, Transport Canada is the main federal department focusing on regulating the transportation system, while Global Affairs Canada considers trade. Other departments, such as Environment Canada, Employment, Workforce Development and Labour, Canada Border Services Agency and Canada Transportation Agency, all have a hand in regulating transportation. This led CTARC to propose an Advisory Committee on Transportation and Logistics chaired by the Minister of Transport and vice-chaired by the Minister of International Trade with members from federal, provincial and municipal governments along with key industry stakeholders (CTARC, 2016a: 28). In their CTARC submission, the Association of Canadian Port Authorities (ACPA) had outlined the need for a multi-departmental forum, including transportation and trade (ACPA, 2015: 6).

Canada's transportation infrastructure requirements received considerable attention from CTARC as they outlined the need for a long-term comprehensive infrastructure plan to create a 'projects pipeline' for the next 20–30 years. This plan would help to attract private sector financing (such as from Canada's many major pension funds) for major transportation infrastructure development (CTARC, 2016a: 24–27). Further, as identified by ports and other transportation providers, there is a critical need to preserve and protect expansion capacity in transportation corridors and on waterfront lands. In response, CTARC recommended a National Corridor Protection Programme within the next five years for corridors and critical gateway ports (CTARC, 2016a: 45).

Canada's transportation system features dominant players (such as the two national railways, CN and CP), captive markets (particularly the railways), a legacy of state-owned systems (such as major airports and ports) and deteriorating critical infrastructure (CTARC, 2016a: 8). This situation has, at times, led to conflicts between commercial oligarchies and the public interest. As an example, in 2014 the Minister of Transport directly intervened in a dispute over the limited rail export grain carriage. Railways are important, as 94 per cent of Canadian grain exports are transported by rail to ports and destinations in the United States and Mexico (Quorum Corporation, 2014). To further exacerbate the dispute, 2013 was a bumper crop year, generating a 37 per cent greater yield than in 2012, and Canada's commercial elevator grain storage capacity is only about 20 per cent of the average annual production (Norbury, 2014; CTARC, 2016a: 157). Thus, efficient railway grain movements were critical in 2014. In the grain case, CN and CP reflected an imbalance in market power by not providing sufficient locomotive capacity to haul grain cars while continuing to ship petroleum products in tanker cars. Grain is a protected market as the railways operate under the federally regulated Maximum Revenue Entitlement Program for this commodity. As a temporary measure addressing the grain crisis, the Minister of Transport tabled legislation to issue fines if the railways failed to move minimum weekly grain allotments to address this unique surge in demand (Deveau, 2014).

In reviewing the federal government's actions, CTARC's finding that 'Canada has been well served by transportation policies that emphasize competition and market forces' led to their recommendation to modernize and phase out the grain sector's Maximum Revenue Entitlement Program over a seven-year period. Further, CTARC reinforced the importance of having real-time system data for all users and to improve supply chain collaboration to support the long-term growth of Canada's grain transportation system (CTARC, 2016a: 159). Canada's major ports recognized the need for collaboration and recommended to CTARC that they serve as 'honest brokers' to provide this service (ACPA, 2015: 8). CTARC agreed this service is necessary and recommended the Canada Transportation Agency establish a comprehensive data platform to collect, analyse and publish accurate transportation information to ensure logistics system fluidity (CTARC, 2016a: 258).

Canada's freight railroads are vertically integrated private companies responsible for their own capital and operational requirements. They own the rights of way and tracks on which they operate. CTARC's focus was on railway safety and appropriate regulations as well as consideration of taxation measures ensuring Canadian railways remain competitive with their continental counterparts (CTARC, 2016a: 112–47).

As discussed previously, there is a lack of integration among state and provincial authorities on truck weights and dimensions. As pointed out by CTARC, 'greater regulatory harmonization was regarded as a critical step towards realizing a seamless North American transportation network' (CTARC, 2016b: 55). CTARC further recommended the federal government work with provincial leaders to harmonize regulatory trucking standards for the fluid movement of interprovincial and international trade (CTARC, 2016a: 49).

On the air side, CTARC recommended further divestment of smaller federally owned airports and moving to a share-capital structure for larger airports to obtain equity-based financing from large institutional investors. In addition, they recommended that foreign ownership limits for airlines operating all-freight services be increased to 100 per cent (CTARC, 2016a: 194/197).

In terms of short sea shipping, CTARC recognized the challenges of removing North American cabotage restrictions, but did recommend a loosening of Canadian restrictions, particularly in respect to container services and establishing a second international ship registry to allow Canadian vessels to move freely in and out of domestic trades (CTARC, 2016a: 229–30). In addition, CTARC found 'the Canada Port Authority model has been able to strike a reasonable balance between commercial discipline and the public interest in ports as enablers of trade development' (CTARC, 2016a: 227). This is despite limitations CPAs face in obtaining suitable financing to enhance and expand port infrastructure. CTARC recommended adopting a share-capital structure approach including seeking financing from institutional investors (such as pension funds) and private firms. CTARC further recommended the consideration of regional amalgamation of CPAs, particularly on Canada's West Coast (CTARC, 2016a: 228).

CTARC concluded that Canada's largest airports, ports and railways should become 'independent entities, disciplined by competition and market forces, financed by private investment and "user pay", and empowered to act accordingly…' They further concluded that 'Canada has been well served by transportation policies that emphasize competition and market forces in the development of infrastructure and services'. The committee stated their many recommendations are based on three broad fundamental principles: 'strengthened market approaches (reinforcing previous federal initiatives in this direction); renewed regulatory frameworks (providing better information and oversight mechanisms); and enhanced leadership (including a long-term infrastructure plan and strategic coordination)' (CTARC, 2016a: 254–55).

Conclusion

North American international freight transportation operates in a relatively fluid way among the three NAFTA countries and overseas. From a continental perspective, a significant portion of international freight moves by land modes, road, rail and pipeline, while freight movements beyond the continent are primarily by sea. Air cargo plays a small role by volume with a larger role by commodity value.

Despite the existence of free trade agreements such as NAFTA and other collaborative initiatives, continental freight movements are not yet seamless due to various impediments and non-tariff barriers, including non-harmonized regulations, rules and standards (such as varying truck weights and dimensions) and cabotage restrictions protecting domestic cargo movements by all modes.

However, steps are being taken to further liberalize continental and international freight movements in North America. The Beyond the Border programme between Canada and the United States is effectively 'thinning' the border for accelerated commercial international freight transportation. The recent Canada Transportation Act Review provided many far-reaching recommendations aimed at improving international freight transportation efficiency and effectiveness. The federal government, along with its provincial counterparts, will consider these recommendations and many will be adopted over time to establish a future pathway ensuring an improved national and international freight transportation system in Canada and with its NAFTA partners. Similar broad-based analyses of freight transportation in the United States and Mexico would assist in generating a truly seamless integrated continental transportation system. It is hoped that Canada's NAFTA partners will follow its lead.

Acknowledgement

The author wishes to acknowledge continued support from SSHRC's Borders in Globalization Partnership Program and the Department of Civil and Environmental Engineering at Carleton University.

References

ACPA (2015) *Canada's ports are catalysts for change: ACPA response to the CTA review panel*, White Paper, Association of Canadian Port Authorities, Ottawa

Airports (2005) Airports could see route expansion under Canadian open skies, *Airports,* **22** (7), p 1

Association of American Railroads (2014) Class 1 railroad statistics, AAR Statistics-pdf, available at <https://www.aar.org/Documents/Railroad-Statistics.pdf> [accessed March 2016]

Atkins, E (2016) US East Coast ports bank on increased traffic from Panama Canal expansion, *Globe and Mail*, Toronto, 1 January

Blank, S (2008) Trade corridors and North American competitiveness, *American Review of Canadian Studies*, **38** (2), pp 231–37

Boxshall, R, Kupelian, B and Lambe, C (2014) Where will the top goods trade routes be in 2030? *Global Economy Watch*, Price Waterhouse Coopers LLP, p 3

Brooks, M (2008) *North American Freight Transportation: The road to security and prosperity*, Edward Elgar, Cheltenham

Brooks, M (2016) personal communication, 17 February

Brooks, M and Frost, J (2004) Short sea shipping: A Canadian perspective, *Maritime Policy & Management,* **31** (4)

Bruce, H (1997) *The Pig That Flew: The battle to privatise Canadian National*, A M Hakkert, Toronto

Canada's Economic Action Plan (2015) Beyond the Border, available at <http://actionplan.gc.ca/en/page/bbg-tpf/beyond-border-action-plan>

Canada's Gateways (2016) available at <www.canadagagteways.gc.ca>

Council of Ministers of Transportation (2008) Harmonization of transportation policies and regulations: Context, progress and initiatives in the motor carrier sector, available at <http://www.comt.ca/english/coff-report.pdf>

Council of Ministers of Transportation (2013) A vision for transportation in Canada, Ministerial Statement, available at <http://www.comt.ca/english/strategic-vision.pdf>

CTARC (2015) *Pathways: Connecting Canada's transportation system to the world*, Minister of Transport, Ottawa

CTARC (2016a) *Pathways: Connecting Canada's transportation system to the world, Volume 1*, Minister of Transport, Ottawa

CTARC (2016b) *Pathways: Connecting Canada's transportation system to the world, Volume 2 (appendices)*, Minister of Transport, Ottawa

Davis, M (2016) Changing course: Commercialising Canadian airport, port and rail governance – 1975 to 2000, PhD thesis, Faculty of Public Affairs, Carleton University, Ottawa, pp 98–99

Deveau, S (2014) Transport Minister Lisa Raitt on why Ottawa wants Canada's grain to head south, *Financial Post*, 4 April, available at <http://business.financialpost.com/news/transportation/transport-minister-lisa-raitt-on-why-ottawa-wants-canadas-grain-to-head-south>

Drewry (2016) A great exploration into the transpacific? Available at <http://www.drewry.co.uk/news.php?id=459>

Edmonson, R G (2005) Short-sea vs. HMT, *Journal of Commerce*, 24 April, pp 34–35

George, R (2013) *Ninety Percent of Everything: Inside shipping*, Metropolitan Books, Henry Holt and Company, New York, p 18

Houston, G (2008) Vancouver Fraser Port Authority: The making of an amalgamated port, Port/Government Interface Conference, Association of Canadian Port Authorities, Ottawa

IBI Group (2015) Canada's transportation system: Identification of 'critical trade-related' infrastructure and approaches to funding, prepared for and cited in CTARC Report, *Pathways: Connecting Canada's transportation system to the world*, Minister of Transport, Ottawa, p 44

ICAO (2005) *Manual on the Regulation of International Air Transport*, 2nd edn, document 9626, pp 4.1: 8–10, International Civil Aviation Organization, Montreal

Ircha, M (2001a) North American port reform: The Canadian and American experience, *International Journal of Maritime Economics*, 3, pp 198–220

Ircha, M (2001b) *US and Canadian ports: Financial comparisons*, Canada Transportation Act Review Committee, Montreal

Ircha, M (2011) Trade corridors and gateways: An evolving national transportation plan, Chapter 14 in *Integrating Seaports and Trade Corridors*, ed P Hall, R McCalla, C Comtois and B Slack, Ashgate, Surrey, pp 221–34

Levinson, M (2006) *The Box: How the shipping container made the world smaller and the world economy bigger*, Princeton University Press, Princeton

McMillan, C (2006) *Embracing the Future: The Atlantic Gateway and Canada's trade corridors*, Asia Pacific Foundation of Canada, Vancouver

Meyer, B (2016) Container shipping's very BIG future, *American Shipper*, 58 (2), p 34

Norbury, K (2014) Bumper wheat crop taxes transportation systems, *Canadian Sailings: Transportation & Trade Logistics*, 23 June

Premti, A (2016) Liner shipping: Is there a way for more competition? Discussion paper No. 224, p 1, United Nations Conference on Trade and Development (UNCTAD), Geneva

QinetiQ, Lloyd's Register and University of Strathclyde (2013) *Global Marine Trends 2030*, Glasgow

Quorum Corporation (2014) *Grain Supply Chain Study: Grain monitoring program supplemental study*, p 21, available at <http://www.quorumcorp.net/Downloads/SupplementalReports/Grain%20Supply%20Chain%20Study%20-%20Report.pdf>

RAC (2015) *Rail Trends 2015*, Railway Association of Canada, Ottawa, p 6

Rodrigue, J-P *et al* (2013) *The Geography of Transport Systems*, 3rd edn, Routledge, New York

Saul, J (2016) Baltic sea index hits all-time low as shipping crisis deepens, *Reuters*, 13 January

Schuler, M (2016) Senator McCain sets crosshairs on Jones Act build requirements (again!), *Captain*, 30 January, available at < http://gcaptain.com/mccain-sets-crosshairs-on-jones-act-build-requirement-again/>

Statistics Canada (2015a) Table 3-1. Components of population growth, medium-growth – historical trends – Canada, 2009/2010 to 2060/2061, available at <http://www.statcan.gc.ca/pub/91-520-x/2010001/tablesectlist-listetableauxsect-eng.htm>

Statistics Canada (2015b) Gross domestic product at basic prices, utilities, trade, transportation and communications, available at < http://www.statcan.gc.ca/tables-tableaux/sum-som/l01/cst01/trade26-eng.htm>

Stolarik, K (2014) Progress on the Beyond the Border Action Plan, Portsecure – Port Security Conference of Canada, Ottawa

Szakonyi, M (2015) Montreal to expand capacity after seeing healthy container traffic growth, *JOC.com*, 22 January, available at <http://www.joc.com/port-news/international-ports/port-montreal/montreal-expand-capacity-after-seeing-healthy-container-traffic-growth_20150122.html>

Transport Canada (2007) *National Policy Framework for Strategic Gateways and Trade Corridors*, Transport Canada, Ottawa

Transport Canada (2012) *Collaboration in Gateways and Corridors*, available at <https://www.tc.gc.ca/eng/policy/anre-menu-3023.htm>

Transport Canada (2015) *APGCI Investments Map*, available at <http://www.asiapacificgateway.gc.ca/investments.html>

UNCTAD (2015) Review of Maritime Transport 2015, Table 2.3, Ownership of the world fleet, as of January 1 2015 (dwt), p 36, available at <http://unctad.org/en/PublicationsLibrary/rmt2015_en.pdf>

United States Census Bureau (2015) 2014 National population projections: summary tables – Table 1: Projections of population and components of change for the United States: 2015–2060, available at <https://www.census.gov/population/projections/data/national/2014/summarytables.html>

US Department of Transportation, Bureau of Transportation Statistics (2015) Table 3-3: US gross domestic product attributed to transportation functions, available at <http://www.rita.dot.gov/bts/sites/rita.dot.gov.bts/files/publications/national_transportation_statistics/html/table_03_03.html>

World Bank (2015) Logistics performance index – global rankings 2014, available at <http://lpi.worldbank.org/international/global/2014>

World Bank (2016) World Development Indicators: Structure of demand – exports of goods and services (% of GDP), Table 4.8, available at <http://wdi.worldbank.org/table/4.8>

World Trade Organization (2013) Table 1.11: Merchandise trade of Canada by origin and destination, 2013; and Table 1.12: Merchandise trade of the United States by origin and destination, 2013, *International Trade Statistics*, World Trade Organization, Geneva

World Trade Organization (2014a) Table 1.16: Merchandise trade of NAFTA countries by major product group and by origin/destination, 2013, *International Trade Statistics*, World Trade Organization, Geneva

World Trade Organization (2014b) Appendix Table 1: World merchandise trade by region and selected economies, *World Trade Report 2015*, World Trade Organization, Geneva, p 24

World Trade Organization (2015) International trade and market access data, available at <https://www.wto.org/english/res_e/statis_e/statis_bis_e.htm>

Worldometers (2016) World population growth rate, available at <http://www.worldometers.info/world-population/#growthrate>

World's Richest Countries (2015) Top Mexican exports to the world/Top Mexican imports from the world, available at <http://www.worldsrichestcountries.com/top-mexico-exports.html>

International freight transport in South America: the case of Colombia

09

DAVID B GRANT, Hull University Business School, UK

RODRIGO BRITTO, Universidad de los Andes School of Management (UASM), Colombia

JUAN PABLO SOTO, Universidad de los Andes School of Management (UASM), Colombia

MARCUS THIELL, Universidad de los Andes School of Management (UASM), Colombia

Introduction

Logistics and transport are broad, far-reaching functions that have a major impact on a society's standard of living. We have come to expect excellent logistical and transportation services but only tend to notice them when there is a problem, eg materials not arriving at a factory gate when needed or food not being on a store's shelf when consumers want to buy it. The UK Freight Transport Association (FTA) asked its members to rate the public and government's understanding of the logistics and transport sectors (Grant, 2012). They found that more than 80 per cent of FTA members responding believed the public had either 'no understanding' (35 per cent) or only 'a slight understanding' (48 per cent) of this sector's role in the economy. Government fared little better, with the FTA responding members believing the government has 'no understanding' (12 per cent), 'a slight understanding' (39 per cent) or 'some understanding' (38 per cent). Hence, more awareness of this sector is required, but not just in domestic markets. Awareness of other markets and countries is also needed, particularly in less popular or less well-known regions of the world.

In the last few decades, much attention has been focused on global trade and transportation between developed western nations and Asia. But despite trade volumes being highly significant between these regions, trade with and across other continents such as South America, one of the economically most fast-growing regions in the world, has largely been ignored as to its potential, nuances and issues. In 2012 there were 5.1 million twenty-foot equivalent (TEU) container movements into and out of South America (World Shipping Council, 2016). Sixty-nine per cent of this is to and from Brazil as one of the 'BRIC' nations that also includes Russia, India and China. However, Colombia (14 per cent), Chile (10 per cent) and Peru (7 per cent) comprise the remaining volumes (IADB, 2014).

This chapter discusses international freight transport considerations in Colombia. Colombia's US $48.5 billion of exports include coffee, fresh flowers, natural resources and apparel with over a quarter of its products destined for the United States. Thus, it is not an insignificant global trading nation and deserves a look at its current capabilities and future potential. This chapter first discusses different aspects of international freight transport to set the scene regarding situational factors in Colombia. Then, an overview of Colombia's country and transportation statistics and characteristics are presented in the context of its Latin American and Caribbean neighbours and the United States. Two case studies pertaining to Colombian logistics and transport are then offered before conclusions round off the chapter.

The nature of international freight transport

Transportation may be defined as the planning and the undertaking of the movement of goods by a carrier between two points in a cost-effective manner that achieves the times and conditions specified by a shipper. Transportation thus plays a central role in seamless supply chain operations, moving inbound materials from supply sites to manufacturing facilities, repositioning inventory among different plants and distribution centres, and delivering finished products to customers.

Any one or more of five modes – truck or road, rail, air, water (either ocean or inland) and pipeline – may be used to transport products. In addition, there are several intermodal combinations available: rail–road, road–water, road–air, and rail–water. Intermodal combinations offer specialized or lower-cost services not generally available when a single mode is used. Other transportation options offering a variety of services to shippers include freight forwarders, shippers' associations, intermodal marketing companies (or shippers' agents), third-party logistics (3PL) service providers, parcel post, and air express companies.

The strategies of carriers and shippers are inextricably interrelated. Transportation is an integral component of logistics strategy. Carriers must understand the role of transportation in a firm's overall logistics system, and firms must understand how carriers aid them in satisfying customer needs at a profit. The administration of transportation activities, or traffic management, includes issues such as inbound and outbound transportation, carrier–shipper contracts, strategic partnerships and alliances, private carriage/leasing, mode/carrier selection, routing and scheduling, service offerings, and computer technology.

International freight transportation can involve any of the five basic modes of transportation; however, air and ocean carriage are perhaps the most important between nations while truck and rail carriage are the most important freight movements within nations. Firms involved in international markets must also be aware of the services, costs and availability of transport modes between and within the countries where they move their products and consider many factors when comparing alternatives. For example, within other or host countries there are differences due to taxes, subsidies, regulations, government ownership of carriers, and geography. In general, international transportation costs represent a much higher fraction of merchandise value than domestic or home country transportation costs. This is primarily due to the longer distances involved, more complex administrative requirements, and related paperwork that must accompany international shipments.

Globalization has increased tremendously since the 1970s, in large part due to various developments in logistics and supply chain management (SCM), such as the wide-spread adoption of the standard shipping container, the expansion of transport infrastructure of ports, improved roadways and railroads, and trade liberalization. These factors helped to provide production and cost differentials between developed and developing countries. A global financial network has also developed that allows multinational firms to expand their operations and firms have increased new material and component acquisitions from other countries, ie global sourcing.

Thus, global trade has increased significantly since the end of World War II as the world economy has become more interdependent. The World Trade Organization (WTO) reported that total world merchandise exports were US $59 billion in 1948 and grew almost ten-fold to US $579 billion by 1973. However, total world merchandise exports in 2014 were US $19 trillion, or almost a 35-fold increase in 41 years. Following a period of growth and recovery after the 2008–09 global financial crisis, world merchandise trade began to level off in 2011 in both developed and developing economies. In 2014, developing economies showed only a 1 per cent increase in exports and zero growth in imports, and their participation in world merchandise exports remained at around 44 per cent, the same as 2012. Nevertheless, merchandise trade in developing economies grew faster than world trade in both 2013 and 2014 (WTO, 2016).

To support its international markets a firm must have a logistics or supply chain system that satisfies the particular requirements of those markets. For example, developing countries are typically characterized by large numbers of channel intermediaries supplying an even larger number of small retailers. The systems and infrastructures in these nations are marked by inadequate transportation and storage facilities, a large unskilled labour force and an absence of logistics and SCM support systems, whereas developed countries have highly sophisticated systems for transportation, high-technology warehousing and skilled labour markets.

Terms of trade across international borders have become highly standardized since the mid-1930s. Terms of trade provide important information on the actual export documents that state who is responsible for the various stages of delivery, who bears what risks, and who pays for the various elements of transportation. Payment continues to be by a letter of credit, which is a document issued by a bank on behalf of the buyer which authorizes payment for goods received. Once the buyer is satisfied that the terms of the agreement have been met by the seller, payment is made to the seller by the bank instead of the buyer.

The Incoterms (2016) rules, first published in 1936, provide internationally accepted definitions and rules of interpretation for most common commercial terms. They help companies trading internationally to avoid costly misunderstandings by clarifying the tasks, costs and risks involved in the delivery of goods from sellers to buyers. The latest version is known as Incoterms 2010 and three of the more popular Incoterms are:

- EXW or Ex-Works at a named origin. The origin will be identified as factory, plant, etc, and the seller's only responsibility is to make the goods available at their premises. The seller bears the costs and risks until the buyer is obligated to take delivery. The buyer pays for the documents, must take delivery of the shipment when specified, and pay any export taxes.

- DDP or Delivered Duty Paid at a named place of destination. DDP represents the seller's maximum obligation – the seller bears all risks and all costs until the goods are delivered.
- FOB or Free on Board at a named port of shipment. Goods are placed on board a ship by the seller at a port of shipment named in the sales agreement. The risk of loss of or damage to the goods is transferred to the buyer when the goods pass over the ship's rail and the seller pays the cost of loading the goods.

The impact on globalization of logistics and transportation activities has also been significant over the last 40 years. Global container trade has increased on average 5 per cent per year and now comprises over 350 million TEU a year (Grant, 2012). However, the impact of globalization does not only affect ocean-borne containers. Worldwide demand and subsequent fulfilment of smart phones and tablets have led to an increase in air freight volumes and prices. For example, Apple sold a record 74.5 million iPhone 6 and 6Plus units in the last quarter of 2014 and air freight rates rose almost 12 per cent between September and October 2014 to US $3.75 per kilogram (Fernie and Grant, 2015).

Managing a global logistics and transport system is more complex than managing a purely domestic network. Firms must properly analyse the international external environment, plan for it, and develop the correct control procedures to monitor the success or failure of the international system. Elements in a firm's external environment are mostly uncontrollable or exogenous, and include political and legal systems in international markets, economic conditions, technology that is available, and social and cultural norms. Firms involved in international markets will want to minimize logistics and transport costs while providing acceptable service levels to customers just as they do in their domestic markets. However, international logistics is generally more expensive than domestic logistics due to increased shipping distances, documentation costs, larger levels of inventory, extra packaging and containerization, and longer order cycle times. Thus, a firm's cost-service mix will likely vary in international markets.

One way of determining the logistics capability of any country is the World Bank's Logistics Performance Index (LPI), which is a weighted average of individual country scores on six key dimensions with a maximum score of 5.0: the efficiency of clearance processes, quality of trade and transport related infrastructure, the ease of arranging competitively priced shipments, the competence and quality of logistics services, the ability to track and trace consignments and the timeliness of shipments in reaching destination within a scheduled or expected delivery time (Arvis *et al*, 2014). In the 2014 LPI the top performing country was Germany with a score of 4.12, followed by the Netherlands (4.05), Belgium (4.04), the UK (4.01), and Singapore (4.00).

Another way to consider a country's logistics capabilities is the size of its total gross domestic product (GDP), which is an indicator of total economic activity. Global GDP in 2014 was estimated at US $74.2 trillion at official exchange rates (CIA, 2016). Additionally, the efficiency and effectiveness of a country's logistics activities may be judged by the percentage of logistics costs relative to GDP. For example, Wilson (2015) reported that logistics costs were 8.3 per cent of US GDP in 2014. Values in other regions range from 10–12 per cent in Europe to 18–23 per cent in developing areas such as Asia or Latin America. Those countries that have high levels of GDP, high LPI scores, and low values of logistics costs relative to GDP may be considered highly efficient in terms of these activities and hence offer less uncertainty or risk. Conversely, countries with lower levels of GDP, lower LPI scores and high values of logistics costs relative to GDP may be considered risky.

There are also many other types of risk in international markets. Outsourcing, globalization, improved infrastructure and information technology, and cheap labour and raw materials have extended supply chains into longer and more complex networks. This has consequently increased supply chain vulnerability and fragility, and has led to more frequent operational disruptions. There are also other factors such as shorter product life cycles, reduced suppliers, buffers and inventories, increased demand for on-time deliveries, change in consumer tastes and preferences, technology shifts or supplier priorities.

To mitigate such risk and adverse consequences, particularly in international markets, firms can employ a supply chain risk management (SCRM) strategy to avoid delays, reduce costs, improve customer service, avoid major disasters and operational disruptions, increase the chances of quick recovery and enhance resilience. Usual risk management approaches largely depend upon the nature of market, industry, organizational structure and attitude, strategy, culture, leadership and geographic area in which a firm is operating, and thus the SCRM strategy should also take these factors into account.

In summary, increased global activity has increased the propensity for firms to enter international markets to sell and/or source their products.

However, doing so entails risk and requires consideration of various risk factors. The first risk to consider is the appropriate country or market. Here the country's GDP, LPI and logistics costs to GDP can help to determine the level of costs, infrastructure, efficiency, effectiveness and other related factors in the host market. Then, relationship of these factors can be analysed to ensure that the firm is ensuring its cost–service mix is the best it can be.

The international freight transport market in Latin America

The A T Kearney Foreign Direct Investment Confidence Index is a regular measure of company chief executive office sentiment about various markets, and continues to indicate that Latin America, which includes Mexico, Central and South America, remains an attractive location to do business (Burnson, 2013). Erik Peterson, managing director of A T Kearney's Global Business Policy Council noted that emerging markets, particularly Latin America, are developing into complementary markets instead of alternative and temporary safe havens during economic upheavals.

The benefits of logistics investments in South America have been addressed recently by the Inter-American Development Bank's (IADB) Department of Infrastructure and Environment. As noted above, transportation is an inherently crucial factor in supporting trade activities as well as providing opportunities for economic development. However, transport infrastructure capacity may have limited value if not supported by a proportional level of reliability and timeliness in freight distribution supported by transport services.

Latin American ports have seen remarkable growth of containerized traffic handled with the development and expansion of port infrastructure, and their conventional role as an exporter of resources such as agricultural and mining products is being expanded through an increasing sophistication of imports and exports. Hence, port facilities and their hinterland have responded with infrastructure investments with a well-founded anticipation of additional traffic growth. However, Latin America's port infrastructure is still rated 'below average' by the World Bank. Channel capacity at most ports is insufficient, with productivity and berthing delays a continuing issue. Further, while Latin America's exports are growing, their share of domestic GDP is low (Burnson, 2013).

Brazil, Colombia, Chile and Peru handle the largest port freight volumes, with Colombia moving 190 million tonnes per year. Air freight in South

America is less than 1.5 per cent of port freight volumes and Brazil is the leader with 760,000 tonnes per year. However, Colombia only has about 20 per cent less air freight volumes at around 610,000 tonnes per year, which is attributable to Colombia's reliance on this mode for flower and – to a lesser extent – textile-related exports. Road freight tariffs in South America range from US $0.07 per tonne-kilometre in Ecuador to $0.47 in Peru. However, the latter is an outlier and the average excluding Peru is about $0.10; Colombia is $0.08 per tonne-kilometre. Argentina, Brazil, Chile and Colombia are the only countries with intensive rail freight operations, with Colombia moving 1.65 tonnes per capita annually (IADB, 2014).

The Inter-American Development Bank has prepared indices (maximum 100) for road, rail, maritime, air and logistics activities in the United States and Latin America and the Caribbean (LAC) countries (IADB, 2014). The components for road include total road network, paved network, carbon dioxide (CO_2) emissions per heavy goods vehicle and cost. Barbados was ranked first with 100 and Colombia ranked twelfth with a score of 30. The components for rail include the total rail network, domestic freight carried, and cost. The United States was first with 100, and due to the lack of rail freight in all 22 countries being examined, Colombia came last in ninth place with a score of 1. Components for maritime include maximum draft in container terminals, liner shipping connectivity index and port traffic per population. The United States was again first with 100 and Colombia was eighth with a score of 40. The air index includes components of international airports with cargo facilities and international freight carried per population. Barbados was first here with 100 while Colombia was ninth with a score of 9. Finally, the logistics index uses the World Bank LPI infrastructure and services scores. The United States was first here also with 100 and Colombia was eighth was a score of 48.

Arvis *et al* (2016) noted that bilateral issues might play a role in LPI survey respondents' perceptions when rating their respective regions. The regions that LAC rated highest on the total LPI score are North America and the European Union (EU), higher than LAC's self-rating, suggesting that trade with these two regions is easier than within LAC. Moreover, these ratings are not symmetrical; the EU's perception of LAC is quite unfavourable, ranking it sixth of the eight regions in the LPI. Ratings of LAC by North America and East Asia and the Pacific (EAP), LAC's main import partners in 2012, are lower than LAC's ratings of them. However, they are relatively good compared with how other regions have been rated: LAC comes third for North America after North America itself and the EU and fourth for EAP after North America, the EU and EAP itself. Colombia's overall LPI score in 2016 was 2.61 and it was ranked 94th out of 160 countries in the LPI survey.

In summary, LAC, particularly South America, is generally in the lower tier of nations when it comes to logistics performance for several reasons. However, the potential for trade and improvement is good compared to other regions. Brazil is the obvious leader in South America but Colombia is in the running for second place.

Colombia: background, facts and figures

Figure 9.1 shows a map of Colombia (CIA, 2016). It is the only South American country to have coastlines on both the Pacific and Atlantic Oceans, the latter connected via the Caribbean Sea. Basic geographic, demographic

Figure 9.1 Map of Colombia

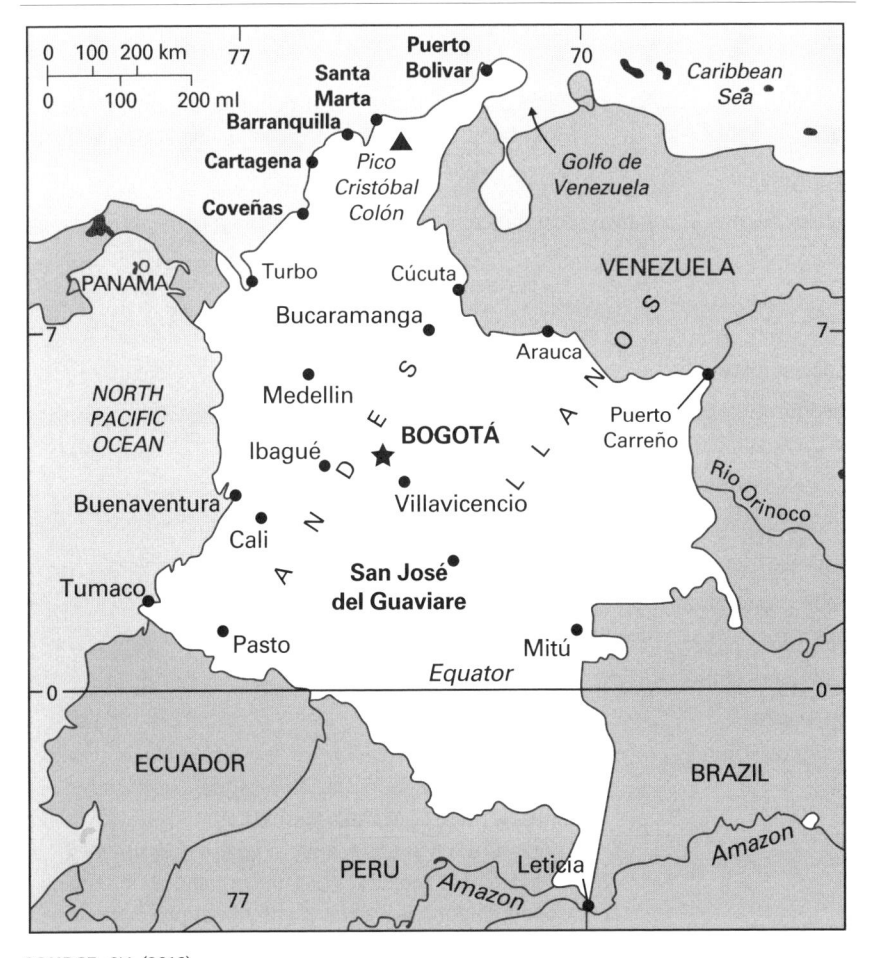

SOURCE CIA (2016)

and economic data for Colombia are shown in Table 9.1 (IADB, 2014; CIA, 2016). Geographically, the country is dominated in the centre by two ranges of the Andes Mountains – the capital Bogotá is on a plateau between them. These ranges inhibit the development of good transport infrastructure, but despite that, transport's share of Colombia's US $274 billion GDP is a little less than 8 per cent. Along the coastline are flat coastal plains where the major seaports are located and there are large lowland plains in the eastern area of the country where a lot of the country's agricultural sector is located.

Table 9.1 Colombia's geographic, demographic and economic statistics

Total area	1,138,910 square kilometres
Coastline	3,208 kilometres
Climate	Tropical along coast and eastern plains, cooler in highlands
Terrain:	Flat coastal lowlands, central highlands, high Andes Mountains, eastern lowland plains (Llanos)
Population	46,736,728
Major cities and capital	Bogotá (capital) – 9.77 million; Medellin – 3.91 million; Cali – 2.65 million; Barranquilla – 1.91 million; Bucaramanga – 1.22 million; Cartagena – 1.10 million
Urbanization	Urban population – 76.4% of total population
Labour force	24.34 million
Labour force by occupation	Services – 62%; Industry – 21%; Agriculture – 17%
Unemployment rate	9.4%
Gross domestic product (GDP)	US $274.2 billion; transport's share is 7.7%
GDP growth rate per annum	2.5%
GDP per capita	US $14,000
GDP sector composition	Services 56.7%. Industry 36.9% consisting of textiles, food processing, oil, clothing and footwear, beverages, chemicals, cement; gold, coal and emeralds. Agriculture 6.4% consisting of coffee, cut flowers, bananas, rice, tobacco, corn, sugarcane, cocoa beans, oilseed, vegetables, shrimp and forest products.

(Continued)

Table 9.1 *(Continued)*

Exports	US $48.5 billion consisting of petroleum, coal, emeralds, coffee, nickel, cut flowers, bananas and apparel
Imports	US $56.1 billion consisting of industrial equipment, transportation equipment, consumer goods, chemicals, paper products, fuels and electricity
Major export partners (est. 2014)	US 26.3%; China 10.5%; Panama 6.6%
Major import partners (est. 2014)	US 28.5%; China 18.4%; Mexico 8.2%

SOURCE Collated from CIA (2016)

Colombia's exports are around US $49 billion per annum and consist of natural resources (petroleum, coal, emeralds and nickel), agricultural products (coffee, cut flowers and bananas) and apparel. Its major export market is the United States at over 26 per cent, followed by China and Panama. Colombia imports just over US $56 billion per annum of industrial and transportation equipment, consumer goods, chemicals, fuels and electricity, and paper products. Again, its major import market is the United States at 28 per cent, followed by China and Mexico.

Data about Colombia's transport networks are shown in Table 9.2 (IADB, 2014; CIA, 2016) while its transportation statistics are in Table 9.3 (IADB, 2014). The majority of Colombia's trade moves through its ports, at 176 million tonnes per annum, and Cartagena on the Atlantic coast is the country's major container port, handling 1.85 million TEU per annum. Buenaventura on the Pacific coast and Santa Maria and Turbo on the Atlantic are the other major seaports. Colombia has 18,300 kilometres of navigable waterways but its most important commercial river is the Magdalena which flows about 1,600 kilometres from north to south traversing the country. Barranquilla at the northern coastal plain is the main port of this system, but the El Canal del Dique in Cartagena provides a direct link to the Magdalena (Gardner and Gómez, 2009).

Freight transport by road is the dominant in-country mode with 199 million tonnes and 65,688 million tonne-kilometres moved annually (IADB, 2014). However, Colombia's challenging terrain means domestic transit times are long. For example, depending on cargo weight and rainfall levels, transporting a 40 ft container (2 TEU) from Cartagena to Bogotá can take longer than five days, the equivalent time to the ocean transit time from Miami to Cartagena

Table 9.2 Colombia's transport networks

Roads	214,946 kilometres; 845 kilometres are motorway or freeway; 7% paved roads
Railways	2,141 kilometres
Inland waterways	18,300 kilometres navigable
Pipelines	Gas – 4,991 kilometres; Oil – 6,796 kilometres Refined products – 3,429 kilometres
Major ports and terminals	Atlantic–Caribbean: Cartagena (container port – 1.85 million TEUs); Santa Maria; Turbo Pacific: Buenaventura River: Barranquilla (Rio Magdalena) Oil terminal: Covenas offshore terminal Dry bulk cargo: Puerto Bolivar (coal)
Airports	121 with paved runways (50 with runways greater than 1,524 meters); 715 with unpaved runways
Major airports	Bogotá; Medellin; Cali; Cartagena; Barranquilla

SOURCE Collated from CIA (2016)

Table 9.3 Colombian transportation statistics

Domestic road freight productivity	65,688 million tonne-kilometres
Domestic road freight carried	199,369,000 tonnes
Average distance per vehicle	64,584 kilometres per year
Domestic rail freight productivity	15,360 million tonnes-kilometres
Domestic rail freight carried	76,800,000 tonnes
Port traffic	176,797,901 tonnes
Container storage facilities area	580,552 square metres
Port traffic exports	127,656,588 tonnes
Port traffic imports	30,141,481 tonnes
International airports with cargo terminal facilities	17
International airport cargo facilities area	115,326 square metres
Domestic air freight carried	145,503 tonnes
International air freight carried	623,792 tonnes

SOURCE Collated from CIA (2016)

(Gardner and Gómez, 2009). Further, guerrilla and paramilitary conflict over the past few decades in several regions has seen transport suppliers and carriers either finding longer and costlier alternative routes around these areas (Gardner and Gómez, 2009) or developing innovative relationship/governance structures and contractual arrangements to enter and use these areas (Vélez Valencia, 2015).

Air freight is a small proportion of transport at just over 769,000 tonnes per annum combined domestic and international (IADB, 2014), and fresh-cut flower exports are the main items transported, making Colombia the largest LAC air export market for the United States. El Dorado Airport in Bogotá has the largest air cargo facilities in the country and serves as Colombia's global hub (Gardner and Gómez, 2009). Medellin, Cali, Cartagena and Barranquilla airports also have cargo handling facilities.

The development of warehousing and distribution (W&D) networks has seen rapid growth in the past decades. Historically, Colombia had broad retail distribution capabilities due its dispersed population and the predominance of small, family-owned businesses. However, the growth of Colombia-owned supermarket chains such as Carulla and the entry of foreign superstores such as Makro and Carrefour due to Colombia obtaining membership in the WTO has seen the creation of a network of W&D facilities that range from 200 to 10,000 square metres. Further, many international 3PLs such as CEVA, DHL, Kuehne + Nagel, Maersk, Panalpina and UPS are now operating in Colombia (Gardner and Gómez, 2009).

In summary, Colombia is a growing market for exports and imports in South America and is moving to second place behind the much larger Brazil. However, it has issues regarding its transport infrastructure and systems. There has been significant inward foreign direct investment in Colombia since 2000 to address these issues, for example US $155 billion in 2015 (CIA, 2016), and Colombia has entered into many trade associations and free trade agreements around the world to develop its economy, the most notable being its membership in the WTO (Gardner and Gómez, 2009). Thus, Colombia's future looks bright, but as noted by Burnson (2013), Erik Peterson of A T Kearney proposed that firms operating in this market should conduct a careful examination of Colombia's business environment and develop nimble strategies to deal with this shifting landscape. The two case studies in the following sections provide an illustration of these issues.

International transport of Colombian cut flowers

Colombia is the second-largest flower exporter country in the world. It started to develop its flower market in the 1960s, and currently, flowers account for 16 per cent of total Colombian exports, representing 72.1 per cent of the global flower production. This sector contributes 0.44 per cent of the GDP (DANE, 2015), resulting in a total of almost US $1.3 billion (Asocolflores, 2015a). Seventy-seven per cent of Colombian flowers are exported to the United States. Nevertheless, Colombia exports to more than 90 countries (Asocolflores, 2015a).

Ninety-seven per cent of total flower exports are shipped using air transportation. Flowers represent 75 per cent of Colombian air traffic cargo exports (Asocolflores, 2015a). According to Avianca Cargo (2016), the main airport hubs for flowers are Bogota and Medellin. Most of these shipments are sent to Miami and Los Angeles (United States), since they have the necessary infrastructure to process the 786 tonnes of flowers exported every day (Avianca Cargo, 2016). Regarding El Dorado, Bogotá's airport, around 2,700 flights are performed to transport flowers and approximately 220,000 tonnes are carried every year (Asocolflores, 2015a).

Colombia has around 19,800 acres of flowers, with 17,300 acres cultivated in greenhouses and the remaining 2,500 acres produced outdoors. The main areas that cultivate flowers are Cundinamarca (75 per cent) and Antioquia (24 per cent) (Asocolflores, 2015b). There are roughly 300 farms; half of them have between 50 and 124 acres and the rest have more than 124 acres (Conlon, 2015). Colombia has become one of the largest exporters of roses, carnations, mini carnations, astromelia, chrysanthemums, pompon, bouquets and more than 15 other species of flowers, meeting the sanitary conditions for the United States, Japan, Australia and the European Union (EU), among other destinations (ICA, 2010). Flower export shares are highly concentrated, with 52 per cent of exports representing only three types of flowers: roses (24 per cent), carnations (17 per cent) and chrysanthemums (11per cent). Other species account for 48 per cent (Asocolflores, 2015a).

St Valentine's Day and Mothers' Day represent 15 per cent and 10 per cent of total year sales respectively (Legiscomex, 2007; Angel and Aranda, 2007). Therefore, this seasonal pattern becomes a key determinant of the supply chain design for the flower industry in Colombia. Other aspects that must be taken into account for the supply chain distribution are the perishability of the flowers, the requirement of cold chain for transportation (between two and four degrees Celsius) and the use of special storage equipment to preserve the quality (Salazar and Córdoba, 2014). As sophisticated equipment is required, transportation costs represent between one-third and two-thirds of total logistics costs in this industry (Escandón, 2009).

With 90,000 direct employees and 40,000 indirect employees, the supply chain structure of the Colombian flower market includes the following stages (Conlon, 2015):

- flower-growing crops;
- postharvest (cutting and storage in cold rooms);
- transportation made by the land cargo operator (LCO) of fresh cut flowers to the airport hubs;
- preparation of flowers and storage in cold rooms by the air cargo operator (ACO);
- transportation to the final destination country by the ACO.

During a peak day, between 500 and 700 truckloads of flowers enter the international load docks of El Dorado airport in Bogotá (González Cardenas, 2013), where they remain in a queue for long periods of time. In this span of time, the trucks are on standby so they must start the engines for at least five minutes each hour to maintain proper temperature in the cargo compartment. Figure 9.2 shows that Antioquia is the area with the lowest average cycle time (11 hours and 34 minutes), followed by Cundinamarca (13 hours and 30 minutes) and other zones (16 hours and 27 minutes) (Asocoflores, 2015b).

Figure 9.2 Average cut flower processing time until loaded onto airplane

Region		Volume				Average Cycle Time	During Valentine' Day	Best Time
C/MARCA	CROP-POSTHARVEST	23.534	LCO 252	ACO 191	ATO 6	13h 30min	9h 58min	5h 56min
	TIME	3h 42min	2h 26min	6h 22min	1h 0min			
ANT	CROP-POSTHARVEST	15.438	LCO 127	ACO 128	ATO 4	11h 34min	9h 1min	5h 6min
	TIME	4h 11min	1h 30min	4h 53min	1h 0min			
CO	CROP-POSTHARVEST		LCO	ACO	ATO	16h 27min	13h 32min	12h 18min
	TIME	34min	8h 30min	6h 21min	1h 2min			

SOURCE Asocolflores (2015b), translation by authors
NOTES C/marca volumes includes west-centre regions (CO). Estimations based on a mathematical model. LCO: Land Cargo Operator; ACO: Air Cargo Operators;
*best average time from the sample

Multiflora is one of the top producers and exporters of fresh cut flowers in Colombia. Its operation started in 1969, planting flowers in Jardines Bacatá, which is one of their most important farms. Since then, it has been sowing and dispatching a wide range of cut flowers and bouquets to major markets around the world. Multiflora has offices in Colombia, the United States and Spain, serving more than 300 direct customers (Multiflora, 2015). The company currently has 70 hectares of production over four farms located in the west of the Sabana de Bogota, where it produces chrysanthemums, carnations, mini carnations and roses. It also sells flowers produced by other farms, with which they hold commercialization and distribution exclusivity agreements (Arango *et al*, 2015).

In its four flower farms, Multiflora employs around 1,000 people, rising to 1,400 depending on the season. Seventy-five per cent of them are single mothers. In general, within the floriculture sector, women constitute 60 per cent of the workforce due to their patience and delicacy in tasks such as irrigation and cutting (Cuartas Rodriguez, 2014). Within its Corporate Social Responsibility programme, Multiflora has two schools where employees' children study for free. The schools include secondary basic, technical and professional education. In addition, labour unions in the farms have created the Solidarity Savings Corporation, Crediflores (Multiflora, 2015).

In particular, the performance of Multiflora's supply chain to serve the US market during St Valentine's Day and Mothers' Day becomes a critical issue to guarantee the profitability of the company. In addition to the previously mentioned product characteristics, the flower sector in Colombia faces several challenges such as:

- absence of workers in postharvest;
- improper forecast of time departure and arrival of trucks;
- lack of qualified workers supporting the job of the ACO to speed up the process done with jet pallets;
- deficiency of a proper EDI platform used by the ATO;
- deficient logistics infrastructure of the country;
- lack of multimodal platforms;
- high transportation costs;
- airport and customs congestion during peak seasonal periods.

All these factors significantly affect the quality of the product, on-time delivery, costs and, finally, profitability of the companies. Therefore, companies strive to design and implement continuous improvement strategies to mitigate the likelihood of supply chain failures. Multiflora has carried out some strategies that helped to significantly improve their supply chain performance, especially during seasonal periods, and these main strategies and the results obtained are described next (Arango *et al*, 2015).

Stage: postharvest cold rooms

- Planning: establishment of due dates for sales orders within the system that lead the postharvest process. Anticipated demand peaks allowed them to flatten, delaying or advancing orders, taking into account operation and storage capacity.

Stage: land transportation

- Temperature control and monitoring: a procedure to randomly measure temperatures of the boxes, at different points:
  - land transportation (a sensor was installed in all trucks to record temperature every 10 minutes);
  - delivery of postharvest trucks;
  - delivery of cargo airlines.

Stage: airport operation

- Customs: multiflora achieved an agreement to assume overtime costs of ICA inspectors (phytosanitary authorities) in case they were needed for Multiflora operations. This allowed Multiflora to introduce flexible schedules in the deliveries.
- Truck scheduling: during peak time, farms were not able to deliver flowers before 7 pm and trucks were scheduled to be at farms at 1 pm. They re-scheduled trucks and achieved an agreement with ACO to accommodate the Multiflora shipments at flights between 2 and 4 am. With this agreement, the speed of the total distribution time of the company was enhanced. Thus, they were able to reduce waiting time at the airport from four hours 55 minutes on average (up to 12 hours), to two hours 16 minutes on average (up to five hours 52 minutes).
- Air Way Bill breakdown: Multiflora divided every single shipment in four different ways, with the aim of:
  - speeding up the documentation process by reducing the number of records per guide;
  - taking advantage of leftover space at ACO, given the smaller size of the loads – during the 2015 Mothers' Day season, 60 per cent of the AWB flew between the third and fourth flight, taking advantage of space leftovers;

- creating AWB by product type, streamlining paperwork times and phytosanitary controls at Miami airport;
- facilitating the operational task of the Miami logistics outsourcing.

- New ACO provider: given long flight delays with the airline (LAN), they decided to seek a better service with another airline (TAMPA). Flight delays were reduced from 22 to 8 hours for St Valentine's Day and from 18 to 7 hours for Mothers' Day. However, this decision increased freight costs by US $0.04 per kilogram.

In summary, the Colombian cut flower market is one of the most challenging markets in terms of time response and transportation conditions. Flowers require a complete cold chain from the farms to the final user. In addition, time is a critical variable to assure the quality and freshness of the product. However, despite Colombia's poor logistics infrastructure, companies are able to implement collaboration strategies that mitigate the negative impact of such conditions and remain competitive in foreign markets. For perishable and delicate products such as flowers in a context with a deficient logistics infrastructure, supply chain coordination arises as a cheap and effective alternative to overcome the restrictions imposed by the environment.

Transportation of oil in Colombia

Contributing to around 7 per cent of the national GDP and 45 per cent of exports in 2015, Colombia produced in the same year around 1.2 million barrels of crude oil per day (BOPD) (Reuters, 2016) leading to a ranking of 20th of the oil producing countries worldwide (CIA, 2016). Columbia is currently ranked 34th, with proven reserves of around 2.6 billion barrels (CIA, 2016; Euromonitor International, 2016), the main areas for oil exploration are Meta in the central region of the country, Arauca at the border of Venezuela, and Putumayo at the border with Ecuador. The main player in this industry is Ecopetrol which is a public–private mixed enterprise that has the objective of developing, in Colombia or abroad, the commercialization, exploration, exploitation, refining, transportation, storage, distribution and marketing of hydrocarbons and their derivatives and products activities (Boletines, 2013). Until 2003, Ecopetrol was in charge of the regulatory duties, after which the National Hydrocarbon Agency (ANH) was established and took its place (PwC, 2014).

Oil, which is Colombia's most important export commodity, is shipped to foreign customers primarily as crude oil from the ports of Coveñas and Barranquilla on the Atlantic coast and is in many cases delivered directly from the tank truck to the ship. While the use of pipelines has increased, with improving security in the country since 2002, the traditional transport mode for oil is tank trucks.

Figure 9.3 shows the distance profile for transporting oil from the Rubiales field in Meta to the port of Barranquilla at the Atlantic coast, visualizing some of the challenges the oil transportation in Colombia is facing:

- Distance: given the location of the oil fields and the main ports for oil export, large distances have to be covered; in the case of Rubiales–Barranquilla 1,393 kilometres. This exposes the trucks and drivers to trips of around three days. Approximately 150,000 BOPD are transported by road, with routes over 1,300 kilometres, which suggests that this mode of transport is inefficient and can result in negative effects on the country's road infrastructure and environmental risks.

- Altitude: the Colombian topography contains three significant mountain chains in which the main cities and consequently main roads are located. In the case of the route Rubiales–Barranquilla, the trucks start at an altitude of around 250 metres and the highest point the trucks pass is 3,231 metres before reaching Bogotá followed by a long, curvy and steep descent on the way to the seaport.

- Road conditions: as mentioned above, a main weakness of Colombia's Logistics Performance Index is that the road conditions are in need of improvement and despite investment, the road infrastructure leads to additional challenges due to pavement conditions, the amount of curves (particularly in the mountains), the road width and also the incline, which in the case of Rubiales–Barranquilla reaches a maximum of 15.2 per cent.

- Security: given the current security conditions of the country, the trucks pass on their way to the coast zones which are not always under governmental control. As security conditions can change with little or no warning, detours cannot always be anticipated. Armed groups as well as more common criminality affect transport and final delivery, as well as the environment, particularly when terrorist groups pollute rivers by dumping truckloads of hijacked oil.

- Visibility: the diversity of nature and geography can lead to problems for the GPS systems which sometimes fail to track the trucks.

- Climate: temperature differences and rain expose the transport to additional challenges. During the transport on the route from Rubiales to Barranquilla, the temperature can be between 6–8 degrees Celsius in the mountains and up to 38–40 degrees on the coast. Tropical rainfall in combination with the road conditions can be an additional challenge, interrupting the transport or increasing the risk of accidents.

Figure 9.3 Distance and elevation profile: Rubiales–Barranquilla

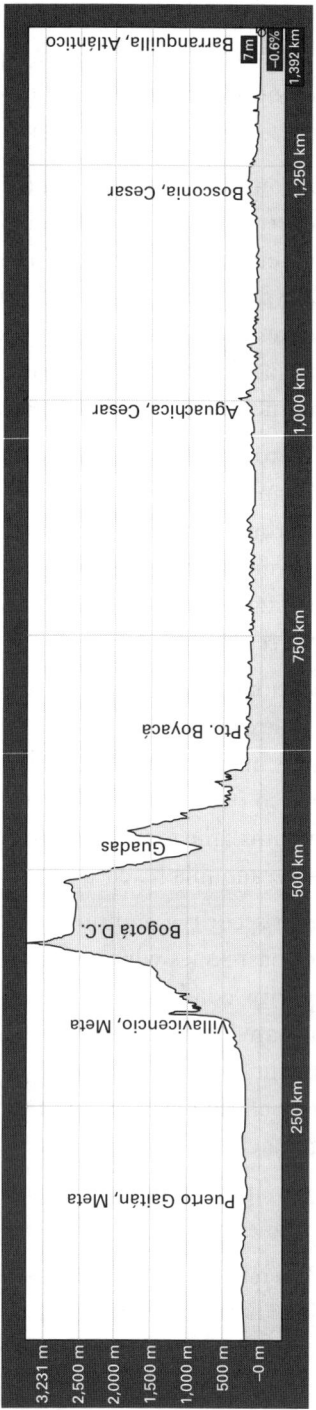

SOURCE Author elaboration using Google Earth elevation profile

In the context of these challenges, the potential impact on competitive parameters and resources involved is manifold, particularly as the above-mentioned challenges combined create high risks of not reaching a perfect order fulfilment.

- Special equipment: to cope with conditions, special suspension, axles, tyres and brakes, as well as the means to protect the trucks against theft are installed. GPS systems to improve visibility are important.
- Cost: to cover the large distances with their extreme distance profiles, costs for gasoline and maintenance (preventive and corrective) are very high. Training needs become relevant and the risk profile leads to higher pay for the truck drivers.
- Timeliness: although supported by sophisticated route planning, the changing conditions on the route lead to problems concerning fulfiling delivery dates.
- Health and wellbeing: drivers are exposed to conditions which on the one hand increase their bargaining power with companies, but on the other hand have a significant impact on their health and wellbeing.

Given the challenges facing tank truck transportation as described above, Ecopetrol has been building pipelines along the whole country and has changed the organizational structure to fulfil the growing transport and logistics needs of the oil business in Colombia. Ecopetrol operates through three business segments: exploration and production; refining and petrochemicals; and transportation and logistics. The transportation and logistics segment includes the transportation of crude oil, motor fuels, fuel oil and other refined products including diesel and biofuels. In June 2012, Ecopetrol's board of directors approved the creation of CENIT, which is in charge of planning and operating the transport infrastructure from the fields to refineries and export centres. They introduced an open operating model, in which all companies in the sector can access the transport infrastructure (Boletines, 2013).

All transportation assets of Ecopetrol (oil and pipelines), including stakes in Central Oil Pipeline SA (Ocensa), Colombia Oil Pipeline SA (ODC), SAS Bicentennial Oil Pipeline, ODL Finance SA, Serviport SA and Ecopetrol Pipelines International Limited, were transferred to be managed by CENIT. Likewise, they will also transfer port concessions. This decision strengthened and expanded the national network of transport of hydrocarbons, meeting high standards for the environment, industrial safety and reliability. In the medium term, this will result in a significant reduction in the deterioration of roads from land transport (Boletines, 2013).

In 2015, CENIT transported 1.2 million BOPD of crude oil and refined products through the crude oil pipelines and multipurpose pipelines. CENIT, directly or indirectly with private sector participants, owned, operated and maintained a network of crude oil and refined products pipelines connecting its own and third-party production centres and terminals to refineries, major distribution points and export facilities in Colombia. CENIT directly owns 46 per cent of the total crude oil pipeline shipping capacity in Colombia. Table 9.4 shows the volumes transported by CENIT during its three years of operation.

In addition to the creation of CENIT, a special unit working together with the national police was established in order to enhance the security of the pipelines, resulting in a reduction in the illegal extraction of crude (through illegal valve installation), and to reduce the number of attacks on the infrastructure. Table 9.5 presents the number of illegal valves identified and attacks recorded during the last three years.

Other possibilities have been explored to improve transportation networks in the country, including participating in business associations in order to pursue and promote infrastructure development projects. For example, Pacific Rubiales, one of the largest private oil companies operating in Colombia, recently joined with other firms in urging the Colombian government to develop initiatives to increase the navigability of the Magdalena River. These initiatives would allow the companies to transport crude oil using the Magdalena River instead of with tanker trucks. The transportation cost reduction using the river was estimated at US $15 per barrel (Ahumada, 2014); a significant reduction in the total logistics cost, particularly when considering oil prices of around US $35–50 in 2015–16.

Table 9.4 CENIT Oil transportation in Kilo Barrels Per Day (KBPD)

	2013	2014	2015
Pipelines	945.85	954.24	976.29
Multipurpose pipelines	237.17	251.2	267.07
Total	1,183.02	1,205.44	1,243.36

SOURCE CENIT (2016)

Table 9.5 Illegal valves and infrastructure attacks on oil installations

	2013	2014	2015
Illegal valves	904	871	807
Infrastructure attacks	185	96	53

SOURCE CENIT (2016)

Colombia has a reserve-to-production ratio of 6.5 years, stressing the importance for the industry and country to discover new reserves in new regions, where the oil transport by trucks will be an integral part of the system. The special context of Colombia remains a challenge for the industry and the oil-transporting companies. The creation of CENIT has allowed the industry to more efficiently manage and develop the transportation network which has led to an increasing trend towards the use of pipelines. CENIT has also allowed the sector to more closely control the transportation infrastructure, leading to the development of contingent strategies with the help of the national police to reduce the attacks and installation of illegal valves through the pipelines. Further, an expected peace agreement could have a positive impact on pipeline security, leading to more construction and use of this alternative and other transportation modes such as river which would result in a more competitive oil industry.

Conclusion

This chapter has discussed issues surrounding international freight transport in light of its rapid growth over the last few decades. This growth has meant that developing regions like South America and nations like Colombia are also experiencing growth in their economies. However, such economic growth is not without its problems and it has a significant impact on logistical and supply chain activities. The case of Colombia generally, and the two case studies of its large export sectors of cut flowers and crude oil, demonstrates that there are challenges in terms of geography, infrastructure and governance to address. However, Colombia is becoming a major global trading nation, but the country must address the aforementioned challenges to ensure its place in global freight business and transportation.

References

Ahumada, O M (2014) El río Magdalena ayudará a capotear crisis del petróleo, *El tiempo*, available at <http://www.eltiempo.com/economia/sectores/crisis-del-petroleo-navegabilidad-por-rio-magdalena/14971085>

Angel, J E and Aranda, Y (2007) Exploración de los principales mercados internacionales para flores tropicales de la provincia del Tequendama, *Revista Colombiana de Ciencias Hortícolas*, 1, pp 81–93

Arango, N, Bernal, J E and Gutierrez, D C (2015) Gestión Cadena de Abastecimiento Multiflora, Master's final project, MBA Uniandes School of Management,

Arvis, J-F, Saslavsky, D, Ojala, L, Shepherd, B, Busch, C, Raj, A and Nola, T (2016) Connecting to compete 2016: Trade logistics in the global economy – the

Logistics Performance Index and its indicators, *World Bank*, available at <https://openknowledge.worldbank.org/handle/10986/24598>

Asocolflores (2015a) *Boletín Estadístico 2015: Dirección de economía y logística*, Asocolflores, Bogotá

Asocolflores (2015b) Plan de desarrollo logístico, infographic, available at <http://www.asocolflores.org/>

Avianca Cargo (2016) Mother's Day Celebration: Avianca cargo shipped more than 11 thousand tons of flowers from Colombia and Ecuador to the United States and Puerto Rico, available at <http://www.avianca.com/en/Documents/press-releases/avianca-cargo-shipped-more-than-eleven-thousand-tons-of-flowers-from-co-and-ec-to-the-us-and-pr.pdf>

Boletines (2013) Recuperado el 10 de 08 de 2013, de Reporte de resultados segundo trimestre del 2013, *Ecopetrol*, available at <http://www.ecopetrol.com.co/contenido.aspx?catID=148&conID=79328&pagID=135388>

Burnson, P (2013) Global Logistics: In South America proceed with care, *Logistics Management*, available at <http://www.logisticsmgmt.com/article/global_logistics_in_south_america_proceed_with_care>

CENIT (2016) Sustainability Report 2015, *CENIT*, available at <http://www.clientestriario.info/Cenit/2016/Mailings/mayo/Informe-sostenibilidad/Cenit_Informe_final-baja.pdf>

CIA (2016) World Factbook, available at <https://www.cia.gov/library/publications/the-world-factbook/geos/xx.html>

Conlon, M (2015) The history of the Colombian flower industry and its influence on the United States, *USDA Foreign Agricultural Service*, available at <http://gain.fas.usda.gov/Recent%20GAIN%20Publications/The%20Colombian%20flower%20industry%20and%20its%20partnership%20with%20the%20U.S._Bogota_Colombia_2-6-2015.pdf>

Cuartas Rodríguez, P (2014) La travesía de las flores, *El Espectador,* available at <http://www.elespectador.com/noticias/actualidad/travesia-de-flores-articulo-491504>

DANE (2015) Banco de la República available at <http://www.banrep.gov.co/es/pib>

Escandón, J (2009) Propuesta logística para el desarrollo de la exportación de rosas y claveles a estados unidos para la comercializadora Export Flexy Ltda, Pontificia Universidad Javeriana – Facultad de Ingeniería, available at <http://www.javeriana.edu.co/biblos/tesis/ingenieria/Tesis238.pdf>

Euromonitor International (2016) Colombia: Country profile, *Euromonitor International*, 22 February

Fernie, J and Grant, D B (2015) *Fashion Logistics*, Kogan Page, London

Gardner, D L and Gómez, H S (2009) *CSCMP Global Perspectives Colombia*, Council of Supply Chain Management Professionals, Lombard, IL

González Cárdenas, A (2013) Intercambio de Información en las cadenas de suministro internacionales. El caso de la cadena de suministro de flor fresca cortada colombiana para la exportación, *Santiago de Chile: CEPAL –*

Naciones Unidas, available at <http://repositorio.cepal.org/bitstream/handle/11362/4350/1/LCL3705_es.pdf>

Grant, D B (2012) *Logistics Management*, Pearson Education Limited, Harlow, UK

IADB (2014) *Freight Logistics Statistics Yearbook for Latin America and the Caribbean*, Inter-American Development Bank available at <http://www.iadb.org/en/inter-american-development-bank,2837.html>

ICA (2010) Flores Colombianas se alistan para celebración del día de las madres en EE.UU, *Agronet*, available at <http://www.agronet.gov.co/Noticias/Paginas/Noticia337.aspx>

Incoterms (2016) *Incoterms 2010*, available at <http://www.iccwbo.org/products-and-services/trade-facilitation/incoterms-2010/>

Legiscomex (2007) Flores y Follajes en EEUU, *Legiscomex*, available at <http://www.legiscomex.com/BancoMedios/Documentos%20PDF/perfilfloresyfollajeseeuu-1.pdf>

Multiflora (2015) Multiflora Farm Direct Experts, *Multiflora*, available at <www.multiflora.com/about>

PwC (2014) Colombia oil & gas industry 2014, *Price Waterhouse Coopers*, available at <http://www.pwc.com/co/es/publicaciones/assets/pwc-oil-gas-colombia.pdf>

Reuters (2016) TABLE-Colombia 2015 oil output up 1.75 pct over year before, *Reuters*, available at <http://www.reuters.com/article/colombia-oil-output-idUSL1N13Z1CC Ecopetrol S.A>

Salazar Castillo, J D and Córdoba Martínez, S E (2014) Análisis de la realidad del sector floricultor colombiano y el potencial del mercado Sur Coreano, Bachelor's Thesis, Universidad del Rosario, available at <http://repository.urosario.edu.co/handle/10336/8707>

Vélez Valencia, C (2015) Doing business amidst conflict: Two essays on the distribution of basic consumer goods, PhD Thesis, Universidad de los Andes: Bogotá

Wilson, R (2015) *Freight moves the economy in 2014: CSCMP's 26th Annual State of Logistics Report*, Council of Supply Chain Management Professionals, Lombard IL

World Shipping Council (2016) Trade Routes, available at <http://www.worldshipping.org/about-the-industry/global-trade/trade-routes>

WTO (2016) StatTalk, available at <https://www.wto.org/english/res_e/statis_e/stattalk_dec15_e.pdf>

Useful online sources

Banco Central de Colombia: http://www.banrep.gov.co/
Ministerio de Transporte: https://www.mintransporte.gov.co/
Departamento Administrativo Nacional de Estadística: www.dane.gov.co
Superintendencia de Puertos y Transportes: http://www.supertransporte.gov.co/super/
Autoridad de Aeronáutica Civil: http://www.aerocivil.gov.co/AAeronautica/Paginas/Inicio.aspx

International freight transport in Southern Africa

CHRISTOPHER SAVAGE, University of Huddersfield, UK

Introduction

The term 'Southern Africa' would seem to be self-explanatory in that it relates to the southernmost region of the African continent and consists of a number of countries determined by geography or geopolitics. Nevertheless, as Tuathail and Toal (1996) state:

> Geography is about power. Although assumed to be innocent, the geography of the world is not a product of nature but a product of the histories of struggle between competing authorities over the power to organize, occupy and administer space.

This certainly applies to the countries of Southern Africa, as they have all been occupied and controlled by other, usually European, powers. For example, Botswana, then known as the Bechuanaland Protectorate, was occupied by the United Kingdom from 1885 to 1966, and Mozambique was colonized by Portugal, not becoming an independent republic until 1975. In some cases this has happened more than once, even during the 20th century. For example, Namibia was colonized by Germany in 1884 but was administered as a Province by the Republic of South Africa (RSA) from 1917 until gaining independence in 1990. The RSA itself only emerged from violent territorial disputes between European settlers and indigenous people to become a self-governing state in 1934 and fully independent in 1994. Thus colonization has left its mark on the culture, political geography of the region and still has a major impact on the logistics and transport patterns of the region. In particular, the RSA (a BRICS nation) dominates much of the trade, and therefore logistics, of the region.

It could even be argued that at a basic level, modern Southern African countries are all artificial as they each contain many diverse tribal groups that dispute, form alliances, compete and often frustrate collaboration within the logistics industry. Nevertheless, for practical purposes it is appropriate to use current geographical nomenclature. The UN and the Southern African Customs Union (SACU) define Southern Africa as the five countries of Botswana, Lesotho, Namibia, RSA and Swaziland (SACU, 2016), whereas the Southern African Development Community (SADC) recognizes a larger group consisting of Angola, Botswana, Democratic Republic of Congo (DRC), Lesotho, Madagascar, Malawi, Mauritius, Mozambique, Namibia, Seychelles, RSA, Swaziland, United Republic of Tanzania, Zambia and Zimbabwe (SADC, 2012). This chapter will concentrate on the SACU countries but will bear in mind the cross-border interaction with neighbouring countries such as Angola, Mozambique, Zambia and Zimbabwe.

Trade, logistics, transport and corridors

Countries trade with each other when they do not have the resources or capacity to satisfy their own needs and wants. By developing and exploiting scarce commodities that are available domestically, countries can produce a surplus and trade this for the resources they need (Economics Online Ltd, 2015). It is generally accepted that trading is beneficial to the trading countries and economic theory shows that there are gains from trade for all countries involved (Ricardo, 1821; WTO E-Learning, 2012). Interestingly, WTO E-Learning (2012) also suggests that although there are financial benefits from trade, there are likely to be disparate effects on the distribution of income. This means that, within any country, some groups will make gains but others may lose. This may be an important factor for the developing countries of Southern Africa, many of which have high Gini coefficients showing that income is unevenly distributed.

Despite the reservations over the possible impact on income distribution, the importance of trade to developing countries is recognized by the World Trade Organization (WTO). As the majority of WTO members are developing countries, one of the main focuses of the organization is to ensure that they are able to participate in international and multilateral trading (World Bank, 2014). The importance of trade in the region has been recognized by local governments and non-government organizations (NGOs). For example, USAID have established the 'Southern African Trade Hub', based in Gaborone (Botswana), with the key objective of 'increasing international competitiveness, intra-regional trade and food security in Southern Africa' (USAID, 2016) and have introduced the web-based 'Trade Information Portal' as a stepping stone to a full 'National Single Window' approach to Customs connectivity to smooth the flow of trade (Anon, 2016). Similarly, the World Bank commissioned a 'Regional trade and transport facilitation assessment for the SACU region', which reported in December 2014 and clearly links trade to transport (Farole, 2014).

The link between freight transport and trade is clear, since if tangible goods cannot be transported they cannot be traded. The exceptions to this are items that can be distributed electronically such as music or literature and, in the future, possibly items suitable for 3D printing. Therefore, trade has been inexorably linked with logistics for as long as human beings have had to move goods to or from a market (Korinek and Sourdin, 2011; World Trade Organization, 2004). For imported goods to become available in a Southern African country, they may have travelled thousands of miles and crossed several borders. Therefore, the price will include freight clearance charges, handling charges, insurance and fuel costs as well as the wages of the drivers and others involved in the transport. As Matsaert (2015) points out, these transport and allied charges can amount to 45 per cent of the cost involved in getting the goods to the point of sale. Nevertheless as OECD/WTO (2013) state, transport and logistics can boost trade performance, which, under appropriate circumstances, leads to higher incomes, employment gains, and lower poverty rates.

It is apparent that logistics can be both an enabler of and a potential barrier to trade development. This is illustrated in Southern Africa, where development has traditionally occurred along routes that connect areas of industry with areas of trade. That is, (predominantly) imported goods flow from ports along roads, railways, waterways and pipelines to end-users in towns and cities, whilst raw materials move back through the same pathways to ports for export. These routes are generically known as corridors and occur in many countries and regions in various forms with a variety of names. For example Brunner (2013) defines economic corridors by their function, saying that they 'connect economic agents along a defined geography. They provide important connections between economic nodes or hubs that are usually centred in urban landscapes'. The major drivers of African trade and corridor development are resources, agriculture and retail (see for example UNCTAD, 2013). Brunner suggests Southern Africa will lead the development of corridors in the short term and predicts that its trade volumes will increase from 240 m tonnes in 2009 to 617 m tonnes in 2030, in terms of tonnes moved. Unfortunately, there is usually a significant imbalance as, for most SACU counties, imports far outweigh exports in both monetary and volume terms. The latter is partially responsible for the shortage of return loads and correspondingly high levels of empty running that prevail across much of the region.

As noted above, infrastructure has mainly developed along corridors and agencies such as the World Bank believe that, as well as trade, these are essential for the development of areas of economic improvement. All Southern African Transport countries rely on corridors as a source or destination of goods but also benefit from the provision of services along the routes as well as from Customs duties and other levies applied at the borders.

Where the country is able to act as an ingress point or gateway to a region, there is usually an opportunity to enhance the access point, eg a harbour or airport, to try to develop a fully configured logistics cluster. On the other hand, where it only functions as a conduit and does not buy or sell the goods, there may be an argument that damage to the infrastructure and side effects such as the spread of animal-borne or human-transmitted diseases such as Dengue virus or HIV/AIDS, could outweigh the benefits. Governments in the region feel that the potential benefits outweigh any risks and actively promote the expansion and improvement of corridors, which have become the focal point for many regional initiatives. Some Southern African countries such as Botswana, Lesotho and Zimbabwe are landlocked and need the transport corridors to access the sea and potential global trading partners.

Whilst transport corridors have been around for hundreds of years, their potential to enhance economic growth by opening up markets to stimulate increased trade and investment has only recently been appreciated fully. Figure 10.1 shows a number of the significant corridors that serve the region. According to the Port & Corridor Cooperation (2012) and the Walvis Bay Corridor Group (WBCG, 2013), these include:

- **North–South (South Africa) Corridor.** The Cape Town–Gauteng and the Durban–Gauteng trade routes connect South Africa's most industrialized ports to Gauteng, the economic heart of the country. It is part of the North–South corridor, running northwards and linking with the Dar es Salaam corridor.
- **Dar es Salaam Corridor.** This plays a key role of serving the needs of Malawi, Zambia and the Democratic Republic of Congo.
- **Trans-Kalahari Corridor.** The Trans-Kalahari Corridor (TKC) was established with a political and economic vision to pursue or contribute

Figure 10.1 Main southern and eastern African transport corridors

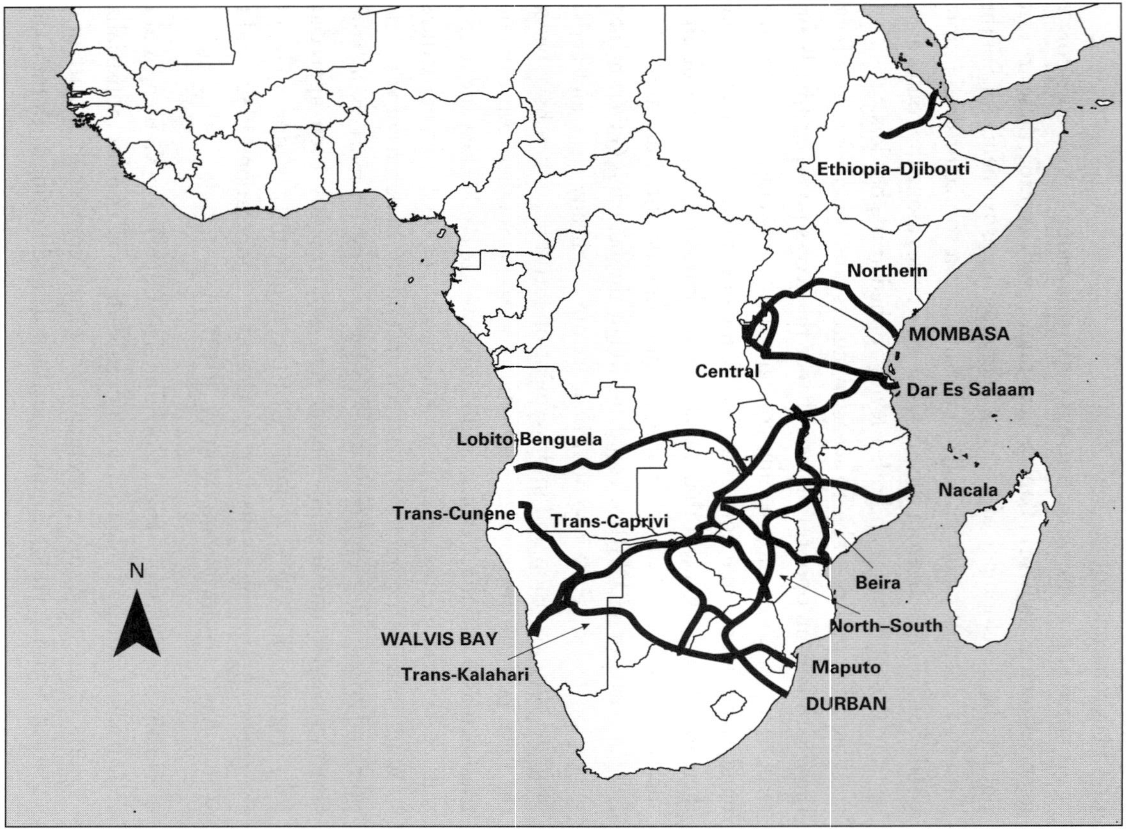

SOURCE Adapted from Transport World Africa (2015)

towards the deeper regional integration programmes of SADC, SACU and NEPAD (New Partnership for Africa's Development). It connects the port of Walvis Bay on Namibia's coast to the port of Maputo, Mozambique.

- **Maputo Corridor.** The Maputo (Development) Corridor (MDC) was launched in 1996 to restore trade and investment ties between RSA and Mozambique.
- **Lobito Corridor.** This is an important array of integrated infrastructure, formed by various enterprises and economic units. It runs west–east to connect Angola with the western state of Southern Africa and thus plays a key role as a platform in the regional and international network system of transport in Southern Africa.
- The group comprising the **Trans-Cunene**, **Trans-Caprivi** and **Trans-Oranje Corridors** (previously known as the Southern Extension). Provides links from the Port of Walvis Bay to:
  - Zambia, the southern Democratic Republic of Congo (DRC) and Zimbabwe;
  - Lubango, southern Angola; and
  - Lüderitz and the Northern Cape Province of South Africa respectively.

As development escalates in the region, these geographic corridors are growing in importance to the SADC as they enable other sectors to maximize their productivity. To support this, the SADC proposed the setting up of 'Spatial Development Initiatives' (SADC, 2012) and this has been adopted by some member states (Boois, 2015). These were first developed in RSA but the model has spread throughout the region. One of the most notable is based around the Maputo Development Corridor, which restored the historic trade route between the landlocked provinces of Gauteng and Mpumalanga in South Africa to the port of Maputo in Mozambique. Its initial upgrades to basic infrastructure proved profitable and drew extensive finance into the sub-region, leading to further public and private investment into transport and communications infrastructure. This led to related industrial projects, such as the BHP Billiton Mozal aluminium smelter in Maputo, which in turn have created jobs and fostered further economic development (Farole, 2014). Meanwhile, the 2012 Regional Infrastructure Development Master Plan suggests that the North–South Corridor and the Dar es Salaam Corridor are a priority for development that, together with medium-priority corridors (eg the Beira and Nacala Multimodal Corridor), offer the greatest potential for regional growth in the future (Farole, 2014).

Unfortunately, infrastructural bottlenecks often restrict the operation of the corridors and have an impact on the associated industries. Constraints include poor roads and bridges, inadequate railways and a lack of facilities for drivers. Despite these more obvious physical issues the Regional Infrastructure Development Master Plan suggests that three-quarters of delays are caused by poor usage of the existing infrastructure. For example, the application of complicated Customs regulations and border procedures can cause delays ranging from hours to several days in extreme cases. The combination of these physical and operational issues adds costs and significantly damages trade in the region. Also, partly because of these problems, not all transport corridors are able to act as economic ones (Mulenga, 2013) and this limits the region's ability to compete on a global scale. Such problems have prompted the SADC to draw up a Protocol on Transport, Communication and Meteorology. The protocol calls for the creation of Corridor Planning Committees to focus on specific strategies for development along the region's key corridors.

Corridor Planning Committees are cross-border bodies made up of both public and private stakeholders from transport, Customs and infrastructure authorities, trade and industry and educational organizations, as well as corridor users. They are tasked with determining specific requirements of their respective corridors and overseeing plans for their development. Some of the corridors are promoted and supported by organizations designed to facilitate their use. For example, the Trans-Kalahari Corridor Secretariat (TKC) is a tripartite trans-boundary corridor management institution that aims to improve the regional integration programmes of SADC, SACU and NEPAD by providing a strategic route-of-choice that gives linkages between the Americas and East European markets and the Southern African hinterland (TKCS, 2014). Similarly, the Walvis Bay Corridor Group serves as a facilitation centre and one-stop shop coordinating trade along the corridors linking Namibia and its ports to the rest of the Southern African region (WBCG, 2009).

The SADC is trying to reduce or eliminate non-tariff barriers to trade, especially unequal border practices (eg by the harmonization of Customs practices throughout the region) to allow and encourage trade to flow freely. While all member states have complied with a region-wide free trade agreement, only Botswana, Lesotho, Namibia, South Africa and Swaziland have thus far joined SACU (SADC, 2012). Some of the individual regional governments, whilst subscribing to the general principles of the SADC, are suspicious that it may have political aspirations that go beyond trade and are perhaps more 'federal in nature'.

This means that although trade facilitation initiatives such as the 'Regional trade and transport facilitation assessment for the SACU region' are well supported, their recommendations, particularly where they may appear not to be to an individual country's perceived immediate advantage, are often not adopted or 'put on a back burner'. Similarly, whilst the declared aims of the Corridor Planning Committees include the provision of coordinated and harmonious freight transport across the region, they cannot eliminate national rivalry and competition. There are many examples of the aims of one group of countries conflicting with those of another. For example: Angola and Zambia plan to construct a railway line to link them (Masawi, 2012); if successful, this may result in a decline in the usage of the Trans-Caprivi Highway Corridor and a concomitant loss of revenue and jobs along parts of its 2,500-kilometre length (eg in Namibia).

Demand and supply: trading volumes

Freight requirements across Southern African nations are influenced by internal trade and trade with other regional members as well as with the rest of the world. According to the SADC (2012), their main 'SADC trade export items' include petroleum oils, agricultural products, electricity and some clothing and textile products. In contrast, the key exports to the rest of the world consist of predominantly raw material resources (eg coal, ferrochromium, manganese ores, platinum and uranium as well as precious metals and gemstones), resource-intensive manufactured goods, mainly for the automotive industry, some clothing and textiles, and tobacco. Intra-African exports make up only a small portion of the exports, whilst the greatest volumes over time go to the Asia-Pacific, followed by the EU markets. Table 10.1 gives an estimate of the volume of intra-SACU trade and illustrates the severity of the freight imbalance across the region, whilst Table 10.2. shows the percentage of SADC exports by destination.

Table 10.2 uses aggregated and generalized figures and, although the SADC constitutes a significant trading bloc, there are difficulties in assembling reliable and compatible statistics for the member states, particularly at a detailed level. This is illustrated by the statement on their website which, whilst acknowledging that 'relevant, timely and accurate statistical information is essential for effective planning, policy formulation, protocol monitoring and decision making in the... region', goes on to say that (although) the SADC Regional Indicative Strategic Development Plan

Table 10.1 Estimated volumes of intra-SACU trade showing the imbalance (2012)

	Trade totals				
	Export	Import	Balance	Ratio	
Botswana	228,812	1,538,714	(1,309,902)	6.7	Import/Export
Lesotho	9,723	336,192	(326,469)	34.6	Import/Export
Namibia	421,575	1,151,259	(729,684)	2.7	Import/Export
South Africa	3,158,413	731,586	2,426,827	4.3	Export/Import
Swaziland	105,712.00	166,485.00	(60,773)	1.6	Import/Export

SOURCE Adapted from World Bank (2014)

Table 10.2 Overall direction of SADC Exports (2000–2010)

Regional economic community/ continent	Asian Pacific (APEC)	Europe (EU)	Rest of the world	Intra-SADC	Rest of Africa
Percentage export	45	27	15	10	3

SOURCE Adapted from International Monetary Fund (2012)

(RISDP) identifies statistics as one of the cross-cutting issues, there will be a 15-year implementation framework (SADC, 2016). The reality of this issue is reinforced by Global Edge (2016), who are able to offer quite detailed import/export information for Botswana and RSA (see Table 10.3), but not for other SACU countries such as Namibia or Lesotho (although their general features and contacts are listed).

Despite the limitations of this data, there are a number of general, interesting deductions that can be made, which can be applied to most of the Southern African countries to a greater or lesser extent. These include:

- **Dominance of the RSA.** The size of the RSA population, its relatively more sophisticated port and logistics infrastructure compared to most of its neighbours, its colonial history and relative political stability enable it to dominate much of the trade flows in the region.

Table 10.3 Botswana's and RSA's top 10 import and export partners (UN Comtrade, 2014)

	Botswana's trade partners				RSA's trade partners			
Top 10 import partners	Import volumes ($)	Top 10 export partners	Export volumes ($)	Top 10 import partners	Import volumes ($)	Top 10 export partners	Export volumes ($)
RSA	4,952,700,852	Belgium	2,040,988,365	China	15,449,362,413	China	8,680,021,942
Namibia	944,325,922	India	1,179,639,430	Germany	10,003,241,740	United States	6,420,025,627
Canada	783,749,128	RSA	932,895,711	Saudi Arabia	7,129,423,486	Japan	4,869,325,871
Belgium	312,365,944	Israel	662,200,810	United States	6,595,504,413	Botswana	4,774,961,315
Israel	118,734,678	Namibia	583,847,794	Nigeria	5,135,808,001	Namibia	4,529,160,727
United States	112,361,447	UAE	372,630,642	India	4,551,486,012	Germany	4,236,185,162
China	88,221,885	Singapore	347,374,638	Japan	3,777,363,593	India	3,769,815,070
India	76,352,569	Canada	323,239,367	United Kingdom	3,271,703,012	United Kingdom	3,458,918,635
Germany	76,074,312	Switzerland	281,230,446	Italy	2,641,239,165	Mozambique	3,001,627,305
United Kingdom	64,646,213	Hong Kong	235,972,758	Thailand	2,376,335,344	Netherlands	2,995,893,00

SOURCE Data extracted from Global Edge (2016)

- **Imbalance of trade.** In all cases, there is a significant imbalance between imports and exports (usually with imports exceeding exports). Although the physical volumes do not always match the values (eg where precious stones are exported and manufactured goods imported), this shows that balancing freight traffic is likely to be a significant problem leading to empty running, inefficient loads/routes, high costs and environmental damage as well as impacting upon long-term sustainability.
- **Continuing colonial influence.** Links are often retained with former colonizer countries, which may become key trading partners. This can be complicated by historical event. For example, the country that is now the RSA was colonized by the UK and the Netherlands but, in turn, it occupied Namibia. Apart from the direct effects, this also gives both countries links to English- and Afrikaans-speaking territories. Mozambique was colonized by Portugal, giving it links to both Portugal and its former colonies such as Brazil.
- **Investor countries.** Most Southern African countries rely on inward investment for their major development projects, often in the form of Foreign Direct Investment (FDI), which can be from former colonizers, but in the 21st century is tending to be from China, India or Japan, which feature in the trading lists.

The lack of reliable statistical data is a common problem across the region and is particularly prevalent in the case of transport and logistics, which makes both planning and research difficult. Although data are available in individual countries, much of them may be neither accurate nor consistent over time. An exception is South Africa's 'Logistics Barometer', which is now managed by Stellenbosch University and provides annual up-to-date and historical information. There are plans to extend this to other countries, which if adopted may provide invaluable information in the future.

Trade agreements

Southern Africa, like the rest of the continent, needs a step change in economic growth and performance. The constituent countries tend to have a very low manufacturing base so the structural transformation of their economies can only be achieved by making use of the symbiotic relationship between trade and industrialization (United Nations Economic Commission for Africa, 2015). In order that this can be both inclusive and sustainable they have negotiated trading agreements with other countries;

Southern African, African and worldwide. In some instances, these are at a country-to-country level whilst in others there are also agreements between countries and trading blocs and between trading blocs.

Individual country-to-country arrangements are often difficult to agree due their disparate colonial history, other political factors and pre-existing agreements. In addition, trading bloc agreements are complicated by mixed allegiances. For example, according to European Commission (2016), the EU signed an Economic Partnership Agreement (EPA) on 10 June 2016 with the SADC EPA Group comprising Botswana, Lesotho, Mozambique, Namibia, South Africa and Swaziland, with Angola holding an option to join the agreement in future. But the other six members of the SADC (The Democratic Republic of the Congo (DRC), Madagascar, Malawi, Mauritius, Zambia and Zimbabwe) are negotiating EPAs with the EU as part of other regional groups – the Preferential Trade Area (PTA) for Eastern and Southern African States and the Common Market for Eastern and Southern Africa (COMESA). This complexity makes negotiations difficult, may lead to issues with import or export documentation and exacerbates the problems associated with border procedures. The situation is often further complicated by the aspirations of individual countries, which may not align with those of the trading bloc they subscribe to or the other member countries of it. This is particularly apparent when organizations such as SADC try to harmonize Customs' systems or gain agreement on tariffs or cabotage and similar regulations.

One of the main mechanisms used by SADC to facilitate and control the trade within the region is the establishment of protocols. For example, the 2005 Protocol on Trade was intended to create a Free Trade Area in the SADC region by 2008. According to SADC (2012), its purpose was to liberalize intra-regional trade in goods and services, improve production efficiency, develop the climate for domestic, cross-border and foreign investment, as well as enhancing the economic development, diversification and industrialization of the region. This would lead to the creation of a bigger market with greater potential for trade, economic growth and employment. This partially succeeded by 2008, when 85 per cent of intra-regional trade amongst the partner states had attained zero duty, but maximum tariff liberalization was only attained in early 2012, when the tariffs for sensitive products were phased in fully. Nevertheless, this was still only a qualified success because a) some individual countries (eg RSA and Mozambique) did not complete their agreements in the targeted timeframe and b) the underpinning mechanisms for operating the Customs' systems have yet to be harmonized.

Infrastructure

The infrastructure across the SACU region can perhaps best be described as adequate. There are parts that are of quite a high standard, but others that are rather poor. The distances that have to be covered in some of the countries are vast but the infrastructure does manage to link ports and airports with major cities and rural areas, albeit sometimes at a fairly basic level. There are capacity constraints that mitigate against the completely successful development of regional value chains capable of interfacing smoothly with their global equivalents.

The road and rail infrastructure varies considerable across Southern Africa. It has been influenced by previous colonial powers and the priorities of incoming governments so, for example, whilst Botswana has approximately 80 per cent metalled roads, Namibia has only about 12 per cent. SACU as a whole has only 27 per cent metalled roads, but this is partly ameliorated because of the dry climates which make gravel roads more viable. In addition, the region's roads have some 'quirky' issues; for example, many of the major roads in Botswana are unfenced, which means that animals ranging from domestic small stock to fully grown kudus or even elephants can stray on to them at night. A collision with such an animal can extensively damage any vehicle, even an interlink truck, so hauliers moving goods from (for example) central Namibia to Gauteng Province in northern RSA may drive on a 'dog-leg' route to avoid Botswana but add 500 km to their journey. Perhaps the main issue with Southern African logistics infrastructure is that most the countries are very large but have small populations. This means that the ratio of (tax-paying) people to kilometre of road or rail is very low; for example, Namibia has 21.3 road kilometres per 1,000 people compared to 4 km/1,000 in Lesotho and less than 3.8 km/1,000 in India. These ratios mean that the cost of building new or maintaining existing infrastructure is a heavy burden on the countries' economies and is therefore often not of the standard that would be acceptable in more developed countries.

One issue is the balance between road and rail freight usage, especially on long hauls. The railways for the most part are 'Cape Gauge', which causes restrictions in terms of loading and the availability of reasonably priced replacement rolling stock. In addition, signalling systems are often rather basic or non-existent, which leads to inefficient usage particularly where there are long stretches of single track lines. Some of the railway tracks were originally laid down to facilitate troop movements in the early 20th century and may not follow the best routes for present-day commercial use. In some cases, they are operated and/or maintained by parastatal organizations such as Portos e Caminhos de Ferro de Moçambique in Mozambique, TransNamib in Namibia and Transnet in the RSA.

These state-controlled companies, faced with difficult infrastructure-to-people ratios, are often underfunded and do not usually have a good record of maintenance and replacement. The associated freight services are often considered to be unreliable and very slow. Generally, SACU regional rail networks are characterized by inefficiency, continually lose ground to road transport and struggle to survive commercially. This means that even high-volume, low-value commodities such as maize meal are often moved long distances (1,000 kilometres or more) by truck rather than rail. This is undesirable from an environmental as well as a commercial viewpoint, but many rail customers, such as the major retailers, prefer road because of the perceived better reliability and shorter travel times.

Port facilities within SACU are restricted to the countries with coastlines, ie the RSA and Namibia, although other Southern African countries such as Mozambique and Angola also have harbours and the corridors enable goods to be imported or exported through ports that are further afield such as Dar es Salaam in Tanzania, if the haulage costs and timescale are acceptable. Although these non-SACU ports are available, their use is restricted because of Customs regulations. For example, although the port of Maputo (Mozambique) is used for exporting bulk goods such as coal or sugar, it handles very few imports because of the need for a bond. The most important commercial ports in SACU are Durban, Port Elizabeth, Ngqura, East London and Cape Town in the RSA and Walvis Bay in Namibia, although there are a number of smaller harbours such as Mossel Bay (RSA) and Lüderitz (Namibia). Figure 10.2 shows the bulk and container tonneage at the main regional ports. All these ports compete for tonnage on the basis of position relative to shipping routes, the hinterland for which they wish to act as a gateway as well as service and price.

One interesting concept is that of the SADC Mall, where the proponents (WBCG) suggest that the region should be treated as a giant 'Mall' giving access to its population of almost 258 million. WBCG's view is for a single point of entry through Walvis Bay, but in reality, any of the major ports could fill such a role and it is more likely that there would be multiple ingress/egress points with volumes reflecting their location relative to the transport corridors, potential demand and the shipping routes (Smith, 2015).

There are capacity constraints, for example when in 2012 the Walvis Bay port, which had not previously been regarded as a bottleneck, experienced

Figure 10.2 Main SACU regional port volumes (2012)

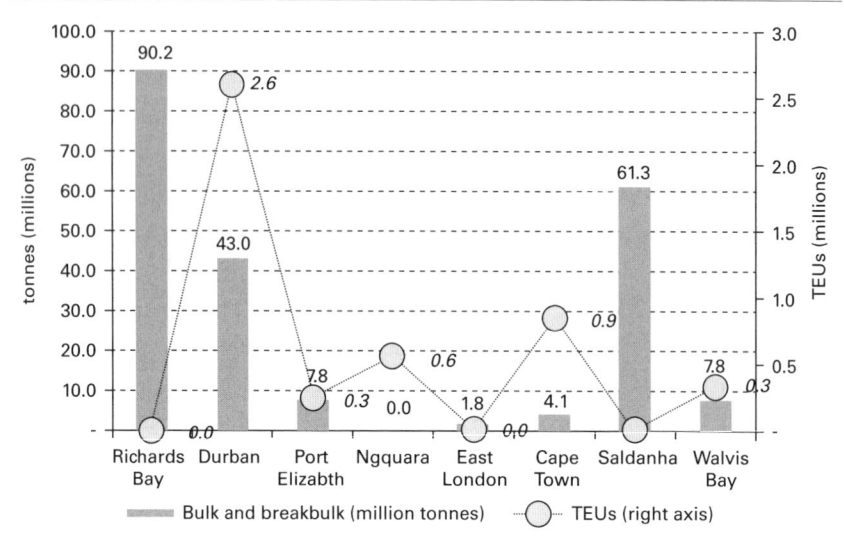

[Bar and line chart showing bulk and breakbulk (million tonnes) and TEUs (millions) for the following ports:
- Richards Bay: 90.2 tonnes, 0.0 TEUs
- Durban: 43.0 tonnes, 2.6 TEUs
- Port Elizabeth: 7.8 tonnes, 0.3 TEUs
- Ngquara: 0.0 tonnes, 0.6 TEUs
- East London: 1.8 tonnes, 0.0 TEUs
- Cape Town: 4.1 tonnes, 0.9 TEUs
- Saldanha Bay: 61.3 tonnes, 0.0 TEUs
- Walvis Bay: 7.8 tonnes, 0.3 TEUs]

SOURCE Farole (2014)
NOTE Walvis Bay data shows volumes from September 2011 to August 2012

significant congestion leading up to the busy Christmas period; Durban's inbound freight congestion is also a significant problem. The Durban issue is being addressed by an expansion plan that will incorporate part of the old airport to give increased potential volume on the east coast of the continent, whilst Walvis Bay is currently the subject of a proposed expansion plan that seeks to raise its capacity to 1 million TEUs, thus enhancing the west coast option.

One major concern is the bulk capacity that will be required to service Botswana's coal exports. Some five alternative routes have been considered, most of which entail the building of new railway lines, possibly of a wider gauge and all of which would have a significant impact on the chosen export port. One difficulty with this new business is that this export volume is unlikely to help rebalance the inbound tonnage because the rolling stock needed for the coal will almost certainly be unsuitable for carrying imports such as retail commodities.

Port pricing in the RSA is another issue because the port tariffs are still based on a system designed to support imports and cross-price subsidies, which leads to confused costs. For example, in 2012, container port tariffs were four times the global average but those for bulk were 18 to 42 times below the global average (Farole, 2014). In general, transport operations costs are considerably higher than in Europe and the United States and this

Table 10.4   Selected SADC countries' LPI (2016)

Logistics performance index of SADC countries (2016)		
Country	Rank	Score
South Africa	20	3.78
Botswana	57	3.05
Namibia	79	2.74
Mozambique	84	2.68
Zambia	114	2.43

SOURCE Adapted from World Bank (2016)
NOTE Other SADC countries are ranked below 160th in the listing

is reflected in their Logistics Performance Index (LPI) scores and rankings, where only the RSA appears in the top 50 countries (Table 10.4).

LPIs are often regarded as somewhat subjective, but they do give an indication that the service levels offered by Southern African countries are likely to be significantly lower than those expected by major global players. Some Southern African logistics operators, their stakeholders and their regional customers may not see this as a problem because their competitors may only offer the same things so their customers have little choice. If the Southern African countries want to engage fully with the international logistics community to reap the benefits from global trade and enable the economic and social development of the region, they may have to re-engineer their infrastructure, operations and service offering.

Another transportation aspect influenced by infrastructure is the adoption and use of intermodal transport. Whilst stakeholders from government and private sectors frequently talk about the benefits of intermodal transport, in most Southern African countries there is a shortage of harbour-based transfer facilities, eg for moving containers easily from ship to train, which exacerbates the limitations of the rail services available. Therefore, although many of the Southern African-based multinational logistics companies such as Imperial Logistics, FP du Toit or TransWorld Cargo advertise and operate intermodal services, they are restricted by the infrastructure issues and have acknowledged that (in Southern Africa) intermodal transport is in its infancy and it will be some years before the benefits are realized (Foulds, 2013).

Perhaps the final pieces in the infrastructure jigsaw are the hubs, clusters, ports and dry ports that serve as the nodes of the supply chains. As already mentioned, Southern African countries have a number of coastal ports that facilitate import and export, but there are also a number of landlocked countries such as Botswana, Lesotho, Zambia and Zimbabwe that do not have direct access to the sea. Some goods are flown by air direct to these countries and others arrive by inland waterway but by far the majority are transported overland by rail or truck using the transport corridors. In some cases, these goods are unloaded and cleared for Customs at the port of entry, but where appropriate Customs agreements are in place, goods may be transported in their sealed containers to a dry port in the destination country where they can be unloaded and cleared.

Recently, a number of the landlocked countries have acquired land at coastal ports to build their own dry ports where goods can be inspected by the receiving country's Customs and then transported as 'cleared goods' to their destination. Examples include Botswana and Zambia, which have dry ports of, respectively, 36,233 and 30,152 square metres at Walvis Bay (Namibia), whilst Zimbabwe has been granted an 18,332-square-metre area at the same location that it hopes to have on-stream by mid-2018. The format of the hubs varies considerably from simple points of cargo exchange to more complex facilities that exhibit some of the features of full logistics clusters that are able to enhance corridor and trade development. Few of them have the sophistication of their European or North American equivalents, but all have an essential role to play in the facilitation of the region's freight transport.

Ancillary factors

There are a number of issues, apart from those already mentioned, that assist or inhibit development of the region's transport industry.

Trade, logistics and transport appear to be recognized by all of the regional governments as being essential to the development and future success of their countries. Organizations such as the World Bank, USAID and the UN agree with this, support the countries' endeavours and try to encourage cross-regional cooperation, which will be vital to the future success of the countries' freight transport industry. Although most of the countries have limited financial resources, there are a plethora of overseas investors who, recognizing the potential of the region, are willing to finance projects by FDI or donation.

One area of great concern is human capital issues, in particular the skills shortage that affects the Southern African transport industry at all levels from warehouse operatives and drivers to senior managers and directors. Organizations ranging from professional institutions to universities throughout the region are trying to address these issues but they are seriously hampered by the poor level of basic numeracy and literacy being provided by the national education systems.

Political stability in the region is also of relevance as it can be both a blessing in, for example, attracting investment and trade, but it can also pose problems. For example, both Namibia and the RSA have enjoyed extensive periods of stable government since their independence in 1990 and 1994 respectively, whilst Mozambique is considered to be a post-conflict success story, but behind these optimistic façades there are some problems. Namibia's SWAPO party has enjoyed over a quarter of a century of continuous government but has failed to have a significant impact on the country's poor distribution of wealth, education or infrastructure, although the situation may improve as a result of the 2014 election. The RSA's African National Congress party (ANC) has been in power since independence, but has presided over a period of high currency devaluation and may be under threat from opposition parties that are gaining support as the probity of some ANC leaders has been called into question.

Whilst nominally stable, Mozambique experienced a civil war that started two years after independence in 1975 and ended in 1992. There followed a period of economic prosperity with a high rate of GDP growth but problems such as poverty, inequality and corruption persisted, which led to a RENAMO party-led armed insurrection that is still ongoing. So although there is a tenuous peace and industry thrives in most areas, problems occur, with rail transport of coal between the provinces of Tete and Beira dropping by half and the Rio Tinto coal mining operation briefly suspending shipments due to security concerns (Manning, 2016). All of these issues show that, whilst the region's countries are generally benefiting from political stability, governmental behaviour can and does limit the development and operation of the freight industry.

Conclusion

The Southern African region boasts a functioning and successful freight transport network that provides connectivity within the individual countries, across the region and to the outside world. It is not homogeneous and its features range from the relatively primitive, particularly in the more remote hinterlands with their sparse populations and harsh climatic conditions, to the comparatively sophisticated operations serving the industrial conurbations and densely populated cities of the more developed countries.

The industry is subject to internal influences such as the dominance of the RSA with the issues of its trading power but unstable currency, as well as external influences such as potential investors and the interface with global trade as well as its shipping routes. It serves a huge area with many countries both large and small, covers vast distances and has to deal with extremes of topographical and climatic conditions.

It serves the region well, but is in need of investment in people, vehicles, equipment and infrastructure. There are issues to do with intraregional collaboration as well as service levels that need to be addressed if the countries of Southern Africa are to maximize their potential and engage fully with the global trading community. Fortunately, there is a growing awareness at both industry and governmental levels of the importance of the industry and its potential to contribute to the generation and distribution of income. There is great potential to cultivate the industry so that it can drive development though trade. Whether, separately and collectively, the individual country governments will allocate the funding and attention needed for the industry and the region to flourish, only time will tell.

References

Anon (2016) Namibia launches online Trade Information Portal, *The Southern Times*, available at <http://southernafrican.news/2015/07/28/namibia-launches-online-trade-information-portal/>

Boois, G (2015) Namibia spatial development initiatives program, Paper presented at the NGCL 7th Annual logistics and transport workshop, Walvis Bay, 30 September

Brunner, H-P (2013) What is economic corridor development and what can it achieve in Asia's subregions? *Asian Development Bank*, available at <https://www.adb.org/sites/default/files/publication/100110/reiwp-117-economic-corridor-development.pdf>

Economics Online Ltd (2015) Why do countries trade? Available at <http://www.economicsonline.co.uk/Global_economics/Why_do_countries_trade.html>

European Commission (2016) Southern African Development Community (SADC), available at <http://ec.europa.eu/trade/policy/countries-and-regions/regions/sadc/>

Farole, T (2014) Regional trade and transport facilitation assessment for the SACU region, *World Bank*, available at <https://openknowledge.worldbank.org/handle/10986/23819>

Foulds, S (2013) Intermodal transport has big benefits, *Transport World Africa*, May 2013, p 3

Global Edge (2016) Botswana: trade statistics, available at <http://globaledge.msu.edu/countries/botswana/tradestats>

International Monetary Fund (2012) Regional economic outlook: Sub-Saharan Africa maintaining growth in an uncertain world, available at <http://www.imf.org/external/pubs/ft/reo/2012/afr/eng/sreo1012.pdf>

Korinek, J and Sourdin, P (2011) To what extent are high quality logistics services trade facilitating? *OECD Trade Policy Papers*, **108**

Manning, C (2016) Political tensions threaten Mozambique's tenuous peace, *World Politics Review*, 21 January

Masawi, T (2012) Zambia, Angola ditch Trans-Caprivi Corridor, *The Villager*, available at <http://www.thevillager.com.na/articles/1440/Zambia--Angola-ditch-Trans-Caprivi-Corridor/>

Matsaert, F (2015) Delivering development: why better logistics is critical for Africa's growth, *Trade Mark East Africa*, available at <http://www.trademarkea.com/blog/delivering-development-why-better-logistics-is-critical-for-africas-growth/>

Mulenga, G (2013) Developing economic corridors in Africa: Rationale for the participation of the African development bank, *AfDP*, available at <http://www.afdb.org/fileadmin/uploads/afdb/Documents/Publications/Regional_Integration_Brief_-_Developing_Economic_Corridors_in_Africa_-_Rationale_for_the_Participation_of_the_AfDB.pdf>

OECD/WTO (2013) Aid for trade and value chains in transport and logistics, *WTO*, available at <https://www.wto.org/english/tratop_e/devel_e/a4t_e/global_review13prog_e/transport_and_logistics_28june.pdf>

Port & Corridor Cooperation (2012) Trade corridors, available at <http://portandcorridor.org/sector-information/sector-information-2/trade-corridors>

Ricardo, D (1821) *On the Principles of Political Economy and Taxation* (3rd edn), London, John Murray

SACU (2016) About SACU, available at <http://www.sacu.int/show.php?id=396>

SADC (2012) Towards a common future, available at <http://www.sadc.int/themes/infrastructure/transport/transport-corridors-spatial-development-initiatives/>

SADC (2016) Statistics, available at <http://www.sadc.int/issues/statistics/>

Smith, C (2015) Logistics hub for southern Africa (and beyond), presentation at the 7th Annual NGCL logistics and transport workshop, Walvis Bay, 30 September

TKCS (2014) Trans-Kalahari Corridor Secretariat, available at <http://www.tkcmc.com/index.php/about-us>

Transport World Africa (2015) Transport infrastructure to get massive cash injection, available at <http://www.transportworldafrica.co.za/2015/10/05/transport-infrastructure-to-get-massive-cash-injection>

Tuathail, G Ó and Toal, G (1996) *Critical Geopolitics: The politics of writing global space*, University of Minnesota Press

UNCTAD (2013) Economic Development in Africa: Intra-African Trade – unlocking private sector dynamism, *UN*, Geneva, 148 pp, available at <http://unctad.org/en/PublicationsLibrary/ aldcafrica2013_en.pdf>

United Nations Economic Commission for Africa (2015) Economic report on Africa 2015: Industrializing through trade, *UNECA*, available at <http://www.uneca.org/publications/economic-report-africa-2015>

USAID (2016) About the Trade Hub, available at <http://www.satradehub.org/about>

WBCG (2009) Walvis Bay Corridor Group (home page), available at <http://www.wbcg.com.na/>

WBCG (2013) N$3 Billion Walvis Bay port expansion project signed, available at <http://www.wbcg.com.na/news-info/news/detail//n3-billion-walvis-bay-port-expansion-project-signed-2/login.html>

World Bank (2014) Connecting to compete 2014: Trade logistics in the global economy, available at <http://lpi.worldbank.org/report>

World Bank (2016) International Global LPI Rankings, available at <http://lpi.worldbank.org/international/global>

World Trade Organization (2004) Infrastructure in trade and international development, available at <https://www.wto.org/ENGLISH/res_e/booksp_e/anrep_e/wtr04_2b_e.pdf>

WTO E-Learning (2012) The WTO and trade economics: Theory and policy, available at <https://ecampus.wto.org/admin/files/course_389/CourseContents/tec-e-print.doc>

Freight transport in Korea and Taiwan

11

SU-HAN WOO, Chung-Ang University, South Korea
PO-LIN LAI, Chung-Ang University, South Korea
DOORI KIM, Chung-Ang University, South Korea
JUNGEUN KIM, Chung-Ang University, South Korea

Introduction

East Asian countries such as Korea and Taiwan have a significant role in global production chains (Kimura *et al*, 2007). While firms in Korea and Taiwan have competence in some industries as producers of final products, their participation in the global value chain is remarkable as a producer of intermediate goods through subcontracting in the form of vertical specialization in such industries as machinery, electronics and car manufacturing (Lee and Song, 2016). Freight transport systems in these countries are regarded as major infrastructure to facilitate product movements internationally as well as domestically. Development of an efficient freight transport system is also commercially important since transport is one of the logistics drivers affecting operational costs and customer services of firms (Chopra, 2003).

Recently, transport sectors have been challenged to respond to changes in manufacturing and consumption trends and to address environmental concerns. A rapid increase in online purchasing has brought about the re-structuring of distribution networks requiring more use of road transport for customized and quicker delivery services. In contrast, transport sectors are under pressure to reduce greenhouse gas (GHG) with increasing concern about environment; transport policy has taken actions to adapt to these changes. This chapter, therefore, reviews the current situation concerning the transport sectors in Korea and Taiwan and discusses how the transport sectors respond to the changes and challenges.

Freight transport in South Korea

Development of transport infrastructure

Through continuous investment in roads, railways, airports and seaports, the capacity of transport infrastructure in Korea has increased substantially over the past 16 years or so, as shown in Table 11.1. There has been increase in capacity in every transport mode ranging from 8 per cent to 191 per cent over this time. The total length of road has increased but there has been no capacity improvement in freight lines, as shown in Table 11.2.

Table 11.3 shows the change in cargo handling capacity of the Korean seaports; there has been 6 per cent capacity improvement annually since 2001. The Korean government has made efforts to support international trade by establishing infrastructure for international logistics, focusing on major Korean seaports. Particularly in focus has been the port of Busan, the world's 6th-largest container port in container cargo volume, which handled 19.47 million TEU with 21 berths in 2014.

Cargo-handling capacity at Korean airports has increased gradually and Korea has become the world's third-largest country in air cargo capacity. In 2010, Korean airports handled 3.59 million tonnes in total, which includes 3.3 million tonnes through international routes and 260,000 tonnes through domestic routes (Table 11.4).

Table 11.1 Transportation infrastructure of South Korea

Transportation facilities		1998(A)	2014(B)	B/A
Road	Total length of road (km)	86,990	105,673	1.21
	Total length of highway (km)	1,996	4,139	2.07
Railway	Total length of railway (km)	3,125	3,590	1.15
	Total length of high-speed railway (km)		346	
Port	Cargo handling capacity (million tonne)	157,387	170,101	1.08
Aviation	Transport capacity	357	1,039.4	2.91

SOURCE KOTI (2016); MOLIT (2015)
NOTE Transport capacity of aviation is based on frequency of flights

Table 11.2 Length of road and railway network, 2001–2014

	Road					Rail		
Year	Total length (m)	Opened length (m)	Pavement ratio (%)	Investment status (KRW 100 million)		Total length (km)	Passenger lines	Freight lines
2001	91,396	83,651	83.9			3,125	3,031	3,052
2002	96,037	87,613	84.1			3,129	3,034	3,062
2003	97,252	87,816	85.0			3,140	3,041	3,062
2004	100,277	89,624	85.2			3,374	3,255	3,047
2005	102,293	90,816	86.5			3,392	3,264	3,060
2006	10,200	90,832	87.2			3,392	3,264	3,060
2007	103,018	91,751	87.9			3,399	3,258	3,067
2008	104,236	92,743	88.2			3,381	3,240	3,049
2009	104,983	93,826	88.7	94,069		3,378	3,239	3,044
2010	105,565	94,230	89.4	77,817		3,557	3,377	3,092
2011	105,930	94,656	89.9	72,638		3,559	3,361	3,078
2012	105,702	96,948	91.0	76,896		3,572	3,379	3,054
2013	106,413	96,418	91.1	90,688		3,590	3,383	3,054
2014	105,672	97,919	91.6	85,373				

SOURCE KOTI (2016); MOLIT (2015)

Table 11.3 Seaport capacity, 2001–2013

Year	No of national seaports			No of berths			Cargo handling capacity (million tonne)		
	Total	International seaport	Coastal seaport	Total	International seaport	Coastal seaport	Total	International seaport	Coastal seaport
2001	51	28	23	639	596	43	470	462	8
2002	51	28	23	624	582	42	487	478	8
2003	51	28	23	656	609	47	510	501	9
2004	51	28	23	717	669	48	524	514	9
2005	52	28	24	723	675	48	650	641	9
2006	52	28	24	747	697	50	683	673	10
2007	52	28	24	761	713	48	729	721	7
2008	52	28	24	775	722	39	759	751	8
2009	54	29	25	793	745	48	801	793	8
2010	55	30	25	820	772	48	915	909	7
2011	57	31	26	827	787	40	944	937	7
2012	60	31	29	840	799	41	1,017	1,010	7
2013	60	31	29	884	843	41	1,064	1,057	7

SOURCE KOTI (2016); MOLIT (2015)
NOTE International seaports are mainly for ocean-going vessels and coastal seaports are mainly for vessel operating domestically

Table 11.4 Aviation capacity, 2001–2013

Year	No of airports	No of runways	Area of apron (m²)	Area of terminal (m²) Passenger	Area of terminal (m²) Cargo	Area of parking (m²)	Area of site (m²)
2001	16	24	3,173,490	902,924	334,643	1,533,986	26,762,530
2002	17	24	3,183,958	855,667	256,004	1,434,654	26,894,434
2003	16	24	3,983,204	831,665	258,552	1,603,991	27,407,427
2004	15	24	3,983,204	831,665	258,552	1,603,991	27,407,427
2005	15	24	3,869,852	856,735	355,647	1,405,671	67,891,404
2006	15	23	3,869,852	869,569	297,492	1,413,416	67,974,518
2007	15	24	3,950,944	928,242	300,404	1,502,710	70,279,262
2008	15	24	5,427,944	928,242	429,604	1,502,710	79,847,262
2009	15	24	5,522,102	940,937	439,981	1,528,054	80,252,535
2010	15	24	5,522,102	940,937	439,981	1,528,054	80,252,535
2011	16	26	5,645,861	949,350	442,781	1,606,223	82,011,535
2012	16	26	5,645,710	1,143,069	439,758	1,606,223	82,011,535
2013	16	26	5,645,710	1,143,069	439,758	1,606,223	82,011,535

SOURCE KOTI (2016); MOLIT (2015)

Freight transport by transport mode

According to MOLIT (2016), Korean domestic freight volumes reached a total of more than 810 million tonnes at the end of 2014 with a 3.35 per cent increase compared with 2011. The domestic freight traffic was heavily reliant on road transport, as shown in Table 11.5. Road transport had the highest percentage of freight transport by mode, ranging from 79.1 per cent to 90.7 per cent. The share of coastal shipping and railway transport was 14.6 per cent and 4.6 per cent respectively in 2014. The aviation transport sector represents only around 0.3 per cent by volume, but much more by value.

International freight volumes have shown a steady increase, as shown in Table 11.6. Shipping is the dominant transport mode for international freight traffic, accounting for 99.7 per cent. The share of air transport is, again only on average, 0.3 per cent by weight, but much more by value, as for domestic freight referred to above.

It is not surprising that shipping is dominant, as South Korea is effectively an island with very little cross-border trade.

Freight transport in Taiwan

Development of transport infrastructure

Over the past 40 years, Korea and Taiwan have shared identical growth paths and historical backgrounds but have achieved quite different degrees of success in their economies. As with Korea, by continuous investment in the infrastructure of roads, railways, airports and ports, the capacity and usage of Taiwan's transport network grew well in the beginning. However, due to the relative small population and land area of the territory, the development of transport facilities has been slower than that of Korea (See Tables 11.1 and 11.7).

The total length of roads has increased (Table 11.8) and since 1998 the average increase rate has been 0.1 per cent. Regarding the railway system, the total length of railway line has decreased due to the abolition of some freight-only lines, with the total length becoming 1,064 km. Included in the overall total length of line has been an increase in the length of passenger line since 2007, in particular due to the opening of a high-speed railway line.

Table 11.5 Freight transportation by mode in Korea

Mode	2010 volume	%	2011 volume	%	2012 volume	%	2013 volume	%	2014 volume	%
Total	783,234		1,605,507		1,727,985		1,704,342		810,628	
Railway	39,217	5.01	40,012	2.49	40,309	2.33	39,822	2.34	37,379	4.61
Road	619,529	79.10	1,439,658	89.67	1,563,487	90.48	1,546,407	90.73	655,046	80.81
Shipping	124,225	15.86	125,588	7.82	119,057	6.89	117,860	6.92	117,920	14.55
Air	262	0.03	281	0.02	265	0.02	253	0.01	283	0.03

SOURCE KOTI (2016); MOLIT (2015)

Table 11.6 International freight transport in Korea

Year/Mode	Total		Shipping		Aviation	
	Tonne (000s)	Growth rate (%)	Tonne (000s)	Growth rate (%)	Tonne (000s)	Growth rate (%)
2010	969,520	13.9	966,193	13.9	3,327	15.8
2011	1,068,331	10.2	1,065,093	10.2	3,238	−2.7
2012	1,111,747	4.1	1,108,538	4.1	3,209	−0.9
2013	1,126,451	1.3	1,123,205	1.3	3,246	1.2
2014	1,188,052	5.5	1,184,641	5.5	3,411	5.1

SOURCE KOTI (2016); MOLIT (2015)

Table 11.7 Transportation infrastructure of Taiwan

Transportation network		1998(A)	2014(B)	B/A
Road	Total length of road (km)	34,916	41,916	1.20
	Total length of highway (km)	559	1,050	1.87
Railway	Total length of railway (km)	3,125	3,590	1.15
	Total length of high-speed railway (km)		345	
Port	Cargo handling capacity (million tonne)	221,284	255,481	1.15
Aviation	Transport capacity	67,534	99,144	1.47

SOURCE Ministry of Transportation and Communication (MOTC) Statistics System
NOTE Transport capacity of aviation is on the basis of aircraft international departures data

Table 11.8 Length of road and railway network in Taiwan, 2001–2014

	Road		Rail			
Year	total length (km)	Pavement ratio (%)	total length (km)	Passenger lines	Freight lines	High speed rail
2001	36,466	88	1,097	1,053	1,095	
2002	37,037	88	1,097	1,053	1,095	
2003	37,310	89	1,097	1,053	1,095	
2004	37,028	89	1,101	1,053	1,101	
2005	37,336	90	1,094	1,053	1,093	

(*Continued*)

Table 11.8 (Continued)

	Road		Rail			
Year	total length (km)	Pavement ratio (%)	total length (km)	Passenger lines	Freight lines	High speed rail
2006	38,297	90	1,094	1,053	1,093	
2007	38,526	98	1,093	1,052	1,093	345
2008	39,315	98	1,090	1,052	1,090	345
2009	39,849	98	1,085	1,046	1,085	345
2010	40,353	98	1,085	1,046	1,085	345
2011	40,995	98	1,086	1,053	1,078	345
2012	41,924	98	1,067	1,053	1,058	345
2013	42,520	98	1,061	1,053	1,058	345
2014	41,916	98	1,064	1,057	1,051	345

SOURCE Ministry of Transportation and Communication (MOTC) Statistics System

Table 11.9 shows the change in the cargo-handling capacity of Taiwanese seaports and, perhaps surprisingly, there has been a decreasing trend since 2007. This is largely related to the rise of China, with the ranking of Kaohsiung port falling from 6th in 2006 to 13th in 2014 due to declining container volumes. While in 2013, cargo handling capacity in Taiwanese ports increased slightly, the average rate of increase between 2001 and 2013 has only been around 10 per cent. The Taiwanese government has tried to support imports and exports by establishing infrastructure for international logistics, so it has focused on improving infrastructure and facilities at major ports such as Kaohsiung and Taipei. The second phase of construction for these ports was approved to meet the needs of petrochemical transporters and to accommodate the increasing size of container ships.

Table 11.10 shows the decrease of international shipment in the overall ranking of the Logistics Performance Index (LPI) from 20 to 25. However, logistics quality and competence increased from 22 to 13. It provides some good signs for the Taiwanese government that they are heading in the right direction.

With regards to improving aviation infrastructure, raising the quality and efficiency of service, the airport authority in Taiwan has continued to upgrade the airport facilities, eg to safeguard the air-side operational

Table 11.9 Port capacity, 2001–2013

Year	No of national registered ports Total	International ports	Domestic ports	Cargo handling capacity (million tonnes) Total	International ports	Domestic ports
2001	10	6	4	223	221	2
2002	10	6	4	238	236	2
2003	10	6	4	280	278	2
2004	11	7	4	250	247	3
2005	11	7	4	269	265	3
2006	11	7	4	266	264	2
2007	11	7	4	276	274	2
2008	11	7	4	268	266	2
2009	11	7	4	237	235	2
2010	11	7	4	249	246	3
2011	11	7	4	247	244	3
2012	11	7	4	242	238	4
2013	11	7	4	246	243	3

SOURCE Ministry of Transportation and Communication (MOTC) Statistics System

safety of Taoyuan International Airport. In addition, both core and support aviation businesses have expanded. At the end of 2015, there were nine civil air transport enterprises and 11 general aviation enterprises in Taiwan. Peripheral businesses include five airport ground handling services providers, five catering service companies, 1,215 air freight forwarders and seven air cargo entrepots (CAA, 2016).

Cargo handling capacity has increased gradually since 2008 due to the establishment of free trade zones at airports. According to Airports Council International, in 2014, Taiwan Taoyuan airport handled 35 million tonnes of cargo in total, which ranks it as the 10th-busiest airport in the world. Along with the completion of the third runway and new terminals over the next 10 years, cargo volumes and the number of passengers are predicted to increase by between 30 and 50 per cent (Table 11.11).

Table 11.10 Logistics Performance Index (LPI)

Country	Overall score	Overall rank	Customs score	Customs rank	Infrastructure score	Infrastructure rank	International shipment score	International shipment rank	Logistics quality and competence score	Logistics quality and competence rank	Tracking and tracing score	Tracking and tracing rank	Timeliness score	Timeliness rank
2010 Taiwan	3.71	**20**	3.35	**25**	3.62	**22**	3.64	**10**	3.65	22	4.04	**12**	3.95	30
2016 Taiwan	3.70	25	3.23	34	3.57	26	3.57	28	3.95	**13**	3.59	31	4.25	**12**

SOURCE World Bank (2016)

Table 11.11 Taiwan's aviation capacity, 2001–2014

Year	No of airports	No of runways	Area of apron (m²)	Area of terminal (m²) Passenger	Area of terminal (m²) Cargo
2001	16	17	2,585,922	777,479	218,060
2002	16	17	2,585,922	777,479	218,060
2003	16	17	2,585,922	777,479	218,060
2004	18	19	2,612,382	782,051	218,060
2005	18	19	2,612,382	782,051	218,060
2006	18	19	2,612,382	782,051	218,060
2007	18	19	2,612,382	782,051	218,060
2008	18	19	2,612,382	782,051	635,659
2009	18	19	2,612,382	782,051	635,659
2010	18	19	2,612,382	782,051	635,659
2011	18	19	2,612,382	782,051	635,659
2012	17	18	2,578,348	774,584	635,659
2013	17	18	5,645,710	774,584	635,659

SOURCE Ministry of Transportation and Communication (MOTC) Statistics System

Freight transport by transport mode

Regarding the freight statistics report of the Ministry of Transport and Communication (MOTC), the domestic freight traffic of Taiwan reached a total of more than 810 million tonnes by the end of 2014. It had increased by approximately 3.35 per cent compared with 2011, but traffic has shown a steady downward trend since 2013. Road transport carried the highest percentage of freight transport by mode, accounting for 95 per cent of total carried goods. Aviation, coastal and railway transport together account for the remaining 5 per cent as shown in Figure 11.1. In 2013, the share of road transport declined from 95 per cent to 90 per cent, but it is clear that the domestic transport system is still heavily reliant on road transport. Coastal shipping's share increased slightly between 2011 and 2014 while rail transport's share has continued on a downward path. International freight traffic has increased steadily, and almost 99.7 per cent of export and import cargoes are handled by shipping; coincidentally this is almost exactly the same modal split as in Korea.

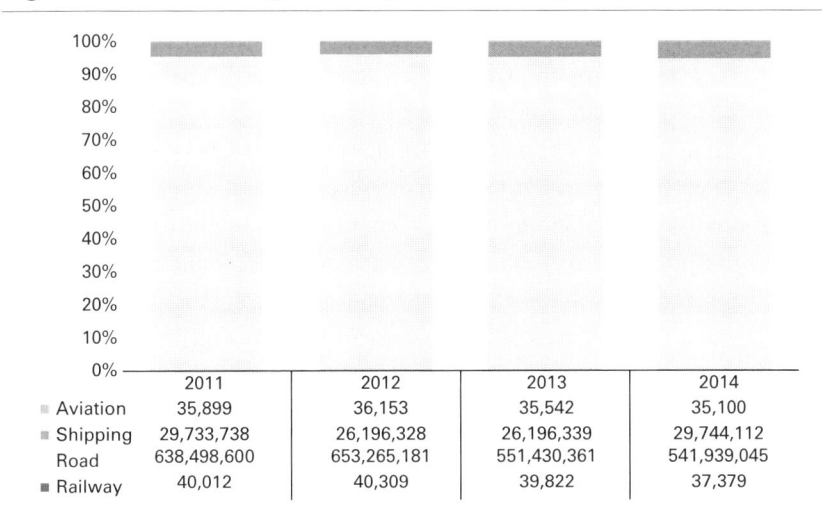

Figure 11.1 Annual freight traffic by mode in Taiwan, 2011–2014

	2011	2012	2013	2014
Aviation	35,899	36,153	35,542	35,100
Shipping	29,733,738	26,196,328	26,196,339	29,744,112
Road	638,498,600	653,265,181	551,430,361	541,939,045
Railway	40,012	40,309	39,822	37,379

SOURCE Ministry of Transportation and Communication (MOTC) Statistics System

Challenges and responses in the transport sectors of Taiwan and Korea

Challenges

Changes in logistics and supply chain structures

Transport operations are significantly influenced by the arrangement of logistics and supply chain structures. Transport modes and routes are decided by logistics and supply chain managers based on their supply chain strategies. In the era of global supply chains, just-in-time (JIT) logistics became the norm in many industries and fast and efficient goods movement is often seen as an economic imperative (Kamakaté and Schipper, 2009). JIT systems tend to increase frequency of delivery and encourage the use of trucking.

The emergence of e-business in the 2000s and the rapid increase in online purchasing provides e-business firms and transport operators with new challenges. Consumers expect a quicker response to their orders despite orders involving small numbers of items with higher diversity, requiring e-business firms to innovate in last-mile services (Colliers, 2015; Oh and Woo, 2016). Sophisticated last-mile services tend to rely on road transport more, having a negative impact on the environment.

Industrial challenges

Economic development in Korea and Taiwan relies heavily on imports and exports. Therefore shipping, which accounts for over 99 per cent of Korea and Taiwan's total trade volume, is the lifeblood of the economic development of both countries. The maritime service providers have been confronted with the severe economic downturn in recent years. Under such severe international economic circumstances, container shipping firms are under pressure to implement structural change. Alliances are being re-formed and container ship size has been increasing, making it even more difficult to fill capacity and hence secure consistent returns on investment. Top shipping companies have made efforts to increase market share and therefore firms operating in marginal areas in the market are at severe risk.

Environmental concerns

In the era of the global economy, supply chains have become more sophisticated, with wider geographical coverage, and more complicated, with more suppliers and customers involved. Due to a growing awareness of the environmental impact of manufacturing and service operations, governments and companies are concerned about sources of greenhouse gas (GHG) emissions and measures to mitigate them (McKinnon and Piecyk, 2012; Rodrigues et al, 2015). Among logistics activities, transport is considered to be a primary source of GHG emissions with a large portion of CO_2 emissions emanating from road transport (Léonardi and Baumgartner, 2004; Liao et al, 2010). Transport constitutes the largest portion of CO_2 emissions and it accounts for 21 per cent of total national greenhouse gas emissions in Korea. Road transport causes higher air pollution than other transport modes in both countries, as shown in Tables 11.12 and 11.13.

Table 11.12 CO_2 emission by mode in Korea (Unit: 1,000 tonne CO_2)

Mode	1990	2000	2010	2011	2012	2013
Air	824	1,411	1,151	1,215	1,215	1,314
Road	30,872	64,412	80,987	80,621	82,053	84,670
Rail	876	969	556	506	507	448
Ocean	2,441	2,750	2,269	2,263	2,143	1,407

SOURCE KOTI (2016); MOLIT (2015)

Table 11.13 CO_2 emission by mode in Taiwan (Unit: 1,000 tonne CO_2)

Mode	1990	2000	2010	2011	2012	2013
Air	280	902	231	257	259	
Road	18,552	30,968	33,744	34,249	33,775	
Rail	214	392	696	727	735	
Ocean	695	1226	866	806	487	

SOURCE Institute of transportation data system, MOTC

Emergence of new corridors

Commercialization of the Northern Sea Route (NSR) has been discussed in the international community and tested by various countries including South Korea (Liu and Kronbak, 2010). This can pose a challenge to traditional transport systems based on the Suez Canal route, as well as an opportunity to countries and areas through which the NSR travels. The Chinese 'One Belt, One Road' initiative also sheds light on the Tuman River Area where China, Russia and North Korea share borders (Ahn *et al*, 2016; Swaine, 2015). The Chinese Government, the Jilin provincial governments in particular, have endeavoured to use the Tuman River Area (Hunchun from the Chinese side) as a platform for transport routes to the Pacific Ocean (Jo and Ducruet, 2007). Therefore, this area has attracted the attention of the governments of countries nearby and logistics firms who sense new business opportunities.

Transport policy adjustments

South Korea

The emphasis of transport policy is on the establishment of efficient transport systems and the development of facilities to respond to new trends in logistics and supply chains. Due to the emergence of e-commerce, firms innovate and actively use last-mile delivery services as a source of competitive advantage. Therefore, urban logistics have become an important part of the whole distribution network and logistics facilities need to be established in cities. The government is developing urban logistics hubs in five main cities and provides e-commerce firms and logistics firms with the facilities. In addition, logistics distri-parks that have been developed adjacent to airports and seaports during the 2000s are being expanded so that e-commerce firms and logistics companies use the facilities for logistics activities including value-added operations.

Korean firms in the transport and logistics industries have sought opportunities to enter into emerging markets in Northern East Asia, expanding their networks and linkages in the region. The Korean government promotes and supports their efforts in various ways. Expecting NSR commercialization, *Hyundai Glovis* completed a test voyage in 2013 and *CJ Korea Express* performed the Northern Sea Route operations commercially for the first time in Korea in 2015 with the help of the government in the area of, for example, seafarer training. A Eurasia initiative was announced by the government in 2013 and this includes collaborative projects such as the Rajin-Hassan logistics project and the Hunchun POSCO-Hyundai logistics centre development.

Elsewhere, there is support for the transport industry to mitigate the negative impact of the global recession in the international freight transport market, particularly the shipping industry. Korea Maritime Guarantee Insurance was established, and the Tonnage Bank was started to strengthen the financial security of shipping companies. Technology advancement is supported through strong research and development (R&D) investment in the transport and logistics sectors as shown in Table 11.14.

Table 11.14 Investments on R&D in transportation (Unit: 100 mil. KRW)

	2007–2011	2012	2013	2014	2015	total
Logistics R&D	357	70	120	137	136	820
Transportation research	2,572	490	566	424	415	4,467
% of investments	13.9	14.3	21.2	32.3	32.8	18.4

SOURCE KOTI (2016)

Table 11.15 GHG reduction estimation in transportation

Scheme	Scenario	Estimation (10,000 tonnes CO_2)
Shift to railway transportation	Railway transport proportion increases from 7% to 15%	292
Shift to short sea shipping	Proportion from 16.7% to 22%	134
Transport integration	Loading factor from 69% to 75%	197
Usage of larger vehicles	Changes vehicles with below 1 tonne load to above 1 tonne load	56
LNG-fuelled vehicle support	Up to 10,000 vehicles	16

SOURCE KOTI (2010)

Korea has adopted several policies to mitigate GHG emissions based on the Framework Act on Low Carbon Green Growth enacted in 2013. These include support schemes for modal shift and LNG-fuelled vehicles, and regulatory measures such as taxation and carbon emission exchange (KOTI, 2010). Table 11.15 shows GHG emission mitigation measures and estimated reductions of CO_2 emissions. These measures intend to reduce the proportion of transport modes emitting more GHG (such as road transport) and increase the proportion of transport modes emitting less GHG (such as railway and short sea shipping).

Taiwan

According to the *Transport Policy White Book* which was released by the Ministry of Transport and Communication (MOTC) in 2012, the main objective for transport policy in Taiwan is 'Sustainable Transport'. The *White Book* highlights and critiques the most important public transport initiatives recently exercised in Taiwan, and provides suggestions for future planning. Strategies suggested for Sustainable Transport are the provision of great service, reliable service, environmental service, equitable service, and networked service. The policy portfolio in Taiwan is similar to that of South Korea.

Enhancing transport capability through the development of transport infrastructure comes first. The Taiwanese government are also investing in transport logistics research as a way of enlarging the transport network. To secure the positive development of technical aspects, the transport logistics research budget reached US $8.2 million (MOLIT, 2015). Second, from the middle of the 1980s to the late 1990s, before the economic development of China, the Asia-Pacific region had positive growth that attracted global attention. The Taiwanese administration announced a major national objective: the 'Asia-Pacific Regional Operational Centre (APROC)', but due to political issues this project failed. Recently, however, Asia-Pacific countries are strongly influenced by the increased economic strength of China. In this case, the Taiwanese government has developed a new policy, the 'New Southbound policy', to widen exchanges between countries in the region in areas such as technology, culture and commerce, and expand Taiwan's ties with both ASEAN and India. The main outcome of this policy, related to transport policy, is to reinforce international logistics and competition capability. The geographical location of Taiwan in the Asia-Pacific region is important, and understanding how to benefit from this will be the main issue over the next 10 years.

Taiwan has also put effort into developing low-carbon transport to try to shift the emphasis of the transport and logistics infrastructure to a more effective environmental focus. For this, the government has supported the

Transit Oriented Development (TOD) project for road transport, a green port policy and eco-shipping in maritime transport, and has a green airport policy which will identify reductions in order to achieve airport carbon accreditation. Lastly, combining intelligent transport technology to provide reliable services and enhance security systems will be an essential development for the Taiwanese transport industry. In maritime transport, under the auspices of the Maritime Port Bureau (MPB), innovation and optimization will be achieved through the Maritime Transport Network Portal (MTNet) services. The Future Development Plan of Port Information Systems (2013–2016) was approved by the Executive Yuan in August 2013. The Bureau and Taiwan International Ports Corp were commissioned to oversee implementation of the plan. In road transport, due to rapid economic growth, the number of private vehicles in Taiwan has greatly increased since 1990, while the number of public vehicles has only slightly increased in the same period (Lan et al, 2006). A 'seamless' intercity and urban electric highway system (including an e-pass system and Electronic Toll Collection (ETC)) has also been completed. For air transport, there is also an attempt to strengthen the customs e-system in order to increase efficiency.

Discussion and conclusion

This chapter reviewed the current situation regarding the freight transport sector in Korea and Taiwan and presented policy responses to challenges and changes in logistics and supply chains. Transport capacity has been increasing in both countries, and infrastructure developments are still planned in order to meet new requirements from market developments, for example developing facilities to accommodate larger vessels and aircraft, and the facilities necessary for international e-commerce business. However, policymakers need to have a clear overview of the supply–demand balance. Policymakers tend to avoid market intervention and look towards capacity enhancement, which is traditionally planned and implemented by public sectors in Asian countries. Capacity enhancement often causes oversupply and deteriorating profitability for operators in the market.

Both countries have sought GHG emission mitigation generated from transport using various measures. However, it is questionable whether the measures can achieve their goals, since road transport is still dominant in Korea and Taiwan. It can be argued that policymakers consider transport as a separate part of the logistics system which disregards the influence of logistics and supply chain strategies on transport operations. In particular, a trade-off relationship exists between CO_2 emissions and the number of warehouses in supply chains (McKinnon and Piecyk, 2012). Therefore, a holistic approach should be retained towards environmental policy for transport.

References

Ahn, G S, Woo, S H and Noh, J H (2016) A study on cooperation of logistics network between Jilin Province and Korea, *The Korean Logistics Review*, **26** (2), pp 73–84

Airport Council International (2015) *ACI Airport Economics Survey 2014*, Geneva: ACI

Chopra, S (2003) Designing the distribution network in a supply chain, *Transportation Research Part E: Logistics and Transportation Review*, **39** (2), pp 123–40

Civil Aviation Administration (2016) *2015 Annual Report*, Taipei: CAA

Colliers International (2015) *New Zealand Retail 2015: Retail reality check*, Auckland: Colliers International

Jo, J C and Ducruet, C (2007) Rajin–Seonbong, new gateway of Northeast Asia, *The Annals of Regional Science*, **41** (4), pp 927–50

Kamakaté, F and Schipper, L (2009) Trends in truck freight energy use and carbon emissions in selected OECD countries from 1973 to 2005, *Energy Policy*, **37** (10), pp 3743–51

Kimura, F, Takahashi, Y and Hayakawa, K (2007) Fragmentation and parts and components trade: Comparison between East Asia and Europe, *The North American Journal of Economics and Finance*, **18** (1), pp 23–40

KOTI (2010) *Measures for Greener Logistics System*, Report to Ministry of Land, Transport and Maritime Affairs

KOTI (2016) National Transport Data Base [online] https://www.ktdb.go.kr/www/index.do [accessed 30 September 2016]

Lan, Lawrence W, Wang, Ming-Te and Kuo, April Y (2006) Development and deployment of public transport policy and planning in Taiwan, *Transportation*, **33** (2), pp 153–70

Lee, C S and Song, B (2016) Vertical specialization in the Korean manufacturing sector, *Journal of Korea Trade*, **20** (2), pp 134–48

Léonardi, J and Baumgartner, M (2004) CO_2 efficiency in road freight transportation: Status quo, measures and potential, *Transportation Research Part D: Transport and Environment*, **9** (6), pp 451–64

Liao, C H, Tseng, P H, Cullinane, K and Lu, C S (2010) The impact of an emerging port on the carbon dioxide emissions of inland container transport: an empirical study of Taipei port, *Energy Policy*, **38** (9), pp 5251–57

Liu, M and Kronbak, J (2010) The potential economic viability of using the Northern Sea Route (NSR) as an alternative route between Asia and Europe, *Journal of Transport Geography*, **18** (3), pp 434–44

MOLIT (2015) *Statistical Yearbook*, Ministry of Land, Infrastructure and Transport

MOLIT and MOF (2016) *National Logistics Development Plan*, Ministry of Land, Infrastructure and Transport, Ministry of Oceans and Fisheries

MOTC (2016) Ministry of Transportation and Communication (MOTC) Statistics System [online] http://stat.motc.gov.tw [accessed 10 September 2016]

McKinnon, A C and Piecyk, M I (2012) Setting targets for reducing carbon emissions from logistics: current practice and guiding principles, *Carbon Management*, **3** (6), pp 629–39

Oh, J H and Woo, S H (2016) Evolution of e-business fulfillment model: a case study of South Korea, *e-Business Studies*, **17** (3), pp 27–49

Rodrigues, V S, Pettit, S, Harris, I, Beresford, A, Piecyk, M, Yang, Z and Ng, A (2015) UK supply chain carbon mitigation strategies using alternative ports and multimodal freight transport operations, *Transportation Research Part E: Logistics and Transportation Review*, **78**, pp 40–56

Swaine, M D (2015) Chinese views and commentary on the 'One Belt, One Road' initiative, *China Leadership Monitor*, **47**, pp 1–24

World Bank (2016) *Logistics Performance Index 2016*, Washington: World Bank

PART FOUR
Challenging environments and transport futures

Overcoming international freight transport challenges in a disaster response context

12

PETER TATHAM, Griffith Business School, Gold Coast, Australia

GYÖNGYI KOVÁCS, Hanken School of Economics, Helsinki, Finland

Introduction

The aftermath of a natural disaster (for example Cyclone Winston that struck Fiji in March 2016) or a complex emergency (such as currently taking place in Syria) typically requires those responding to set up an ad hoc supply chain to deliver the goods and services needed by the affected population as efficiently and effectively as possible. In this respect, so-called 'natural disasters' relate to the impact of events such as earthquakes, volcanic eruptions, flooding or wind events (CRED, 2016a), whereas complex emergencies are defined by the United Nations (UN) Inter-Agency Standing Committee (IASC) as:

a humanitarian crisis in a country, region or society where there is total or considerable breakdown of authority resulting from internal or external conflict and which requires an international response that goes beyond the mandate or capacity of any single agency and/or the ongoing United Nations country programme. (OCHA, 1999, p 1)

The humanitarian context is inherently challenging from a transport perspective. Whether as a result of earthquakes or wars, bridges may be down, runways compromised, roads destroyed or reduced in capacity, all of which individually and collectively impact on modal choice, vehicle selection and routing options infrastructure (Tatham and Pettit, 2010). By the same token, floods can equally impact on the availability of certain routes even in a 'regular' wet season (Rest *et al*, 2012). Simultaneously, disasters frequently impact the location of people. Famines, floods and conflicts all result in significant movements of people – be this away from the disaster location or, sometimes, towards it in the hope of gaining employment as part of the response effort. Thus, determining the very location of demand, ie the destination node(s) of the freight movements, is a significant problem in itself.

Given the breadth and depth of the freight transport problem outlined in this introduction, this chapter will focus on a number of the specific challenges that arise for transport in the humanitarian context, together with emerging opportunities that have the potential to improve the efficiency and/or effectiveness of the logistic response process. The chapter, therefore, starts with an introduction to the humanitarian context and then addresses a number of specific issues in humanitarian transport, namely: achieving access to disaster areas and beneficiaries; the very complex nature of transport services in this area; and, last but not least, the rise of new technologies and what they may bring to the practice of humanitarian transport.

The humanitarian context

Unlike the 'for profit' world in which the customer clearly identifies their requirements, those responding in the humanitarian environment constantly face the '4W' challenge of 'who wants what where?' Arguably this should be a relatively simple process of extrapolation from input such as a recent census and integrating this data with an experience-based understanding of the nature and extent of the particular disaster or emergency. But, in reality, the situation is usually significantly more complex – for example, there may have been no recent census or there may have been significant events after the last one took place which have resulted in major population movements. This is frequently the case, not only in complex emergencies where people are fleeing from fighting, but also in natural disasters – particularly those affecting cities – where many individuals will return to their home town or village to escape the disaster's impacts. In parallel, however, others will move into the cities to take up opportunistic work opportunities such as the clearance of rubble from an earthquake.

Furthermore, the actual requirements of those affected will depend on a multitude of factors such as the nature of the disaster itself, the environment (city vs country), the current and future weather-related needs such as hot- or cold-temperature clothing and shelter (Tatham *et al*, 2013), as well as the demographics (male vs female; old vs young) (Tatham and Kovács, 2010). In short, undertaking this 'needs assessment' is significantly more complex than in a commercial environment and this is exacerbated by the challenge of understanding who is the customer of the process – is it those who are affected by the event or is it those who are actually funding the response process, such as governments, the UN, the Red Cross movement or non-government organizations (NGOs)? In short, there is a decoupling of material and financial flows, and as a result, it is frequently the humanitarian logistician who is placed in the difficult position of having to second guess the needs of the beneficiaries whilst simultaneously meeting the increasingly demanding governance requirements of the donor community (Tatham and Christopher, 2014).

An additional aspect of the humanitarian logistics challenge is the recognition that, in an ideal world, the responding organizations should only be providing material (as distinct from financial) support on a temporary basis. Thus, in the aftermath of a disaster and as the response moves from the 'emergency' to the 'recovery' phase at around Day 30 (Safran, 2003), the international organizations who are responding should be transitioning to financial mechanisms through which they can continue to help the affected region recover from the impact of the event. However, at the same time they should be endeavouring to avoid disrupting the normal pattern of trading (Fenton *et al*, 2014). Put simply, if an NGO provides new fish hooks free of charge, what happens to the livelihood of the local fish hook maker?

In summary, therefore, if one takes the most frequently offered definition of humanitarian logistics – 'The process of planning, implementing and controlling the efficient, cost-effective flow and storage of goods and materials as well as related information, from the point of origin to the point of consumption for the purpose of meeting the end beneficiary's requirements'

(Thomas and Mizushima, 2005, p 60) – it can be seen that developing an efficient and effective logistics response is critical to mitigating the impact of a disaster or complex emergency. The importance of efficient and effective logistics can be even more starkly underscored if one analyses the cost of this aspect of an NGO's activities.

The current best evidence would indicate that some 60–80 per cent of the income of an NGO is spent on undertaking the activities implied by the above definition (van Wassehove, 2006; Tatham and Pettit, 2010). In short, based on an overall sector that expends some US $25 billion per year (Scriven, 2016), procurement, transport into the country/region, warehousing, internal transport and 'last mile' distribution to the beneficiaries are estimated to have an annual cost of some US $15–20 billion. Furthermore, in extreme cases, freight transport alone can account for 60 per cent of costs, whether this is because of the sheer length of transport around the world, the limited modal choice in light of the urgency of the response, or the paucity of routing options due to daunting security considerations in conflict zones. So, the key question that emerges is: 'how can these sums be better spent in providing the logistics response to a disaster or complex emergency?'

Furthermore, based on the last decade's data, some 350–450 natural disasters will take place in a given year (CRED, 2016b) – but, to date, the timing and location of an event is impossible to predict other than in a general sense. For example, in 2015, 156 disasters took place in the Asian region compared with 23 in Europe (CRED, 2016b), and thus it is reasonable to predict that a similar pattern will continue in the short term at least, but this cannot be guaranteed. Thus, much as one might like to improve the preparatory activities as they relate to a specific potential event, the reality is that this is challenging in the extreme – not least as governments in the round (as well as individuals) are reluctant to expend money on a disaster that may never occur. The resultant model is, typically, retrospective with the consequential challenge facing the humanitarian logistician being that of transitioning from dormant to action (Kovács and Tatham, 2009), whilst also operating – at least in the initial stages of the response, ie until greater information is available as a result of the needs assessment process – on a 'push' (as distinct from 'pull') basis.

Daunting though this challenge undoubtedly is, not least because the price of failure can be counted in terms of unnecessary loss of life or continued hardship rather than reduced profits, the actual size of the inventory is not enormous. For example, the catalogue of the International Federation of Red Cross and Red Crescent Societies (IFRC, 2016) comes in three volumes, of which two are focused on medical supplies and equipment. Thus, the number of Stock Keeping Units (SKUs) contained in the non-medical section is only around 5,000. By the same token, the Oxfam catalogue contains some 300 SKUs, which is two orders of magnitude less than the 30–40,000 found in a typical supermarket (Fernie and Sparks, 2004). Indeed, of these SKUs, some are alternatives – for example, hot vs cold temperature shelter – whilst others, such as washing or cooking equipment, are ubiquitous. Indeed, some researchers have argued that there is, indeed, a degree of predictability about the 'what?' component of the 4W problem (Everywhere et al, 2011), but this still leaves the 'who?' and 'where?' elements to be satisfied as efficiently and effectively as is possible.

Access to the disaster area

Humanitarian aid can only be as effective if and when it reaches the people most in need. To date, however, most transport models assume both (a) knowledge of the nodes and links in terms of demand and supply, and (b) knowledge about the arches between these in terms of the usability of different types of vehicles. Unfortunately, neither of these are a given in the humanitarian context. Importantly, even in regions with a well-developed transport infrastructure, the impact of a disaster can, and frequently does, result in significant damage (Haavisto and Vaillancourt, 2016). As a result, humanitarian logisticians (together with national governments) need to start with establishing, and constantly updating, their understanding of the state of the transport infrastructure and its potential to bear different vehicle sizes and loads. With this in mind, it will come as no surprise that humanitarian organizations have frequently been heavily involved in the reconstruction, or even the initial construction, of roads and bridges, and the rehabilitation of ports and air fields, whether in South Sudan, Haiti or Nepal.

Access to the disaster area also cannot be guaranteed, especially in a complex emergency where it is often a question of negotiation. Indeed, Larson (2009) found that the skill of 'negotiation with warlords' often figured in job ads for humanitarian logisticians! Furthermore, in conflict zones, there is an added layer of security concerns in relation to the negotiations for corridors to be considered for vehicle routing. The problem is also a dynamic one; even where access has been successfully negotiated beforehand with all parties to a crisis, the sudden appearance of road blocks may require the rerouting of convoys.

As a crucial point of differentiation with the 'for profit' area of transport, in the humanitarian context cost efficiency is not always the most important consideration. Rather, actually reaching the beneficiaries (ie coverage and equity) and the security of the convoys often supersede efficiency considerations. This is starkly illustrated when one considers the challenges of, for example, reaching beneficiaries in Homs or Aleppo in Syria, or in remote villages in the jungles of the Central African Republic. Saving and sustaining lives is the maxim. Importantly, as in the example of meeting health care needs, the underpinning aim of providing overall coverage requires logisticians to do their utmost to reach remote locations, and humanitarian transport providers cannot shy away from delivering aid to villages simply because they are difficult or not cost-effective to reach.

Access, and coverage, can also be a function of time. Floods and rainy seasons can compromise access to particular areas during specific time periods, whereas access can be free at other times. Transport schedules may therefore depend on weather forecasts and, in order to maximize coverage, deliveries may be scheduled ahead of time, both in order to actually be able to access an area and also to reduce the costs of transport as cheaper transport modes can be available before and after a rainy season rather than during it. That said, modal choice decisions in disasters are unfortunately much tainted by political decisions. When investigating the feasibility of sea-basing, we found that air transport was often a preferred mode, notwithstanding the higher costs as, in the political environment that existed at the time, any other mode of transport could be seen as not 'urgent enough' to qualify as humanitarian transport. This resulted it items being stuck in a lengthy customs clearance process, rather than being exempted from it. Another important consideration of humanitarian transport is the establishment of corridors that often go through several other countries, rather than via the shortest route to the disaster area. Beresford and Pettit (eg 2013) have investigated numerous humanitarian corridors for various landlocked countries and compared these with sea port access, clearly demonstrating some of the issues in this complex, but critical, area.

In the distribution of aid, and especially in relation to the 'last mile', local logistics service providers (LSPs) or those employed by local implementing partners (IPs) are frequently used. Therefore, interestingly, humanitarian organizations typically consider 'transport' to reflect just the inbound side of logistics, ie the movement of goods to a port or warehouse within a country. By contrast, the transport activities of IPs or LSPs (and occasionally a responding agency's own fleet) are considered to be 'distribution' or 'relief'.

Nevertheless, whatever the chosen terminology, this latter aspect of the overall challenge boils down to understanding the optimum way(s) of getting both an appropriate vehicle as well as its freight load to a disaster area.

On the one hand, use of an agency's own vehicles leads (potentially) to a greater level of control over the operation, whereas the use of partners who are more familiar with the terrain etc, may result in a swifter and more effective response. Thus, whilst working through local partners may have a negative impact on the end-to-end tracking of the cargo, LSPs bring their knowledge to the table; they know the transport network and its potential shortcomings, the socio-economic environment, and possibly also ways of overcoming an adverse security situation. For example, they are likely to be better equipped to negotiate their way through road blocks etc if that is an option.

At the same time, as Balcik and Beamon (2008) cogently observed, many facets of the demand picture are unknown in the humanitarian area. In addition to the questions of quantity, location, size and shape summarized earlier, this also includes questions around the choice of beneficiaries. Needs assessment is, therefore, not only the first key activity of humanitarian organizations in the aftermath a disaster, but also an art, especially when it comes to populations on the move – whether due to a flood or in a refugee crisis – and it must also reflect consideration of the vulnerability vs capacity of beneficiaries themselves. What is more, in conflict situations, beneficiaries may be actively hiding as, for example, Choi *et al* (2010) found in the Rwanda genocide.

That said, depending on the particular circumstances of the disaster it can be possible to determine and even optimize the location of suitable points of distribution (PODs) (eg Boudhoum, 2014). However, access to aid is not simply a function of demand and supply, or even the location of a POD, but also whether a person is able, or even allowed to collect aid from such a location. The logistic challenge also reflects other issues such as the gendered access to aid, where the ability or the cultural norms of beneficiaries may impact on who actually can receive aid, and from whom (Tatham and Kovács, 2010). Similarly, beneficiaries may have difficulties in accessing aid due to their age, disability, or some kind of discrimination that they face in a community – yet, importantly, these may be the most vulnerable groups of people, and thereby high on the priority list of preferred aid recipients.

A complex system of humanitarian transport services

Humanitarian organizations are constantly criticized for a lack of co-ordination, notwithstanding an abundance of coordination mechanisms and activities targeting this area which even extends to the coordinated purchasing of logistics services (Pazirandeh and Herlin, 2014), and the relations between humanitarian organizations and groups of commercial LSPs. The United Nations World Food Programme (WFP) Logistics Cluster is the most prominent of these coordination mechanisms, and works with the United Nations Network of Humanitarian Response Depots (UNHRDs) to optimize joint pre-positioning. However, two further aspects of coordination mechanisms are important in terms of humanitarian transport: one is the very complex nature of contracting and service tiering, and the other is the joint operation of convoys in conflict zones.

Similar to many commercial transport services, those in the humanitarian domain also use a complex system of services and service tiering. Not only are there various third- and fourth-party LSPs in this area, but also humanitarian organizations themselves have been likened to LSPs in the sense that they act as intermediaries between the governments who are responding to a disaster and the beneficiaries. With this in mind, it is perhaps unsurprising that humanitarian organizations have started to offer their logistics services to one another, whether this is in the area of customs clearance, kitting, procurement, tracking and tracing or, indeed, freight transport.

This development stems from a drive to improve the professionalization of the discipline and adopt commercially proven practices, alongside a restructuring of some organizations into service centres that need to recover their costs. For example, the IFRC, when supporting national chapters in disaster relief, does so on a cost-recovery basis. Taking a slightly different approach, the Logistics Cluster offer free capacity on their vehicles on the basis of 'service request forms'. Overall, as Heaslip (2013) has noted, there is a steady servitization of the sector which has the potential to add yet another layer of complexity to the transport management challenge.

Offering such free capacity is, however, not only a good way to improve the vehicle fill rates, but also increasingly a necessity in areas in which only convoys can operate. Thus, we see a rise in convoys and a consequential improvement in the actual coordination of humanitarian transport in areas where access is difficult. Conflict zones are a case in point, but so too are areas in which access is limited for political reasons. But there are some new challenges that have emerged with the operation of joint convoys, First, and unsurprisingly, donors like to see their flag of choice in media reporting, but this is not a given in such operations as this flag may be unacceptable both to other convey participants as well as to those who control the area that the convoy must pass through. However, this can be overcome through innovative solutions for which humanitarian logistics, and their transport specialists, are famed.

Second, not even humanitarian Enterprise Resource Planning (ERP) systems are built to support such coordination; in fact, their growing use has actually introduced even more rigidity to deliveries. International Public Sector Accounting Standards (IPSAS) compliance may, on the one hand, be a noble aim, but such transaction-based transparency and compliance can inhibit system optimization as well as the cross-utilization of assets or even the use of First In, First Out (FIFO) and First Expired, First Out (FEFO) principles. Third, when negotiating the loading of a convoy's vehicles, the normal situation is that demand outstrips supply, and this leads to questions of prioritization – in essence, which organization's cargo will be prioritized in a given delivery – with a resultant benefit not only to the recipients, but, arguably, also to the supplying organization in terms of both meeting their mandate and the potential for positive publicity and the consequential improvement in donation rates.

New technology in humanitarian transport

As outlined earlier, the humanitarian logistician is faced with challenges on both sides of the supply versus demand equation, but emerging technologies have the potential to mitigate these. In relation to the latter, as outlined above, the loss of physical and information-related infrastructure places significant barriers to the needs assessment process. Indeed, as an example, in the 2005 Pakistan earthquake, it was not until 10 days after the event that an area of 10,000 people was actually accessed (Tatham *et al*, 2016a).

The emergence of Long Endurance Remotely Piloted Aircraft Systems (LE-RPAS) (otherwise known as 'drones' or 'unmanned aerial vehicles/systems' (UAV/S)) has the potential to help understand the impact of a disaster and the resultant needs of those affected. Such aircraft have an endurance of 8–10 hours and a range of some 1,000 km (at a cruising speed of 90–110 kph), and can carry a variety of payloads including video or still, daylight and infra-red cameras, mobile phone relay technology or droppable items such as satellite phones or medicines (Tatham *et al*, 2016b).

Thus, using their internal satellite navigation systems, such LE-RPAS are able to undertake surveillance of the disaster area and produce highly detailed and accurate photography (5 cm resolution) as the basis for decision making by the National Disaster Management Organization (NDMO). Furthermore, this data can be shared in real time with other adjacent countries, thereby helping to transform the logistic response from 'push' to a needs-based pull model.

In addition, such aircraft can also fly in a geo-stationary mode and, as such, mimic the operations of a cell phone tower in the event that the regular one is no long functioning – as was the case in two major wind-related disasters that recently took place in the South East Pacific region (Cyclone Pam – Vanuatu, March 2015; Cyclone Winston – Fiji, February 2016). Furthermore, they also have the capability to use a 'find your phone' system that can initiate a call from the NDMO to an individual on the ground in order that a more detailed understanding of the local needs can be ascertained (Tatham *et al*, 2016b).

Such aircraft come in at around 50 per cent of the capital cost of the most obvious alternative of a light helicopter, require a similar crew size (pilot, camera operator and maintainer), but consume only some 6 litres of fuel in a 10-hour mission. Thus, responding authorities can use manned fixed-wing aircraft or helicopters for more appropriate activities such as search and rescue, leaving the LE-RPAS to meet the surveillance demands to support the needs assessment process.

Turning to the 'supply' side of the equation, it is unsurprising that, given the nature of most rapid onset disasters, in which one has between zero notice in the case of earthquakes and some 48–72 hours for wind events (cyclones, hurricanes, etc), the immediate response is frequently air transport based. This is epitomized by the response to the 2005 Pakistan earthquake in which some 200 cargo planes landed at Islamabad airport in the first 30 days after the event carrying around a total of around 3,900 mt (Tatham *et al*, 2016a).

However, such an approach – whilst having the clear benefit of simplicity – is also extremely costly, with a broad order estimate of US $100,000 per flight being frequently quoted. Thus, the IFRC component of the response, which saw 70 cargo flights carrying 1,750 mt cost the organization some US $7 million – whereas the use of container shipping for the period from day 15 onwards, could have reduced this figure by some 50 per cent (Tatham, *et al*, 2016a).

Furthermore, the availability of runways and cargo handling facilities to manage the aircraft and their loads cannot be guaranteed. For example, in the aftermath of the 2010 Haiti earthquake, the main international airfield was initially unusable due to the damage to the air traffic control tower, and subsequently was overwhelmed by the number of relief flights. As a result, many were diverted to Santo Domingo in the neighbouring Dominican Republic, with the WFP setting up a truck-based transit service to the Haitian capital that was free of charge for UN agencies and NGOs. By the same token, the international airport in Kathmandu was placed under severe pressure after the 2015 earthquake, reflecting the fact that it has only nine aircraft parking slots and limited customs facilities. This resulted in major restrictions on aircraft size, frequency and arrival times and, in turn, led to a significant use of truck routes from India, but this involved a journey time of 7–10 days for the 850 km one-way trip from Kolkota to Kathmandu (Logcluster, 2015).

As a result, consideration is being given to the potential benefits of the next generation of 'Hybrid Cargo Airships' (HCAs). Examples of such HCAs include the Aeroscraft ML866, which has a payload of 60 tonnes and a range of some 6,000 km at 185 kph, and the larger ML868 (payload 220 tonnes, range 9,500 km), which are scheduled to be operational in the 2018–2021 timeframe (Aeroscraft, 2016). The actual lifting capacity is attained through a combination of helium for aerostatic lift and thrust vectoring for aerodynamic lift, and they are typically powered by four engines (one at each corner) which can be tilted to provide directional stability. They also operate with 'state of the art' electronics which help to ensure the most efficient flight plan etc.

Key to the potential value of HCAs in a humanitarian context is that they operate in a vertical take-off/landing mode. Thus, in principle, they could transfer relief supplies directly from a regional warehouse (or UNHRD) directly to the affected area. This has clear benefit in terms of avoiding the need to undertake time-consuming and costly inter-modal transfers, as can be exemplified by the response to Typhoon Haiyan (known locally as Yolanda) in 2013.

This was one of the strongest typhoons ever to be recorded and the deadliest to strike the Philippines in modern history, with winds gusting close to 315 kph (200 mph). It resulted in the death of over 6,300 people, and 11 million were affected, many of whom were made homeless. The main area of the country impacted by the typhoon was the Eastern Visayas, and in particular the regional capital of Tacloban. Unfortunately, due to damage from the typhoon, access to the city's airport was restricted to light aircraft, together with some military assets from the Philippines and US air forces. As a result, the majority of cargo flights were routed to the city of Cebu, which is located on an adjacent island. From Cebu airport, it was necessary to transport the relief goods to the docks, then via Ro-Ro ferry to Tacloban (some five hours away), before subsequent movement from the ferry to the Tacloban distribution centre (Tatham *et al*, 2016a).

Given that the exemplar HCAs can operate from sand, earth, water bodies and grass areas (provided they are clear of obstacles), and that the launch/land zones do not need to be totally flat (a degree of slope and/or undulation is acceptable), they are significantly more flexible than their fixed-wing counterparts. That said, the physical size of the required take-off and landing areas is significant – in the case of the ML868 it would require a circle of some 360 m diameter. Nevertheless, this spatial requirement should be set against their internal capacity of over 7,000 cum (ML866) and 30,000 cum (ML868) (Aeroscraft, 2016). Furthermore, not only do HCAs have the potential to launch from a location close to the regional warehouse and deliver in the vicinity of the final destination, but they can also achieve this in a very environmentally friendly way. For example, the International Air Transport Association (IATA) suggests that 'airships produce 80–90 per cent fewer emissions than conventional aircraft' (Air Cargo News, 2010).

A final observation in relation to the potential use of alternative and emerging transport modes to support the supply of material in the aftermath of a disaster is to return to the potential use of RPAS. Their capabilities were outlined earlier in the discussion of ways in which the needs assessment process might be improved, but they are also able to support, either directly or indirectly, the delivery process. Thus, they can use the same camera-enabled reconnaissance method to overfly a prospective supply route and check that it is not compromised by, for example, fallen trees, landslides or broken bridges. Clearly, in the case of the latter, the fact that a bridge appears to be physically intact is no guarantee that it will take the weight of a loaded truck, but overflying the route will support an initial go/no go decision.

Second, there has recently been some quite considerable hype over the potential use of RPAS to achieve last-mile deliveries by, for example, Amazon (Amazon, 2016) or Domino's (Griffith, 2016). This capability is already being actively tested in a humanitarian context to support the delivery of vaccines and blood samples in Africa (Kuo, 2016). Clearly, the payloads that can be carried in this way, as well as the associated endurance, are relatively limited, but the approach as a whole has potential to provide life-saving support in areas where the road network (to the extent that it exists) is compromised.

Grand challenges

As we have outlined in this chapter, the provision of efficient and effect transport in a humanitarian environment faces multiple challenges. Concepts and models from commercial or business transport can, of course, be applied to an extent, but rather than copying them, they need to be adapted to this specific context. That said, the two contexts have much to learn from one another, and in addition they frequently come together via the commercial LSP interface.

New technology is often paraded as 'the answer to all humanitarian problems' and, to an extent, this must be true. Thus, much more could clearly be achieved by adopting RPAS, using 3D printing, or even using better tracking and tracing devices for the protection of humanitarians and humanitarian cargo. However, there are limitations to the use of these technologies, most of which stem from privacy and security concerns. For example, tracking humanitarians raises questions such as (a) whether they want to be tracked at all times, and (b) who has access to such data.

Similarly, the use of RPAS can easily run into problems in geographic areas in which RPAS are commonly used as military assets – how are beneficiaries to know which ones to hide from and which ones are bringing them aid? By the same token, social media has given rise to numerous apps designed to resolve all sorts of real or perceived problems. However, let's just bear in mind for a second that (a) the loss of infrastructure in the aftermath of a disaster may well include supporting energy and telecoms systems; (b) not all people in the world have access to cell phones, Internet and the like – we still live in a world with a digital divide; and (c) he or she who shouts the loudest is not necessarily the one most in need.

There are, however, other ongoing challenges that new technologies could and should address. One of these is the eternal problem of temperature control in the supply chain. A substantial part of medical aid and, to a lesser extent, food aid, requires temperature-controlled supply chains. Both the actual maintenance of the cold chain, and the assurance that is has indeed been maintained, are problematic both in a physical sense as well as in a process one. For example, and rightly, customs clearance authorities as well as end users need to be clear that temperature-sensitive cargos are 'fit for purpose' when they reach the intended beneficiaries. An obvious alternative is, however, the development of medicines, especially vaccines, that do not need such a cold chain. This has been a 'grand challenge' for a long time, but while we are waiting for these to arrive, ensuring the integrity of the cold chain reverts to those with responsibility for the management of the life-giving humanitarian transport.

In this chapter, we have highlighted a broad range of challenges that fall to humanitarian logisticians and, in particular, those overseeing the transport component. We have also suggested areas where potential solutions are being developed, as well as those that are firmly in the 'unfinished business' category. With this, we hope to inspire researchers and practitioners to take a leap in their thinking and introduce passion and innovation, as well as rational decision making into the management of humanitarian transport.

References

Aeroscraft (2016) Fleet, available at: http://aeroscraft.com/fleet-copy/4580475518 (accessed 30 May 2016)

Air Cargo News (2010) Airfreight must embrace dirigibles, available at: http://www.aircargonews.net/news/single-view/news/airfreight-must-embrace-dirigibles-says-iata.html (accessed 20 June 2016)

Amazon (2016) Amazon Prime Air, available at: http://www.amazon.com/b?node=8037720011 (accessed 29 April 2016)

Balcik, B and Beamon, B M (2008) Facility location in humanitarian relief, *International Journal of Logistics: Research and Applications*, **11** (2), pp 101–21

Beresford, A K C and Pettit, S J (2013) Humanitarian aid logistics: The Wenchuan and Haiti earthquakes compared, in *Supply Chain Management: Concepts, methodologies, tools, and applications*, IGI Global, Ch 39

Boudhoum, O (2014) Disaster relief models: Location of points of distribution, *University of Arkansas*, available at: http://hdl.handle.net/10826/938 (accessed 12 June 2016)

Choi, A K Y, Beresford, A K C, Pettit, S J and Bayusuf, F (2010) Humanitarian aid distribution in East Africa: A study in supply chain volatility and fragility, *Supply Chain Forum*, **11** (3), pp 20–31

CRED (Centre for Research on the Epidemiology of Disasters) (2016a) EM-DAT Glossary, available at: http://www.emdat.be/Glossary (accessed 29 April 2016)

CRED (Centre for Research on the Epidemiology of Disasters) (2016b) Disasters in Numbers 2015, *CRED Crunch 41*, available at: http://www.emdat.be/#pager (accessed 29 April 2016)

Everywhere, Jahre, M and Navangul, K A (2011) Predicting the unpredictable: Demand forecasting in international humanitarian response, *Proceedings of NOFOMA 2011*, Harstad University College, 9–10 June, available at: http://aveniranalytics.com/wp-content/uploads/2014/11/Everywhere-Jahre-and-Navangul-2011.pdf (accessed 29 April 2016)

Fenton, G, Goodhand, M, and Vince, R (2014) What next for humanitarian logistics? in P H Tatham and M G Christopher (eds) *Humanitarian Logistics: Meeting the challenge of preparing for and responding to disasters*, 2nd edn, Kogan Page, London

Fernie, J and Sparks, L (2004) *Logistics and Retail Management*, Kogan Page, London

Griffith, C (2016) Domino's unveils robot delivery boy, *The Australian*, 18 March, available at: www.theaustralian.com.au/business/technology/dominos-pizza-unveils-robot-delivery-boy/news-story/04d9f15f076ab624454190489b4dda45 (accessed 29 April 2016)

Haavisto, I and Vaillancourt, A (2016) Country logistics performance and disaster impact, *Disasters*, **40** (2), pp 262–83

Heaslip, G (2013) Services operations management and humanitarian logistics, *Journal of Humanitarian Logistics and Supply Chain Management*, 3 (1), pp 37–51

IFRC (International Federation of Red Cross and Red Crescent Societies) (2016) *Emergency Items Catalogue*, available at: http://procurement.ifrc.org/catalogue/#1_101 (accessed 29 April 2016)

Kovács, G and Tatham, P H (2009) Responding to disruptions in the supply network: from dormant to action, *Journal of Business Logistics*, 30 (2), pp 215–29

Kuo, L (2106) Drone delivery could give Africa's HIV-positive babies a fighting chance at survival, *Quartz Africa*, 15 March, available at: http://qz.com/639417/drone-delivery-could-give-africas-hiv-positive-babies-a-better-chance-at-survival/ (accessed 29 April 2016)

Larson, P D (2009) *Proceedings of the 2nd Cardiff/Cranfield Humanitarian Logistics Initiative Conference*, 24–26 March 2009, Faringdon, UK

Logcluster (United Nations Logistics Cluster) (2105) Operational Update, 14 May, available at: http://www.logcluster.org/ops/nepal (accessed 29 April 2016)

OCHA (Office for the Coordination of Humanitarian Affairs) (1999) *OCHA Orientation Handbook on Complex Emergencies*, available at: http://reliefweb.int/sites/reliefweb.int/files/resources/3D153DA3049B322AC1256C30002A9C24-ocha__orientation__handbook_on__.html (accessed 29 April 2016)

Pazirandeh, A and Herlin, H (2014) Unfruitful cooperative purchasing: a case of humanitarian purchasing power, *Journal of Humanitarian Logistics and Supply Chain Management*, 4 (1), pp 24–42

Rest, K-D, Trautsamwieser, A and Hirsch, P (2012) Trends and risks in home health care, *Journal of Humanitarian Logistics and Supply Chain Management*, 2 (1), pp 34–53

Safran, P (2003) A strategic approach to disaster and emergency assistance, 2nd UN-ISDR Asian Meeting, 15–17 Jan, Kobe Japan, available at: http://www.adb.org/sites/default/files/institutional-document/32118/disaster-emergency.pdf (accessed 23 Jun 2016)

Scriven, K (2016) Humanitarian innovation and the art of the possible, *Humanitarian Practice Network – Humanitarian Exchange*, 26, pp 5–7

Tatham, P H, Ball, C, Wu, Y and Diplas, P (2016a) Using Remotely Piloted Aircraft Systems (RPAS) to support for humanitarian logistic operations – benefits and challenges, *Australia and New Zealand Academy of Management (ANZAM) Operations, Supply Chain and Services Management Symposium*, University of Technology, Sydney, 13–15 June

Tatham, P H and Christopher, M G (2014) An Introduction to Humanitarian Logistics, in P H Tatham, and M G Christopher (eds) *Humanitarian Logistics: Meeting the challenge of preparing for and responding to disasters*, 2nd edn, Kogan Page, London

Tatham, P H and Kovács, G (2010) The impact of gender on humanitarian logistics, *International Journal of Mass Emergencies and Disasters*, 28 (2), pp 148–69

Tatham, P H, Kovács, G and Vaillancourt, A (2016b) Evaluating the applicability of sea basing to support the preparation for, and response to, rapid onset disasters, *Transactions on Engineering Management*, **63** (1), pp 67–77

Tatham, P H, L'Hermitte, C, Spens, K M and Kovács, G (2013) Humanitarian logistics: development of an improved disaster classification framework, *Proceedings of ANZAM OM/SC Conference*, Brisbane, 20–21 June 2013, ISBN: 978-0-646-90576-1

Tatham, P H and Pettit, S J (2010) Transforming humanitarian logistics: the journey to supply network management, *International Journal of Physical Distribution and Logistics Management*, **40** (8/9), pp 609–22

Thomas, A and Mizushima, M (2005) Logistics training: necessity or luxury? *Forced Migration Review*, **22**, pp 60–61

Van Wassenhove, L N (2006) Humanitarian aid logistics: supply chain management in high gear, *Journal of the Operational Research Society*, **57**, pp 475–58

13

Transport futures: reconciling the on-demand economy with global production chains

PETER WELLS, Cardiff Business School, UK

Introduction

It might appear surprising to some, but it could be claimed in retrospect that both freight and passenger transport have enjoyed substantial stability and continuity over the 70 years or so to 2020. Notwithstanding several generations of incremental technological improvements over these decades, and the usual processes of supply, demand and competition, the overwhelming narrative is one of evolutionary growth within well-understood operational and regulatory boundaries. This chapter, however, seeks to make the case that the next few decades will be radically different except with regard to one key issue: that the majority of transport is a derived demand. Transport is called for in order to achieve other things, and to this extent can be considered undesirable waste that is justified because it unites efficient production via economies of scale, low cost via global production chains, and consumer material demands. Underneath this fundamental concern, however, lies a nascent tension between the localized on-demand economy and global production chains that are held together mainly by maritime transport, and also in part by high-geared airfreight services.

This chapter is necessarily speculative, and, rather than seeking to provide a definitive answer to the question of 'what is the future for transport?'

the stance taken is that there is likely to be a multiple set of co-existing, complementary and contradictory futures in which the activity of transport is contested and politicized as never before. Transport not only emerges out of these futures as a residual; changes in transport provision, in technologies and business models, and in the rules governing transport use will all act to varying degrees as enablers of diverse futures. Theoretically then, the chapter proposes a dialectic and evolutionary perspective that seeks to understand historic change, and somewhat on the basis of this considers the likely trajectories of future change, as an emergent property of wider socio-technical systems that have to date been relatively self-stabilizing but are fracturing and morphing into new futures. The first part of this chapter therefore outlines this theoretical framework, which is derived ultimately from socio-technical transitions theory (Geels, 2002; 2012). It is argued that such transitions, layered into and mediated by distinct institutional settings or varieties of capitalism, are also definitively shaped by the actions of elite or privileged actors that may intervene either to constrain or to promote change. In this conceptualization, then, the technologies of freight transport are neither entirely neutral nor entirely determining.

Freight transport fundamentally acts to bridge the spatial separation of production and consumption. The second section of this chapter therefore considers how the spatial separation of production and consumption has changed in the recent past, and how the possible future pathways of such change may map out. There are powerful tensions in this separation, between the demands of the market for late-configuration, customized and on-demand supply on the one hand, and the demands of the production system for similarity and modularity, spatially concentrated economies of scale, least-cost production locations, and the necessity for high levels of capacity utilization. More recently, the voices calling for a return to the 'local', however that is defined, have become stronger, as has the more profound challenge emerging from proponents of degrowth. It would appear that the palliatives of eco-efficiency and corporate social responsibility, while delivering instances of improvement, do more to enable the continuing separation of production and consumption at the price of increased external costs mainly in the form of environmental impacts.

This section therefore presents a brief consideration of the case of maritime cargo trades in the realm of long-distance transport but also discusses the uneasy interface between global production chains and the on-demand economy as expressed at the urban level. Hence there are two empirical foci for the chapter: Maritime transport over long distances as the 'conveyor belt' of the global economy; and the short-range, fragmented and increasingly customized transport of products within urban areas. It is recognized that in so doing there are important gaps in coverage within this chapter of the logistics systems that enable global value chains. The chapter excludes an analysis of, for example, truck and distribution centre operations that a holistic analysis would normally demand. However, the purpose of this chapter is to identify those aspects of freight transport in which change is likely to be the greatest or the most significant, and those aspects which will have a determining impact on the whole system.

The final section offers some thoughts, based on the preceding analysis, on the limited utility of the traditional tools of forecasting in a chaotic and turbulent world. In a sense, this final section therefore presents a post-hoc consideration of methodology and theorization. In particular, the idea of a single (and stable) future is questioned as an unrealistic idealization. Rather, it is argued that the underlying principles of sustainability suggest that at the very least transport solutions need to be sensitive to the peculiarities of place and of specific applications, and hence the quest for greater transport efficiency is likely to result in a greater diversity of such solutions. A greater challenge, however, is the idea that the fundamentals of the neo-liberal capitalist model will implode under population and resource pressures, resulting in a new 'de-growth' economy.

Technologies, transitions, varieties and elites: a theoretical framework for transport futures

While socio-technical transitions theory is reasonably well established in academic discourse, and is increasingly finding application in policy arenas, recent research utilizing this framework has sought more recently to integrate other theoretical insights in a search for stronger accounts of agency and causality. Penna and Geels (2015), for example, have invoked a dialectic form of Product Life Cycle Theory to explain the historic emergence of safety as a concern in the US automotive industry. That is, the theory has offered a useful lens through which to describe and envisage the ways in which technological change permeates and helps transform society over extended periods of time, but has lacked locational specification and a sense in which social and technical change may be conflictual, intermittent and contextual (Shove and Walker, 2007).

Researchers interested in socio-technical transitions have engaged with both urbanism and transport as key themes. Transport emerges as an area of interest because it is heavily enmeshed into contemporary economies and societies, and directly implicated in a wide range of environmental problems including global warming and air pollution. Urbanism is seen as the crucial arena in which socio-technical transitions in many aspects of life, including freight transport, are enacted.

Still, there has been a relative neglect of the significance of differences between places within socio-technical transitions research. Many case studies in the literature are indeed 'located' within nation state jurisdictions or other geo-political boundaries, but this mostly appears to be a matter of narrative convenience: data tend to be collected and available at distinct spatial levels. In part to offer a critical alternative to the universalism of management theory and research, the 'varieties of capitalism' school of thought has emerged in the search for explanations of distinctly different trajectories and qualitative content (for example in labour practices; labour-management relations; relations between manufacturing and finance capital; and the role of the state) as evidenced in firms in different countries and regions (Gereffi and Wyman, 1990; Hall and Soskici, 2001). Some of this research has been about the integration of locations into increasingly global value chains (Sturgeon *et al*, 2008; Pierre, 2015), but the actual mechanism of achieving this integration in the form of the maritime industry has been neglected. The central theme of the 'varieties of capitalism' approach, however, is that of institutions in their specific settings, or what is sometimes termed the 'institutional regime' (Hancke *et al*, 2008) where it is argued that institutional complementarities form the basis of national comparative advantage. Thus, it is held that France has exhibited a distinct variety of capitalism as compared with, for example, that prevailing in Germany or the UK (Schmidt, 2003; Clift, 2012; Haipeter *et al*, 2012).

Intriguingly, as the preponderance of international freight transport is undertaken on the high seas, and flags of convenience blur vessel ownership boundaries, much of maritime transport is effectively stateless, which poses unique governance issues with regard to shipping and environmental performance, among other concerns (Lister *et al*, 2015). The 'varieties of capitalism' school of thought has yet to be applied to maritime activities, yet in some regards there are in this setting distinct governance practices, labour relations, cultures, and norms of behaviour just as there are in national states. Hence, for this chapter, the dualism in the contrast between the spatially specific on-demand economy, and the globally embracing maritime transport industry is somewhat reflected in the theoretical framework used here. That is to say, socio-technical transition theory is broadly an attempt to explain the permeation of technologies into society, and increasingly to look for ways to achieve a more sustainable pattern of production and consumption.

However, while the early analysis from Geels (2002) indeed used shipping as a case study of transition, specifically from sail to steam, the analysis largely related to distinct national interests prevalent at that time. So, while transitions theory, along with varieties of capitalism theory, may help provide insights into the diffusion of on-demand technologies in urban contexts, there is considerable scope to develop both further for the analysis of international maritime transport. This chapter can only hint at the possibilities in this regard.

Similar comments may apply to the role played by elite actors, be they corporate or individual, in shaping historical outcomes. The significance of individual agency is a hotly debated issue for historians, but there can be little doubt that there are some social actors with more power and influence than others who can at least try to enact outcomes that would not have otherwise happened, or perhaps bring such outcomes to pass more rapidly than would otherwise be the case. The relationship between elite actors and their structural or institutional setting is again a matter for much debate, and for which it is difficult to prove a direct cause and effect linkage. Counterfactual narratives may sometimes be invoked to explore what the world would have been like had 'x' not happened. While this chapter cannot explore such issues in any depth, it is at least notable that innovators are often accorded an elite status in historical narratives, and it could be argued that the introduction of the standardized shipping container by Malcolm McLean in 1956 represents the actions of just such an innovator.

A feature that unites contemporary urban and maritime transport is that of air pollution, specifically that related to diesel emissions. In broad terms, it would appear that land-based emissions from cars, vans and trucks have had more regulatory attention than shipping. In part this is logical – vehicles and people are in close proximity in urban areas, and there has been a rapid growth in vehicle use over the last 50 years or so. However, the globalization process has also resulted in expansion of the maritime fleet, and jumboization of vessels in most sectors. With that has come a concern to understand and ultimately rectify the health consequences of maritime transport-derived air pollution (Corbett *et al*, 2007). Regulatory control is often considered a key force in propelling technological innovation (particularly for sustainability), and hence a key trigger for broader socio-technical change. Again, the consequences to date and policy options for the future are arguably more evident in land transport than maritime transport, with fewer technological solutions available to the maritime sector (Lué et al, 2016).

Finally, it is worth noting that the physical flows of materials and products are the corporeal manifestation of embedded flows of energy, water and even knowledge (Sheller, 2014), and are accompanied by hidden flows of information and finance. Attempts to expand or restrict the physical flows, for whatever reason, are also therefore related to power and politics, and to the ability of some social entities to achieve their ends over and above others. The movement of materials and products, whether over water or land, is thus susceptible to and in part a tool of these geo-political, economic and military concerns. It is this feature that elevates the futures of transport beyond the merely technical, or beyond the merely commercial.

Freight transport: bridging the spatial separation of production and consumption

Typically, freight transport involves multiple stages and a variety of modes, with periods of movement interspersed with periods of stasis, and at a range of spatial scales. There are flows of products from rural areas to the cities, from smaller settlements up the urban spatial hierarchy to bigger cities, and across vast distances from one country to another. This chapter highlights just two aspects of freight transport for deeper consideration: shipping and urban delivery. In part this is a deliberate juxtaposition because of the desire to highlight the potential schisms that may arise out of the non-alignment of global production systems with burgeoning on-demand deliveries of products. The comfortable resolution of the resultant tensions is by no means certain, but it is argued to be key to understanding the future of freight transport.

Global logistics chains: shipping

The major bulk flows of materials, foods, product components and finished products are conducted via a global shipping fleet of increasing scale and specialization. The flows of raw materials such as iron ore and bauxite are achieved by dedicated ship designs, as are the bulk commodity flows of items such as wheat, rice and soy bean. The flows of petroleum and related products are achieved by dedicated tankers, and Ro-Ro vessels provide fast-response, simplified inter-island trades, eg the 'marine motorways' of the

European Union. In turn, the movement of finished goods has been revolutionized by the invention of the container, resulting in ever-larger container ships. All of these flows are achieved by the use of marine diesel (bunker) fuels. Significant reductions in shipping time, cost and environmental burden have been delivered through these ship technologies, and the detailed attention to eco-design and operational innovations (such as slow steaming, or the use of onshore electricity while at harbour).

Inevitably, these processes have also seen parallel developments in terms of the growth of scale of shipping companies, and in levels of industrial concentration in the sector. The incremental integration of previously isolated economies, from the former Council for Mutual Economic Assistance countries (COMECON), India, China and elsewhere, has been one of the most important political and economic processes of the last 30 years or so. In tandem with the technology, operational and structural changes noted above, this neo-liberal trade and market process has been key to accelerating the spatial separation of production and consumption, along with allowing the pursuit of economies of scale at multiple points in the global value chains so created (De Marchi *et al*, 2014). Hence, mining operations for iron ore and other raw materials have become more concentrated into fewer, larger sites along with a process of merger and acquisition into fewer but bigger companies. Similar events have occurred involving many of the materials production industries such as steel and aluminium, all the way through to companies producing finished products for the retail market. Similarly, the infrastructures of shipping, from ports to storage depots and the land-based movement of products, have also become increasingly concentrated on key points around the world (Birtchnell and Urry, 2015; Cidell, 2012).

There is a widespread expectation of increased regulation of the global maritime fleet, at a range of spatial scales, and with uncertain impacts in terms of the cost and competitiveness of shipping (Makkonen and Repka, 2016; Poulsen *et al*, 2016).

Local logistics chains: the on-demand revolution

The interactive impact of the Internet, mobile telecommunications, online shopping, and the local purchase of products or services continues to grow, but with differential impacts on different areas of consumption. In the realm of media (music, films, etc) the process of digitization has transformed consumption, with online downloading and streaming of content via a bewildering array of providers and intermediaries offering a vast range of service packages and prices. In other areas, such as groceries, the penetration of online shopping has been less dramatic, but continues to grow by taking share from the more traditional practice of shoppers visiting retail outlets and 'delivering' their own products home. In addition, hybrid solutions such as 'click and collect' have become more popular and exhibit a strong growth rate.

In all this, it is easy to be carried away by the populist media and enthusiastic experts and imagine a radical transformation is unfolding before our eyes, but some caution is needed. It is worth recalling, for example, that in many regards the home delivery of products was the norm before dispersed sub-urbanization and the arrival of the large supermarket chains. Products such as milk, meat and fish, vegetables, ice-cream, ready meals (eg fish and chips), and more were routinely delivered door-to-door by mobile retail outlets (mostly medium-sized vans, or delivery bikes, or of course the classical electric milk floats in the UK), as were services such as libraries. In this regard, it may be that the normal practice of the last 50 years or so, whereby we buy and transport the goods ourselves, is the anomaly. Moreover, non-motorized urban delivery remains important in many cities in countries such as India (Sadhu *et al*, 2014) and China (Zacharias and Zhang, 2015). It is notable that Zacharias and Zhang (2015) found that motorized alternatives to the tricycle were uncompetitive in terms of time, financial cost and energy efficiency.

It is also worth remembering that many in the population are excluded from these new on-demand opportunities because they lack certain prerequisites such as being able to forecast with precision when they will be home to receive goods, or perhaps even lack bank accounts through which payments can be made. Others may lament the loss of human contact in the traditional shopping experience, and refuse to participate.

Despite these caveats, it would appear that the on-demand economy is growing fast, and in turn there are enormous implications for the character of local logistics chains at all scales; international, national, regional and local. For example, one possible area of development identified by Fatnassi *et al* (2015) is the dual use of metro systems for people (by day) and freight (by night).

According to Felsted (2014), the UK was one of the largest markets in the world for non-food click and collect, with about 11 per cent of the UK market by volume, but with an expectation of reaching 30 per cent by 2017, equivalent to compound annual growth of 60 per cent between 2012 and 2017 compared with just 5 per cent for home delivery. With time, the number of transactions is growing, though the per-unit value is falling. Asda, one of the supermarket majors in the UK, announced in 2015 their plan to have 1,000 click-and-collect points by 2018 at locations as diverse as transport hubs, high streets, universities, office blocks or even airports (Asda, 2015). As another example, the consultants The Centre for Retail Research (CRR, 2015) considered that retail online spending in Europe was expected to grow from £132.05 billion (€156.28 billion) in 2014 to £156.67 billion (€185.39 billion) in 2015 (+18.4 per cent), reaching £185.44 billion (€219.44 billion) in 2016. It is notable, however, that CRR define a 'mature' online market as having more than 9.5 per cent of all retail transactions conducted online, and with 55 per cent or more of the population as online shoppers. Thus, while there is an expectation of disruption to traditional retail outlets, and to the attendant transport flows, online retailing remains a significant niche rather than the new mainstream.

Even if the growth area is 'click and collect', it is arguable that the largest logistics impact of the on-demand economy has been the rapid increase in deliveries to individual residential addresses (Wang and Zhou, 2015). It is this practice that has supported the rapid growth in sales of light delivery vans and car-derived vans in Europe, for example, while also providing the demand basis for many of the new delivery and courier services that are becoming a feature of the urban context.

Of particular interest is the way in which what used to be known as the 'sharing' economy has become an area for commercial innovation, with the arrival of peer-to-peer systems hosted by intermediary companies seeking to offer low-cost package delivery services. An ongoing example is 'UBERrush', a package service offered by the Uber taxi hire business in some locations in North America (Uber, 2015). It is interesting to note that the press release from Uber quotes a customer:

> I RUSH keys to my guests right when they arrive, ensuring no waiting around, and a higher rating for me – Carlos M, Airbnb host.

This is indicative of how the virtual world and physical world of the on-demand economy come to be realized through the application of innovative transport solutions, even for items as small as a set of house keys. Uber will also employ bicycle couriers on this sort of service in some locations. Inevitably, as with the original dotcom boom, there are many new businesses with a range of business models in this realm of peer-to-peer delivery, and not all will prosper into the future. One that is apparently gaining a foothold is Nimber, based in Norway (see https://www.nimber.com/). In some regions of the world, the bicycle, or moped, is one of the main modes of transport, moving small freight in large volumes but in small consignments and, in many instances, passengers.

Layered into this technological opportunity is also a growing desire to foster 'smart' and 'clean' cities, with the exclusion of a range of transport technologies being a prime candidate for action. In Europe, the growing concerns over air pollution in major cities such as London and Paris is leading to a succession of increasingly restrictive policies, notably with regards to emissions from vehicles. Major building programmes for urban land transport are unlikely as a feature of the future in the mature cities of Europe, Japan and North America, except perhaps mass transit for people. As a result, the application of telematics is seen as potentially significant to squeeze more efficiency out of available urban infrastructures, though Walker and Manson (2014) argue that such optimism may be misplaced in certain circumstances. For enthusiasts, the opportunities for 'green' local logistics are immense: for example Streeter (2013) claims that up to 50 per cent of urban freight could be replaced by bicycles. The EU-funded project, Cyclelogistics Ahead, running for three years to May 2017, is intended to promote the adoption of bicycle and other zero-emissions cargo delivery (see http://www.cyclelogistics.eu/index.php?id=11). Products considered viable were those with less than 7 km between origin and destination, less than 200 kg in weight, and not part of a 'complex logistics chain'. Certainly, however, barriers to cargo bicycles remain, including safety concerns for the riders and lack of awareness among potential consumers (Schliwa et al, 2015). In similar vein, there would appear to be natural 'synergies' between the performance envelope of electric vehicles and the requirements of zero-emissions urban delivery (Nordtømme et al, 2015a), but issues of the development of an appropriate infrastructure and the design of delivery routes require strategic planning at an early stage (Juan et al, 2016; Melo et al, 2014; Taefi et al, 2015).

In between the global logistics systems and the local urban on-demand economy there needs to be some sort of buffer that mediates the 'shock' of erratic orders and compensates for the slowness of response that long-range shipping entails, while serving environmental goals by reducing urban traffic (Allen et al, 2012). A more 'national' form of this buffer may be seen in the operations of the Ocado online supermarket group in the UK, whose pivotal investment is not a retail outlet, but a huge semi-automated warehouse and distribution centre. As Nordtømme et al (2015b) observe, establishing urban-scale consolidation centres seems a logical step, but may be difficult to establish in practice. Other 'rational' measures such as ensuring maximum load capacities are filled for urban delivery (as in the 'milk run' concept) may also result in unintended negative consequences (Arvidsson, 2013).

Forecasting in a chaotic and diverse world

As noted above, it is argued that the bigger picture on product logistics is the global-scale separation of production and consumption enabled and stimulated by efficient and low-cost shipping, ever-more sophisticated airfreight networks and super-agile and responsive, normally road-based 'last mile' delivery, and attendant low fuel prices. Similar advances have been made in terms of truck logistics and warehousing systems on land. As De Marchi *et al* (2014) observe, global value chains are usually dominated by major retailers, whose concern for reputational risk may drive enhanced governance of maritime and airfreight systems. Other studies argue that enhanced sustainability performance in shipping operations also enhances competitiveness, which may also then propel greater uptake of sustainability practices (Yang *et al*, 2013). It can be argued that some eco-efficiency measures such as slow-steaming are rather susceptible to volatility depending upon the value of the cargo: an increasingly expensive cargo may provide the stimulus for higher speed, because cargo owners have working capital tied up (Lindstad and Eskeland, 2015). Some studies suggest that shipping flows could be increased substantially without growth in environmental burdens either at sea or in ports (Bal and Vleugel, 2015).

The eco-efficiency impact of new technologies, the adoption of cost-reducing management practices and shipping automation, along with the opening up of new routes (through the Arctic, and through the proposed Nicaragua canal), will all serve to lower the costs of shipping and thereby continue to underpin growing demand (Yip and Wong, 2015). The environmental implications of such developments are largely negative (Lindstad *et al*, 2016). It is pertinent to ask, therefore, what events or developments could change the current likely trajectory of shipping, land-based road/rail transport and airfreight capability-based logistics?

At a global level, shifts in the major bulk flows of materials and products could have a profound impact on the future of maritime transport over the period to 2050. Such shifts may include, for example, a reduction in shipping of crude oil from the Middle East to Europe and North America as alternative energy sources and energy-saving measures take effect, perhaps to be replaced by flows to China, Africa and India. Bulk petroleum accounts for 25 per cent of global total freight movements by weight, so changes in this one commodity will make a substantial difference. Bulk flows of food and commodities are also likely to change as the mature economies pursue greater self-reliance, and as emerging economies develop a greater capacity to consume. In turn, the movement of finished products may also change, particularly as the drive to establish circular economies may by the latter stages of this time period begin to make a measurable impact on virgin material and product consumption. Put simply, the untrammelled growth in shipping to which we have been witness over the last 30 years is very unlikely to be repeated in the next 30 years, and simultaneously those flows are likely to become more fragmented and diverse. As a result, short sea shipping is likely to become relatively more important (Morales-Fusco *et al*, 2012; 2013).

However, those retailers dominating global value chains also face major changes in the urban markets in which they primarily operate, and this too may drive changes in maritime systems. From an operations management perspective, then, the emergent digital design and manufacturing possibilities (Holmström *et al*, 2016) carry also enormous implications for the structure of global logistics. No matter how efficient global maritime and airfreight systems may be, and how low the cost-per-unit transported is driven down, the movement of materials and products imposes a cost that is ideally best avoided. Put another way, if a combination of market pressures via the on-demand economy, new technology advances in terms of responsive manufacturing, and regulatory pressures to bring to reality the circular economy and a 90 per cent reduction in carbon emissions by 2050 all are combined, then the tension between existing global production and supply chains and the nature of local demand will become unbearable; those production chains will break and in so doing will take down the demand for shipping.

At the local or urban scale, a combination of on-demand markets and growing requirements around reverse logistics, recycling and product take-back are likely to underpin the further growth in urban transport, but this cannot be achieved by contemporary trucks and vans. It is already the case that many, if not most, large cities around the world (and not just in Asia) routinely fail to meet World Health Organization standards on air pollution, and the use of internal combustion engine vehicles in those urban areas is one of the major reasons. As knowledge about the health effects of such poor air quality becomes more developed and widespread, so the basis for action will increase. Additional pressures brought about by autonomous vehicles offering cheap and flexible on-demand transport will further stretch infrastructures and enhance air quality concerns unless and until alternative powertrain technologies are brought in. Just as car-sharing schemes are becoming significant for private motorists, so will van-sharing schemes become important for future logistics operations.

In addition, such developments are very much in the 'mainstream' of contemporary expectations. The circular economy, for example, is a primary policy target for the European Union and countries such as China (Yuan *et al*, 2006; EMF, 2012: see also http://ec.europa.eu/environment/circular-economy/index_en.htm). It is entirely possible that much more profound shocks are delivered at a regional or global level. In particular, at the global environmental level the rapid overshoot of the 450 ppm tipping point for carbon concentrations in the atmosphere, which is likely to occur around 2035 at current rates of accumulation, may, in time, trigger stronger policy responses. Aviation and shipping, along with land transport, are areas of continued growth in carbon emissions and prime targets for regulatory control. Even more profoundly, there is an emergent 'degrowth' movement that argues for the controlled and sustained reduction in consumption and production (Boonstra and Joosse, 2013; Kallis, 2011). In this degrowth analysis, it is contended that eco-efficiency and regulation are ineffective palliatives, and that the only way to return humanity to living within planetary boundaries is a massive net reduction in consumption – and almost inevitably the end of the extension of neo-liberal capitalism. In this vision for the future, the circular economy only exists as an indicator of failure, and specifically as the overt sign of over-production, leading to over-consumption and then premature disposal via eBay, Gumtree, or charity and thrift shops. Low-cost freight transport is key to the viability of over-supply and to the movement of low-value second-use goods and materials.

Most of the answers offered to the sustainability issues focus on technology, and perhaps on transport policy, yet, as Baindur and Macário (2013) argue with the case of the Mumbai lunchbox (tiffin) delivery system, there is much that can be achieved with a low-technology, low-cost system – and by implication much that can be learned from established traditional practices. The Mumbai case also points to the importance of understanding the significance of place. Different locations will continue to see different solutions, depending upon their historically-constructed urban form, cultural preferences, economic circumstances, climate, topography, and much more. While the pervading theme of the future for freight is one of reduced environmental burden per unit carried, the manifestation of this future is likely to be extremely diverse – more so than at present.

Conclusions

We may conclude therefore, that freight transport as we currently know and understand it does not have a future… rather it has multiple futures dependent upon many contextual factors, and on the outcomes of many contested processes. In some respects, the technological possibilities are the least problematic to consider. It is much more difficult to know whether key contradictions in our production and consumption practices can be reconciled, and if so on whose terms. These are social and political issues; the answers are likely to emerge out of distinct cultural preferences, behaviours and beliefs as much as technological rationality or indeed market forces. The existing global production and consumption system must change, and as transport remains a derived demand, it too must change.

In view of this, it might be argued that human history has reached a point where the growth in transport, and freight transport in particular, must cease and that a reduction in such activities is the only truly viable way forward. This is especially true for certain forms of freight transport, ie those which are most environmentally obtrusive, or simply those which are the most expensive in the longer term.

Similarly, viewed in aggregate, it is hard to conclude that urban transport is at all efficient even if individual operators may say that they are. The key future innovations, therefore, are not so much in fundamental technologies, but in social, institutional or organizational structures that allow a closer approximation to collective efficiency and the concept of satisficing rather than maximizing consumption. Thus far, socio-technical transitions theory and its application in policy has not embraced such a future. The idea of an orchestrated or managed transition remains prominent, but without questioning the underlying assumptions of materialism that are a feature of contemporary cultures. Whether an orderly transition can be achieved without substantive social and economic cost must be in doubt. Moreover, the freight industry, the logistics service providers, retailers and other parties are now much more powerful and have greater vested interests than 30 years ago, while the entrenched global production chains act to reinforce structural inter-dependency. Hence, in thinking about futures, when it is tempting to focus mostly on what will change, it may be more pertinent to focus on what will remain broadly the same.

References

Allen, J, Browne, M, Woodburn, A and Leonardi, J (2012) The role of urban consolidation centres in sustainable freight transport, *Transport Reviews*, 32 (4), pp 473–90

Arvidsson, N (2013) The milk run revisited: A load factor paradox with economic and environmental implications for urban freight transport, *Transportation Research Part A: Policy and Practice*, 51, pp 55–62

Asda (2015) Asda brings more value to more people as it purchases 15 standalone petrol stations from Rontec LTD [online] http://your.asda.com/press-centre/asda-brings-more-value-to-more-people-as-it-purchases-15-standalone-petrol-stations-from-rontec-ltd [accessed 6 June 2015]

Baindur, D and Macário, R M (2013) Mumbai lunch box delivery system: A transferable benchmark in urban logistics? *Research in Transportation Economics*, **38** (1), pp 110–21

Bal, F and Vleugel, J (2015) Container ship calls: triple throughput without an increase in marine CO_2, NOx and PM10 emissions? *European Transport – Trasporti Europei*, **58**, copy obtained from: http://repository.tudelft.nl/islandora/object/uuid:2cc1b7df-e56a-4d5f-9cb1-ccf62ca28117?collection=research [accessed 20 May 2016]

Birtchnell, T and Urry, J (2015) The mobilities and post-mobilities of cargo, *Consumption Markets and Culture*, **18** (1), pp 25–38

Boonstra, W J and Joosse, S (2013) The social dynamics of degrowth, *Environmental Values*, **22** (2), pp 171–89

Cidell, J (2012) Flows and pauses in the urban logistics landscape: The municipal regulation of shipping container mobilities, *Mobilities*, **7** (2), pp 233–45

Clift, B (2012) Comparative capitalisms, ideational political economy and French post-dirigiste responses to the global financial crisis, *New Political Economy*, **17** (5), pp 565–90

Corbett, J J, Winebrake, J J, Green, E H, Kasibhatla, P, Eyring, V and Lauer, A (2007) Mortality from ship emissions: A global assessment, *Environmental Science and Technology*, **41** (24), pp 8512–18

CRR (2015) Online retailing: Britain, Europe, US and Canada 2015, *Centre for Retail Research* [online] http://www.retailresearch.org/onlineretailing.php [accessed 6 June 2015]

De Marchi, V, Maria, E D and Ponte, S (2014) Multinational firms and the management of global networks: Insights from global value chain studies, *Advances in International Management*, **27**, pp 463–86

EMF (2012) *Towards the Circular Economy Vol. 1: An economic and business rationale for an accelerated transition*, Cowes: Ellen MacArthur Foundation

Fatnassi, E, Chaouachi, J and Klibi, W (2015) Planning and operating a shared goods and passengers on-demand rapid transit system for sustainable city-logistics, *Transportation Research Part B: Methodological*, **81**, pp 440–60

Felsted, A (2014) 'Click and collect' poised to overtake home delivery, *Financial Times* [online] http://www.ft.com/cms/s/0/3ac9e120-c653-11e3-ba0e-00144feabdc0.html#axzz3w4WOAaNf [accessed 6 June 2015]

Geels, F W (2002) Technological transitions as evolutionary reconfiguration processes: A multi-level perspective and a case-study, *Research Policy*, **31** (8/9), pp 1257–74

Geels, F W (2012) A socio-technical analysis of low-carbon transitions: Introducing the multi-level perspective into transport studies, *Journal of Transport Geography*, **24**, pp 471–82

Gereffi, G and Wyman, D L (eds) (1990) *Manufacturing Miracles: Paths of industrialization in Latin America and East Asia*, Princeton, NJ: Princeton University Press

Haipeter, T, Jürgens, U and Wagner, K (2012) Employment relations in the banking and automotive industries in Germany, *International Journal of Human Resource Management*, 23 (10), pp 2016–33

Hall, P A and Soskice, D (2001) *Varieties of Capitalism: The institutional foundations of comparative advantage*, Oxford: Oxford University Press

Hancke, B, Rhodes, M and Thatcher, M (2008) *Beyond Varieties of Capitalism: Conflict, contradictions, and complementarities in the European economy*, Oxford: Oxford University Press

Holmström, J, Holweg, M, Khajavi, H S and Partanen, J (2016) The direct digital manufacturing (r)evolution: Definition of a research agenda, *Operations Management Research*, 9 (1), pp 1–10

Juan, A A, Mendez, C A, Faulin, J, De Armas, J and Grasman, S E (2016) Electric vehicles in logistics and transportation: A survey on emerging environmental, strategic, and operational challenges, *Energies*, 9 (2), pp 1–21

Kallis, G (2011) In defence of degrowth, *Ecological Economics*, 70 (5), pp 873–80

Lindstad, H and Eskeland, G S (2015) Low carbon maritime transport: How speed, size and slenderness amounts to substantial capital energy substitution, *Transportation Research Part D: Transport and Environment*, 41, pp 244–56

Lindstad, H, Bright, R M and Strømman, A H (2016) Economic savings linked to future Arctic shipping trade are at odds with climate change mitigation, *Transport Policy*, 45, pp 24–30

Lister, J, Poulsen, R T and Ponte, S (2015) Orchestrating transnational environmental governance in maritime shipping, *Global Environmental Change*, 34, pp 185–95

Lué, A, Bresciani, C, Colorni, A, Lia, F, Maras, V, Radmilović, Z, Whitmarsh, L, Xenias, D and Anoyrkati, E (2016) Future priorities for a climate-friendly transport: A European strategic research agenda toward 2030, *International Journal of Sustainable Transportation*, 10 (3), pp 236–46

Makkonen, T and Repka, S (2016) The innovation inducement impact of environmental regulations on maritime transport: A literature review, *International Journal of Innovation and Sustainable Development*, 10 (1), pp 69–86

Melo, S, Baptista, P and Costa, Á (2014) The cost and effectiveness of sustainable city logistics policies using small electric vehicles, *Transport and Sustainability*, 6, pp 295–314

Morales-Fusco, P, Saurí, S and De Melo, G (2013) Short sea shipping in supply chains: A strategic assessment, *Transport Reviews*, 33 (4), pp 476–96

Morales-Fusco, P, Saurí, S and Lago, A (2012) Potential freight distribution improvements using motorways of the sea, *Journal of Transport Geography*, 24, pp 1–11

Nordtømme, M E, Andersen, J, Sund, A B, Roche-Cerasi, I, Levin, T, Eidhammer, O and Bjerkan, K Y (2015a) Green urban distribution: Evaluation of adapted measures for the city of Oslo, *International Journal of Transport Economics*, **42** (1), pp 61–85

Nordtømme, M E, Bjerkan, K Y and Sund, A B (2015b) Barriers to urban freight policy implementation: The case of urban consolidation center in Oslo, *Transport Policy*, **44**, 179–86

Penna, C C R and Geels, F W (2015) Climate change and the slow reorientation of the American car industry (1979–2012): An application and extension of the Dialectic Issue Life Cycle (DILC) model, *Research Policy*, **44** (5), pp 1029–48

Pierre, J (2015) Varieties of capitalism and varieties of globalization: Comparing patterns of market deregulation, *Journal of European Public Policy*, **22** (7), pp 908–26

Poulsen, R T, Ponte, S and Lister, J (2016) Buyer-driven greening? Cargo-owners and environmental upgrading in maritime shipping, *Geoforum*, **68**, pp 57–68

Sadhu, S L N S, Tiwari, G and Jain, H (2014) Impact of cycle rickshaw trolley (CRT) as non-motorised freight transport in Delhi, *Transport Policy*, **35**, pp 64–70

Schliwa, G, Armitage, R, Aziz, S, Evans, J and Rhoades, J (2015) Sustainable city logistics: Making cargo cycles viable for urban freight transport, *Research in Transportation Business and Management*, **15**, pp 50–57

Schmidt, V (2003) French capitalism: Transformed, yet still a third variety of capitalism, *Economy and Society*, **32** (4), pp 526–54

Sheller, M (2014) Global Energy Cultures of Speed and Lightness: Materials, mobilities and transnational power, *Theory, Culture and Society*, **31** (5), pp 127–54

Shove, E and Walker, G (2007) Caution! Transitions ahead: Politics, practice and sustainable transition management, *Environment and Planning A*, **39**, pp 763–70

Streeter, A K (2013) More than 50% of city freight could shift from truck to bike, *Treehugger* [online] http://www.treehugger.com/bikes/50-percent-of-city-freight-could-shift-from-truck-to-bike.html [accessed 6 June 2015]

Sturgeon, T, Biesebroeck, J van and Gereffi, G (2008) Value chains, networks and clusters: Reframing the global automotive industry, *Journal of Economic Geography*, **8** (3), pp 297–321

Taefi, T T, Kreutzfeldt, J, Held, T and Fink, A (2015) Strategies to increase the profitability of electric vehicles in urban freight transport, *Green Energy and Technology*, **203**, pp 367–88

Uber (2015) A reliable ride for your deliveries [online] https://newsroom.uber.com/nyc/a-reliable-ride-for-your-deliveries/ [accessed 22 January 2015]

Walker, G and Manson, A (2014) Telematics, urban freight logistics and low carbon road networks, *Journal of Transport Geography*, **37**, pp 74–81

Wang, X C and Zhou, Y (2015) Deliveries to residential units: A rising form of freight transportation in the U.S., *Transportation Research Part C: Emerging Technologies*, **58**, pp 46–55

Yang, C-S, Lu, C-S, Haider, J J and Marlow, P B (2013) The effect of green supply chain management on green performance and firm competitiveness in the context of container shipping in Taiwan, *Transportation Research Part E: Logistics and Transportation Review*, **55**, pp 55–73

Yip, T L and Wong, M C (2015) The Nicaragua canal: Scenarios of its future roles, *Journal of Transport Geography*, **43**, 1–13

Yuan, Z, Bi, J and Moriguichi, Y (2006) The circular economy: A new development strategy in China, *Journal of Industrial Ecology*, **10** (1–2), pp 4–8

Zacharias, J and Zhang, B (2015) Local distribution and collection for environmental and social sustainability: Tricycles in central Beijing, *Journal of Transport Geography*, **49**, pp 9–15

INDEX

3D printing 152, 153, 258, 311
3PL 203, 233

AAR 221, 227
ACI 286
ADB 24, 177, 178, 179, 193, 202
Adriatic 163
AEC 26, 185, 202
AEO 62, 63
Aeroscraft ML866 2, 309
Afghanistan 82
AFRA 106, 121
Africa 7, 18, 21, 24, 28, 29, 30, 53, 81, 102, 116, 117, 118, 127, 131, 160, 162, 163, 256, 257, 258, 259, 260, 261, 262, 263, 264, 266, 267, 268, 271, 274, 275, 276, 310, 312, 313, 325
African National Congress (ANC) 273
agents 3, 65, 188, 233, 258
agribulks 21
AGTC 214
Air Canada 204, 221
Airbus A380 2
Airports Council International (ACI) 286
Ak Bidai Grain Terminal 85
Aktau 80, 81, 82, 84, 85, 86, 87, 88, 91, 94, 95, 96
Alaska 109, 111, 112, 114, 220
Alaska pipeline 109
alliance(s) 7, 29, 37, 41, 46, 55, 56, 135, 136, 137, 138, 140, 143, 144, 153, 155, 156, 233, 257
Almaty 90, 97, 98, 99
Altynsarin 85
alumina 15, 18, 21
Amazon 26, 310, 312
Amirabad 82, 84, 86, 87, 94, 95, 96
Amoco Cadiz 113, 120
ANC 273
Angola 8, 28, 116, 257, 261, 263, 267, 269, 275
Anti-Bribery Act 2010 65
anti-dumping measures 59
Antioquia 244, 245
Antonov 225, 2
Antwerp 25, 149, 160, 163
Antwerp Port Community System (APCS) 25, 149, 160, 163
APCS 149

APGCI 213, 214, 229
APL 137, 138, 157
APM Terminals 131, 141, 142, 144, 153
APROC 293
Arauca 248
Arctic Ocean 117
ASEAN 3, 6, 26, 55, 67, 167, 181, 185, 202, 293
ASEAN Economic Community (AEC) 26, 55, 185, 202
Asia 7, 18, 21, 22, 23, 24, 27, 28, 29, 30, 33, 41, 53, 80, 81, 82, 92, 97, 101, 102, 112, 115, 116, 117, 126, 129, 131, 137, 138, 140, 141, 146, 152, 153, 159, 164, 165, 168, 171, 181, 187, 202, 203, 208, 211, 213, 228, 232, 236, 238, 263, 274, 292, 293, 295, 326, 330
Asia-Pacific Gateway and Corridor Initiative (APGCI) 213
Asia-Pacific Regional Operational Centre (APROC) 293
Asian Development Bank (ADB) 24, 178, 202, 274
Association of American Railroads (AAR) 221, 227
Association of Southeast Asian Nations (ASEAN) 3, 181
Astana 89, 90, 97, 98, 99
Astrakhan Grain Terminal 92
Atlantic 41, 101, 113, 116, 117, 214, 218, 228, 239, 241, 248, 249
Atlantic Gateway and Trade Corridor (AGTC) 214
Australia 2, 6, 82, 158, 167, 172, 244, 313
Authorised Economic Operator (AEO) 62, 63
Auto-Pact 205
Average Freight Rate Assessment (AFRA) 106, 121
Azerbaijan 81, 87, 88

Baku 81, 82, 88, 101
Baltic Clean Tanker Index 46, 48
Baltic Dry Index (BDI) 44, 45, 208
Banda Aceh–Medan–Pekanbaru–Palembang Economic Corridor 179
Bandah Aceh 179, 182, 195, 196, 197
Bandar Abbas 79, 80, 82, 83, 84, 86, 87, 88, 89, 90, 91, 93, 94

Index

Bangladesh 27, 28, 33, 203
banks 118, 142
Bantry Bay 106, 111
Barbados 238
Barcelona 163
Barranquilla 240, 241, 243, 248, 249, 250
bauxite 15, 18, 21, 320
BDI 44, 45, 208
Beaufort scale 112
Beineu 82, 85
Belawan 189, 190, 191, 195
Belgium 141, 162, 163, 236
Benjamin Franklin 208
Berge Stahl 2
BIMCO 32, 54, 119, 121
biomass 116
Black Sea 82, 84, 85, 88, 95, 97, 98, 101
BMW 163, 165, 167, 173
Bocimar International 46
Boeing 747 2
Bogotá 240, 241, 243, 244, 245, 246, 249, 254, 255
border agencies 66, 72
Botswana 7, 256, 257, 258, 259, 262, 264, 265, 267, 268, 270, 271, 272, 275
Braefoot Bay 111
Braer 113, 114, 122
Brazil 2, 24, 28, 102, 116, 131, 232, 237, 238, 239, 243, 266
Bremerhaven 159, 163
BRIC 232
Bunker 41, 114
Busan 278
BYB 217

CAA 221, 286, 295
cabotage 30, 205, 207, 217, 218, 219, 220, 222, 225, 226, 267
Cali 240, 243
Canada 6, 7, 82, 95, 161, 204, 205, 206, 207, 208, 209, 210, 211, 213, 214, 215, 216, 217, 218, 219, 220, 221, 222, 223, 224, 225, 226, 227, 228, 229, 230, 329
Canada Border Services Agency (CBSA) 217, 223
Canada Marine Act 216
Canada Transportation Act 7, 214, 222, 223, 226, 228
Canada Transportation Act Review Committee (CTARC) 214, 222, 223, 224, 225, 226, 227, 228
Canada Transportation Act Review report 214
Canada Transportation Agency 223, 224
Canada–US Regulatory Cooperation Council 217

Canadian Airport Authorities (CAA) 221, 286, 295
Canadian National Railway 221
Canadian Port Authorities 216, 223, 227, 228
capacity 1, 4, 8, 14, 15, 21, 25, 26, 29, 35, 36, 37, 38, 41, 42, 48, 54, 82, 83, 84, 85, 87, 88, 90, 91, 92, 94, 95, 108, 125, 126, 133, 136, 137, 143, 145, 146, 156, 160, 162, 164, 165, 166, 167, 200, 208, 223, 224, 229, 237, 247, 252, 257, 268, 269, 270, 278, 280, 281, 282, 284, 285, 286, 288, 290, 294, 300, 305, 306, 309, 310, 316, 325
Capesize 44, 45, 46, 47
Car-Equivalent Units (CEU) 159, 160, 164, 166
Car shipping 158
cargo characteristics 3
cargo owners 2, 325
Cars 158, 159, 172
Cartagena 240, 241, 243
Caspian Sea 81, 82, 84, 86, 92, 95, 101, 122
CBSA 217
CENIT 252, 253, 254
Centre for Retail Research (CRR) 323, 329
CETA 205
CEU 159, 160, 164, 166
CFS 189
charter rates 42
charterers 118
Chengdu 167
Chennai 162, 172
Chile 28, 232, 237, 238, 254
China 1, 18, 21, 22, 24, 25, 26, 27, 28, 29, 30, 32, 33, 53, 54, 80, 81, 82, 95, 102, 115, 116, 117, 127, 131, 137, 138, 141, 142, 156, 160, 161, 162, 165, 167, 206, 210, 232, 241, 266, 285, 291, 293, 296, 321, 322, 325, 327, 332
China Ocean Shipping Group Company (COSCO) 137
Clarksons Research 15, 16, 17, 22, 23, 24, 37, 38, 40, 41, 42, 44, 48, 54, 119
classification societies 119
CMA CGM 29, 136, 137, 138, 142, 154, 157, 208
CNSHI 137
CO_2 168, 169, 173, 238, 290, 291, 292, 293, 295, 329
coal trade 21
coarse grain 21
Coasting Trade Act 1992 218
Colombia 6, 7, 30, 231, 232, 237, 238, 239, 240, 241, 242, 243, 244, 246, 248, 249, 251, 252, 253, 254, 255

COMECON 321
commodity traders 118
Common Market for Eastern and Southern Africa 267
Compañía Chilena de Navegación Interoceánica 137
Comprehensive Economic and Trade Agreement (CETA) 205
comprehensive port 138
concentration 42
consumer demand 18
consumer goods 1, 18, 241, 255
consumption 26, 91, 101, 116, 129, 146, 152, 277, 301, 316, 319, 320, 321, 325, 326, 327, 328
container freight rates 37
Container Freight Station (CFS) 189
container ship(s) 2, 28, 29, 33, 34, 36, 37, 41, 42, 44, 126, 127, 128, 143, 144, 145, 146, 157, 207, 208, 285, 290, 321
container shipping 29, 123, 135, 143, 164, 290
containerization 5, 6, 123, 124, 127, 156, 157, 235
containerized freight 2, 195
contemporary economies 318
corporate social responsibility 316
COSCO 29, 137, 138
costs 1, 2, 25, 26, 33, 34, 35, 36, 41, 42, 44, 46, 54, 58, 63, 67, 68, 72, 73, 74, 80, 81, 83, 86, 87, 91, 92, 93, 97, 106, 109, 123, 125, 135, 137, 143, 144, 148, 153, 155, 167, 179, 190, 200, 207, 219, 233, 234, 235, 236, 237, 245, 246, 247, 248, 251, 258, 262, 266, 269, 270, 277, 302, 304, 306, 316, 325
Council for Mutual Economic Assistance countries 321
CPA 216, 221
CRED 299, 302, 312
Crediflores 246
Crimea 118
crisis conditions 8
cross-border trade 2
CRR 323, 329
crude oil 18, 48, 100, 101, 102, 105, 106, 109, 111, 112, 116, 118, 251, 252
cruise ship 2
CSAV 29, 137
CTARC 214, 222, 223, 224, 225, 226, 227, 228
C-TPAT 63
CTM 46
Cundinamarca 244, 245
customs 4, 7, 57, 58, 59, 60, 61, 63, 64, 65, 66, 67, 68, 70, 71, 72, 73, 74, 75, 85, 88, 98, 133, 143, 150, 186, 197, 198, 216, 246, 294, 304, 306, 309, 311
Customs Agency 59
Customs and Trade Partnership Against Terrorism (C-TPAT) 63
customs brokers 65, 70
Customs management practices 63
Cyclone Pam 308
Cyclone Winston 299, 308

DAKOSY 149
Dar es Salaam Corridor 259, 261
DDP 59, 133, 235
Delivered Duty Paid 59, 133, 235
demand 1, 4, 9, 13, 14, 15, 18, 21, 22, 24, 25, 26, 27, 29, 32, 33, 34, 35, 36, 37, 38, 41, 42, 44, 46, 48, 53, 54, 55, 56, 81, 85, 90, 92, 94, 95, 97, 100, 105, 114, 115, 116, 131, 133, 140, 143, 145, 148, 152, 154, 161, 162, 164, 165, 166, 167, 171, 173, 181, 188, 189, 224, 230, 235, 236, 247, 263, 269, 294, 300, 303, 305, 307, 312, 315, 316, 317, 318, 319, 320, 321, 322, 323, 324, 325, 326, 329
Democratic Republic of Congo 8, 257, 261
demurrage 67, 68
derived demand 9, 200, 315, 328
developing countries 15, 18, 19, 26, 27, 28, 30, 34, 53, 71, 120, 129, 233, 234, 257
developing economies 24, 53, 127, 138, 234
Dirty Tanker Index (DTI) 46, 48
disaster 9, 106, 119, 299, 300, 301, 302, 303, 304, 305, 306, 307, 310, 311, 312, 313, 314
distri-parks 291
distribution networks 8, 166, 277
door-to-door logistics services 135
double-stack wagons 2
DPW 142
DRC 257, 261, 267
dry bulk 18, 32, 33, 37, 44, 45, 46, 87, 106
dry-term leases 133
DTI 46, 48
Dubai Ports World (DPW) 142
Dubai World sovereign wealth fund 142
Dumai 179, 182, 194, 195, 196, 198

earthquakes 109, 111, 299, 300, 308, 312
East–West trades 129
eco-efficiency 316, 325, 327
ecological impacts 112
e-commerce 14, 25, 26, 54, 55, 135, 151, 291, 294
Economic Community of West African States (ECOWAS) 3

Index

economic growth 6, 14, 68, 178, 192, 193, 198, 206, 211, 217, 253, 259, 266, 267, 294
Economic Partnership Agreement 267
economies of scale 2, 3, 9, 33, 37, 65, 93, 96, 106, 123, 136, 137, 146, 154, 208, 315, 316, 321
Ecopetrol 248, 251, 254, 255
ECOWAS 3
Ecuador 238, 248, 254
Egypt 28, 30
El Canal del Dique 241
Electric Toll Collection 294
embedded flows 320
Emden 163
emergency 8, 299, 300, 301, 302, 304, 313
emergency aid 8
emissions regulation 168, 169
Emma Maersk 146
Employment, Workforce Development and Labour 223
Empty container logistics 146, 155
Enterprise Resource Planning (ERP) 65, 307
Environment Canada 223
Environmentally Sound Ship (E/S) 170, 171
ERL 160, 173
ERP 65, 307
E/S 170, 171
Esso Bernicia 114, 122
ETC 294
EU 3, 59, 60, 61, 62, 63, 67, 142, 161, 165, 205, 238, 244, 263, 267, 324
Eukor 166
Eurogate 143
Europe 2, 18, 21, 22, 23, 24, 25, 28, 37, 41, 46, 71, 80, 81, 91, 92, 95, 101, 102, 106, 109, 110, 115, 116, 117, 118, 126, 129, 131, 137, 138, 142, 146, 154, 158, 162, 163, 164, 165, 166, 167, 168, 169, 171, 173, 208, 236, 270, 295, 302, 323, 324, 325, 329
European Commission 60, 72, 137, 151, 154, 267, 274
European Container Terminals 150
European Union 3, 55, 72, 73, 81, 137, 161, 205, 210, 218, 238, 244, 321, 327
Evergreen 29, 137
evolutionary growth 9, 315
exotic products 1
exploration 118, 228, 248, 251
EXW 59, 133, 234
Ex-Works (EXW) 59, 133, 234
Exxon Valdez 106, 113, 114, 119, 122

Fairplay 119
Famines 300
Far East 2, 37, 82, 131, 146, 162, 165, 169, 181
FCC 82, 83, 144
FDI 237, 266, 272
FEFO 307
FEU 39, 125
Fiat 163
FIFO 307
financial crisis 14, 234, 329
financial holdings 142
finished product 9
Finnart 111
First Expired, First Out (FEFO) 307
First In, First Out (FIFO) 307
fleet management 133
floating Spar 109
FOB 59, 84, 85, 95, 133, 235
Food Contract Corporation (FCC) 82, 83, 144
Ford 158, 162, 163
Foreign Corrupt Practices Act 65
Foreign Direct Investment (FDI) 237, 266, 272
Forty-foot Equivalent Unit (FEU) 125
Framework Act on Low Carbon Green Growth 2013 292
France 29, 81, 318
Fraser River 213
Free on Board (FOB) 59, 84, 85, 95, 133, 235
Free Trade Agreement (FTA) 67, 205, 219
freight forwarders 65, 83, 85, 86, 88, 90, 133, 134, 135, 157, 195, 233, 286
freight rate(s) 13, 33, 34, 36, 37, 41, 42, 44, 46, 48, 53, 54, 55, 86, 95, 133, 135, 136, 152, 206, 208, 235
freight transport 8, 241, 277, 278, 282, 288, 316, 320
FTA 67, 205, 219
fully cellular container ships 144
Future Development Plan of Port Information Systems 294

G6 Alliance 137
gas 5, 15, 18, 28, 33, 100, 101, 102, 104, 105, 107, 109, 110, 111, 112, 114, 115, 116, 117, 118, 119, 120, 121, 122, 163, 219, 255, 277, 290
GATT 60, 72, 75
GDP 14, 26, 127, 157, 206, 209, 229, 230, 236, 237, 240, 244, 248, 273
General Agreement on Tariffs and Trade (GATT) 60, 72, 75
general cargo 28
Genk 162
geothermal 116

German 30, 69, 142
Germany 27, 29, 82, 123, 126, 142, 143, 158, 159, 163, 165, 169, 236, 256, 318, 330
GHG 277, 290, 292, 293, 294
Gioa Tauro 162
Global Affairs Canada 223
global container transport 5, 124
global instability 118
global marketplace 2, 148
global outsourcing 5
global production chains 9, 315
global sourcing 233
Global Terminal Operator (GTO) 140, 141, 142
global trade 4, 5, 7, 13, 22, 34, 74, 123, 127, 144, 160, 204, 214, 232, 234, 271, 274
global value chains 8, 317, 318, 321, 325, 326
global warming 318
globalization 1, 2, 13, 80, 211, 235, 236, 319, 331
GM 162, 163, 167
Golden Ocean Group Limited 46
Golden Union Shipping 46
grain transport 4, 83
Great Lakes 206, 214, 219
Greater Mekong Sub-region 7, 179
Greece 27, 32, 97
greenhouse gas (GHG) 277, 290, 292, 293, 294
Grimsby 163
gross domestic product (GDP) 14, 26, 127, 157, 206, 209, 229, 230, 236, 237, 240, 244, 248, 273
gross weight 2, 90
GSX World Terminals 142
GTO 140, 141, 142
Gulf 46, 82, 91, 101, 102, 109, 114, 117, 211
Gulf War 114
Gulftainer 142

Halifax Gateway Council 214
Hamburg 25, 42, 43, 111, 137, 148, 149, 154, 155, 159
Hanjin Shipping 34, 41
Hapag-Lloyd 29, 137
Harbor Maintenance Tax (HMT) 220, 228
Harmony of the Seas 2
Hat Yai 182, 188, 189, 190, 191, 198, 201
Hat Yai/Songkhla 182
Hawaii 220
HCAs 309, 310
Hesse-Noord Natie 141

HHLA 148
High Cube Container 126
HMT 220, 228
Höegh 159, 164, 168, 172, 173
Höegh Target 164, 168, 172
Honda 163, 167
Hong Kong 27, 55, 108, 141
HPH 141, 142, 154
humanitarian 8, 9, 300, 301, 302, 303, 304, 305, 306, 307, 309, 310, 311, 312, 313, 314
Hutchison Ports Holdings (HPH) 141, 142, 154
Hybrid Cargo Airship (HCA) 309, 319
hybrid solutions 322
hydrocarbons 5, 100, 105, 109, 114, 115, 116, 118, 120, 248
hydroelectricity 116
hydrology 112
Hyundai 56, 137, 160, 162, 163, 167, 172, 173, 292

IACS 119, 121
IADB 232, 237, 238, 240, 241, 243, 255
IASC 299
IATA 71, 310
ICAO 71, 73, 228
ICT 5, 148, 154, 155
Ideal-X 123
IFRC 392
ILO 120, 121
IMB 119, 121
IMB Piracy Reporting Centre 119
IMG-GT 6
Immingham 163
IMO 63, 71, 73, 74, 107, 120, 122, 171
IMT-GT 6, 7, 177, 178, 179, 180, 181, 182, 183, 184, 185, 186, 187, 188, 189, 191, 192, 194, 195, 196, 197, 198, 199, 200, 201, 202, 203
Incoterms 2010 73, 234, 255
India 27, 28, 30, 32, 33, 115, 116, 162, 167, 232, 266, 268, 293, 309, 321, 322, 325
Indian Ocean 25, 91
indirect costs 68
Indonesia 6, 21, 24, 27, 28, 30, 32, 101, 116, 167, 177, 178, 179, 180, 181, 185, 186, 187, 202
Indonesia–Malaysia–Thailand Growth Triangle (IMT-GT) 6, 177, 179
industry interests 118
Information and communication technology (ICT) 5, 148, 154, 155
Infrastructure 24, 53, 99, 155, 183, 184, 185, 199, 201, 237, 252, 261, 262, 268, 276, 296

initial public offering (IPO) 221
Inland terminal operator 143
inland transport operations 135
Institutional Framework 183
insurance 34, 119, 199, 258
Inter-Agency Standing Committee (IASC) 299
Inter-American Development Bank (IADB) 237, 238, 255
intermodal integration 135
Intermodal Surface Transportation Efficiency Act 211
International Air Transport Association (IATA) 71, 310
International Association of Independent Tanker Owners 118
International Civil Aviation Organization (ICAO) 71, 73, 228
International Federation of Red Cross (IFRC) 302
international freight transport 2, 3, 4, 6, 7, 77, 207, 211, 232, 237, 284, 299, 318
International Labour Organization (ILO) 120, 121
international logistics 4, 271, 278, 285, 293
International Maritime Bureau 119
International Maritime Organization (IMO) 63, 71, 73, 74, 107, 120, 122, 171
International Oil Pollution Compensation (IOPC) 119, 122
International Organization for Standardization (ISO) 125, 126, 131, 155
International Public Sector Accounting Standards (IPSAS) 307
International Road Transport Union 71
International Tanker Owners Pollution Federation (ITOPF) 118, 122
INTERTANKO 118, 122
Intra-Asian trade 24
Intraregional trades 129
IOPC 119, 122
IPO 221
IPSAS 307
Iran 79, 80, 81, 82, 83, 84, 85, 86, 87, 88, 89, 90, 91, 94, 95, 96, 98, 117
iron ore 1, 2, 18, 45, 106, 320, 321
Islamic Republic of Iran 53
ISO 125, 126, 131, 155
ISTEA 211
ITOPF 118, 122

Jaguar Landrover (JLR) 163
Japan 24, 27, 32, 33, 95, 102, 108, 115, 116, 117, 126, 158, 160, 161, 165, 210, 244, 266, 313, 324

JLR 163
Jones Act 218, 219, 220, 229
jumboization 319
Just-In-Time 85

Kantang 192, 193, 194
Kaohsiung 285
Karaganda 89
Kartaly 92, 93
Kazakhstan 4, 5, 79, 80, 81, 82, 83, 84, 85, 87, 88, 89, 90, 91, 92, 93, 94, 95, 96, 97, 98, 99, 116
Kazmortransflot 88
Khromtau 85
Kokshetau 79, 80, 83, 84, 86, 87, 88, 89, 91, 92, 93, 95, 96
Koper 163
Korea 6, 8, 24, 27, 30, 32, 33, 67, 95, 115, 116, 117, 160, 161, 162, 165, 167, 277, 278, 282, 283, 285, 288, 289, 290, 291, 292, 293, 294, 295, 296
Korea Maritime Guarantee Insurance 292
Kuwait 29
Kyrgyzstan 80, 98

LAA 221
Lake Nicaragua 117
landbridge 2, 80
landlord port 138
last mile 302, 304
last mile delivery 325
Latin America 24, 55, 232, 236, 237, 238, 255, 330
LCL 133
LDCs 30
Le Havre 160
leaks 112
least-cost sourcing 1
Least Developed Countries (LDCs) 30
LE-RPAS 307, 308
Lesotho 7, 257, 259, 262, 264, 267, 268, 272
less-than-container load (LCL) 133
Lhokseumawe 194, 196, 197
Liberia 27, 30, 32
Lift-on, Lift-off (Lo-Lo) 6
liner companies 29
liner conferences 136
liquefied petroleum gas (LPG) 102, 105, 107, 108, 111, 115
liquid bulk transport 5
liquid bulk vessels 1
liquid natural gas (LNG) 18, 102, 103, 107, 108, 111, 113, 116, 117, 168, 292, 293
Lloyd's List 119
LNG 18, 102, 103, 107, 108, 111, 113, 116, 117, 168, 292, 293

Index

LNG tanker 103, 107, 111, 113, 117
Lobito Corridor 261
Local Airport Authorities (LAA) 221
logistic service providers 133
Logistics Cluster 306, 313
Logistics Performance Index (LPI) 207, 235, 236, 237, 238, 249, 254, 271, 285, 287
Logistics Service Providers (LSP) 183
Lo-Lo 6
London 45, 47, 48, 54, 68, 73, 106, 121, 122, 154, 157, 163, 172, 173, 254, 269, 270, 275, 312, 313, 324
Long Beach 168, 212
Long Endurance Remotely Piloted Aircraft Systems (LE-RPAS) 307, 308
low-cost production 9
low-cost shipping 325
LPG 102, 105, 107, 108, 111, 115
LPI 207, 235, 236, 237, 238, 249, 254, 271, 276, 285, 287
LSP 183

M&A 101, 136, 137, 153
Maasvlakte II 151
macroeconomic 14, 73, 156
Madagascar 8, 257, 267
Maersk 29, 41, 55, 136, 137, 141, 142, 144, 146, 243
Malacca 146, 182, 192, 193, 194, 195, 198
Malawi 8, 257, 259, 267
Malaysia 6, 28, 30, 160, 167, 177, 178, 179, 180, 181, 182, 185, 186, 187, 188, 189, 192, 193, 194, 199, 200, 201, 202
Malaysian Northern Corridor Economic Region (NCER) 192
Malcolm McLean 124, 319
manufacturing 1, 6, 9, 13, 18, 24, 60, 65, 101, 109, 133, 138, 162, 164, 167, 168, 169, 206, 211, 232, 266, 277, 290, 295, 318, 326, 330
manufacturing processes 1, 9, 18
Maputo Corridor 261
Maputo Development Corridor 261
marine insurance 119
Maritime Container Transportation Chain 5, 124, 131, 132
maritime industry 318
Maritime Port Bureau (MPB) 294
maritime transport 4, 9, 13, 14, 25, 26, 53, 55, 105, 120, 203, 294, 315, 318, 319, 320, 325, 330
Maritime Transport Network Portal 294
Maritime Unmanned Navigation through Intelligence in Networks (MUNIN) 151
MARPOL 120, 168
Marshall Islands 27, 30, 32

Master leases 133
Mauritius 8, 257, 267
Maximum Revenue Entitlement Program 224
MCTC 124, 131, 133, 135, 140, 144, 149, 150
Medan 179, 182, 188, 189, 190, 191, 195, 196, 198, 201
Medellin 240, 243, 244
Mediterranean 136, 163, 166
megaships 34, 37
Melaka–Dumai Economic Corridor 179
Melbourne 167, 172
Memorandum of Cooperation on Sharing Short Sea Shipping Information and Experience 219
Memorandums of Understanding (MOU) 120, 214
Mercedes 163
Merchant Marine Act 1920 218
mergers and acquisitions (M&A) 101, 136, 137
Meta 248, 249
metal pigs 111
metals 21, 263
Mexico 101, 102, 109, 116, 161, 167, 204, 205, 207, 209, 210, 211, 215, 219, 220, 224, 226, 237, 241
Middle East 81, 82, 101, 102, 106, 108, 115, 116, 117, 118, 127, 131, 163, 325
minerals 21, 209
Ministry of Land, Infrastructure and Transport (MOLIT) 278, 279, 280, 281, 282, 283, 284, 290, 293, 296
Ministry of Transportation and Communication (MOTC) 284, 285, 286, 288, 289, 291, 292, 296
Mitsubishi 163
MLC 120
modal combinations 4, 84
Modern Express 160, 173
MOL 137, 160, 166, 171
MOLIT 278, 279, 280, 281, 282, 283, 284, 290, 293, 296
Morocco 30
Moscow 80, 88, 99
MOTC 284, 285, 286, 288, 289, 291, 292, 296
MOU 120, 214
Mozambique 8, 256, 257, 261, 266, 267, 269, 271, 273, 275
MPB 294
MSC 29, 136, 137, 142, 207
MTNet 294
Multiflora 246, 247, 253, 255

Index

multimodal 5, 79, 80, 83, 84, 96, 135, 150, 191, 214, 246, 296
multimodal transport 5, 79, 80, 84, 96, 143, 191, 202
multi-trailer road trains 1
MUNIN 151

NAFTA 3, 7, 205, 206, 207, 209, 210, 211, 218, 219, 222, 226, 230
Namibia 7, 256, 257, 261, 262, 263, 264, 266, 267, 268, 269, 271, 272, 273, 274
NAS 221
National Airports System 221
National Disaster Management Organization (NDMO) 307, 308
National Hydrocarbon Agency (ANH) 248
National Policy Framework for Strategic Gateways and Trade Corridors 214, 229
natural disasters 8, 299, 301, 302
natural gas 18, 100, 102, 105, 109, 111, 112, 115, 116
NCER 192
NDMO 307, 308
needs assessment 301, 302, 307, 308, 310
neo-liberal capitalism 327
Neo-Panamax (NPX) 146
NEPAD 261, 262
Netherlands 126, 158, 236, 266
New Partnership for Africa's Development (NEPAD) 261, 262
New Zealand 159, 295, 313
NGO 301, 302
Nigeria 28, 116, 118
Nimber 323
Ningbo 138
Nissan 160, 163, 167
nitrogen oxides (NOx) 168
NOL 29, 137, 138, 154
Non-Government Organisation (NGO) 301, 302
non-tariff barriers 7, 205, 226, 262
Nordtømme 324, 331
North America 2, 6, 33, 106, 115, 116, 129, 131, 137, 138, 164, 169, 171, 181, 204, 205, 206, 207, 209, 210, 211, 213, 214, 215, 217, 218, 219, 220, 221, 223, 225, 226, 227, 229, 238, 323, 324, 325
North American Free Trade Agreement (NAFTA) 3, 7, 205, 206, 207, 209, 210, 211, 218, 219, 222, 226, 230
North Fraser River 213
North Korea 291
North Sea 102, 116, 168
Northern Sea Route (NSR) 291, 292, 295
North–South corridor 259

North–South Economic Corridor 7, 179
North–South trades 129
NOx 168, 169, 329
NPX 146
NSR 291, 292, 295
nuclear energy 116

OBO 106
OBOR 24, 25, 26, 53
Ocado 324
Ocean Alliance 137, 138
Oceania 18
OECD 66, 67, 74, 81, 98, 127, 156, 258, 275
oil 5, 14, 15, 18, 25, 33, 36, 37, 46, 48, 53, 55, 100, 101, 102, 103, 104, 105, 106, 109, 110, 111, 112, 113, 114, 115, 116, 117, 118, 119, 120, 121, 122, 123, 163, 167, 168, 181, 240, 248, 249, 251, 252, 253, 255, 325
oil companies 101, 102, 118
oil-bulk-ore (OBO) 106
Oil Pollution Act (OPA 90) 107, 114, 119
Olya 84, 92, 93, 96
One Belt, One Road 24, 291, 296
Ontario–Quebec Continental Gateway and Trade Corridor 214
OPA 90, 107, 114, 119
operators 3, 4, 8, 29, 58, 118, 138, 140, 141, 142, 143, 144, 153, 166, 171, 194, 196, 197, 215, 221, 271, 289, 294, 328
Orcelle 170, 171
Organisation for Economic Co-operation and Development (OECD) 66, 67, 74, 81, 98, 127, 156, 258, 275
over-consumption 327
overinvestment 34
Oxfam 303

P&I 119
P&O Ports 142
Pacific 22, 26, 39, 41, 67, 97, 116, 117, 131, 144, 187, 203, 205, 208, 213, 228, 238, 239, 241, 252, 263, 291, 293, 308
Pakistan 27, 28, 32, 33, 307, 308
Palembang 179, 182, 195, 196, 197, 198
Panama 1, 24, 27, 30, 32, 53, 106, 145, 146, 155, 164, 207, 208, 227, 241
Panama Canal 1, 24, 53, 145, 146, 164, 227
Panamax 24, 42, 44, 45, 47, 48, 106, 144, 145, 146, 154, 164, 165, 172, 173
passenger transport 2, 315
PCC 158
PCS 149
PCTC 158, 159

Index

Penang 179, 180, 181, 182, 188, 189, 191, 192, 193, 194, 199
Persian Gulf 46, 80, 84, 90, 91, 96, 122
Peru 232, 237, 238
petrochemicals 101, 251
petroleum 15, 18, 48, 102, 105, 116, 224, 241, 263, 320, 325
Philippines 24, 27, 30, 32, 33, 202, 309
phosphate 15, 18
Phuket 179, 182, 196, 197
physical flows 320
Pipavav 162
pipelines 5, 100, 102, 105, 109, 110, 111, 112, 116, 118, 119, 120, 121, 248, 251, 252, 253, 258
Piraeus 25
PODs 305, 312
points of distribution (POD) 305, 312
political instability 118
pollution 112, 114, 119, 120, 121, 169, 290, 318, 319, 324
port community system (PCS) 149
Port Klang 182, 188, 189, 191, 194, 199
Port Metro Vancouver 213
port pricing 270
Port of Singapore Authority (PSA) 141, 142, 163, 169
Port State Control (PSC) 120
port tariffs 270
Portnet 149
Ports America 142
Portugal 256, 266
post-Panamax 144, 145, 164
Preferential Trade Area (PTA) 267
Prince Rupert 213
Prince William Sound 114, 119
Product Life Cycle Theory 317
production 1, 5, 9, 21, 53, 81, 101, 102, 104, 105, 109, 111, 115, 116, 118, 120, 123, 129, 152, 158, 161, 162, 164, 166, 167, 169, 171, 173, 185, 192, 205, 224, 244, 246, 251, 252, 253, 267, 277, 315, 316, 319, 320, 321, 325, 326, 327, 328
products 1, 5, 7, 8, 15, 18, 21, 48, 55, 59, 100, 102, 105, 106, 107, 109, 112, 116, 121, 127, 148, 152, 159, 163, 180, 181, 188, 189, 194, 209, 211, 224, 232, 233, 236, 237, 240, 241, 242, 248, 251, 252, 255, 263, 267, 277, 317, 320, 321, 322, 325, 326
Protection and Indemnity Clubs (P&I) 119
Protocol on Transport, Communication and Meteorology 262
PSA 141, 142, 163, 169
PSC 120
PTA 267

public port authority 138
Puerto Rico 220, 254
Pure Car and Truck Carrier (PCTC) 158, 159
Pure Car Carrier (PCC) 158
Putumayo 248

rail routes 1, 90
Railway Clearing House (RCH) 124
Ranong–Phuket–Bandah Aceh Economic Corridor 179
raw materials 1, 4, 18, 80, 152, 169, 206, 236, 258, 320, 321
RCEP 26
RCH 124
recovery 5, 46, 53, 127, 153, 164, 234, 236, 301, 307
Red Crescent 302, 313
Red Cross 301, 302, 313
refining 105, 118, 168, 251
Regensburg 167
Regional Comprehensive Economic Partnership (RCEP) 26
Regional Indicative Strategic Development Plan (RISDP) 263, 264
regulatory authorities 118
Remotely Piloted Aircraft Systems (RPAS) 310, 311, 313
RENAMO 273
Renault 163
renewables 116, 121
Republic of South Africa (RSA) 256, 257, 261, 264, 265, 266, 267, 268, 269, 270, 271, 273, 274
RISDP 263, 264
risk 3, 4, 63, 70, 75, 112, 114, 118, 119, 152, 167, 235, 236, 237, 249, 251, 290, 325
road bridges 1
Roll-on, Roll-off (Ro-Ro) 6
Rolls-Royce 151, 152
Ro-Ro 6, 87, 164, 309
Rotterdam 2, 25, 111, 126, 150, 151
RPAS 310, 311, 313
RSA 7, 256, 257, 261, 264, 265, 266, 267, 268, 269, 270, 271, 273, 274
Russia 80, 81, 82, 83, 84, 85, 91, 92, 93, 94, 98, 118, 167, 173, 232, 291
Russian Federation 21, 32, 98, 116, 117
Russian Railways (RZD) 92, 93, 95, 99
RZD 92, 93, 95, 99

SACU 7, 8, 257, 258, 259, 261, 262, 263, 264, 268, 269, 270, 274, 275
SADC 3, 7, 257, 261, 262, 263, 264, 267, 269, 271, 274, 275
Sarakhs 84, 88, 89, 90, 96

Saryagash 88, 89, 92
scale economies 1
SCM 63, 233, 234, 332
SDGs 13
sea freight market 133, 135
sea routes 1, 160, 207
seaborne trade 14, 15, 16, 17, 18, 19, 20, 24, 27, 53, 116, 127, 128, 157, 206
seafarers 32, 55
SECAs 168, 171
Serhetyaka 91
service 1, 2, 5, 9, 29, 30, 34, 37, 42, 53, 59, 65, 70, 83, 85, 101, 119, 124, 133, 135, 143, 144, 148, 149, 163, 164, 172, 182, 184, 187, 188, 189, 191, 192, 193, 195, 202, 207, 215, 219, 224, 233, 235, 236, 237, 248, 269, 270, 271, 274, 285, 286, 290, 293, 304, 306, 308, 321, 323, 328
Seychelles 8, 257
ship building 32
ship owners 28, 30, 34, 35, 36, 46, 118, 119, 207
ship scrapping 27, 33, 44
shippers 34, 65, 118, 133, 135, 155, 168, 171, 185, 187, 188, 192, 215, 233
shippers and consignees 183
shipping 4, 5, 6, 13, 18, 25, 26, 27, 28, 29, 30, 31, 32, 34, 36, 38, 42, 44, 46, 53, 54, 55, 67, 68, 70, 87, 91, 94, 100, 105, 106, 107, 108, 117, 118, 119, 120, 121, 123, 124, 125, 126, 127, 129, 131, 133, 135, 136, 137, 138, 140, 141, 142, 143, 145, 146, 148, 149, 152, 153, 154, 155, 156, 158, 159, 160, 161, 162, 163, 164, 166, 167, 168, 169, 170, 171, 172, 173, 188, 194, 198, 204, 206, 207, 208, 209, 213, 215, 217, 218, 219, 220, 225, 227, 228, 229, 233, 235, 238, 252, 269, 274, 282, 288, 290, 292, 293, 294, 308, 318, 319, 320, 321, 324, 325, 326, 327, 329, 330, 331, 332
shipping line 67
shipping networks 5
short sea shipping 218, 219, 326
short-term leases 133
SIDS 30
Singapore 27, 28, 29, 30, 68, 72, 74, 107, 137, 141, 149, 181, 182, 189, 202, 236
Single Window 68, 70, 74, 258
SKUs 303
slow steaming 37, 41, 146, 321
small and medium-sized enterprises (SMEs) 26, 187, 200
Small Island Developing States 30
SMEs 26, 187, 200

socio-technical transitions theory 316, 317, 328
solar 116, 170, 171
SOLAS 73, 120
Solidarity Savings Corporation 246
Songkhla 178, 179, 180, 188, 191
Songkhla–Penang–Medan Economic Corridor 179
South America 6, 7, 28, 53, 129, 131, 231, 232, 233, 235, 237, 238, 239, 241, 243, 245, 247, 249, 251, 253, 254, 255
South Korea 278
Southampton 159, 163
Southeast Asia 6, 28, 30, 117, 131, 177, 179, 181, 183, 185, 187, 189, 191, 193, 195, 197, 199, 201, 202, 203
Southern Africa 6, 256, 257, 259, 261, 263, 266, 267, 269, 271, 273, 275
Southern African Customs Union (SACU) 7, 8, 257, 258, 259, 261, 262, 263, 264, 268, 269, 270, 274, 275
Southern African Development Community (SADC) 3, 7, 257, 261, 262, 263, 264, 267, 269, 271, 274, 275
Southern African Trade Hub 258
South–South trade 53
Soviet Union 4, 79, 80
SOx 167, 168, 169
soybean 21
Spain 162, 163, 173, 246
spills 112, 113, 114, 119
St Gothard base tunnel 1
St Lawrence River 206
Star Bulk Carriers 46
state regulation 118
STCW 120
Stevedores 141
Stock Keeping Units (SKU) 303
Strait of Malacca 146
Straits of Melaka Economic Corridor 179
Sub-Panamax 42
Suez Canal 24, 25, 53, 55, 91, 101, 106, 116, 117, 146, 207, 214, 291
Sullom Voe 111, 114
Sulphur Emissions Control Areas (SECA) 168, 171
sulphur oxide (SOx) 167, 168, 169
Sumatra 177, 178, 180, 181, 182, 184, 186, 188, 189, 191, 195, 196, 199, 200, 201
supply 1, 4, 5, 13, 14, 18, 25, 34, 35, 36, 37, 38, 41, 42, 44, 46, 53, 54, 59, 61, 63, 71, 73, 82, 92, 95, 100, 101, 105, 109, 110, 115, 116, 133, 135, 142, 143, 151, 152, 153, 155, 169, 171, 178, 203, 206, 208, 224, 232, 233, 234, 236, 244,

245, 246, 247, 248, 253, 263, 271, 289, 290, 291, 294, 295, 296, 299, 303, 305, 307, 308, 310, 311, 312, 313, 314, 315, 316, 326, 327, 330, 332
supply chain management (SCM) 63, 233, 314, 332
sustainability 14, 216, 223, 266, 317, 325, 327, 332
Sustainable Development Goals 13
sustainable transport 4, 292, 293
SWAPO 273
Swaziland 7, 257, 262, 264, 267
Switzerland 1, 155
Syria 299, 304
Syrian civil war 117

Taipei 285, 295
Taiwan 6, 8, 277, 278, 282, 284, 285, 286, 288, 289, 290, 291, 292, 293, 294, 295, 332
Taiwan International Ports Corp 294
Tajikistan 80
tanker freight rates 46
tankers 5, 33, 36, 48, 53, 100, 101, 102, 105, 106, 107, 108, 109, 112, 114, 116, 117, 118, 119, 121, 144, 320
Tanzania 8, 257, 269
Taoyuan International Airport 286
tariff quotas 59
Tarragona 163
taxes 58, 59, 70, 215, 216, 228, 233, 235
technological solutions 320
terminal handling 67
Terminal Operating System (TOS) 150
TEU 21, 22, 29, 31, 33, 35, 36, 37, 38, 41, 42, 43, 87, 92, 93, 96, 125, 126, 129, 136, 140, 141, 144, 146, 147, 185, 186, 189, 191, 192, 208, 212, 232, 235, 241, 278
Thailand 6, 160, 167, 177, 178, 179, 180, 181, 182, 185, 186, 187, 188, 189, 191, 192, 193, 196, 199, 200, 201, 202
the Americas 18, 28, 29, 262
third-party logistics (3PL) 203, 233
time charter 43, 45, 47
TOD 294
Tonnage Bank 292
Torrey Canyon 113, 119
TOS 150
Toyota 160, 163
TPP 26, 67, 205
trade 2, 3, 4, 7, 13, 14, 15, 18, 21, 22, 23, 24, 25, 26, 27, 34, 37, 41, 42, 44, 48, 53, 54, 57, 58, 59, 60, 66, 67, 68, 69, 70, 71, 72, 73, 74, 75, 79, 80, 81, 87, 88, 95, 96, 98, 101, 106, 116, 117, 118, 119, 122, 123, 124, 126, 127, 129, 130, 131, 136, 137, 148, 153, 154, 155, 156, 157, 158, 161, 162, 164, 168, 172, 178, 179, 180, 181, 182, 185, 186, 187, 188, 191, 192, 194, 199, 200, 201, 204, 205, 206, 207, 208, 209, 210, 211, 212, 213, 214, 215, 217, 219, 221, 222, 223, 225, 226, 227, 228, 229, 230, 232, 233, 234, 235, 237, 238, 239, 241, 243, 255, 257, 258, 259, 261, 262, 263, 264, 265, 266, 267, 272, 273, 274, 275, 276, 278, 282, 286, 290, 295, 321, 330
trade blocs 4
trade facilitation 3, 25, 26, 58, 66, 67, 68, 69, 70, 71, 72, 73, 74, 75, 186, 217
trading protocols 2
Trang 178, 182, 192, 193, 194, 198
Trans–Atlantic 2
Transatlantic Trade and Investment Partnership (TTIP) 26, 67
Trans-Canada Highway 204
Trans-Canada pipeline 204
Trans-Caprivi corridor 261
Trans-Cunene corridor 261
transhipment 88, 131, 133, 143, 181, 196
Transit-Oriented Development 294
Trans-Kalahari Corridor 259, 262, 275
Trans-Oranje Corridor 261
Trans–Pacific 2, 22, 23
Trans-Pacific Partnership (TPP) 26, 67, 205
Transport Canada 213, 221, 229
transport futures 8, 9, 297, 317
transport solutions 3, 79, 317, 323
Transports Internationaux Routiers (TIR) 60
Triple E 146
trucks 1, 84, 90, 124, 126, 188, 189, 208, 220, 245, 246, 247, 249, 251, 252, 253, 319, 326
TTIP 26, 67
Turkey 84, 91, 162
Turkmenistan 80, 83, 84, 88, 89, 90, 91, 94, 95, 96, 99
Twenty-foot Equivalent Unit (TEU) 125
Tyne 163

UASC 29, 137
UAV/S 307
Uber 323, 331
UK 54, 58, 59, 65, 66, 67, 73, 97, 114, 119, 159, 163, 172, 231, 236, 255, 266, 296, 313, 318, 322, 324
UK Chamber of Shipping 119
UK Freight Transport Association (FTA) 231, 232
Ukraine 32, 82, 91, 98, 118
ULCC(s) 1, 106, 116

Index

ULCV(s) 146, 207
Ultra-Large Container Vessels (ULCV) 146, 207
Ultra-Large Crude Carriers (ULCC) 1, 106, 116
UN 7, 68, 71, 74, 168, 257, 265, 272, 276, 299, 301, 308, 313
uncertainty 3, 4, 8, 14, 144, 236
UNCTAD 13, 14, 15, 16, 17, 19, 20, 22, 26, 29, 30, 31, 32, 38, 43, 45, 47, 53, 55, 56, 66, 74, 116, 120, 122, 123, 127, 131, 136, 137, 138, 157, 207, 228, 229, 258, 276
UNESCAP 80, 94, 99
UNHRDs 306
United Kingdom 256
United Nations 26, 66, 71, 74, 120, 122, 157, 203, 228, 266, 276, 299, 300, 306, 313
United Nations Conference on Trade and Development (UNCTAD) 13, 14, 15, 16, 17, 19, 20, 22, 26, 29, 30, 31, 32, 38, 43, 45, 47, 53, 55, 56, 66, 74, 116, 120, 122, 123, 127, 131, 136, 137, 138, 157, 207, 228, 229, 258, 276
United Nations Network of Humanitarian Response Depots (UNHRD) 306
United States 6, 7, 22, 30, 53, 63, 81, 101, 109, 115, 116, 117, 120, 123, 124, 126, 146, 158, 161, 204, 205, 206, 207, 208, 209, 210, 211, 214, 215, 216, 217, 219, 220, 221, 224, 226, 229, 230, 232, 238, 241, 243, 244, 246, 254, 270
unmanned aerial vehicles/systems (UAV/S) 307
urban transport 326, 328
urbanism 318
US Coastguard 120
US shale boom 117
USAID 258, 272, 276
Uzbekistan 80, 83, 84, 88, 89, 90, 91, 94, 95, 96, 98

VAG 163
value-added services 133
value-addition 3
Vancouver 212, 213, 214, 219, 221, 228
Vancouver Gateway Council (VGC) 213
varieties of capitalism 316, 318, 319
vehicle 1, 6, 46, 124, 158, 162, 163, 164, 165, 167, 168, 171, 172, 173, 199, 238, 268, 293, 300, 303, 304, 306, 319
Venezuela 28, 101, 116, 122, 248
Very Large Crude Carrier(s) (VLCC) 48, 50, 53, 101, 106, 116
vessel operating cost 37

vessel size 1, 31, 34, 53
Vessel Traffic Service (VTS) 150
Vietnam 22, 24, 126
Vigo 162, 163
VLCC(s) 48, 50, 53, 101, 106, 116
volcanic eruptions 299
Volga–Don–Caspian canal 92
Volkswagen Audi Group (VAG) 163
VTS 150

W&D 243
Wallenius Wilhelmsen Logistics (WWL) 160, 164, 166, 170
Wal-Mart 26
Walvis Bay 259, 261, 262, 269, 270, 272, 274, 275, 276
Walvis Bay Corridor Group (WBCG) 259, 262, 269, 276
warehousing and distribution (W&D) 243
wars 8, 300
waste 9, 59, 116, 315
wave power 170
WBCG 259, 262, 269, 276
WCO 59, 60, 63, 70, 71, 74, 75
WEF 66, 75, 127, 157
WFP 306, 308
wheat 21, 81, 82, 92, 98, 228, 320
wind 116, 170, 299, 308
World Bank 66, 72, 73, 75, 207, 209, 229, 230, 235, 237, 238, 254, 257, 258, 259, 264, 271, 272, 274, 276, 287
World Customs Organization (WCO) 59, 60, 63, 70, 71, 74, 75
World Economic Forum (WEF) 66, 75, 127, 157
world fleet 27, 28, 30, 32, 229
World Food Programme (WFP) 306, 308
World Trade Organization (WTO) 25, 56, 60, 66, 67, 70, 71, 72, 73, 74, 75, 205, 210, 230, 234, 243, 255, 257, 258, 275, 276
Worldscale 46, 49, 50, 51, 52
WTO 25, 56, 60, 66, 67, 70, 71, 72, 73, 74, 75, 205, 210, 230, 234, 243, 255, 257, 258, 275, 276
WWL 160, 164, 166, 170

Yemeni civil war 117
Yilport 142

Zacharias 322
Zambia 8, 257, 259, 261, 263, 267, 271, 272, 275
Zeebrugge 163
Zimbabwe 8, 257, 259, 261, 267, 272